WORLD QUALITY OF LIFE INDICATORS

WORLD QUALITY OF LIFE INDICATORS

Edited by
Rose Schumacher
Gail K. Sevrens
Timothy S. O'Donnell
Lee Torrence
Kate Carney

ABC-CLIO
Santa Barbara, California
Oxford, England

ISBN 0-87436-549-X

10 9 8 7 6 5 4 3 2 1

ABC-CLIO, Inc.
P. O. Box 1911
Santa Barbara, California 93116-1911

Clio Press Ltd.
55 St. Thomas' Street
Oxford, OX1 1JG, England

This book is printed on acid free paper ∞ .
Manufactured in the United States of America.

Contents

Introduction

Written for librarians, teachers, students, and those seeking information on a variety of factors affecting quality of life, World Quality of Life Indicators provides extensive current data for 172 countries and territories throughout the world. Compiled from documents not readily available to the general reader, this book will assist in the study and analysis of worldwide living conditions. The convenient, uniform format used for reporting the data provides for easy comparison between countries and fosters greater understanding of the various factors within countries.

SCOPE AND ARRANGEMENT

The data and information contained in this work are taken from ABC-CLIO's KALEIDOSCOPE: CURRENT WORLD DATA database. Countries are arranged alphabetically under their familiar names followed by their official names in English. Cross-references are provided for countries with more than one familiar name.

A wealth of information on each country is presented. Each category reflects a different aspect of life that influences the living conditions for the citizens of that country. The data can answer many questions for teachers and students:

Where is the country located? Who are its neighbors?

How is its land used? What percentage is arable?

What is the population density and growth rate?

What is the average life expectancy?

What are the maternal and infant mortality rates?

How many doctors and hospital beds are available?

What is the ethnic and religious composition?

Is there a common language?

What is the illiteracy rate?

How does the country spends its money?

What is the gross domestic product per capita?

What is the country's climate?

What health precautions should travelers take?

What system of government is in place?

GATHERING AND INTERPRETATION OF DATA

In all compilations of international scope, there are problems to be addressed in the gathering and interpretation of data; namely, the availability, reliability, currency, and consistency of information. Terminology, methods of reporting, and categories of information usually vary among countries, and one frequently finds discrepancies between publications for the same data. The time lag between collection of data and their availability in published form varies, depending upon the methods of data gathering and frequency of reporting. Discontinuities in the publication of collected data resulting from internal political strife within countries is also a factor in the currency and availability of data (where applicable, this is indicated). Not all categories of information are available for all countries. This is also indicated.

In all cases, reliability, objectivity, accuracy, and currency of information are used as guidelines for selecting sources that are regularly consulted for this compilation. A bibliography of regularly consulted sources is provided on the last page of this book.

FUTURE PUBLICATION PLANS

As always in a work of this nature and scope, changes will have taken place between the time the information was collected, analyzed, edited, and published, and the time the work reaches the shelves. Future editions of this work are planned as necessary to maintain currency. ABC-CLIO remains committed to providing and maintaining high-quality reference sources and welcomes recommendations furthering this commitment.

AFGHANISTAN
Democratic Republic of Afghanistan

LOCATION: Afghanistan is a landlocked country strategically located between Central Asia, the Indian subcontinent and the Middle East. It is bounded by the Soviet Union to the north, Iran to the west, China to the northeast and Pakistan to the east and south.

AREA: 251,773 sq. miles

Land Use: 12.44% cropland; 46.33% permanent pasture; 2.93% forests and woodland; 38.30% other.
Arable Land: 12.44%
Arable Land per capita: 1.11 acres

POPULATION: 18,110,000 (1987 estimate)

Population Density: 72 inhabs. per sq. mile (1987 estimate)
Population Distribution: 18.50% urban (1985)
Population Growth Rate: 4.83% per year (1985-90 projection)

VITAL STATISTICS

Average Life Expectancy: 39.00 years (1985-90 projection)
Male: 38.60 years (1985-90 projection)
Female: 39.40 years (1985-90 projection)
Age Distribution: (1985)

0-14	41.80%
15-64	55.50%
65+	2.70%

Median Age: 18.80 years (1985)
Maternal Mortality: (not available)
Infant Mortality: 183 per 1,000 live births (1985-90 projection)

HEALTH CARE

Hospital Beds: 4.09 per 10,000 population (1982)
Doctors: 0.72 per 10,000 population (1982)

ETHNIC COMPOSITION: Pushtun - 50%; Tajik - 25%; Uzbek - 9%; Hazara - 9%; other - 7%.

RELIGION: Sunni Moslem - 74%; Shiite Moslem - 25%; other - 1%.

LANGUAGE: The two principal languages are Pashtu and Dari. Other languages include Uzbek, Turkmen, Baluchi and Pashai.

EDUCATION: Illiteracy: 88%. In 1981/82, there were 3,824 elementary schools with 1,115,993 students; 447 secondary schools with 124,488 students; 45 vocational and technical colleges with 14,431 students; 14 teacher training institutes with 4,427 students; and 5 schools of higher education with 12,868 students.

ECONOMIC DATA

Expenditures by Function [as % of total]: (not available)
GDP per capita: $172 (1986)

TRAVEL NOTES

Climate: Afghanistan experiences a wide range of temperatures, with the southwest highlands peaking at 120°F in the summer, and the mountains in the northeast dropping to 15°F.
Health Precautions: Immunizations against smallpox, cholera and yellow fever are required. The water is not potable.
Miscellaneous: Tourists are generally not permitted to travel outside of Kabul due to the ongoing civil war. However, potential tourist attractions include numerous mosques, painted caves, suspended lakes and the mountains of Hindu Kush.

GOVERNMENT

Afghanistan (Republic of Afghanistan—De Afghanistan Jamhuriat [Pushtu]—Jonhuri-ye Afghanestan [Dari]) has been a republic since Jun 17, 1973, when the previous parliamentary constitutional monarchy was overthrown in a military coup led by the deposed monarch's cousin, Lt. Gen. Sardar Mohammad Daud Khan, who became President and Premier. On Apr 27, 1978, President Daud was overthrown and killed in a military coup, and a hard-line Communist regime took power, prompting a December 1979 invasion by the Soviet Union. Since 1978, Afghanistan has been engaged in a civil war fought between traditionalist Moslem insurgents and the Soviet-backed Government.

Constitution: The 1977 Constitution was abolished after the 1978 coup. A declaration of *Basic Principles* was ratified by the Revolutionary Council in 1980 and a Constitution closely resembling the Basic Principles was approved by the National Assembly in April 1985. A new Constitution, approved on Nov 30, 1987, changed the post of the president from a largely figurehead position to that of commander-in-chief of the army. The president was also granted a broad range of emergency powers.

ALBANIA
People's Socialist Republic of Albania

LOCATION: Albania is located on the west coast of the Balkan Peninsula and is bordered by Yugoslavia to the north and east, Greece to the southeast and the Ionian and Adriatic Seas to the west.

AREA: 11,100 sq. miles

Land Use: 43% forest; 21% cultivable; 19% meadow and pasture; 5% permanent crop; 5% inland water; 7% other.
Arable Land: 26%
Arable Land per capita: 0.61 acres

POPULATION: 3,020,000 (1986)

Population Density: 272 inhabs. per sq. mile (1986)
Population Distribution: 33.40 urban (1985)
Population Growth Rate: 2% per year (1986)

VITAL STATISTICS

Average Life Expectancy: 69 years (1983)
Male: (not available)
Female: (not available)
Age Distribution: (1985)
0-14: 35.40%
15-64: 59.70%
65+: 4.90%
Median Age: 22.10 years (1985)
Maternal Mortality: (not available)
Infant Mortality: 87 per 1,000 live births (1971)

HEALTH CARE

Hospital Beds: 62 per 10,000 population (1983)
Doctors: 17 per 10,000 population (1983)

ETHNIC COMPOSITION: Albanian - 96%; Greek, Vlach, Gypsy, Serb and Bulgarian - 4%.

RELIGION: The Government recognizes no religion and supports atheism. Before World War II, about 70% of Albanians practiced Islam, while about 20% were Albanian Orthodox and 10% were Roman Catholic.

LANGUAGE: Most people speak Albanian, and the official dialect is Tosk. The other principal dialect is Gheg, and there is also a small Greek-speaking minority.

EDUCATION: Illiteracy: 25%. In 1983, there were 1,621 primary schools with 532,300 students; 20 general secondary schools with 32,500 students; 313 vocational secondary schools with 123,500 students; and 8 institutions of higher learning with 17,500 students.

ECONOMIC DATA

Expenditures by Function [as % of total]: (not available)
GDP per capita: (not available)

TRAVEL NOTES

Climate: The climate is Mediterranean throughout the country with frequent cyclones in winter months.
Health Precautions: (not available)
Miscellaneous: Tourist attractions include the scenic coast and interior, the resort city of Durres and the castles of Berat, Kruje and Kuculla.

GOVERNMENT

Albania (Republika Popullore Socialiste e Shqiperise—The Socialist People's Republic of Albania) is a Communist one-party state.

Constitution: The political structure of Albania is based on the Constitution of 1946 as revised and formally adopted on Dec 27, 1976. The Constitution vests supreme authority in the People's Assembly, under the guidance of the Communist Albanian Labor Party. Effective policy-making power rests with the party politburo.

ALGERIA
Democratic and Popular Republic of Algeria

LOCATION: Algeria is located in northern Africa and is bounded by the Mediterranean Sea to the north, Tunisia to the northeast, Libya to the east, Niger to the southeast, Mali to the southwest and Mauritania, the Western Sahara and Morocco to the west.

QUALITY OF LIFE INDICATORS

AREA: 919,595 sq. miles

Land Use: 3.10% cropland; 13.40% permanent pasture; 1.84% forests and woodland; 81.66% other (mainly desert).
Arable Land: 3%
Arable Land per capita: 0.75 acres

POPULATION: 23,546,000 (1988 estimate)

Population Density: 26 inhabs. per sq. mile (1988 estimate)
Population Distribution: 42.60% urban (1985)
Population Growth Rate: 3.10% per year (1988 estimate)

VITAL STATISTICS

Average Life Expectancy: 62.50 years (1985-90 projection)
Male: 61.00 years (1985-90 projection)
Female: 64.10 years (1985-90 projection)
Age Distribution: (1985)
0-14 .... 45.42%
15-64 .... 50.94%
65+ 3.64%
Median Age: 17 years (1985)
Maternal Mortality: (not available)
Infant Mortality: 80 per 1,000 live births (1985)

HEALTH CARE

Hospital Beds: 20 per 10,000 population (1983)
Doctors: 4 per 10,000 population (1983)

ETHNIC COMPOSITION: Arab-Berber - 99%; European - 1%.

RELIGION: Sunni Moslem - 99%; Christian and Jewish - 1%. The state religion is Islam.

LANGUAGE: Arabic is the official language, but French and several Berber dialects are also spoken.

EDUCATION: Illiteracy: 48%. In 1983, there were 10,453 primary schools with 3,336,536 students and 13 institutions of higher learning with 95,867 students. In 1982, there were 1,250 middle and secondary schools with 1,420,303 students and 174 technical schools with 32,086 students. There were 40 teacher training schools in 1979 with 20,664 students in 1983.

ECONOMIC DATA

Expenditures by Function [as % of total]: (not available)

GDP per capita: $2,200 (1987)

TRAVEL NOTES

Climate: Algeria has a mild Mediterranean climate in the coastal areas, although there are frequent cyclones during the winter. The inland mountain regions have hot summers and cold winters, while the Sahara is extremely hot throughout the year. The average annual temperature is 57°F in the northeast and 64°F in the southwest.
Health Precautions: Typhoid and gamma globulin immunizations are recommended, along with inoculations against polio, diphtheria and tetanus. Yellow fever vaccination certificates are required of visitors coming from infected areas. The water is not potable.
Miscellaneous: Points of interest in Algeria include the Mediterranean coastline, the desert, the Atlas mountains, numerous thermal springs and boar-hunting reserves.

GOVERNMENT

Algeria (al-Jumhuriyah al-Jaza' iriyah al-Dimuq-ratiyah al-Sha' biyah—Democratic and Popular Republic of Algeria) gained independence from France on Jul 3, 1962, following an 8-year war of liberation led by the indigenous National Liberation Front (FLN). A civilian government under the leadership of Ahmed Ben Bella was set up in September 1963, but was deposed in June 1965 in a bloodless military coup led by Col. Houari Boumedienne. Colonel Boumedienne ruled as President of the National Council of the Algerian Revolution until his death in 1978. Col. Chadli Bendjedid was selected by the FLN, the country's sole legal political party, as the presidential designee, and after a brief interim government, Bendjedid was elected President in a national referendum on Feb 7, 1979.

Constitution: A new Constitution, adopted in November 1976, provided for a single-party socialist state with the National Liberation Front (FLN) serving as the vanguard force. The document was based on a National Charter approved earlier in the year in a popular referendum. The National Charter committed the state to the goal of creating a socialist society, with Islam as the official religion and the FLN as the leading force in society. The Constitution (which was amended by the National People's Assembly in 1979) gave sweeping powers to the presidency,

3

established Arabic as the official language and reaffirmed the state's control of the means of production, while guaranteeing respect for non-exploitative private property. The liberation of women and their full participation in the political, economic, social and cultural life of the nation was also guaranteed in the Constitution, along with the freedom of expression and assembly. A new National Charter, approved by referendum in 1986, reaffirmed the Government's commitment to socialism and Islam, and provided the opportunity for a more pragmatic approach to economic and social problems, including the partial privatization of the public sector.

ANDORRA
Valleys of Andorra

LOCATION: A landlocked country located in Western Europe, Andorra lies in the eastern Pyrenees mountain range, bounded by France to the north and Spain to the south.

AREA: 180 sq. miles

Land Use: 2% cropland; 56% permanent pasture; 22% forests and woodland; 20% other.
Arable Land: 2%
Arable Land per capita: 0.06 acres

POPULATION: 54,000 (1988 estimate)

Population Density: 300 inhabs. per sq. mile (1988 estimate)
Population Distribution: (not available)
Population Growth Rate: 3.90% per year (1988 estimate)

VITAL STATISTICS

Average Life Expectancy: (not available)
Male: (not available)
Female: (not available)
Age Distribution: (1987)
0-14 .... 27.00%
15-59 .... 60.50%
60+ 12.50%
Median Age: (not available)
Maternal Mortality: (not available)
Infant Mortality: 12 per 1,000 live births (1985)

HEALTH CARE

Hospital Beds: (not available)
Doctors: (not available)

ETHNIC COMPOSITION: Spanish - 61%; Andorran - 30%; French - 6%; other - 3%.

RELIGION: Virtually all of the population is Roman Catholic.

LANGUAGE: Catalan is the official language. Spanish and French are also widely spoken.

EDUCATION: Illiteracy: 0%. In 1986/87, there were 5,642 students in the 7- to 15-year-old age group and 1,328 students aged 15 years and over.

ECONOMIC DATA

Expenditures by Function [as % of total]: (not available)
GDP per capita: (not available)

TRAVEL NOTES

Climate: Andorra experiences an Alpine climate with temperate summers and much snowfall during the winter.
Health Precautions: (not available)
Miscellaneous: Tourists enjoy skiing in the winter and the mountain climate during the summer.

GOVERNMENT

Andorra (Valls d'Andorra—Les Vallees d'Andorre—Principado de Andorra—Valleys of Andorra) is a co-principality established in 1278 under the joint suzerainty of the President of the French Republic and the Spanish Bishop of Urgel. In April 1984, the Government of Oscar Ribas Reig was forced to resign following controversial proposals for indirect taxes. Josep Pintat Solans was appointed the new head of government on May 21, 1984.

Constitution: Andorra has no written Constitution, but the Plan of Reform, which was adopted in 1866, serves the function of a constitution.

ANGOLA
People's Republic of Angola

LOCATION: Lying on the west coast of Africa, Angola is bordered by Zaire to the north, Zambia to the east and Namibia to the south. The Cabinda district is separated from the rest of the country by the estuary of the River Congo and Zairian territory, with the Congo Republic to the north of it. On the east of both parts of the country is the Atlantic Ocean.

AREA: 481,354 sq. miles

Land Use: 44% forest; 22% meadow and pasture; 1% cultivated; 33% other (including fallow).
Arable Land: 2%
Arable Land per capita: 0.76 acres

POPULATION: 8,164,000 (1986)

Population Density: 16.96 inhabs. per sq. mile (1986)
Population Distribution: 24.50% urban (1985)
Population Growth Rate: 3.20% per year (1986)

VITAL STATISTICS

Average Life Expectancy: 42 years (1985)
Male: 40.40 years (1985)
Female: 43.60 years (1985)
Age Distribution: (1985)
0-14 .... 44.60%
15-64 .... 52.40%
65+ 3.00%
Median Age: 17.70 years (1985)
Maternal Mortality: (not available)
Infant Mortality: 148.50 per 1,000 live births (1984)

HEALTH CARE

Hospital Beds: 25.91 per 10,000 population (1980)
Doctors: 0.56 per 10,000 population (1980)

ETHNIC COMPOSITION: Ovimbundu - 37%; Kimbundu - 25%; Bakongo - 13%; Mestico - 2%; European - 1%; other - 22%.

RELIGION: Roman Catholic - 68%; Protestant - 20%; indigenous beliefs - 10%; other - 2%.

LANGUAGE: The official language is Portuguese. Various Bantu dialects, such as Ovimbundu, Kimbundu, Bakongo and Chokwe, are widely spoken.

EDUCATION: Illiteracy: 80%. In 1982, there were 1,258,858 primary school students; 136,466 general secondary school students; 2,564 teacher training school students; 2,642 vocational college students; and 374 higher college students.

ECONOMIC DATA

Expenditures by Function [as % of total]: (not available)
GDP per capita: $457 (1985)

TRAVEL NOTES

Climate: The climate is tropical, with two distinct seasons (wet and dry) but little seasonal variation in temperature. While it is very hot and rainy in the coastal region, temperatures are lower inland.
Health Precautions: While medical care is free, it is hampered by a shortage of trained personnel and medicines.
Miscellaneous: Security is continually hindered by guerrilla activity in southern and central Angola.

GOVERNMENT

Angola (Republica Popular de Angola—People's Republic of Angola) became an independent state on Nov 11, 1975, following the formal end of over 400 years of Portuguese colonial rule. Independence came amid civil war among Angolan nationalist groups (partly based on differing tribal loyalties), who immediately proclaimed the establishment of two rival governments. By February 1976, the forces of the Marxist-oriented Movimento Popular de Libertacao de Angola (MPLA—Popular Movement for the Liberation of Angola), led by Agostinho Neto, emerged triumphant. In December 1977, the MPLA was renamed the MPLA—Partido de Trabalho (Workers' Party), or MPLA-PT.

Constitution: The 1975 Constitution as amended in 1976 and 1980 vests responsibility for the political, economic and social leadership of the nation in the MPLA-PT. The MPLA-PT's supreme organ is the Congress, which meets every 4 years. It elects the MPLA-PT's president and a 75-member Central Committee to direct the party's work.

ARGENTINA
Argentine Republic

LOCATION: Argentina occupies most of South America south of the Tropic of Capricorn and east of the Andes. It has a long border with Chile on the west and is bordered by Bolivia and Paraguay on the north and Brazil and Uruguay on the east, with a long Atlantic coast on the eastern side.

AREA: 1,068,302 sq. miles

Land Use: 46% meadow and pasture; 11% crop; 25% forest; 18% mountain, urban and waste.
Arable Land: 12%
Arable Land per capita: 2.63 acres

POPULATION: 31,186,000 (1986)

Population Density: 29 inhabs. per sq. mile (1986)
Population Distribution: 80% urban (1983)
Population Growth Rate: 1.50% per year (1986)

VITAL STATISTICS

Average Life Expectancy: 70 years (1983)
Male: 66.80 years (1983)
Female: 73.20 years (1983)
Age Distribution: (1985)
0-14 .... 30.40%
15-59 .... 57.80%
60+ 11.80%
Median Age: 27.40 years (1985)
Maternal Mortality: 85 per 100,000 live births (1979)
Infant Mortality: 36 per 1,000 live births (1986)

HEALTH CARE

Hospital Beds: 52.40 per 10,000 population (1977)
Doctors: 19.20 per 10,000 population (1977)

ETHNIC COMPOSITION: Caucasian - 85%; Mestizo, Indian and other - 15%.

RELIGION: Roman Catholic - 92%; Protestant and other - 8%.

LANGUAGE: Spanish is the official language, while English, Italian, French and German are also spoken.

EDUCATION: Illiteracy: 6%. In 1982, there were 23,034 primary schools with 4,382,351 students; 4,896 secondary schools with 1,425,648 students; and 1,041 colleges and universities with 53,166 students.

ECONOMIC DATA

Expenditures by Function [as % of total]: (1983)
General public services 8.76%
Defense 9.09%
Education 7.64%
Health 1.37%
Social security and welfare 33.37%
Housing and community amenities 0.58%
Other community and social services 0.47%
Economic services 22.75%
Agriculture, forestry, fishing and hunting . 0.87%
Roads 3.15%
Other transport and communication 6.72%
Other purposes 27.30%
GDP per capita: $2,472 (1984)

TRAVEL NOTES

Climate: The climate varies from sub-tropical in the north to sub-antarctic in Patagonia in the south.
Health Precautions: No particular health risks exist in most areas of Argentina, though in the area near the Bolivian border there is some instance of malaria. Sanitary conditions are good and the water is safe. Tourists are advised to acquire all standard immunizations.
Miscellaneous: Argentina's many attractions include the Andes mountains, the lake district around Bariloche, Patagonia, the Perito Moreno glacier, the beaches on the Atlantic, Mar del Plata, the Iguazu falls, the Pampas, Buenos Aires and Tierra del Fuego.

GOVERNMENT

Argentina (Republica Argentina—Argentine Republic) won its independence from Spain in 1816. Its history has been marked by alternations of civilian and military rule. The latest period of military rule (1976-83) ended with presidential and legislative elections and the restoration of the 1853 Constitution. President Alfonsin, on Jun 8, 1987, signed into law a measure to move the capital (beginning late 1990) from Buenos Aires to the twin cities of Viedma and Carmen de Patagones, located in the southern region of Patagonia.

Constitution: The 1853 Constitution provides for separation of executive, legislative and judicial powers. It was suspended in 1976 after a military coup, but was reinstated (with some electoral changes) with the return of civilian rule in December 1983. In September 1987 President Alfonsin postponed a plan to reform the Constitution.

AUSTRALIA
Commonwealth of Australia

LOCATION: Australia is an island continent lying between the Indian and Pacific Oceans. Indonesia is to the north, across the Timor and Arafura Seas, while Papua New Guinea lies to the north across the Coral Sea. In addition to the principal island, Australia also includes numerous offshore islands, the most important of which is Tasmania to the southeast.

AREA: 2,966,151 sq. miles

Land Use: 6.11% cropland; 57.82% permanent pasture; 13.92% forests and woodland; 22.15% other.
Arable Land: 6.11%
Arable Land per capita: 7.20 acres

POPULATION: 16,102,000 (1987 projection)

Population Density: 5.43 inhabs. per sq. mile (1987 projection)
Population Distribution: 85.50% urban (1985)
Population Growth Rate: 1.25% per year (1985-90 projection)

VITAL STATISTICS

Average Life Expectancy: 75.70 years (1985-90 projection)
Male: 72.30 years (1985-90 projection)
Female: 79.30 years (1985-90 projection)
Age Distribution: (1985)
0-14 . . . . 23.60%
15-64 . . . . 66.30%
65+ 10.10%
Median Age: 30.60 years (1985)
Maternal Mortality: 25 per 100,000 live births (1981)
Infant Mortality: 8 per 1,000 live births (1985-90 projection)

HEALTH CARE

Hospital Beds: 107 per 10,000 population (1984)
Doctors: 22 per 10,000 population (1984)

ETHNIC COMPOSITION: Caucasian - 96%; other - 4% (including Asian and Aborigine).

RELIGION: Anglican - 26.10%; Roman Catholic - 26.00%; other Christian - 24.30%; other - 23.60%.

LANGUAGE: English is the official language, but aboriginal languages are also spoken in certain regions.

EDUCATION: Illiteracy: 1.50%. In 1983, there were 7,546 primary and secondary government schools with 2,281,022 students; 2,362 non-government schools with 734,784 students; 209 technical colleges with 1,027,052 students; 19 universities with 169,350 students; and 45 colleges of advanced education with 179,893 students.

ECONOMIC DATA

Expenditures by Function [as % of total]: (1984)
General public services 7.34%
Defense 9.25%
Education 7.53%
Health 7.83%
Social security and welfare 28.91%
Housing and community amenities 1.37%
Other community and social services 1.08%
Economic services 8.62%
Agriculture, forestry, fishing and hunting . 1.29%
Roads 2.19%
Other transport and communication 1.20%
Other purposes 28.07%
GDP per capita: $10,350 (1986)

TRAVEL NOTES

Climate: The northern part of Australia experiences tropical monsoons in the summer and dry winters. The northwest and northeast coasts sometimes have tropical cyclones between December and April, while in the south the wet season is winter. The inland is very dry, and extremely high temperatures (over 122°F) occur during the summer in the interior, and in the north during the pre-monsoon months.
Health Precautions: None
Miscellaneous: Quicker and cheaper international air transport is contributing to a growing Australian tourist industry. Popular attractions include the Pacific beaches, the Great Barrier Reef, the Australian Alps, the Blue Mountains and the sandstone monolith of Ayers Rock.

GOVERNMENT

Australia (Commonwealth of Australia) became an independent dominion under the British Crown on Jan 1, 1901, when a federation of 6 former British colonies was inaugurated. It is a constitutional monarchy with a parliamentary form of government. On Mar 2, 1986, Queen Elizabeth II signed into law the Australia Act, which gives Australia full legal independence from Britain, including the removal of the right of appeal from Australian courts to the Privy Council in London. The Queen remains the sovereign, however.

Constitution: The Constitution (promulgated on Jul 9, 1900) provides for a federal system with a strong central Government, but with a wide range of independent authority vested in the member states. The governments at both state and federal levels are patterned after the British parliamentary system. Amendments to the Constitution must receive the approval of an absolute majority in both houses of Parliament and must be submitted within 6 months to voters in each state for approval. However, if an amendment twice receives an absolute majority in one house, but not in the other, the Governor General may submit the proposal to the electorate for ratification, which requires approval by a majority of electors and a majority of states. Amendments affecting the territorial limits of a state or diminishing its proportional representation in Parliament require the approval of a majority of voters in that state. The Constitution forbids the establishment of an official religion or prohibiting the exercise of any religion.

AUSTRIA
Republic of Austria

LOCATION: Austria is located in central Europe and is bordered by West Germany and Czechoslovakia to the north, Switzerland and Liechtenstein to the west, Italy and Yugoslavia to the south and Hungary to the east.

AREA: 32,377 sq. miles

Land Use: 38% forested; 26% meadow and pasture; 20% agricultural; 15% waste and urban; 1% inland water.

Arable Land: 20%
Arable Land per capita: 0.55 acres

POPULATION: 7,564,000 (1986)

Population Density: 234 inhabs. per sq. mile (1986)
Population Distribution: 55% urban (1985)
Population Growth Rate: 0% per year (1986)

VITAL STATISTICS

Average Life Expectancy: 73 years (1986)
Male: 69.30 years (1981)
Female: 76.40 years (1981)
Age Distribution: (1985)
0-14 .... 19.10%
15-59 .... 60.50%
60+ 20.40%
Median Age: (not available)
Maternal Mortality: 11.10 per 100,000 live births (1983)
Infant Mortality: 11.50 per 1,000 live births (1984)

HEALTH CARE

Hospital Beds: 112 per 10,000 population (1981)
Doctors: 23 per 10,000 population (1981)

ETHNIC COMPOSITION: German - 99.40%; Croatian - 0.30%; Slovene - 0.20%; other - 0.10%.

RELIGION: Roman Catholic - 88%; Protestant - 6%; other - 6%

LANGUAGE: German is the official language, while there are small Croat and Slovene-speaking minorities.

EDUCATION: Illiteracy: 2%. In 1984/85, there were 3,414 primary schools with 349,030 students; 1,715 secondary schools with 500,281 students; 1,194 compulsory vocational schools with 372,518 students; 73 teacher training schools with 16,823 students; and 18 colleges and universities with 151,934 students.

ECONOMIC DATA

Expenditures by Function [as % of total]: (1983)
General public services 6.95%
Defense 3.21%
Education 9.64%
Health 11.48%
Social security and welfare 45.55%
Housing and community amenities 3.05%

Other community and social services 1.33%
Economic services 13.15%
Agriculture, forestry, fishing and hunting . . 2.86%
Roads 3.47%
Other transportation and communication . . 3.79%
Other purposes 5.62%
GDP per capita: $10,461 (1985)

TRAVEL NOTES

Climate: The average annual temperature is between 45°F and 48°F, though the climate varies
greatly with the vast differences in altitude.
Health Precautions: No special precautions are
necessary. The tap water is potable.
Miscellaneous: Austria's forests and mountain
scenery attract visitors the year round, while the
ski resorts are popular during the winter. Vienna
is a great cultural and historical center famous
for its opera houses, museums and art galleries.

GOVERNMENT

*Austria (Republik Oesterreich - Republic of
Austria)* is a federal republic with a parliamentary form of government.

Constitution: The Austrian federal Constitution
divides the jurisdictions of the central and
provincial governments into 4 categories: areas
belonging exclusively to the central Government (e.g., foreign affairs); areas in which
policy-making authority is vested in the central
Government, but administration is the responsibility of the province (e.g., elections, population matters, road affairs); areas where the
Central Government has laid down the rudi-
ments of the law, but the provinces make and
administer the law (e.g., land reform, agricultural workers' rights, charities); and areas not
expressly reserved to the central Government
which are the responsibility of the province
(e.g., municipal affairs).

BAHAMAS
Commonwealth of the Bahamas

LOCATION: The Bahamas are an archipelago of
more than 2,700 islands, rocks and keys spread
over 90,000 square miles of the western Atlantic
Ocean, extending southeastward from off the coast
of Florida to just north of Cuba and Haiti.

AREA: 5,382 sq. miles

Land Use: 29% forest; 1% cultivated; 70% urban,
waste and other.
Arable Land: 2%
Arable Land per capita: 0.29 acres

POPULATION: 235,000 (1986)

Population Density: 43.66 inhabs. per sq. mile
(1986)
Population Distribution: 75% urban (1986)
Population Growth Rate: 1.80% per year (1986)

VITAL STATISTICS

Average Life Expectancy: 67 years (1985)
Male: 64 years (1985)
Female: 70 years (1985)
Age Distribution: (1985)
0-14 . . . . 43.60%
15-59 . . . . 50.90%
60+ 5.50%
Median Age: 27.30 years (1985)
Maternal Mortality: 38.10 per 100,000 live
births (1981)
Infant Mortality: 22.20 per 1,000 live births
(1984)

HEALTH CARE

Hospital Beds: 45 per 10,000 population (1980)
Doctors: 9 per 10,000 population (1980)

ETHNIC COMPOSITION: Black - 85%; white -
15%.

RELIGION: Baptist - 29%; Anglican - 23%; Roman
Catholic - 22%; other - 26%.

LANGUAGE: The official language is English.

EDUCATION: Illiteracy: 11%. In 1982/83, there
were 78 primary schools with 27,728 students; 37
junior and senior high schools with 23,495 students and 4 special schools with 264 students. In
1981, there were 3,963 students at the College of
the Bahamas.

ECONOMIC DATA

Expenditures by Function [as % of total]: (1979)
General public services 19.33%
Defense 1.29%
Education 23.11%
Health 13.92%
Social security and welfare 7.37%

9

Housing and community amenities 0.29%
Other community and social services 0.67%
Economic services 24.40%
Agriculture, forestry, fishing and hunting . . 2.25%
Roads 1.44%
Other transportation and communication . . 3.83%
Other purposes 9.62%
GDP per capita: $6,899 (1981)

TRAVEL NOTES

Climate: The climate in the Bahamas is sub-tropical, with summertime temperatures averaging about 86°F and wintertime temperatures about 68°F.

Health Precautions: Health care in the Bahamas is good, as is the sanitation. The food, most of which is imported from the US, is thoroughly inspected. There is a high incidence of respiratory ailments in Nassau, and typhoid and dysentery occur periodically in some of the poorer areas of the country.

Miscellaneous: The mild climate and beautiful beaches are the primary tourist attractions. Tourism is the principal source of income.

GOVERNMENT

Bahamas (Commonwealth of the Bahamas) became an independent state on Jul 10, 1973. A former British colonial territory, it recognizes the British monarch as head of state. Effective political authority rests with the majority party or coalition in Parliament.

Constitution: The Constitution of Jul 10, 1973 set up a parliamentary system modeled on the British system of government. Amendments to central features of the Constitution (such as the parliamentary system itself) require an extraordinary majority or three-fourths in both houses of Parliament and must be approved by a majority of the popular vote in a national referendum.

BAHREIN
State of Bahrein

LOCATION: Bahrein consists of an archipelago in the Arabian Gulf, with the peninsula of Qatar to the east and the coast of Saudi Arabia to the west.

AREA: 240 sq. miles

Land Use: 3.23% cropland; 6.45% permanent pasture; 0% forests and woodland; 90.32% other (mostly desert).
Arable Land: 3%
Arable Land per capita: 0.01 acres

POPULATION: 470,000 (1988 estimate)

Population Density: 1,958 inhabs. per sq. mile (1988)
Population Distribution: 81.71% urban (1985)
Population Growth Rate: 2.70% per year (1988)

VITAL STATISTICS

Average Life Expectancy: 70.60 years (1985-90 projection)
Male: 68.30 years (1985-90 projection)
Female: 73.00 years (1985-90 projection)
Age Distribution: (1985)
0-14 . . . . 33.80%
15-64 . . . . 64.35%
65+ 1.85%
Median Age: 24.20 years (1985)
Maternal Mortality: (not available)
Infant Mortality: 34 per 1,000 live births (1985)

HEALTH CARE

Hospital Beds: 32 per 10,000 population (1981)
Doctors: 11 per 10,000 population (1982)

ETHNIC COMPOSITION: Bahreini - 63%; Asian - 13%; other Arab - 10%; Iranian - 8%; other - 6%.

RELIGION: Shiite Moslem - 60%; Sunni Moslem - 40%.

LANGUAGE: Arabic is the official language; English is widely spoken.

EDUCATION: Illiteracy: 27%. In 1986, there was a total of 139 schools with 50,936 students enrolled in primary schools, 19,838 students enrolled in intermediate schools, 12,349 students enrolled in secondary schools, 2,630 students enrolled in technical schools and 114 students in religious schools. Bahrein has 2 universities and 1 college for nurses and paramedics.

ECONOMIC DATA

Expenditures by Function [as % of total]: (1987)
General public services 22.99%
Defense 12.20%

Education 10.70%
Health 6.42%
Social security and welfare 2.18%
Housing and community amenities 8.34%
Other community and social services 1.54%
Economic services 27.91%
Agriculture, forestry, fishing and hunting . . 1.68%
Roads 6.81%
Other transportation and communication . . 2.10%
Other purposes 7.72%
GDP per capita: $8,322 (1986)

TRAVEL NOTES

Climate: The climate is temperate between the months of November and April, but hot and humid the rest of the year. Daytime temperatures regularly reach 100°F in the summer, with the relative humidity averaging 70% to 80%. Bahrein receives less than 4 inches of rainfall annually.

Health Precautions: Inoculations for cholera, typhoid, tetanus/diphtheria and polio are recommended, and care should be taken to avoid heat exhaustion.

Miscellaneous: Bahrein has several interesting archaeological sites, and is the home of the Arabian Gulf University, an institution funded jointly with several neighboring countries. The recently completed causeway linking Bahrein with Saudi Arabia has quadrupled the annual number of visitors to the island.

GOVERNMENT

Bahrein (Dawlat al-Bahrayn—State of Bahrein) is an hereditary emirate ruled since 1782 by the Al Khalifa family. The British established a protectorate over Bahrein in 1861, which endured until Aug 14, 1971, when Bahrein formally declared its independence.

Constitution: Bahrein's first written Constitution was adopted on Dec 6, 1973. It declares Bahrein to be an Islamic State, whose laws must conform to the Sharia (traditional Islamic legal principles). The Constitution guarantees all citizens the right of free speech and the right to assemble peaceably, and provides for freedom of the press and the equality of all citizens before the law. Other provisions in the Constitution include compulsory free primary education and free medical care for the people of Bahrein. The 1973 Constitution also established a National Assembly, which was later dissolved by the Emir.

BANGLADESH
People's Republic of Bangladesh

LOCATION: Situated in southern Asia, Bangladesh shares a small portion of its southeastern border with Burma; it has a southern coast on the Bay of Bengal.

AREA: 55,598 sq. miles

Land Use: 68% cropland; 5% permanent pasture; 16% forests and woodland; 11% other.
Arable Land: 68%
Arable Land per capita: 0.23 acres

POPULATION: 106,651,000 (1987 projection)

Population Density: 1,918 inhabs. per sq. mile (1987)
Population Distribution: 11.90% urban (1985)
Population Growth Rate: 2.61% per year (1985-90 projection)

VITAL STATISTICS

Average Life Expectancy: 49.60 years (1985-90 projection)
Male: 50.10 years (1985-90 projection)
Female: 49.10 years (1985-90 projection)
Age Distribution: (1985)
0-14 . . . . 45.70%
15-64 . . . . 51.20%
65+ 3.10%
Median Age: 17 years (1985)
Maternal Mortality: (not available)
Infant Mortality: 119 per 1,000 live births (1985-90 projection)

HEALTH CARE

Hospital Beds: 2.17 per 10,000 population (1981)
Doctors: 1.12 per 10,000 population (1981)

ETHNIC COMPOSITION: Bengali - 98%; other (including non-Bengali Moslems, or Biharis) - 2%.

RELIGION: Moslem - 83%; Hindu - 16%; Buddhist, Christian and other - 1%.

LANGUAGE: The official language is Bengali; English is also widely used.

EDUCATION: Illiteracy: 71%. In 1984/85, there were 44,423 primary schools with 9,914,000 students; 8,594 secondary schools with 2,657,000 students; 123 technical colleges with 23,606 students; and 6 universities with 41,215 students.

ECONOMIC DATA

Expenditures by Function [as % of total]: (1980)
General public services 19.56%
Defense 9.44%
Education 11.49%
Health 6.37%
Social security and welfare 5.04%
Housing and community amenities 0.30%
Other community and social services 0.83%
Economic services 46.95%
Agriculture, forestry, fishing and hunting . 13.02%
Roads .... (not available)
Other transportation and communication .. 4.28%
Other purposes 10.57%
GDP per capita: $148 (1986)

TRAVEL NOTES

Climate: Bangladesh has a tropical monsoon climate with an average annual temperature of 84°F, and periodic cyclones.

Health Precautions: Immunization against cholera is required of travelers. Immunizations against typhoid, tetanus, diphtheria and polio are also recommended, as are gamma globulin shots. Precautions against malaria are also necessary in some areas. Water should be boiled before being used for human consumption. Care should be taken in choosing restaurants since some may not sterilize the water they use.

Miscellaneous: Tourist attractions include the world's longest beach (75 miles) at Cox's Bazar on the Bay of Bengal and the cities of Dhaka and Chittagong.

GOVERNMENT:

Bangladesh (Ganaprojatantri Bangladesh—People's Republic of Bangladesh), formerly the Eastern Province of Pakistan, proclaimed its independence on Mar 26, 1971 and achieved full independence in early 1972, after a civil war and military intervention by India against Pakistani forces. Since Aug 17, 1975, when President Sheik Mujibur Rahman was assassinated in a junior officers' coup, effective political power has rested with the armed forces, who have generally ruled under martial law regimes. The most recent military coup, on Mar 24, 1982, was led by Lt. Gen. Hussain Mohammed Ershad. Ershad suspended the Constitution and declared himself armed forces commander-in-chief and chief martial law administrator. Ershad declared himself President on Dec 11, 1983, and extended his term for one more year on Apr 30, 1985. Martial law was lifted in November 1986 and constitutional government was revived.

Constitution: The Constitution came into effect on Nov 4, 1972 and was subsequently amended. It was suspended when martial law was imposed following the March 1982 military coup but was revived on Nov 10, 1986 when martial law was lifted.

BARBADOS

LOCATION: Barbados is the easternmost Caribbean island, located about 200 miles northeast of Trinidad.

AREA: 166 sq. miles

Land Use: 77% cropland; 9% permanent pasture; 0% forests and woodland; 14% other.
Arable Land: 77%
Arable Land per capita: 0.32 acres

POPULATION: 256,000 (1987 projection)

Population Density: 1,542 inhabs. per sq. mile (1987 projection)
Population Distribution: 42.20% urban (1985)
Population Growth Rate: 0.60% per year (1985-90 projection)

VITAL STATISTICS

Average Life Expectancy: 73.50 years (1985-90 projection)
Male: 70.70 years (1985-90 projection)
Female: 76.40 years (1985-90 projection)
Age Distribution: (1985)
0-14 .... 27.10%
15-64 .... 62.20%
65+ 10.70%
Median Age: 26.20 years (1985)
Maternal Mortality: 24.10 per 100,000 live births (1980)
Infant Mortality: 11 per 1,000 live births (1985-90 projection)

HEALTH CARE

Hospital Beds: 85.04 per 10,000 population (1980)
Doctors: 8.04 per 10,000 population (1979)

ETHNIC COMPOSITION: African - 80%; mixed African and European - 16%; European - 4%.

RELIGION: Anglican - 70%; Methodist - 9%; Roman Catholic - 4%; other - 17% (including Moravian).

LANGUAGE: English

EDUCATION: Illiteracy: 1%. In 1984/85, there were 138 primary schools with 33,906 students; 21 secondary schools with 21,474 students; 15 state-aided independent schools with 4,227 students; 1 technical institute with 1,600 students; 1 teacher training institute with 186 students; 1 theological school with 20 students; 1 community college with 1,806 students; and 1 university with 1,617 students.

ECONOMIC DATA

Expenditures by Function [as % of total]: (1983)
General public services 16.37%
Defense 2.88%
Education 18.49%
Health 10.59%
Social security and welfare 17.46%
Housing and community amenities 4.70%
Other community and social services 1.46%
Economic services 19.30%
Agriculture, forestry, fishing and hunting . . 3.69%
Roads 4.98%
Other transportation and communication . . 2.47%
Other purposes 8.75%
GDP per capita: $4,920 (1985)

TRAVEL NOTES

Climate: The climate is warm most of the year, except during the rainy season, which lasts from July to November. The average annual temperature is 78°F.

Health Precautions: Health conditions in Barbados are generally good, with adequate medical and surgical services. Typhoid shots, tetanus boosters and polio immunizations are recommended. The water is good and does not require boiling.

Miscellaneous: The natural attractions of Barbados consist primarily of the beautiful scenery and pleasant climate. There are also many facilities for a variety of outdoor sports. Bathsheba, a well-known health resort, is located on the east coast of the island.

GOVERNMENT

Barbados has historically been a planter-dominated island, and has been shaped by a British tradition extending back to 1639. While a British colony, Barbados was often referred to as the Little England of the Caribbean. It became an independent sovereign state within the Commonwealth of Nations on Nov 30, 1966, following several unsuccessful attempts to form a federation of various Caribbean states.

Constitution: The independence Constitution established a governmental structure based on the British parliamentary system.

BELGIUM
Kingdom of Belgium

LOCATION: Lying in northwestern Europe, Belgium is bordered by the Netherlands to the north, West Germany and Luxembourg to the east, France to the south and the North Sea to the northwest.

AREA: 11,780 sq. miles

Land Use: 25.23% cropland; 20.48% permanent pasture; 21.39% forests and woodland; 32.90% other.
Arable Land: 25%
Arable Land per capita: 0.19 acres

POPULATION: 9,888,000 (1988 estimate)

Population Density: 840 inhabs. per sq. mile (1988 estimate)
Population Distribution: 96.28% urban (1985)
Population Growth Rate: 0.10% per year (1988 estimate)

VITAL STATISTICS

Average Life Expectancy: 74.30 years (1985-90 projection)
Male: 70.90 years (1985-90 projection)
Female: 77.90 years (1985-90 projection)
Age Distribution: (1985)
0-14 . . . . 18.93%

15-64 .... 67.64%
65+ 13.43%
Median Age: 35.10 years (1985)
Maternal Mortality: 8.60 per 100,000 live births (1984)
Infant Mortality: 10 per 1,000 live births (1985)

HEALTH CARE

Hospital Beds: 93 per 10,000 population (1983)
Doctors: 29 per 10,000 population (1984)

ETHNIC COMPOSITION: Flemish - 55%; Walloon - 33%; other - 12%.

RELIGION: Roman Catholic - 75%; other - 25% (mainly Protestant).

LANGUAGE: Flemish (Dutch) - 56%; French - 32%; bilingual - 11%; German - 1%. Flemish and French are official languages.

EDUCATION: Illiteracy: 2%. In 1983/84, there were 4,383 primary schools with 755,576 students; 827,839 secondary school students and 143,408 university and higher learning students. In 1982/83, there were 314 secondary schools; 250 technical schools with 84,588 students; 168 teacher training schools with 25,166 students; and 19 universities and other higher institutions of learning.

ECONOMIC DATA

Expenditures by Function [as % of total]: (1985)
General public services 5.27%
Defense 5.21%
Education 12.92%
Health 1.71%
Social security and welfare 39.35%
Housing and community amenities 1.74%
Other community and social services 0.73%
Economic services 11.82%
Agriculture, forestry, fishing and hunting .. 0.67%
Roads 1.50%
Other transportation and communication .. 5.24%
Other purposes 20.29%
GDP per capita: $16,203 (1987)

TRAVEL NOTES

Climate: The Belgian climate is moderate; summer temperatures average 60°F. The weather along the coast is more temperate than the weather inland.

Health Precautions: There are no special health precautions and the water is potable.
Miscellaneous: Gothic and Renaissance architecture, numerous art museums with works of the Flemish masters and the annual summer Festival of Flanders are among the many tourist attractions.

GOVERNMENT

Belgium (Royaume de Belgique—Koninkrijk Belgie—Konigreich Belgien—Kingdom of Belgium) became independent from the Netherlands on Oct 4, 1830. It is a constitutional monarchy with a parliamentary form of government. Effective political authority rests with an elected Parliament and a Cabinet responsible to it. Throughout its history, the country has been subject to ethnic and linguistic tensions between Dutch-speakers (Flemish), French-speakers (Walloons) and a small German-speaking minority. This strife has caused several constitutional crises and forced the change of several administrations. The most recent such crisis occurred in late 1987 when Prime Minister Wilfried Martens was forced to resign, although he formed a new coalition Government several months later.

Constitution: The Constitution of 1931 established a constitutional, representative and hereditary monarchy. Since then, it has been frequently amended, mostly at the expense of royal prerogatives, in favor of more representative political institutions and procedures. Recent changes in the Constitution have been designed to decentralize the central government and to grant greater authority to new regional governments, and to reflect the interests and desires for autonomy of Belgium's cultural and linguistic communities. Constitutional amendments are proposed by a simple majority of both houses of Parliament, after which elections for a new Parliament are held. The newly-elected Parliament may approve the amendments by a two-thirds vote in both houses, provided that a special quorum of two-thirds of the members of each house is observed.

BELIZE

LOCATION: Belize is located on the east coast of Central America, with Mexico to the northwest, Guatemala to the southwest and the Gulf of Honduras to the east.

AREA: 8,865 sq. miles

Land Use: 2% cropland; 2% permanent pasture; 44% forests and woodland; 52% other.
Arable Land: 2%
Arable Land per capita: 0.66 acres

POPULATION: 176,000 (1988 estimate)

Population Density: 20 inhabs. per sq. mile (1988 estimate)
Population Distribution: (not available)
Population Growth Rate: 2.10% per year (1988 estimate)

VITAL STATISTICS

Average Life Expectancy: 66 years (1988)
Male: (not available)
Female: (not available)
Age Distribution: (1986)
0-14 .... 45.30%
15-59 .... 47.60%
60+ 7.10%
Median Age: (not available)
Maternal Mortality: (not available)
Infant Mortality: 19 per 1,000 live births (1985)

HEALTH CARE

Hospital Beds: 35 per 10,000 population (1985)
Doctors: 5 per 10,000 population (1985)

ETHNIC COMPOSITION: Creole - 39.70%; Mestizo - 33.10%; Maya - 9.50%; Garifuna - 7.60%; East Indian - 2.10%; other - 7.00%.

RELIGION: Roman Catholic - 60%; Protestant - 40%.

LANGUAGE: English is the official language, but Spanish is widely spoken. Other languages are Maya and Garifuna (Carib).

EDUCATION: Illiteracy: 7%. In 1985, there were 225 primary schools with 38,512 students; 24 secondary schools with 6,676 students; and 5 institutions of higher learning with 765 students.

ECONOMIC DATA

Expenditures by Function [as % of total]: (1985)
General public services 16.07%
Defense 5.69%
Education 15.46%
Health 8.99%
Social security and welfare 7.83%
Housing and community amenities 2.89%
Other community and social services 0.79%
Economic services 25.76%
Agriculture, forestry, fishing and hunting . 9.76%
Roads 10.60%
Other transportation and communication .. 1.38%
Other purposes 16.52%
GDP per capita: $1,284 (1986)

TRAVEL NOTES

Climate: The Belizean climate is subtropical. Temperatures generally range from 70°F to 90°F, while a rainy season occurs from June through November.
Health Precautions: Precautions should be taken against hepatitis, malaria and typhoid. Tap water is not potable.
Miscellaneous: Tourists are attracted by beautiful beaches as well as relics of the Mayan civilization.

GOVERNMENT

Belize (previously British Honduras) was settled in the 1600s by the British, and became a British colony in 1862. In 1964, it assumed autonomy over its internal affairs, and finally became an independent nation within the British Commonwealth on Sep 21, 1981. The country is locked in a dispute with neighboring Guatemala, which claims sovereignty over the country. Various negotiations have resulted in proposals that Guatemala drop this claim in exchange for access to the Caribbean Sea, although the dispute has yet to be definitively settled.

Constitution: The independence Constitution, in effect since Sep 21, 1981, preserves the internal democratic institutions of the Constitution that came into force on Jan 1, 1964. It bars discrimination on the basis of race or sex, and guarantees freedom of expression, association, assembly and movement.

BENIN
People's Republic of Benin

LOCATION: Benin is located in West Africa, with a short southern coastline on the Bight of Benin, an arm of the Atlantic Ocean. Nigeria lies to the east, Niger to the north, Burkina Faso to the northwest and Togo to the west.

AREA: 43,484 sq. miles

Land Use: 16.35% cropland; 4.00% permanent pasture; 34.53% forests and woodland; 45.12% other.
Arable Land: 80%
Arable Land per capita: 5.17 acres

POPULATION: 4,307,000 (1987)

Population Density: 99 inhabs. per sq. mile (1987)
Population Distribution: 33.13% urban (1985)
Population Growth Rate: 3.12% per year (1985-90)

VITAL STATISTICS

Average Life Expectancy: 46.00 years (1985-90)
Male: 44.40 years (1985-90)
Female: 47.60 years (1985-90)
Age Distribution: (1985)
0-14 .... 46.80%
15-64 .... 50.40%
65+ 2.90%
Median Age: 16.60 years (1985)
Maternal Mortality: (not available)
Infant Mortality: 110 per 1,000 live births (1985-90)

HEALTH CARE

Hospital Beds: 11 per 10,000 population (1981)
Doctors: 0.57 per 10,000 population (1980)

ETHNIC COMPOSITION: Africans - 99% (42 ethnic groups, the most important being Fon, Adja, Yoruba and Bariba); 1% other.

RELIGION: Indigenous beliefs - 70%; Christianity - 15%; Islam - 15%.

LANGUAGE: French is the official language, though each indigenous group speaks its own language. Bariba and Fulani are widely spoken in the south, while Fon and Yoruba are prevalent in the north.

EDUCATION: Illiteracy: 80%. In 1982, there were 2,723 primary schools with 428,185 students; 133 general secondary schools with 117,724 students; 30 vocational secondary schools with 6,543 students; and 13 institutions of higher learning with 6,302 students.

ECONOMIC DATA

Expenditures by Function [as % of total]: (1979)
General public services 13.09%
Defense 8.75%
Education 20.48%
Health 5.56%
Social security and welfare 8.70%
Housing and community amenities 2.55%
Other community and social services 0.46%
Economic services 20.84%
Agriculture, forestry, fishing and hunting . 7.92%
Roads 6.90%
Other transportation and communication .. 0.05%
Other purposes 9.04%
GDP per capita: $248 (1983)

TRAVEL NOTES

Climate: The northern interior of Benin is tropical with a maximum temperature of about 115°F, and with a rainy season lasting from June to October. The coastal areas in the south are less warm, with temperatures usually between 68°F and 93°F. The main coastal rainy season lasts from March until July, while there is a shorter, less intense rainy season from September to November.
Health Precautions: Water should be boiled and filtered, and fresh vegetables should be treated in a solution of potassium permanganate or chlorine before being rinsed in sterilized and filtered water. Valid vaccinations for cholera and yellow fever are necessary for entering Benin, and precautions against hepatitis and malaria are recommended as well. The nation's proximity to the equator also necessitates precautions against sun exposure.
Miscellaneous: Safaris in Benin can be arranged in the country's two national parks, and on numerous other hunting reserves.

GOVERNMENT

Benin (Republique Populaire du Benin—People's Republic of Benin) gained independence from France as the republic of Dahomey on Aug 1, 1960. Since Oct 26, 1972, political power has rested with a group of left-wing military officers (led by President Brig. Gen. Ahmed [Mathieu] Kerekou) committed to the establishment of a socialist society in Benin with Marxism-Leninism as its revolutionary philosophy and basis. On Nov 30, 1975, President Kerekou announced that Dahomey would henceforth be called the People's Republic of Benin. With the adoption of a Loi Fondamentale in 1977, the Kerekou regime converted itself into a civilian Government.

Constitution: A Loi Fondamentale (Basic Law) was announced on May 23, 1977 by the Party of the People's Revolution of Benin. Approved that August by the ruling military National Revolutionary Council, the Loi provided for the replacement of the Council by an elected National Revolutionary Assembly. The Loi was amended in 1984.

BERMUDA

LOCATION: Comprising about 150 islands, the Bermudas (or Somers) form an isolated archipelago in the Atlantic Ocean, about 570 miles off the coast of South Carolina in the US.

AREA: 20.65 sq. miles

Land Use: 60% forest; 21% built on or waste land; 11% leased for air and naval bases; 8% cultivable.
Arable Land: 8%
Arable Land per capita: 0.02 acres

POPULATION: 59,000 (1986)

Population Density: 2,857 inhabs. per sq. mile (1986)
Population Distribution: (not available)
Population Growth Rate: 0.60% per year (1986)

VITAL STATISTICS

Average Life Expectancy: 72.55 years (1980)
Male: 68.81 years (1980)
Female: 76.28 years (1980)
Age Distribution: (not available)
Median Age: (not available)
Maternal Mortality: (not available)
Infant Mortality: 7.10 per 1,000 live births (1985)

HEALTH CARE

Hospital Beds: 84.48 per 10,000 population (1985)
Doctors: 13.10 per 10,000 population (1985)

ETHNIC COMPOSITION: Black - 61%; white and other - 39%.

RELIGION: Anglican - 37%; other Protestant - 21%; Roman Catholic - 14%; Black Moslem and other - 28%.

LANGUAGE: English is the official language.

EDUCATION: Illiteracy: 2%. Education is free and compulsory from age 5 to 16. There are 5 private secondary schools, and there is a Bermuda College. Extramural degree courses are available through a few Canadian and US universities.

ECONOMIC DATA

Expenditures by Function [as % of total]: (not available)
GDP per capita: $17,293 (1983/84)

TRAVEL NOTES

Climate: With average annual rainfall at 58 inches and temperatures usually between 46°F and 90°F, Bermuda is mild and humid.
Health Precautions: None
Miscellaneous: The main tourist attractions are the climate, outdoor entertainment facilities and scenery.

GOVERNMENT

Bermuda is a British colony which enjoys a large measure of internal self-government.

Constitution: The 1968 Constitution, amended in 1973 and 1979, provides for a parliamentary government.

BHUTAN
Kingdom of Bhutan

LOCATION: A landlocked country in Asia's Himalayan mountains, Bhutan is bordered by India to the south and China to the north.

AREA: 17,950 sq. miles

Land Use: 2.09% cropland; 4.62% permanent pasture; 69.79% forests and woodland; 23.50% other.
Arable Land: 2%
Arable Land per capita: 0.17 acres

POPULATION: 1,507,000 (1988 estimate)

Population Density: 84 inhabs. per sq. mile (1988 estimate)
Population Distribution: 4.52% urban (1985)
Population Growth Rate: 2.00% per year (1988 estimate)

VITAL STATISTICS

Average Life Expectancy: 47.90 years (1985-90 projection)
Male: 48.60 years (1985-90 projection)
Female: 47.10 years (1985-90 projection)
Age Distribution: (1985)
0-14 .... 40.01%
15-64 .... 56.67%
65+ 3.32%
Median Age: 19.90 years (1985)
Maternal Mortality: (not available)
Infant Mortality: 122 per 1,000 live births (1985)

HEALTH CARE

Hospital Beds: 6 per 10,000 population (1983)
Doctors: 0.48 per 10,000 population (1983)

ETHNIC COMPOSITION: Bhote (of Tibetan origin) - 60%; Nepalese - 25%; indigenous tribes - 15%.

RELIGION: Lamaistic (Mahayana) Buddhism - 75%; Hindu - 25%.

LANGUAGE: The official language is Dzongkha, which belongs to the Tibeto-Burman group of languages. Other Tibetan dialects, as well as Nepalese, are spoken.

EDUCATION: Illiteracy: 95%. In 1987, there were 148 primary schools, 21 junior high schools, 9 high schools, 2 teacher training institutes, 1 junior college, 1 college and 6 technical schools, with a total enrollment of 57,262 students.

ECONOMIC DATA

Expenditures by Function [as % of total]: (1984)
General public services 18.74%
Defense .... (not available)
Education 11.39%
Health 5.55%
Social security and welfare 1.40%
Housing and community amenities 7.67%
Other community and social services 0%
Economic services 52.48%
Agriculture, forestry, fishing and hunting 21.68%
Roads 13.92%
Other transportation and communication .. 3.49%
Other purposes 2.77%
GDP per capita: $207 (1986)

TRAVEL NOTES

Climate: The mountainous northern part of Bhutan is cold, while the valleys in the center of the country are more temperate and the heavily forested south is semi-tropical. Rainfall averages between 60 and 120 inches per year; monthly temperature averages 62°F during July and 40°F during January.
Health Precautions: Precautions should be taken against tuberculosis and malaria.
Miscellaneous: Bhutan boasts beautiful mountains and wildlife preserves.

GOVERNMENT

Bhutan (Druk-yul—Kingdom of Bhutan) is a hereditary monarchy. The first hereditary King, Ugyan Wangchuk, began his reign on Dec 17, 1907. On Aug 8, 1949, India and Bhutan signed a treaty requiring Bhutan to be guided by India in foreign affairs and India to refrain from interfering in Bhutan's internal affairs. King Jigme Singye Wangchuk (the Dragon King) is of the 4th generation of the current dynasty.

Constitution: Bhutan has no written constitution. Responsibility for governing is divided among the monarch (who acts as the executive), the Council of Ministers, the Royal Advisory Council, the National Assembly and the monastic head of Bhutan's Buddhist monks.

BOLIVIA
Republic of Bolivia

LOCATION: Bolivia is a landlocked country located in South America; it is bordered by Brazil to the north and east, Chile and Peru to the west, and Argentina and Paraguay to the south.

AREA: 424,164 sq. miles

Land Use: 3% cropland; 25% permanent pasture; 52% forests and woodland; 20% other.
Arable Land: 3%
Arable Land per capita: 1.20 acres

POPULATION: 6,730,000 (1987 projection)

Population Density: 15.87 inhabs. per sq. mile (1987)
Population Distribution: 47.80% urban (1985)
Population Growth Rate: 2.76% per year (1985-90 projection)

VITAL STATISTICS

Average Life Expectancy: 53.10 years (1985-90 projection)
Male: 50.90 years (1985-90 projection)
Female: 55.40 years (1985-90 projection)
Age Distribution: (1985)
0-14 .... 43.80%
15-64 .... 53.00%
65+ 3.20%
Median Age: 18 years (1985)
Maternal Mortality: (not available)
Infant Mortality: 110 per 1,000 live births (1985-90 projection)

HEALTH CARE

Hospital Beds: 22.80 per 10,000 population (1977)
Doctors: 5.30 per 10,000 population (1985)

ETHNIC COMPOSITION: Quechua - 30%; Aymara - 25%; Mestizo - 31%; European - 14%.

RELIGION: Roman Catholic - 95%; the remainder include an active Protestant minority, especially Methodist.

LANGUAGE: Spanish, Quechua and Aymara are the official languages.

EDUCATION: Illiteracy: 37%. In 1981, there were 10,662 primary and elementary schools with 1,115,259 students; 548 higher schools with 178,217 students; and 39 specialized schools with 16,206 students.

ECONOMIC DATA

Expenditures by Function [as % of total]: (1984)
General public services .... (not available)
Defense 5.40%
Education 12.23%
Health 1.48%
Social security and welfare 5.21%
Housing and community amenities 0.20%
Other community and social services 0.10%
Economic services 5.29%
Agriculture, forestry, fishing and hunting . 0.53%
Roads 1.60%
Other transportation and communication .. 2.29%
Other purposes .... (not available)%
GDP per capita: $579 (1986)

TRAVEL NOTES

Climate: Depending on the altitude, the climate varies from cool and cold in the Andes mountains to humid and tropical in the eastern and northern lowlands.
Health Precautions: Due to the altitude, newcomers should rest the first three days. Tap water is not potable.
Miscellaneous: Lake Titicaca offers excellent fishing, and the famous Roman Catholic sanctuary of Copacabana is located on its shore. The highest ski run in the world is located on the Andean peak of Chacaltaya. Tiwanaku offers pre-Incan ruins.

GOVERNMENT

Bolivia (Republica de Bolivia—Republic of Bolivia) proclaimed its independence from Spain on Aug 6, 1825. It has had a turbulent political history marked by nearly 200 military coups. The most recent military regime restored power to a civilian Government (originally elected in June 1980) on Oct 10, 1982.

Constitution: Since its first Constitution in November 1826, Bolivia has promulgated many new ones. The February 1967 Constitution is the nation's 16th since independence, and vests executive authority in a popularly elected President and legislative authority in a bicameral National Congress.

BOTSWANA
Republic of Botswana

LOCATION: Situated in southern Africa, Botswana is bordered by South Africa to the south and east, Namibia to the west and north, Zambia to the north and Zimbabwe to the east.

AREA: 224,711 sq. miles

Land Use: 2.32% cropland; 75.17% permanent pasture; 1.64% forests and woodland; 20.87% other (mostly desert).
Arable Land: 2%
Arable Land per capita: 2.44 acres

POPULATION: 1,180,000 (1988 estimate)

Population Density: 5 inhabs. per sq. mile (1988 estimate)
Population Distribution: 19.24% urban (1985)
Population Growth Rate: 3.30% per year (1988 estimate)

VITAL STATISTICS

Average Life Expectancy: 56.50 years (1985-90 projection)
Male: 54.90 years (1985-90 projection)
Female: 58.10 years (1985-90 projection)
Age Distribution: (1985)
0-14 .... 49.14%
15-64 .... 48.87%
65+ 1.99%
Median Age: 15.40 years (1985)
Maternal Mortality: (not available)
Infant Mortality: 63 per 1,000 live births (1985)

HEALTH CARE

Hospital Beds: 22 per 10,000 population (1981)
Doctors: 1 per 10,000 population (1981)

ETHNIC COMPOSITION: Botswana - 95%; various indigenous tribal groups - 4%; white - 1%.

RELIGION: Indigenous beliefs - 85%; Christian - 15%.

LANGUAGE: English is the official language. Setswana is widely spoken.

EDUCATION: Illiteracy: 29% (1985). In 1986, there were 537 primary schools with 235,941 students; 73 secondary schools with 35,966 students; 2 technical colleges with 652 students; 5 teacher training colleges with 1,633 students; and 1 university with 1,700 students.

ECONOMIC DATA

Expenditures by Function [as % of total]: (1985)
General public services 21.69%
Defense 6.43%
Education 17.69%
Health 4.97%
Social security and welfare 2.79%
Housing and community amenities 4.53%
Other community and social services 1.33%
Economic services 29.65%
Agriculture, forestry, fishing and hunting . 9.79%
Roads 6.21%
Other transportation and communication .. 3.01%
Other purposes 10.92%
GDP per capita: $1,538 (1987)

TRAVEL NOTES

Climate: Botswana's climate is hot and arid, with desert claiming large sections of the country. The northern and eastern portions of the country receive an average annual rainfall of 21 inches, but rainfall in the west is erratic, with as little as 10 inches falling in some years. Temperatures range from summer daytime highs of over 100°F to winter nighttime lows of 29°F.
Health Precautions: Recommended inoculations include typhoid, measles, tetanus, diphtheria and gamma globulin. Tap water is potable in Gaborone, but not in rural areas.
Miscellaneous: Visitors admire Botswana's 6 large game reserves, which offer a wide variety of wildlife and scenic beauty.

GOVERNMENT

Botswana (Republic of Botswana), formerly the British Protectorate of Bechuanaland, gained independent status within the British Commonwealth on Sep 30, 1966 with Prime Minister Seretse Khama, an exiled former Chief of the Bamangwanto tribe, being named Botswana's first President. Khama was a popular leader, winning reelection in 1969, 1974 and 1979. At his death in July 1980 he was succeeded as President by his Vice President and Finance Minister, Dr. Quett Masire, who has retained the office since that time.

Constitution: The 1966 Botswana Constitution is based on the Bechuanaland Constitution of 1965, with minor alterations. The 1966 Constitution institutes a modified parliamentary form of government, replacing the office of Prime Minister with a President, who serves as head of state and government. The Constitution also includes a bill of human rights.

BRAZIL
Federative Republic of Brazil

LOCATION: Situated in central and northeastern South America, Brazil is bounded on the north by Venezuela, Colombia, Guyana, Suriname and French Guiana, on the west by Peru and Bolivia and on the south by Paraguay, Argentina and Uruguay.

AREA: 3,286,488 sq. miles

Land Use: 60% forest; 13% pasture; 4% cultivated; 23% urban, waste and other.
Arable Land: 17%
Arable Land per capita: 2.53 acres

POPULATION: 141,459,000 (1987)

Population Density: 43 inhabs. per sq. mile (1987)
Population Distribution: 72.70% urban (1985)
Population Growth Rate: 2.07% per year (1985-90)

VITAL STATISTICS

Average Life Expectancy: 64.90 years (1985-90)
Male: 62.30 years (1985-90)
Female: 67.60 years (1985-90)
Age Distribution: (1985)
0-14 .... 36.40%
15-64 .... 59.30%
64+ 4.30%
Median Age: 21.60 years (1985)
Maternal Mortality: 92.10 per 100,000 live births (1980)
Infant Mortality: 63 per 1,000 live births (1985-90)

HEALTH CARE

Hospital Beds: 41 per 10,000 population (1980)
Doctors: 6.80 per 10,000 population (1980)

ETHNIC COMPOSITION: The vast majority of people are Portuguese, mulattoes and African; there are also Italian, German, Japanese, Indian, Jewish and Arabic minorities.

RELIGION: 80% are nominally Roman Catholic.

LANGUAGE: The official language is Portuguese. English is also widely spoken.

EDUCATION: Illiteracy: 24%. In 1984, there were 216,220 first grade schools with 24,120,924 students; 8,624 second grade schools with 3,003,671 students; and 847 higher schools with 1,453,354 students.

ECONOMIC DATA

Expenditures by Function [as % of total]: (1983)
General public services 11.68%
Defense 4.11%
Education 3.73%
Health 7.29%
Social security and welfare 34.91%
Housing and community amenities 0.22%
Other community and social services 0.23%
Economic services 23.81%
Agriculture, forestry, fishing and hunting . 7.65%
Roads 1.59%
Other transportation and communication .. 1.76%
Other purposes 18.14%
GDP per capita: $1,579 (1984)

TRAVEL NOTES

Climate: In the Amazon basin tropical rain forest, the climate is hot and wet; in the savannah grasslands of the central and southern uplands, it is temperate, with warm summers and mild winters.
Health Precautions: Immunizations against yellow fever, polio, typhoid, tetanus, diphtheria and infectious hepatitis are recommended.
Miscellaneous: The modern capital, Brasilia, is a showpiece of contemporary city planning. Towns like Salvador and Recife have excellent examples of Portuguese colonial and modern architecture. Among the natural attractions are the Iguacu Falls, the 7th largest by volume in the world, and the tropical Amazon basin forests.

GOVERNMENT

Brazil (Republica Federativa do Brasil— Federative Republic of Brazil) is a federal republic. A Portuguese colony until 1815, it was ruled by a military-backed Government from 1964 to 1985, after which a civilian President, Tancredo Neves, was indirectly elected. He died before assuming office and his position was filled by his Vice President-elect, Jose Sarney Costa.

Constitution: After military rule ended in 1985, a new draft Constitution was proposed in 1986 and was written by a Special Assembly of the

National Congress. It replaced the authoritarian military Constitution of 1967. The Constitution was adopted on Oct 6, 1988 and further democratized the Government by calling for direct elections, allowing more political parties, abolishing censorship and giving Congress broader economic powers, as well as abolishing Presidential decrees. The Constitution also provides basic health care for the public and ensures secret balloting. It is the 7th Constitution since 1822.

BRITAIN
United Kingdom of Great Britain and Northern Ireland

LOCATION: Britain and Northern Ireland lie off the northwest coast of Europe. England, Scotland and Wales, making up Great Britain, are on the main island. Northern Ireland, consisting of the northeastern part of the island of Ireland, is to the west of Great Britain. Together the countries are called the United Kingdom.

AREA: 99,714 sq. miles

Land Use: 28.94% cropland; 48.44% permanent pasture; 9.02% forests and woodland; 13.60% other.
Arable Land: 28.94%
Arable Land per capita: 0.33 acres

POPULATION: 56,160,000 (1987 estimate)

Population Density: 563 inhabs. per sq. mile (1987 estimate)
Population Distribution: 91.50% urban (1985)
Population Growth Rate: 0.02% per year (1985-90 projection)

VITAL STATISTICS

Average Life Expectancy: 74.50 years (1985-90 projection)
Male: 71.40 years (1985-90 projection)
Female: 77.80 years (1985-90 projection)
Age Distribution: (1985)
0-14 .... 19.50%
15-64 .... 65.40%
65+ 15.10%
Median Age: 35.40 years (1985)

Maternal Mortality:
8.60 per 100,000 live births (England and Wales — 1983)
14.60 per 100,000 live births (Northern Ireland — 1983)
12.30 per 100,000 live births (Scotland — 1984)
Infant Mortality: 9 per 1,000 live births (1985-90 projection)

HEALTH CARE

Hospital Beds: 76.32 per 10,000 population (1984)
Doctors: 14.82 per 10,000 population (1984)

ETHNIC COMPOSITION: English - 81.50%; Scottish - 9.60%; Irish - 2.40%; Welsh - 1.90%; Ulster - 1.80%; other (including West Indian, Indian, Pakistani) - 2.80%.

RELIGION: Anglican - 27,000,000; Roman Catholic - 5,300,000; Presbyterian - 2,000,000; Methodist - 760,000; Jewish - 450,000.

LANGUAGE: English is the primary language. About 26% of the population in Wales speaks Welsh, while about 1% of Scots speak a Scottish form of Gaelic.

EDUCATION: Illiteracy: 1%. In 1985, there were 3,559 primary schools and 719 secondary schools in Scotland and Northern Ireland. There were 30,748 total schools in England and Wales. In the United Kingdom, there were 4,413,234 primary students; 4,139,672 secondary students; and 47 universities with 340,992 students (excluding Open University students and part-time students in Northern Ireland).

ECONOMIC DATA

Expenditures by Function [as % of total]: (1985)
General public services 6.27%
Defense 13.25%
Education 2.06%
Health 12.55%
Social security and welfare 28.55%
Housing and community amenities 1.66%
Other community and social services 0.40%
Economic services 8.91%
Agriculture, forestry, fishing and hunting . 1.14%
Roads 1.01%
Other transportation and communication .. 0.89%
Other purposes 26.33%
GDP per capita: $9,700 (1986)

TRAVEL NOTES

Climate: Generally temperate, the climate is also variable. The average temperature is 59°F in summer and about 41°F in winter. Average rainfall is 35-40 inches. The average number of hours of sunshine per day is 6 to 7 in summer and 1 to 2 in winter.

Health Precautions: None

Miscellaneous: London is renowned for its museums, galleries and as a center of government and commerce. Edinburgh is known for beautifully preserved Georgian and Victorian architecture. Northern Ireland, and all of the United Kingdom, attracts tourists with its pastoral countryside.

GOVERNMENT

Britain (United Kingdom of Great Britain and Northern Ireland) is a constitutional monarchy with a democratic parliamentary system of government. Geographic and ethnic divisions have resulted in differences of participation in the government by the various constituent parts of the Kingdom—England, Wales, Scotland and Northern Ireland. England has been the dominant region, with more than half the land area and 80% of the population. Wales, under English control since medieval times, has its own capital, Cardiff, and a Cabinet ministry advised by a Council for Wales. Scotland, a separate kingdom until 1707, has a Cabinet ministry and separate legal and local government systems, but not a separate legislature. Northern Ireland, which joined the Kingdom in 1800, had its own legislature and executive branch until 1974, when, amid increasing political violence, the Secretary of State for Northern Ireland and his ministers assumed control of government, responsible to the United Kingdom Parliament at Westminster. In November 1985, Britain and Ireland signed the Anglo-Irish Agreement, which for the first time gave Dublin a consultative role in the governing of Northern Ireland. Ireland's participation extends to Northern Irish legal, political, cross-border and security matters. The British Constitution is unwritten. It is based in part on statute, in part on common law and in part on the traditional rights of Englishmen. Constitutional changes may come about through Acts of Parliament or through the acceptance of new usage or judicial precedent. The Magna Carta, signed in 1215, began the process whereby the law of the land acquired a status of its own, independent of the Sovereign and Parliament. The Bill of Rights of 1689 ended a long-standing rivalry between Crown and Parliament, while the 1832 Reform Bill dramatically broadened the basis of representative government.

BRUNEI
Sultanate of Brunei

LOCATION: Brunei is located on the northern coast of the island of Borneo, off the coast of Southeast Asia. It is bounded on three sides by the Malaysian state of Sarawak, and on the north by the South China Sea.

AREA: 2,243 sq. miles

Land Use: 75% forest; 3% cultivable; 22% industry, urban, waste or other.
Arable Land: 0.70%
Arable Land per capita: 0.42 acres

POPULATION: 240,000 (1986)

Population Density: 109 inhabs. per sq. mile (1986)
Population Distribution: 64% urban (1971)
Population Growth Rate: 3.70% per year (1986)

VITAL STATISTICS

Average Life Expectancy: 62 years (1973)
Male: (not available)
Female: (not available)
Age Distribution: (1973)
0-14 . . . . 42.80%
15-59 . . . . 52.20%
60+ 5.00%
Median Age: (not available)
Maternal Mortality: (not available)
Infant Mortality: 30 per 1,000 live births (1979)

HEALTH CARE

Hospital Beds: 32.64 per 10,000 population (1981)
Doctors: 5 per 10,000 population (1981)

ETHNIC COMPOSITION: Malay - 64%; Chinese - 20%; other - 16%.

RELIGION: Moslem - 60% (official); Christian - 8%; indigenous and other - 32%.

LANGUAGE: Malay is the official language. English and Chinese are also spoken.

EDUCATION: Illiteracy: 55%. In 1984, there were 177 primary schools with 34,373 students; 28 secondary schools with 18,565 students; 2 teacher training colleges with 591 students; and 4 vocational colleges with 748 students.

ECONOMIC DATA

Expenditures by Function [as % of total]: (not available)
GDP per capita: $17,987 (1984)

TRAVEL NOTES

Climate: The climate is tropical with consistent humidity. Annual rainfall ranges from about 110 inches in lowland areas to over 150 inches in the interior. Temperatures range from 73°F to 96°F.
Health Precautions: Cholera and yellow fever vaccination certificates are required of travelers arriving from infected areas. There is no malaria risk.
Miscellaneous: Free medical services are provided by the Government. Tourism is virtually non-existent.

GOVERNMENT

Brunei (Brunei Darussalam—Brunei, Abode of Peace), a sultanate dating back some 500 years, gained full independence from Britain on Jan 1, 1984. It had been a British protectorate since 1888; the British relinquished responsibility for internal affairs in 1959, retaining responsibility for defense and foreign affairs until Brunei attained full independence.

Constitution: The 1959 Constitution vests supreme authority in the Sultan and Yang Di-Pertuan (head of state). Since a rebellion in 1962, however, several provisions of the Constitution have been suspended and the Sultan has ruled by decree.

BULGARIA
People's Republic of Bulgaria

LOCATION: In the eastern Balkans in southeastern Europe, Bulgaria is bordered by Rumania to the north, Turkey and Greece to the south and by Yugoslavia to the west. The Black Sea lies to the east.

AREA: 42,823 sq. miles

Land Use: 33% forest; 11% agricultural; 56% other.
Arable Land: 41%
Arable Land per capita: 1.25 acres

POPULATION: 8,990,000 (1986)

Population Density: 209.93 inhabs. per sq. mile (1986)
Population Distribution: 66.50% urban (1985)
Population Growth Rate: 0.20% per year (1986)

VITAL STATISTICS

Average Life Expectancy: 71.50 years (1986)
Male: 69 years (1986)
Female: 74 years (1986)
Age Distribution: (1985)
0-14 .... 22.30%
15-64 .... 66.40%
65+ 11.30%
Median Age: 34.90 years (1985)
Maternal Mortality: 27 per 100,000 live births (1983)
Infant Mortality: 16.20 per 1,000 live births (1984)

HEALTH CARE

Hospital Beds: 8.99 per 10,000 population (1983)
Doctors: 2.68 per 10,000 population (1983)

ETHNIC COMPOSITION: Bulgarian - 85.30%; Turk - 8.50%; Gypsy - 2.60%; Macedonian - 2.50%; Armenian - 0.30%; Russian - 0.20%; other - 0.60%.

RELIGION: Bulgarian Orthodox - 85.00%; Moslem - 13.00%; Jewish - 0.80%; Roman Catholic - 0.70%; Protestant, Gregorian-Armenian, other - 0.50%.

LANGUAGE: Bulgarian, a Slavonic language, is the official language.

EDUCATION: Illiteracy: 5%. In 1984, there were 5,551 kindergarten schools with 391,902 students; 3,521 unified secondary polytechnics with 1,202,558 students; 130 special schools with 2,356 students; 274 secondary vocational technical schools with 115,038 students; 229 technical colleges and art schools with 91,102 students; 16 semi-higher institutes with 7,305 students; and 30 higher educational institutions with 86,275 students.

ECONOMIC DATA

Expenditures by Function [as % of total]: (not available)
GDP per capita: (not available)

TRAVEL NOTES

Climate: Winters are cold and summers are hot.
Health Precautions: There are no special precautions necessary.
Miscellaneous: Black Sea coastal resorts are very popular, with most visitors coming from the Soviet Union and Eastern Europe. Bulgaria is also successfully promoting tourism in the West.

GOVERNMENT

Bulgaria (Narodna Republika Bulgariya— People's Republic of Bulgaria) is an independent state in which effective political control rests with the Bulgarian Communist Party. Bulgaria was proclaimed a People's Republic on Sep 15, 1946, after a referendum (Sep 8, 1946) decided against the existing Bulgarian monarchy.

Constitution: The Constitution of May 18, 1971, which replaced the Constitution of December 1947, defines Bulgaria as a socialist state and declares the Communist Party to be the leading force in society and the state.

BURKINA FASO

LOCATION: Burkina Faso is located in western Africa, and is a landlocked country bordered by the Cote d'Ivoire, Ghana, Togo and Benin to the south, Niger to the northeast and Mali to the northwest.

AREA: 105,870 sq. miles

Land Use: 9.62% cropland; 36.52% permanent pasture; 25.64% forests and woodland; 28.22% other.
Arable Land: 9.62%
Arable Land per capita: 1.02 acres

POPULATION: 7,310,000 (1987 estimate)

Population Density: 69.05 inhabs. per sq. mile (1987)
Population Distribution: 7.90% urban (1985)
Population Growth Rate: 2.65% per year (1985-90 projection)

VITAL STATISTICS

Average Life Expectancy: 47.20 years (1985-90 projection)
Male: 45.60 years (1985-90 projection)
Female: 48.90 years (1985-90 projection)
Age Distribution: (1985)
0-14 .... 43.90%
15-64 .... 53.20%
65+ 2.90%
Median Age: 17.90 (1985)
Maternal Mortality: (not available)
Infant Mortality: 139 per 100,000 live births (1985-90 projection)

HEALTH CARE

Hospital Beds: 3.32 per 10,000 population (1980)
Doctors: 0.18 per 10,000 population (1984)

ETHNIC COMPOSITION: Mossi - 65%; other (including Fulani, Lobi, Gurunsi, Bobo, Samo, Mande and Senufo) - 35%.

RELIGION: Animist - 65%; Moslem - 25%; Christian (mostly Roman Catholic) - 10%.

LANGUAGE: While French is the official language, many native dialects, especially Mossi, are spoken.

EDUCATION: Illiteracy: 86.80%. In 1985, there were 1,537 primary schools with 313,520 students; 92 general secondary schools with 39,369 students; 21 vocational schools with 4,213 students; 2 teacher training schools with 199 students; and 19 higher education schools with 4,100 students.

ECONOMIC DATA

Expenditures by Function [as % of total]: (1984)
General public services 10.76%
Defense 18.23%
Education 16.88%
Health 5.53%
Social security and welfare 6.73%
Housing and community amenities 0.27%
Other community and social services 1.63%

Economic services 14.44%
Agriculture, forestry, fishing and hunting . . 4.31%
Roads 0%
Other transportation and communication . . 0.78%
Other purposes 20.44%
GDP per capita: $69 (1985)

TRAVEL NOTES

Climate: There are three main seasons: the weather from March to May is hot and dry; the rainy season lasts from June to October; and from November to February the climate is dry and relatively cool. During the hot season, daily temperatures may be higher than 100°F, while the high temperatures during the cooler season will reach approximately 85°F.

Health Precautions: Yellow fever and cholera vaccination certificates are required. Malaria risk is present.

Miscellaneous: Big game hunting is a major tourist attraction.

GOVERNMENT

Burkina Faso, which means the Land of Upright Men, was formerly known as Upper Volta and was renamed in August 1984 by then-President Thomas Sankara on the one-year anniversary of his coup. A former French Overseas Territory, the country became an independent state on Aug 5, 1960. Burkina Faso's politics are strongly influenced by ethnic loyalties and rivalries. Although it has a tradition of democratic political activity, the armed forces have frequently intervened in the political affairs of the country. Since its independence, there have been 5 successful coups. On Oct 15, 1987 President Thomas Sankara was overthrown and executed by forces representing his boyhood friend and second-in-command, Capt. Blaise Compaore, who subsequently proclaimed himself head of state.

Constitution: The 1977 Constitution was suspended in November 1980, following the assumption of power by Col. Saye Zerbo.

BURMA
Socialist Republic of the Union of Burma

LOCATION: Situated in the northwest region of Southeast Asia, Burma is bordered by Bangladesh and India to the northwest, by China and Laos to the northeast and by Thailand to the southeast. Toward the southwest, Burma has an extensive coastline that runs along the Bay of Bengal and the Andaman Sea.

AREA: 261,148 sq. miles

Land Use: 15.31% cropland; 0.56% permanent pasture; 48.87% forests and woodlands; 35.27% other (including urban areas).
Arable Land: 15%
Arable Land per capita: 0.64 acres

POPULATION: 39,140,000 (1988 estimate)

Population Density: 150 inhabs. per sq. mile (1988 estimate)
Population Distribution: 23.90% urban (1985)
Population Growth Rate: 1.90% per year (1988 estimate)

VITAL STATISTICS

Average Life Expectancy: 60.00 years (1985-90 projection)
Male: 58.30 years (1985-90 projection)
Female: 61.80 years (1985-90 projection)
Age Distribution: (1985)
0-14 . . . . 37.60%
15-64 . . . . 58.20%
65+ 4.20%
Median Age: 20.90 years (1985)
Maternal Mortality: (not available)
Infant Mortality: 89 per 1,000 live births (1985)

HEALTH CARE

Hospital Beds: 7 per 10,000 population (1987)
Doctors: 3 per 10,000 population (1987)

ETHNIC COMPOSITION: Burman - 68%; Shan - 9%; Karen - 7%; Raljome - 4%; Chinese - 3%; Indian - 2%; other - 7% (including Chins, Kachins, Mons and Arakanese).

RELIGION: Theravada Buddhist - 85%; other - 15% (including Moslem, Christian, Hindu and animist).

LANGUAGE: The official language is Burmese; a number of tribal languages are found among the minority ethnic groups.

EDUCATION: Illiteracy: 12%. In 1984/85, there were 29,061 primary and middle schools with

5,849,548 students; 676 secondary schools with 257,897 students; 18 teacher training colleges with 3,834 students; 56 technical/vocational schools with 10,736 students; and 35 universities and colleges with 174,279 students.

ECONOMIC DATA

Expenditures by Function [as % of total]: (1985)
General public services 13.85%
Defense 18.84%
Education 11.74%
Health 7.71%
Social security and welfare 5.27%
Housing and community amenities 3.13%
Other community and social services 1.48%
Economic services 35.09%
Agriculture, forestry, fishing and hunting . 24.55%
Roads 6.44%
Other transportation and communication . . 1.42%
Other purposes 2.91%
GDP per capita: $221 (1986)

TRAVEL NOTES

Climate: The climate is tropical, with an average temperature of 80°F and high relative humidity except in the mountainous dry zone. Burma receives most of its annual average rainfall of 100 inches during the May-September monsoon season.

Health Precautions: Vaccinations against cholera and yellow fever (if traveling from endemic areas) are required of visitors. Cholera, tuberculosis, plague, hepatitis, dengue fever and polio are found in Burma, along with a variety of intestinal parasites, and malaria is a threat in rural regions. Tap water is not potable.

Miscellaneous: Burma is replete with sites of historic and cultural interest, including shrines, palaces and several thousand pagodas, but tourism remains undeveloped.

GOVERNMENT

Burma (Pyidaungsu Myanma Nainggan-Daw— Socialist Republic of the Union of Burma), formerly annexed to British India, became an independent state on Jan 4, 1948, with a parliamentary form of government. On Mar 2, 1962, the armed forces, under Gen. Ne Win, ousted the parliamentary Government in a bloodless coup, suspended the Constitution and placed supreme authority in a Revolutionary Council dominated by the military. The military regime introduced a one-party system, wherein effective political authority rested with the Burma Socialist Program Party (BSPP), with the backing of the military. The summer of 1988 saw a turbulent series of events staged against a background of widespread and violent street protests: in the two months following Ne Win's resignation as BSPP Chairperson on Jul 23, the nominal leadership of the country changed hands three times and, on Sep 10, it was announced that the one-party system would end. On Sep 18, 1988, the military, led by Gen. Saw Maung, officially took over the reins of power. The new regime immediately dissolved all Government bodies including the Council of State and the People's Assembly, and subsequently appointed a new Cabinet, headed by Gen. Saw Maung. Soon afterwards the name of the BSPP was changed to the National Unity Party.

Constitution: The Constitution of Jun 4, 1974 (Burma's second) was approved in a national referendum in December 1973. It declares Burma to be a socialist state and guarantees freedom of religion. The Constitution was amended by the People's Assembly on Sep 11, 1988 to allow opposition political parties to form, in a transition from one-party rule.

BURUNDI
Republic of Burundi

LOCATION: Situated a little south of the Equator in east central Africa on Lake Tanganyika, Burundi is bounded by Rwanda to the north, Tanzania to the south and east and Zaire to the west.

AREA: 10,747 sq. miles

Land Use: 24% cultivated, 23% pasture, 10% scrub and forest, 43% other.
Arable Land: 37%
Arable Land per capita: 0.53 acres

POPULATION: 4,807,000 (1986)

Population Density: 447.29 inhabs. per sq. mile (1986)
Population Distribution: 7.10% urban (1984)
Population Growth Rate: 2.80% per year (1986)

VITAL STATISTICS

Average Life Expectancy: 46.95 years (1983)
Male: 45.30 years (1983)
Female: 48.60 years (1983)
Age Distribution: (1985)
0-14 . . . . 44.80%
15-64 . . . . 51.90%
65+ 3.30%
Median Age: 17.90 years (1980)
Maternal Mortality: (not available)
Infant Mortality: 137.30 per 1,000 live births (1984)

HEALTH CARE

Hospital Beds: 35.20 per 10,000 population (1981)
Doctors: 0.17 per 10,000 population (1980)

ETHNIC COMPOSITION: Hutu (Bantu) - 85%; Tutsi (Hamitic) - 14%; Twa (Pygmy) - 1%. There is also a large presence (around 70,000) of refugees, mostly from Rwanda and Zaire, and about 5,000 Europeans and South Asians.

RELIGION: Roman Catholic - 62%; Protestant - 5%; indigenous beliefs - 32%; Moslem - 1%.

LANGUAGE: The official languages are French and Kirundi. Swahili is also widely used.

EDUCATION: Illiteracy: 75%. In 1984, there were 337,329 primary school students; 9,765 secondary school students; 7,782 teacher training school students; and 4,514 vocational school students.

ECONOMIC DATA

Expenditures by Function [as % of total]: (not available)
GDP per capita: $251 (1985)

TRAVEL NOTES

Climate: Hot and humid in the lowlands, the climate is cool in the highlands with an irregular rainfall.
Health Precautions: None
Miscellaneous: The Government plans to develop tourism. There is a 150-bed hotel complex on the shores of Lake Tanganyika.

GOVERNMENT

Burundi (Republika y' u Burundi—Republique du Burundi—Republic of Burundi) obtained independence as a monarchy on Jul 1, 1962. A military coup in 1966 deposed the King (Mwami) and established a republic. Another coup in November 1976 resulted in a gradual restoration of civilian government under a single legal political party, the Union for National Progress (UPRONA).

Constitution: A national referendum approved a new Constitution on Nov 18, 1981. Besides providing for a single legal political party, the Constitution establishes a separate executive and legislature.

CAMBODIA
Democratic Kampuchea

LOCATION: Located in Southeast Asia, Cambodia is bordered by Thailand on the north and west, Laos on the north, Vietnam on the east and the Gulf of Thailand on the south.

AREA: 69,898 sq. miles

Land Use: 74% forest; 16% cultivated; 10% urban, waste and other.
Arable Land: (not available)
Arable Land per capita: (not available)

POPULATION: 7,688,000 (1987)

Population Density: 110 inhabs. per sq. mile (1987)
Population Distribution: 10% urban (1985)
Population Growth Rate: 2.48% per year (1985-90)

VITAL STATISTICS

Average Life Expectancy: 48.40 years (1985-90)
Male: 47.00 years (1985-90)
Female: 49.90 years (1985-90)
Age Distribution: (1985)
0-14 . . . . .32.50%
15-59 . . . . .64.80%
60+ 2.60%
Median Age: 22.20 years (1985)
Maternal Mortality: (not available)
Infant Mortality: 160 per 1,000 live births (1986)

HEALTH CARE

Hospital Beds: 24.50 per 10,000 population (1985)
Doctors: 0.69 per 10,000 population (1985)

ETHNIC COMPOSITION: Khmer - 90%; Chinese - 5%; other - 5%.

RELIGION: Theravada Buddhism - 95%; other - 5%.

LANGUAGE: Khmer is the official language, while small minorities speak Chinese and Vietnamese. French is also spoken.

EDUCATION: Illiteracy: 52%. In 1983/84, there were 1,504,840 primary school students; 207 junior secondary schools with 145,730 students; and 13 senior secondary schools with 7,334 students.

ECONOMIC DATA

Expenditures by Function [as % of total]: (not available)
GDP per capita: (not available)

TRAVEL NOTES

Climate: The Cambodian climate is tropical and humid with a long rainy season lasting from June to November, with the heaviest rainfall in September. The temperature is generally between 68°F and 97°F.
Health Precautions: Yellow fever and smallpox vaccinations are required.
Miscellaneous: Due to the tumultuous political situation in Cambodia, travel has been unsafe for foreign tourists since the early 1970s.

GOVERNMENT

Cambodia (Kampuchea Pracheatipateyy—Kampuchea Democratique—Democratic Kampuchea) gained its independence from France as the Kingdom of Cambodia on Nov 9, 1953. It was proclaimed the Khmer Republic on Oct 9, 1970, after the ouster of Prince Norodom Sihanouk by right-wing leader Lt. Gen. Lon Nol. It was renamed Democratic Kampuchea in the Jan 5, 1976 Constitution after the pro-Communist Khmer Rouge takeover. On Jan 7, 1979, Phnom Penh fell to Vietnamese-backed insurgents of the Kampuchean National United Front for National Salvation, who proclaimed a People's Republic of Kampuchea.
Exiled Government: *Democratic Kampuchea.* Although the People's Republic of Kampuchea still controls Cambodia, the Government of Democratic Kampuchea has continued to receive recognition from the UN General Assembly as the legitimate Government. Under the terms of a declaration signed in Kuala Lumpur (Malaysia) on Jun 22, 1982, three groups opposed to the People's Republic of Kampuchea Government — followers of Prince Norodom Sihanouk, the Communist Khmer Rouge and the anti-Communist Khmer People's National Liberation Front — joined to form the Democratic Kampuchea coalition Government, whose stated purpose is to force the withdrawal of Vietnamese troops. The coalition Government is administered by a Council of ministers, which includes an inner Cabinet and 4 coordination committees with representatives from the three coalition groups.

Constitution: The Constitution, approved Jun 27, 1981, consists of a preamble and 10 chapters, divided into 93 articles. It establishes the People's Republic of Kampuchea as an independent sovereign state, "gradually advancing towards socialism." It provides for a Council of State elected from among the National Assembly, a Council of Ministers, a judicial system and Local People's Committees.

CAMEROON
United Republic of Cameroon

LOCATION: Cameroon is located on the bight of Biafra on the west coast of Africa, with Chad and the Central African Republic to the east, Nigeria to the west and the Congo Republic, Equatorial Guinea and Gabon to the south.

AREA: 183,569 sq. miles

Land Use: 15% cropland; 18% permanent pasture; 54% forests and woodland; 13% other.
Arable Land: 14%
Arable Land per capita: 1.63 acres

POPULATION: 10,438,000 (1987 projection)

Population Density: 57 inhabs. per sq. mile (1987)
Population Distribution: 42.40% urban (1985)
Population Growth Rate: 2.80% per year (1985-90 projection)

VITAL STATISTICS

Average Life Expectancy: 52.90 years (1985-90 projection)
Male: 51.20 years (1985-90 projection)

Female: 54.70 years (1985-90 projection)
Age Distribution: (1985)
0-14 .... 43.30%
15-64 .... 52.80%
65+ 3.90%
Median Age: 18.40 years (1985)
Maternal Mortality: (not available)
Infant Mortality: 94 per 1,000 live births (1985-90 projection)

HEALTH CARE

Hospital Beds: 27 per 10,000 population (1979)
Doctors: 0.70 per 10,000 population (1979)

ETHNIC COMPOSITION: Cameroon Highlanders - 31%; Equatorial Bantu - 19%; Kirdi - 11%; Fulani - 10%; Northwestern Bantu - 8%; Eastern Nigritic - 7%; other African (including over 200 different peoples) - 13%; non-African - 1%.

RELIGION: Indigenous beliefs - 51%; Christian - 33%; Moslem - 16%.

LANGUAGE: English and French are the official languages; there are approximately 24 major African language groups.

EDUCATION: Illiteracy: 35%. In 1984/85, there were 5,742 primary schools with 1,638,629 students; 376 secondary schools with 238,075 students; and 164 technical colleges with 77,555 students; In 1985/86 there were 5 institutions of higher learning with 17,113 students.

ECONOMIC DATA

Expenditures by Function [as %of total]: (1984)
General public services 23.29%
Defense 8.40%
Education 3.77%
Health 4.38%
Social security and welfare 4.25%
Housing and community amenities 5.54%
Other community and social services 2.94%
Economic services 28.69%
Agriculture, forestry, fishing and hunting .. 6.79%
Roads 11.85%
Other transportation and communication .. 7.51%
Other purposes 11.78%
GDP per capita: $675 (1984)

TRAVEL NOTES

Climate: The west and southwest of Cameroon are hot and humid, with an average temperature of around 80°F. The north is drier, with more extreme temperatures.

Health Precautions: Malaria, filariasis, dysentery, parasites, bilharzia, jaundice, hepatitis and fungus infections are threats. Polio, yellow fever, tetanus and infectious hepatitis immunizations are recommended for visitors. Water can be contaminated.

Miscellaneous: The tourist trade is currently being expanded and the main attractions are the national parks, sandy beaches and game reserves.

GOVERNMENT

Cameroon (Republique du Cameroun—Republic of Cameroon) traces its independence to Jan 1, 1960, when the Republic of Cameroon was proclaimed in what is now the eastern half of the country, ending a French Trusteeship of the territory. On Oct 1, 1961, a part of the former British Cameroon Trusteeship united with the Republic to form the Federal Republic of Cameroon. On Jun 2, 1972, the federal structure of the country was dismantled and replaced with a unitary state. Cameroon is a highly centralized, one-party state with a strong executive branch. Effective political authority rests with the ruling Rassemblement Democratique du Peuple Camerounais. Tentative steps toward democracy were taken during an election on Apr 24, 1988, when secret balloting and multiple candidacy were implemented.

Constitution: The present Constitution, establishing a unitary state, was proclaimed on Jun 2, 1972 and subsequently amended in 1974 and 1981. It replaced the Federal Constitution of Oct 1, 1961. The Constitution may be amended by special act of the National Assembly. Amendments may be proposed by the President or by the National Assembly. The President may choose to submit any amendment to the voters in a national referendum. The Constitution specifically bars amendments that impair the republican character of the Government or the unity and territorial integrity of the state.

CANADA

LOCATION: The second largest country in the world, Canada occupies the northern part of North America, excluding Alaska and Greenland. It extends from the Atlantic Ocean to the Pacific, with its southern border with the US formed along the upper St. Lawrence and the Great Lakes, continuing west along latitude 49°N.

AREA: 3,849,674 sq. miles

Land Use: 5.03% cropland; 2.59% permanent pasture; 35.37% forests and woodland; 57.01% other (waste, urban and inland water).
Arable Land: 5.03% (cultivated only)
Arable Land per capita: 4.77 acres

POPULATION: 25,963,000 (1987)

Population Density: 6.74 inhabs. per sq. mile (1987)
Population Distribution: 75.90% urban (1985)
Population Growth Rate: 1.01% per year (1985-90)

VITAL STATISTICS

Average Life Expectancy: 75.70 years (1985-90)
Male: 72.80 years (1985-90)
Female: 80.10 years (1985-90)
Age Distribution: (1985)
0-14 .... 21.50%
15-64 .... 68.10%
65+ 10.40%
Median Age: 31.40 years (1985)
Maternal Mortality: 1.90 per 100,000 live births (1982)
Infant Mortality: 8 per 1,000 live births (1985-90)

HEALTH CARE

Hospital Beds: 69 per 10,000 population (1982)
Doctors: 15.64 per 10,000 population (1982)

ETHNIC COMPOSITION: British origin - 45%; French origin - 29%; other European - 23%; indigenous Indian and Eskimo - 1.5%; other 1.5%.

RELIGION: Roman Catholic - 46%; United Church - 16%; Anglican - 10%; other - 28%.

LANGUAGE: The official languages are French and English.

EDUCATION: Illiteracy: 1%. In 1984/85, there were 15,624 primary and secondary schools with 4,956,280 students; 197 post-secondary non-university schools with 329,800 students; and 66 universities and colleges with 471,370 students.

ECONOMIC DATA

Expenditures by Function [as % of total]: (1983)
General public services 8.33%
Defense 7.98%
Education 3.61%
Health 6.27%
Social security and welfare 35.58%
Housing and community amenities 2.07%
Other community and social services 0.76%
Economic services 16.69%
Agriculture, forestry, fishing and hunting ..2.03%
Roads 0.19%
Other transportation and communication ...4.53%
Other purposes 20.11%
GDP per capita: $13,436 (1985)

TRAVEL NOTES

Climate: The climate is extreme, particularly in the interior, with winter temperatures falling well below freezing and snowfalls heavy. Summers are generally warm. Rainfall is moderate to light.
Health Precautions: None
Miscellaneous: Beautiful scenery and cultural and ethnic diversity attract tourists.

GOVERNMENT

Canada became a self-governing Dominion within the British Empire on Jul 1, 1867. It became an autonomous member state of the Commonwealth of Nations under the British Statute of Westminster of 1931. Because it recognizes the British sovereign as head of state, Canada is a monarchy. The Canadian system has been strongly influenced by British political institutions. Like Britain, Canada has a Constitution and a Parliament that in practice limit the monarch's power. Unlike Britain, however, Canada is a federation in which the member provinces exercise a wide range of powers independently of the federal Government. Effective political authority thus rests with the democratically elected parliamentary majorities, organized in political parties, at both federal and provincial levels.

Constitution: The "living" Constitution of Canada, like that of most of the older constitutional democracies, cannot be found in a single document. It consists of a series of written documents, judicial pronouncements, "unwritten" customs and usages and other sources.

CAPE VERDE
Republic of Cape Verde

LOCATION: Cape Verde is an archipelago of 10 islands and 5 islets situated in the Atlantic Ocean about 400 miles west of Senegal.

AREA: 1,557 sq. miles

Land Use: 9.93% cropland; 6.20% permanent pasture; 0.25% forests and woodland; 83.62% other (mainly volcanic terrain).
Arable Land: 10%
Arable Land per capita: 0.31 acres

POPULATION: 331,000 (1988 estimate)

Population Density: 213 inhabs. per sq. mile (1988 estimate)
Population Distribution: 5.30% urban (1985)
Population Growth Rate: 2.10% per year (1988 estimate)

VITAL STATISTICS

Average Life Expectancy: 61.50 years (1985-90 projection)
Male: 59.90 years (1985-90 projection)
Female: 63.30 years (1985-90 projection)
Age Distribution: (1985)
0-14 . . . . 41.10%
15-64 . . . . 53.68%
65+ 5.22%
Median Age: 18.30 years (1985)
Maternal Mortality: 107.30 per 100,000 live births (1980)
Infant Mortality: 89 per 1,000 live births (1985)

HEALTH CARE

Hospital Beds: 21 per 10,000 population (1980)
Doctors: 2 per 10,000 population (1980)

ETHNIC COMPOSITION: Creole - 71%; African - 28%; European - 1%.

RELIGION: Roman Catholic - 98%; other - 2%. A majority of the population fuses indigenous beliefs with their Roman Catholicism.

LANGUAGE: Portuguese is the official language, but the local form of Creole (Crioulo) is more widely spoken.

EDUCATION: Illiteracy: 63%. In 1986/87, there were 347 primary schools with 49,703 students; 16 preparatory schools with 10,304 students; 4 secondary schools with 5,026 students; 3 teacher-training schools with 211 students; and 1 industrial school with 531 students.

ECONOMIC DATA

Expenditures by Function [as % of total]: (not available)
GDP per capita: $263 (1980)

TRAVEL NOTES

Climate: Cape Verde has a semi-arid climate, with little rainfall and persistently strong northeast winds. September is the warmest month and February the coolest. The average annual temperature is 76°F.
Health Precautions: Inoculations against hepatitis, typhoid, tetanus, typhus and yellow fever are required, while malaria suppressants and gamma globulin injections are recommended. The water is not potable.
Miscellaneous: Tourists are attracted to the beautiful mountain scenery and expansive beaches on the islands of Brava, Fogo, Sao Antao and Sao Tiago. All the islands offer a wide variety of water sports, including fishing, sailing, diving, boating and windsurfing.

GOVERNMENT

Cape Verde (Republica de Cabo Verde—Republic of Cape Verde), granted independence from Portugal on Jul 5, 1975, is a one-party state with effective political power residing in the African Party for the Independence of Cape Verde (PAICV). However, the Government maintains an official policy of tolerating political dissent; it permits an active opposition press and is believed to be holding no political prisoners.

Constitution: Cape Verde's first Constitution was adopted by a vote of the National People's Assembly on Sep 7, 1980. The Constitution declares the nation to be a "sovereign, democratic, unitary, anti-colonialist and anti-imperialist republic." The PAICV is described as the "leading force in society," with the Government established as being subordinate to the ruling party. The Constitution also provides for a number of civil and human rights, including freedom of speech, thought, expression, religion, association, demonstration and assembly.

CENTRAL AFRICAN REPUBLIC

LOCATION: The Central African Republic is located in the center of Africa and is bordered by Chad on the north, Sudan on the east, Zaire and the Congo on the south and Cameroon on the west.

AREA: 240,535 sq. miles

Land Use: 3.16% cropland; 4.82% permanent pasture; 57.59% forests and woodland; 34.43% other (mostly grassland).
Arable Land: 15%
Arable Land per capita: 8.55 acres

POPULATION: 2,701,000 (1987)

Population Density: 11 inhabs. per sq. mile (1987)
Population Distribution: 42.40% urban (1985)
Population Growth Rate: 2.42% per year (1985-90 projection)

VITAL STATISTICS

Average Life Expectancy: 45.00 years (1985-90 projection)
Male: 43.40 years (1985-90 projection)
Female: 46.60 years (1985-90 projection)
Age Distribution: (1985)
0-14 .... 42.52%
15-64 .... 53.63%
65+ 3.84%
Median Age: 18.90 years (1985)
Maternal Mortality: (not available)
Infant Mortality: 132 per 1,000 live births (1985-90 projection)

HEALTH CARE

Hospital Beds: 16 per 10,000 population (1980)
Doctors: 0.45 per 10,000 population (1980)

ETHNIC COMPOSITION: Baya - 34%; Banda - 27%; Mandjia - 21%; Sara - 10%; Mboum - 4%; M'Baja - 4%.

RELIGION: Protestant - 25%; Roman Catholic - 25%; indigenous beliefs - 24%; Moslem - 15%; other - 11%.

LANGUAGE: The national language is Sango, though the official language is French.

EDUCATION: Illiteracy: 80%. In 1985, there were 986 primary schools with 294,312 students; 41 general secondary schools with 914 students; 4 technical secondary schools with 2,233 students; and 2,133 students in institutions of higher education.

ECONOMIC DATA

Expenditures by Function [as % of total]: (1981)
General public services 22.97%
Defense 9.70%
Education 17.62%
Health 5.08%
Social security and welfare 6.15%
Housing and community amenities 0.18%
Other community and social services 1.18%
Economic services 19.60%
Agriculture, forestry, fishing and hunting .10.52%
Roads 4.60%
Other transportation and communication ...0.28%
Other purposes 7.71%
GDP per capita: $303 (1984)

TRAVEL NOTES

Climate: The Central African Republic has a tropical climate with an average temperature of 79°F. The southwestern forest areas receive most of the country's precipitation, with rainfall usually occurring during two seasons, from April to May and from August to November.
Health Precautions: Yellow fever and cholera immunizations are required. Shots for tetanus, typhoid, polio, rabies and hepatitis are recommended. The water is not potable and should be boiled and filtered before drinking. Unwashed fruits and undercooked meat should also be avoided.
Miscellaneous: The primary tourist attractions in the Central African Republic are the waterfalls, the forests and the vast variety of wild animals.

GOVERNMENT

Central African Republic (Republique Centrafricaine) became an independent state on Aug 13, 1960. Before independence, the CAR was the Ubangi-Shari territory of French Equatorial Africa. The independence Constitution provided for a democratically elected Government, but by 1962 a one-party system had emerged. President David Dacko was overthrown in 1966 in a military coup led by the army commander, Jean Bedel Bokassa. In 1976, Bokassa proclaimed himself Emperor Bokassa I. The Imperial Government was overthrown Sep 20, 1979, in a coup led by former President Dacko. About 23 months later, on Sep 1, 1981, the army ousted Dacko and installed a ruling military committee headed by Gen. Andre Kolingba. In November 1986, Kolingba was elected President under a new Constitution, which permitted only one legal political party. National elections were held on Jul 31, 1987 for the first time in 20 years, although all candidates were nominated by the country's only legal party, the Rassemblement Democrate Centrafricaine (RDC).

Constitution: On Nov 21, 1986 a new Constitution was approved by an estimated 90% of the electorate in a national referendum. The Constitution established a one-party state under the Rassemblement Democrate Centrafricaine (RDC), which was launched in May 1986 as the country's sole legal political party.

CEYLON
See Sri Lanka

CHAD
Republic of Chad

LOCATION: A landlocked country in north central Africa, Chad is bounded by Libya to the north, Sudan to the east, the Central African Republic to the south, Cameroon to the southwest and Nigeria and Niger to the west.

AREA: 495,800 sq. miles

Land Use: 2.50% cropland; 35.74% permanent pasture; 10.55% forests and woodland; 51.21% other (mainly desert).
Arable Land: 3%
Arable Land per capita: 1.75 acres

POPULATION: 5,571,000 (1988 estimate)

Population Density: 11 inhabs. per sq. mile (1988 estimate)
Population Distribution: 27% urban (1985)
Population Growth Rate: 2.50% per year (1988 estimate)

VITAL STATISTICS

Average Life Expectancy: 45.00 years (1985-90 projection)
Male: 43.40 years (1985-90 projection)
Female: 46.60 years (1985-90 projection)
Age Distribution: (1985)
0-14 . . . . .42.31%
15-64 . . . . .54.10%
65+ 3.59%
Median Age: 18.80 years (1985)
Maternal Mortality: (not available)
Infant Mortality: 140 per 1,000 live births (1985)

HEALTH CARE

Hospital Beds: 8 per 10,000 population (1980)
Doctors: 0.20 per 10,000 population (1984)

ETHNIC COMPOSITION: Chad has about 200 distinct ethnic groups, with Moslems (Arabs, Baguirmi, Boulala, Fulbe, Hausa, Kanembou, Kotoko, Maba, Toubou) found in the northern and central parts of the country and non-Moslems (Goulaye, Massa, Mbaye, Moudang, Moussei, Ngambaye) located in the south. There are also approximately 150,000 nonindigenous peoples, including 1,000 French.

RELIGION: Moslem - 44%; Christian - 33%; indigenous beliefs - 23%.

LANGUAGE: French and Arabic are the official languages. There are more than 100 different languages and dialects spoken, with Sango and Sara being the most common.

EDUCATION: Illiteracy: 83%. In 1984, there were 1,231 primary schools with 288,478 students; 45,612 secondary school students; and 1,643 students in higher institutions.

ECONOMIC DATA

Expenditures by Function [as % of total]: (not available)

GDP per capita: $81 (1985)

TRAVEL NOTES

Climate: The northern section of Chad, which is part of the Sahara Desert, has a hot and arid climate. The southern half of the country is extremely wet, with an average annual rainfall of 196 inches.

Health Precautions: Immunizations against yellow fever and cholera are required, and gamma globulin shots are recommended. The water is not potable.

Miscellaneous: Chad's beautiful and diverse scenery includes dense, tropical forests in the southern part of the country and the vast Sahara Desert in the north. There is an abundance of wild animals, especially at the two national parks and 5 game reserves.

GOVERNMENT

Chad (Republique du Tchad—Republic of Chad), gained its independence from France on Aug 11, 1960. It has had a history of political instability and turmoil since independence, largely due to conflicts between Moslem herders in the northern part of the country and black animist farmers in the south. A Transitional Government of National Unity (Gouvernement d'Union National de Transition—GUNT) was established in August 1979, with Goukhouni Oueddei being designated as the country's president. Oueddei was overthrown on Jun 7, 1982, by a Moslem rebel group headed by Hissein Habre, who became Chad's new head of state. After his ouster, Oueddei continued to assert GUNT's legitimacy and formed his own government-in-exile in opposition to Habre's regime. Several rebel groups announced in February 1988 that they were switching their allegiance to Habre's government, thereby enabling the President to further consolidate his power base within Chad.

Constitution: The nation's first Constitution, adopted in 1964, was officially nullified in April 1975 following a military coup. A provisional Constitution, called the Fundamental Act, was promulgated on Sep 29, 1982. The document specifies that the President be granted unrestrained powers until a permanent Constitution can be adopted.

CHILE
Republic of Chile

LOCATION: Situated along the western coast of South America, Chile is bounded by Argentina on the east while Peru lies to the north and Bolivia lies to the northeast. Several islands offshore, including Isla de Pascua (Easter Island) also form part of Chile.

AREA: 292,132 sq. miles

Land Use: 7% cropland; 16% permanent pasture; 21% forests and woodland; 56% other (barren mountain, desert and urban).

Arable Land: 7%

Arable Land per capita: 1.08 acres

POPULATION: 12,416,000 (1987)

Population Density: 42.50 inhabs. per sq. mile (1985)

Population Distribution: 83.60% urban (1985)

Population Growth Rate: 1.52% per year (1985-90)

VITAL STATISTICS

Average Life Expectancy: 70.70 years (1985-90)

Male: 67.60 years (1985-90)

Female: 73.90 years (1985-90)

Age Distribution: (1985)

0-14 . . . . .30.20%
15-64 . . . . .64.10%
65+ 5.70%

Median Age: 24.70 years (1985)

Maternal Mortality: 52.40 per 100,000 live births (1982)

Infant Mortality: 20 per 1,000 live births (1985-90)

HEALTH CARE

Hospital Beds: 34.21 per 10,000 population (1980)

Doctors: 5.19 per 10,000 population (1979)

ETHNIC COMPOSITION: Mestizo (mixed Spanish and Indian) - 65%; European, including

German, English, Italian, Yugoslav and French - 30%; Indian, including Araucanian - 5%.

RELIGION: Roman Catholic - 89%; Protestant - 11%.

LANGUAGE: The official language is Spanish.

EDUCATION: Illiteracy: 10%. In 1985, there were 2,062,344 primary school students; 667,797 secondary school students; and 196,460 technical college and university students.

ECONOMIC DATA

Expenditures by Function [as % of total]: (1984)
General public services 11.10%
Defense 11.60%
Education 13.05%
Health 6.18%
Social security and welfare 41.82%
Housing and community amenities 3.44%
Other community and social services 0.71%
Economic services 7.54%
Agriculture, forestry, fishing and hunting .. 1.65%
Roads 2.65%
Other transportation and communication .. 0.78%
Other purposes 4.55%
GDP per capita: $1,161 (1985)

TRAVEL NOTES

Climate: The climate, generally mild, is influenced by both the mountains and the cold Humboldt Current. The average maximum temperature varies by no more than 55°F between Arica in the north and Punta Arenas in the extreme south. Rainfall varies widely between the arid desert in the north and the rainy south.

Health Precautions: Typhoid and gamma globulin shots are recommended.

Miscellaneous: Geographically diverse, Chile has many attractions. Among them are the northern deserts, the labyrinths of channels, inlets, fjords and peninsulas in the south and the Andes.

GOVERNMENT

Chile (Republica de Chile—Republic of Chile) won independence from Spain in 1818. Its 20th century history has been marked by struggles for ascendancy between left-wing and right-wing groups. A military coup on Sep 11, 1973 ousted the elected Marxist Government of Salvador Allende Gossens, and Gen. Augusto

Pinochet Ugarte and a 4-member junta subsequently took power. President Pinochet was defeated for another term in an Oct 5, 1988, yes-no plebiscite and power is scheduled to return to an elected president in March 1990, following December 1989 elections.

Constitution: The 1925 Constitution was suspended after the military takeover of September 1973 and abolished in 1981. A decree of Dec 17, 1974 (under which Gen. Pinochet assumed the presidency) vests executive powers in the President and legislative powers in the junta. A new Constitution was approved by a referendum in September 1980 and entered into effect in March 1981, establishing an 8-year transition period to "authoritarian democracy."

CHINA
People's Republic of China

LOCATION: Located in eastern Asia, China is bordered by Mongolia to the north, the Soviet Union to the north and west, Afghanistan and Pakistan to the west and India, Nepal, Bhutan, Burma, Laos and Vietnam to the south. North Korea also borders China at a northeastern section, while China's coastline is formed along the Pacific Ocean.

AREA: 3,695,500 sq. miles

Land Use: 10.82% cropland; 30.63% permanent pasture; 14.08% forest and woodland; 44.47% other (mostly desert).
Arable Land: 10.82%
Arable Land per capita: 0.25 acres

POPULATION: 1,085,008,000 (1987 estimate)

Population Density: 293.60 inhabs. per sq. mile (1987)
Population Distribution: 20.60% urban (1985)
Population Growth Rate: 1.18% per year (1985-90 projection)

VITAL STATISTICS

Average Life Expectancy: 69.40 years (1985-90 projection)
Male: 68.00 years (1985-90 projection)
Female: 70.90 years (1985-90 projection)
Age Distribution: (1985)
0-14 ....29.70%

15-59 . . . . 65.00%
60+ 5.30%

Median Age: 24.00 years (1985)
Maternal Mortality: (not available)
Infant Mortality: 32 per 1,000 live births (1985-90 projection)

HEALTH CARE

Hospital Beds: 20.63 per 10,000 population (1984)
Doctors: 13.34 per 10,000 population (1984)

ETHNIC COMPOSITION: Han-Chinese - 93.30%; Zhuang, Uygur, Hui, Yi, Tibetan, Miao, Manchu, Mongol, Buyi, Korean and others - 6.70%.

RELIGION: China is officially atheist. However, Confucianism, Taoism, Buddhism and ancestor worship persist as important religious elements. About 2-3% of the population is Moslem, and 1% is Christian.

LANGUAGE: The principal language is Northern (Standard) Chinese or Mandarin (also known as Putonghua and based on the Beijing dialect); also spoken are Yue (Cantonese), Wu (Shanghainese), Minbei (Fuzhou), Minnan (Hokkien - Taiwanese), Xiang, Gan, Hakka dialects and other minority languages. The Constitution stipulates that "all nationalities have the freedom to use their own spoken and written languages."

EDUCATION: Illiteracy: Less than 25%. In 1984, there were 853,740 primary schools with 135,571,000 students; 75,867 lower secondary schools with 38,643,000 students; 17,847 upper secondary schools with 6,898,000 students; 2,293 secondary technical schools with 811,000 students; 1,008 teacher training schools with 511,000 students; 4,622 agricultural schools with 907,000 students; 2,380 vocational schools with 837,000 students; and 902 higher learning institutions with 1,443,000 students.

ECONOMIC DATA

Expenditures by Function [as % of total]: (not available)
GDP per capita: (not available)

TRAVEL NOTES

Climate: The Chinese climate is varied; the climate in the far south is sub-tropical, while the north experiences an annual average tempera-ture of below 50°F. The east has a monsoon climate, while the northwest is dry.
Health Precautions: A cholera vaccination is required for entry.
Miscellaneous: Tourists are drawn by historical monuments such as the Great Wall, the Forbidden City, the Ming Tombs and the Temple of Heaven.

GOVERNMENT

China (Zhonghua Renmin Gongheguo—People's Republic of China) is a unitary multinational state in which effective political power rests with the Chinese Communist Party. However, Deng Xiaoping is generally regarded to be the nation's effective leader, although he holds no post other than Chairman of the Central Military Commission. The armed forces, known as the People's Liberation Army (PLA), also have an important influence in government. The People's Republic was established on Oct 1, 1949, following a civil war in which Chinese Communist forces overthrew the Kuomintang Government of Chiang Kai-shek.

Constitution: China's present Constitution (its 4th under Communist rule) was adopted by the National People's Congress on Dec 4, 1982. The Constitution is divided into a Preamble and 4 Chapters and contains 138 articles. According to the Preamble, "The basic task of the nation in the years to come is to concentrate its effort on socialist modernization." The 1982 Constitution restores many of the articles of the 1954 Con-stitution that were dropped in the 1975 and 1978 versions. It reestablishes the largely ceremonial post of President; abolishes the right to strike (introduced by Mao Zedong in 1975); extends the list of civil rights to include equality before the law, freedom of worship and protection from arbitrary arrest; and makes the practice of family planning a duty of husband and wife. It also limits the President, Premier and other top officials to two 5-year terms in office. The Con-stitution was amended during the 13th National Party Congress of the Chinese Communist Party (CCP). The amendments made it possible for Deng Xiaoping to retain the post of Chairman of the Central Military Commission despite his resignation from the Politburo, established solid power for the Politburo over the Secretariat and also eliminated all mention of the people's com-munes from the Constitution. The functions of the head of state are exercised by the President.

The Constitution grants the National People's Congress Standing Committee authority to send and receive ambassadors and to ratify or abrogate treaties. The direction of the Government is vested in the State Council (Cabinet), headed by a Chairman (Premier—Head of Government). The Council is responsible to the National People's Congress. Despite the provisions of the Constitution, the Chinese Communist Party holds effective political power, and Deng Xiaoping is generally acknowledged to be the country's leader, although he holds no position other than Chairman of the Central Military Commission.

COLOMBIA
Republic of Colombia

LOCATION: Colombia lies in the northwest of South America, with the Caribbean Sea to the north and the Pacific Ocean to the west. It is bordered on the east by Venezuela and Brazil, and on the south by Peru and Ecuador. Panama links Colombia to Central America.

AREA: 439,737 sq. miles

Land Use: 72% forest and savannah; 5% crop and fallow; 14% pasture; 6% forest, swamp and water; 3% urban and other.
Arable Land: 5%
Arable Land per capita: 0.47 acres

POPULATION: 29,956,000 (1986)

Population Density: 68.12 inhabs. per sq. mile (1986)
Population Distribution: 64.20% urban (1985)
Population Growth Rate: 2.10% per year (1986)

VITAL STATISTICS

Average Life Expectancy: 63.70 years (1985)
Male: 61.40 years (1985)
Female: 66.00 years (1985)
Age Distribution: (1985)
0-15 .... 37.20%
15-64 .... 59.10%
64+ 3.80%
Median Age: 20.70 years (1985)
Maternal Mortality: 133.50 per 100,000 live births (1977)
Infant Mortality: 53 per 1,000 live births (1985)

HEALTH CARE

Hospital Beds: 17.19 per 10,000 population (1980)
Doctors: 5.21 per 10,000 population (1977)

ETHNIC COMPOSITION: Mestizo - 58%; white - 20%; mulatto - 14%; black - 4%; mixed black/Indian - 3%; Indian - 1%.

RELIGION: Roman Catholic - 95%; Protestant, Jewish and other - 5%.

LANGUAGE: Spanish

EDUCATION: Illiteracy: 20%. In 1985, there were 34,004 primary schools with 4,039,533 students; 4,540 secondary schools with 1,934,032 students; 225 higher institutions with 389,075 students.

ECONOMIC DATA

Expenditures by Function [as % of total]: (not available)
GDP per capita: $1,198 (1984)

TRAVEL NOTES

Climate: While the coastal climate is that of a tropical rain forest, the plateaus enjoy temperate weather. Areas of the Andes mountains are under permanent snow.
Health Precautions: Travelers to Colombia should be inoculated against typhoid, tetanus, polio, yellow fever and infectious hepatitis. All foods should be washed thoroughly before they are eaten.
Miscellaneous: Tourism is the second biggest foreign exchange earner. Among the tourist attractions in Colombia are the Caribbean coast, the 16th-century walled city of Cartagena, the town of Leticia on the Amazon, the Andes mountains, pre-Colombian relics and monuments of colonial art.

GOVERNMENT

Colombia (Republica de Colombia—Republic of Colombia) is a republic with a presidential form of government. It achieved independence from Spain in 1819 and became a republic in 1830.

Constitution: The present Constitution was originally promulgated on Aug 5, 1886, but it has been amended frequently and substantial changes in its provisions have occurred over the years. It guarantees freedom of religion, speech, assembly and other basic civil, social and economic rights. It provides for a strong presidential form of government, with separation of powers between the executive, legislative and judicial branches. The Constitution provides that in cases of emergency the executive may legislate by decree for periods of not more than 90 days in any one year; the decrees must be addressed to the cause of the emergency. The Constitution also provides for a National Economic Council to advise the Controller-General in charge of the nation's finances.

COMORO ISLANDS
Federal Islamic Republic of the Comoros

LOCATION: Also known as the Comoros, the Comoro Islands are an archipelago of 4 major islands and several islets in the Indian Ocean between northern Madagascar and the east African coast. The 4 major islands are Njazidja (where the capital is located), Nzwani, Mwali and Mayotte (Mahore), which is administered by France as a territorial collectivity but also claimed by the Comoro Islands (see below: Government).

AREA: 719 sq. miles

Land Use: 42.86% cropland; 6.91% permanent pasture; 16.13% forests and woodland; 34.10% other.
Arable Land: 43%
Arable Land per capita: 0.47 acres

POPULATION: 459,000 (1989 estimate)

Population Density: 638 inhabs. per sq. mile (1989 estimate)
Population Distribution: 25.23% urban (1985)
Population Growth Rate: 2.90% per year (1988 estimate)

VITAL STATISTICS

Average Life Expectancy: 52.00 years (1985-90 projection)
Male: 50.30 years (1985-90 projection)
Female: 53.80 years (1985-90 projection)
Age Distribution: (1985)
0-14 .... 46.07%
15-64 .... 51.01%
65+ 2.92%

Median Age: 16.90 years (1985)
Maternal Mortality: (not available)
Infant Mortality: 111 per 1,000 live births (1985)

HEALTH CARE

Hospital Beds: 19 per 10,000 population (1978)
Doctors: 0.56 per 10,000 population (1978)

ETHNIC COMPOSITION: The population is predominantly derived from Arab, African and Malagasy ancestors.

RELIGION: Sunni Moslem - 86%; Roman Catholic - 14%. Islam is the state religion.

LANGUAGE: The official languages are Arabic and French, although the majority speaks Comoran (a blend of Swahili and Arabic).

EDUCATION: Illiteracy: 85%. In 1980, there were 236 primary schools with 59,709 students; 13,528 general secondary students; 151 vocational secondary students; and 119 teacher training students.

ECONOMIC DATA

Expenditures by Function [as % of total]: (not available)
GDP per capita: $316 (1985)

TRAVEL NOTES

Climate: Although the Comoran climate is generally tropical, the climate varies from one island to another, with some islands experiencing more rainfall than others.
Health Precautions: (not available)
Miscellaneous: The Comoros Islands provide the tourist with lovely beaches and opportunities for water activities.

GOVERNMENT

Comoro Islands (Jumhuriyat al-Qumur al-Ittihadiyah al-Islamiyah—Republique Federale Islamique des Comores—Federal Islamic Republic of the Comoros), a French Overseas Territory since 1947, became internally self-governing in 1961 and unilaterally declared its independence from France on Jul 6, 1975. A majority of the people on the island of Mayotte (Mahore), however, voted to remain a French dependency, and France continues to maintain a presence on that island, while recognizing the independence of the rest of the Comoros.

Constitution: A national referendum (in which Mayotte did not participate) approved a new Constitution on Oct 1, 1978. It provides for a federal Islamic system with a degree of autonomy for each island government. The Constitution also provides for an ultimate reunion between the island of Mayotte and the Comoro Islands. Amendments to the Constitution were made in 1982 and 1985, when the position of Prime Minister was abolished.

CONGO
People's Republic of the Congo

LOCATION: Located in west-central Africa, with a small outlet to the Atlantic Ocean on the southwest, the Congo is bordered by Gabon to the west, Cameroon to the northwest, the Central African Republic to the northeast, Zaire to the east and south and Angola to the southeast.

AREA: 132,050 sq. miles

Land Use: 1.97% cropland; 29.28% permanent pasture; 62.37% forests and woodland; 6.38% other.
Arable Land: 2%
Arable Land per capita: 1.02 acres

POPULATION: 1,970,000 (1988 estimate)

Population Density: 15 inhabs. per sq. mile (1988 estimate)
Population Distribution: 39.48% urban (1985)
Population Growth Rate: 3.10% per year (1988 estimate)

VITAL STATISTICS

Average Life Expectancy: 48.50 years (1985-90 projection)
Male: 46.90 years (1985-90 projection)
Female: 50.20 years (1985-90 projection)
Age Distribution: (1985)
0-14 .... 43.62%
15-64 .... 52.99%
65+ 3.39%
Median Age: 18.20 years (1985)
Maternal Mortality: (not available)
Infant Mortality: 110 per 1,000 live births (1985)

HEALTH CARE

Hospital Beds: 348 per 10,000 population (1986)
Doctors: 2 per 10,000 population (1984)

ETHNIC COMPOSITION: Kongo - 48%; Sangha - 20%; Teke - 17%; M'Bochi - 12%; other - 3%.

RELIGION: Christian - 50%; traditional beliefs - 42%; Moslem - 2%; other - 6%.

LANGUAGE: French is the official language, although many indigenous languages, especially dialects of Bantu, are spoken.

EDUCATION: Illiteracy: 37% (1985). In 1984, there were 1,522 primary schools with 458,237 students; 182,294 general secondary school students; 18,959 vocational school students; 1,655 teacher training school students; and 1 university with 9,385 students.

ECONOMIC DATA

Expenditures by Function [as % of total]: (not available)
GDP per capita: $1,140 (1984)

TRAVEL NOTES

Climate: The Congolese climate is tropical and humid. Annual temperatures average between 70°F and 80°F, while annual rainfall—which occurs mainly between March and May—averages between 45 and 80 inches.
Health Precautions: Cholera, yellow fever, smallpox, typhoid, tetanus, polio and rabies vaccinations are recommended, as are gamma globulin inoculations and precautions against cholera. Malaria suppressives are highly recommended as the disease is endemic. Tap water is not potable.
Miscellaneous: Tourists are attracted by the lush vegetation and beautiful natural features, including Foulakari Falls, Pine Forest, Lake Kivu and Lac Bleu.

GOVERNMENT

Congo Republic (Republique Populaire du Congo—People's Republic of the Congo) previously the French colony of Middle Congo, was formerly part of French Equatorial Africa. It became the autonomous Republic of Congo within the French Community in November 1958, and became an independent state on Aug

15, 1960. Effective political power rests with the Council of Ministers, headed by the President and responsible to the Parti congolais du travail (PCT—Congolese Labor Party), the sole legal political organization since Dec 31, 1969, when the country was renamed the People's Republic of the Congo.

Constitution: The 1979 Constitution (the country's 4th since independence) establishes the PCT as the sole legal party and names the Central Committee Chairperson as President of the Republic (head of state). Constitutional revisions adopted by the party in 1984 make the President head of government as well. The Constitution provides for ownership of property and guarantees religious freedom, but prohibits religious-based political groups.

COSTA RICA
Republic of Costa Rica

LOCATION: In the Central American isthmus, Costa Rica is bordered by Nicaragua to the north, Panama to the south, the Caribbean Sea to the east and the Pacific Ocean to the west.

AREA: 19,730 sq. miles

Land Use: 60% forest; 22% meadow and pasture; 8% cultivated; 10% waste, urban and other.
Arable Land: 12%
Arable Land per capita: 0.56 acres

POPULATION: 2,714,000 (1986)

Population Density: 137.56 inhabs. per sq. mile (1986)
Population Distribution: 49.80% urban (1986)
Population Growth Rate: 2.60% per year (1986)

VITAL STATISTICS

Average Life Expectancy: 69.70 years (1986)
Male: 67.50 years (1986)
Female: 71.90 years (1986)
Age Distribution: (1985)
0-14 .... 36.70%
15-64 .... 59.50%
65+ 3.80%
Median Age: 21.10 years (1985)
Maternal Mortality: 22.90 per 100,000 live births (1980)

Infant Mortality: 18.60 per 1,000 live births (1984)

HEALTH CARE

Hospital Beds: 33.22 per 10,000 population (1982)
Doctors: 7.07 per 10,000 population (1979)

ETHNIC COMPOSITION: White and mestizo - 96%; black - 3%; Indian - 1%.

RELIGION: Roman Catholic - 95%; Protestant, Jewish and other - 5%.

LANGUAGE: The official language is Spanish. A Jamaican dialect of English is used around Puerto Limon.

EDUCATION: Illiteracy: 7%. In 1983, there were 3,511 primary schools with 378,222 students; in 1981, there were 242 secondary schools with 153,971 students.

ECONOMIC DATA

Expenditures by Function [as % of total]: (1983)
General public services 8.78%
Defense 3.04%
Education 19.37%
Health 22.48%
Social security and welfare 14.45%
Housing and community amenities 2.67%
Other community and social services 5.11%
Economic services 20.16%
Agriculture, forestry, fishing and hunting ..5.30%
Roads 12.58%
Other transportation and communication ...0.41%
Other purposes 10.28%
GDP per capita: $1,315 (1985)

TRAVEL NOTES

Climate: The lowlands are warm and damp. The Central Plateau, where two-thirds of the population live, are cooler, with an average temperature of 72°F.
Health Precautions: There may be serious tropical diseases in certain areas, with malaria cases reported in coastal areas with altitudes below 2,000 feet. In some places the water is not safe to drink and should be boiled or filtered.
Miscellaneous: The volcanos of Irazu and Poas, the Orosi valley, the ruins of the colonial church at Orosi and the jungle train to Limon are the main tourist features. The beaches of Guanacaste and Puntarenas are also popular.

GOVERNMENT

Costa Rica (Republica de Costa Rica—Republic of Costa Rica) declared its independence from Spain in September 1821. From time to time since 1821 it has been incorporated into Mexico or into Central American federal states. It is a democratic republic in which effective political power is shared by the President and the legislature, both selected by popular vote.

Constitution: The present Constitution (of Nov 7, 1949) provides for three independent branches of government (legislative, executive and judicial) in which the legislature and the President are co-equal. The Constitution forbids the establishment of a permanent military force.

COTE D'IVOIRE
Republic of the Ivory Coast

LOCATION: Cote d'Ivoire lies in West Africa, and is bounded by Liberia and Guinea on the west, Mali and Burkina Faso on the north, Ghana on the east and the Gulf of Guinea on the south.

AREA: 124,503 sq. miles

Land Use: 12.56% cropland; 9.43% permanent pasture; 26.35% forests and woodland; 51.66% other (mostly savanna).
Arable Land: 12.56%
Arable Land per capita: 1.08 acres

POPULATION: 10,529,000 (1987)

Population Density: 84.57 inhabs. per sq. mile (1987)
Population Distribution: 42% urban (1985)
Population Growth Rate: 3.45% per year (1985-90 projection)

VITAL STATISTICS

Average Life Expectancy: 52.50 years (1985-90 projection)
Male: 50.80 years (1985-90 projection)
Female: 54.30 years (1985-90 projection)
Age Distribution: (1985)
0-14 .... 45.60%
15-64 .... 51.50%
65+ 3.00%
Median Age: 17.20 years (1985)
Maternal Mortality: (not available)

Infant Mortality: 100 per 1,000 live births (1985-90 projection)

HEALTH CARE

Hospital Beds: 10.77 per 10,000 population (1980)
Doctors: 0.63 per 10,000 population (1980)

ETHNIC COMPOSITION: Baoule - 23%; Bete - 18%; Senoufou - 15%; Malinke - 11%; other - 33% (including other indigenous groups, foreign Africans, Lebanese and French).

RELIGION: Animist - 63%, Moslem - 25%, Christian (mostly Roman Catholic) - 12%.

LANGUAGE: French is the official language. Over 60 African dialects are spoken, with Dioula the most common.

EDUCATION: Illiteracy: 76%. In 1984/85 there were 1,179,456 students enrolled in primary schools; 245,342 students in secondary schools; and 12,755 in colleges and universities.

ECONOMIC DATA

Expenditures by Function [as % of total]: (1980)
General public services 21.26%
Defense 3.91%
Education 16.34%
Health 3.95%
Social security and welfare 3.05%
Housing and community amenities 1.26%
Other community and social services 1.38%
Economic services 13.41%
Agriculture, forestry, fishing and hunting ..3.40%
Roads 1.99%
Other transportation and communication ...4.26%
Other purposes 7.95%
GDP per capita: $772 (1986)

TRAVEL NOTES

Climate: The Ivorian climate is tropical, with temperatures ranging from 57°F to 103°F. The heavy annual rainfall averages 51-82 inches.
Health Precautions: Vaccinations against cholera and yellow fever are mandatory. There is also risk of typhoid, malaria, encephalitis and dengue fever.
Miscellaneous: Tourists are attracted by the landscape as well as the game reserves.

GOVERNMENT

Cote d'Ivoire (Republique de la Cote d'Ivoire— formerly known also as Republic of the Ivory Coast) gained full independence from France on Aug 7, 1960. It is presently a one-party state with a strong presidential form of government. Effective political authority rests with the *Parti Democratique de la Cote d'Ivoire* led by President Houphouet-Boigny.

Constitution: The Ivory Coast's only Constitution was promulgated on Oct 31, 1960 and amended in 1971, 1975, 1980, 1985 and 1986. Authority to amend the Constitution rests with the National Assembly.

CUBA
Republic of Cuba

LOCATION: Cuba is an archipelago of islands, consisting of two main islands and approximately 1,600 tiny islets, located in the Caribbean Sea. Florida lies about 90 miles to the north, the Bahamas are to the northeast, Haiti is to the east, Jamaica lies to the south, Mexico is to the west and the Gulf of Mexico lies to the northwest.

AREA: 42,800 sq. miles

Land Use: 29.06% cropland; 22.46% permanent pasture; 17.41% forests and woodland; 31.07% other.
Arable Land: 29%
Arable Land per capita: 0.80 acres

POPULATION: 10,462,000 (1988 estimate)

Population Density: 224 inhabs. per sq. mile (1988 estimate)
Population Distribution: 71.75% urban (1985)
Population Growth Rate: 1.20% per year (1988 estimate)

VITAL STATISTICS

Average Life Expectancy: 74.00 years (1985-90 projection)
Male: 72.20 years (1985-90 projection)
Female: 75.80 years (1985-90 projection)
Age Distribution: (1985)
0-14 .... 26.36%
15-64 .... 65.75%
65+ 7.89%

Median Age: 25.80 years (1985)
Maternal Mortality: 45.40 per 100,000 live births (1983)
Infant Mortality: 14 per 1,000 live births (1986)

HEALTH CARE

Hospital Beds: 55 per 10,000 population (1986)
Doctors: 25 per 10,000 population (1986)

ETHNIC COMPOSITION: White (including mestizo) - 96%; black - 3%; Indian - 1%.

RELIGION: Roman Catholic - 95%; other - 5%.

LANGUAGE: Spanish is the official language.

EDUCATION: Illiteracy: 4% (1987). In 1986/87, there were 9,837 primary schools with 1,001,000 students; 1,293 general secondary schools with 800,700 students; 634 professional and technical schools with 317,600 students; and 35 institutions of higher learning with 256,600 students.

ECONOMIC DATA

Expenditures by Function [as %of total]: (1986)
General public services .... (not available)
Defense 10.90%
Education and health 21.89%
Social security and welfare .... (not available)
Housing and community amenities 6.57%
Other community and social services 16.38%
Economic services .... (not available)
Agriculture, forestry, fishing
and hunting .... (not available)
Roads .... (not available)
Other transportation and
communication .... (not available)
Other purposes .... (not available)
Net Material Product per capita: $1,006 (1986)

TRAVEL NOTES

Climate: Cuba has a semitropical climate, with an average annual temperature of 75°F and an average summer temperature of 81°F. The country has two main seasons: a dry period lasting from November to April, and a rainy season, which occurs between May and October. Annual average rainfall is 54 inches.
Health Precautions: Yellow fever, gamma globulin and typhoid inoculations are recommended.
Miscellaneous: Cuba is renowned for its tropical beaches, diving and fishing areas. Also of

interest are the many fine examples of Spanish colonial architecture and art.

GOVERNMENT

Cuba (Republica de Cuba—Republic of Cuba) was under Spanish rule from the 1700s until 1898, when it came under US control. It became an independent republic in May 1902, although the US retained the right for some degree of control in Cuban affairs until 1934. Fidel Castro Ruiz, backed by a group of rebels, seized power in January 1959, and proclaimed Cuba a Communist state in December 1961. Since then, effective political power has rested with the *Partido Comunista Cubano* (PCC—Communist Party of Cuba), under the direction of Castro.

Constitution: The present Constitution, consisting of 141 articles in 12 chapters, was approved in a referendum on Feb 16, 1976, and entered into effect on Feb 24, 1976. It proclaims Cuba a socialist state committed to friendship and cooperation with the Soviet Union and other socialist states, and recognizes the leading role of the Communist Party. The Constitution also deals with political, social and economic principles of the state: citizenship, the family, education and culture, equality of citizens and individual rights and duties. The Constitution may be amended by a two-thirds vote of the National Assembly of People's Power.

CYPRUS
Republic of Cyprus

LOCATION: Cyprus is an island in the eastern Mediterranean Sea. Turkey lies approximately 40 miles to the north and Syria 60 miles to the west.

AREA: 3,572 sq. miles (includes Turkish sector)

Land Use: 46.75% cropland; 10.06% permanent pasture; 18.51% forests and woodland; 24.68% other.
Arable Land: 47%
Arable Land per capita: 1.58 acres

POPULATION: 689,000 (1988 estimate)

Population Density: 193 inhabs. per sq. mile (1988 estimate)
Population Distribution: 49.50% urban (1985)

Population Growth Rate: 1.10% per year (1988 estimate)

VITAL STATISTICS

Average Life Expectancy: 74.60 years (1985-90 projection)
Male: 72.70 years (1985-90 projection)
Female: 76.70 years (1985-90 projection)
Age Distribution: (1985)
0-14 ....25.41%
15-64 ....64.72%
65+ 9.87%
Median Age: 29.60 years (1985)
Maternal Mortality: (not available)
Infant Mortality: 12 per 1,000 live births (1985)

HEALTH CARE

Hospital Beds: 56 per 10,000 population (1981)
Doctors: 10 per 10,000 population (1981)

ETHNIC COMPOSITION: Greek - 78%; Turkish - 18%; other - 4%. (Data includes Turkish sector.)

RELIGION: Greek Orthodox - 78%; Moslem - 18%; other - 4%. (Data includes Turkish sector.)

LANGUAGE: Greek is spoken by 75% of the population, with most of the remaining 25% speaking Turkish. A small minority speak English. (Data includes Turkish sector.)

EDUCATION: Illiteracy: 1%. In 1986/87, there were 373 primary schools with 54,254 students; 94 secondary schools with 40,627 students; 9 technical and vocational institutions with 3,681 students; 1 teacher training institution with 413 students; and 15 post-secondary institutions with 3,006 students.

ECONOMIC DATA

Expenditures by Function [as % of total]: (1986)
General public services 15.31%
Defense 2.86%
Education 10.77%
Health 6.47%
Social security and welfare 20.48%
Housing and community amenities 3.92%
Other community and social services 1.30%
Economic services 21.19%
Agriculture, forestry, fishing and hunting .14.76%
Roads 2.75%
Other transportation and communication ...1.33%

Other purposes 12.43%
GDP per capita: $3,938 (1985)

TRAVEL NOTES

Climate: Cyprus has a mild climate, with temperatures in Nicosia ranging between 41°F and 97°F. The temperature sometimes exceeds 100°F in the summer, but the humidity is low. The rainy season lasts from December to March and snow occasionally falls in the southwestern mountains.

Health Precautions: None

Miscellaneous: Tourists are attracted to Cyprus by its warm climate, archaeological ruins and beautiful beaches, which are considered ideal for skin diving, waterskiing and windsurfing. Places of interest in Nicosia include the Cathedral of St. John, the Cyprus Museum and the Makarios Center.

GOVERNMENT

Cyprus (Dimokratia Kyprou—Kibris Cumhuriyeti—Republic of Cyprus) became an independent state on Aug 16, 1960, under compromise agreements guaranteed by Britain, Greece and Turkey. These agreements were designed to alleviate the long-standing enmity between the island's Greek and Turkish communities by safeguarding the rights of the Turkish minority and expressly prohibiting "Enosis" (union of Cyprus with Greece) or the division of the island between Greece and Turkey. Constitutional changes aimed at modifying the obstructive powers of the Turkish minority were proposed by the Greek Cypriot majority Government in November 1963, resulting in an increase of intercommunal fighting and the withdrawal of Turkish Cypriots from the Government. In 1964, a United Nations (UN) peacekeeping force was established on the island. Following a renewal of conflict in 1967, Turkish Cypriots created the Turkish Cypriot Provisional Administration in the northern (Turkish-dominated) region of the country. Turkish troops were dispatched to northern Cyprus on Jul 20, 1974, 5 days after a successful coup against the civilian Government by Greek Cypriot army officers. Over 1,400 square miles of the island (approximately one-third of the total area) were taken over by Turkish forces before a cease-fire was instituted. In 1975, Turkish Cypriots in the occupied northern sector proclaimed the region an autonomous federal state, and on Nov 15, 1983 it was officially declared the "Turkish Republic of Northern Cyprus" (TRNC). Thus far, Turkey is the only nation to recognize the independent status of the TRNC. The UN continues to supervise negotiations on a unified Cyprus, but little progress has been made.

Constitution: The Constitution of 1960 provided for a Government designed to protect both Greek and Turkish Cypriot interests by allocating political power and representation in proportion to the population of the two communities. Officially, the Constitution continues to remain in effect, but since the Turkish Cypriot withdrawal from the Government in 1963, each group has administered its own affairs and refused to recognize the legitimacy of the other's Government.

REPUBLIC OF CYPRUS: The Government of Cyprus is based on the Constitution of 1960, which created a sovereign and democratic republic. Executive authority is held by a President and a Council of Ministers, while legislative authority rests with a unicameral House of Representatives.

TURKISH REPUBLIC OF NORTHERN CYPRUS: The Constitution of the TRNC, approved by national referendum in May 1985, established a presidential-parliamentary system based on the principles of social justice and the rule of law. A President and a Cabinet hold executive power, with a unicameral Assembly of the Republic wielding legislative authority.

CZECHOSLOVAKIA
Czechoslovak Socialist Republic

LOCATION: Located in central Europe, Czechoslovakia is bounded to the north by Poland, to the northwest by East Germany, to the west by West Germany, to the southwest by Austria, to the southeast by Hungary and to the east by the Soviet Union.

AREA: 49,384 sq. miles

Land Use: 41.20% cropland; 13.27% permanent pasture; 36.52% forests and woodland; 9.01% other.

Arable Land: 41.20%

Arable Land per capita: 0.83 acres

QUALITY OF LIFE INDICATORS

POPULATION: 15,723,000 (1988 estimate)

Population Density:318 inhabs. per sq. mile (1988 estimate)
Population Distribution:65.30% urban (1985)
Population Growth Rate:0.32% per year (1985-90 projection)

VITAL STATISTICS

Average Life Expectancy: 72.00 years (1985-90 projection)
Male: 68.40 years (1985-90 projection)
Female: 75.80 years (1985-90 projection)
Age Distribution: (1985)

0-14 .... 24.40%
15-64 .... 64.60%
65+ 11.00%

Median Age: 32.60 years (1985)
Maternal Mortality: 10 per 100,000 live births (1983)
Infant Mortality: 14 per 1,000 live births (1985-90 projection)

HEALTH CARE

Hospital Beds: 126 per 10,000 population (1985)
Doctors: 35 per 10,000 population (1985)

ETHNIC COMPOSITION: Czech - 64.30%, Slovak - 30.50%, Hungarian - 3.80%; German - 0.40%; Polish - 0.40%; Ukrainian - 0.30%; Russian - 0.10%; other - 0.20%.

RELIGION: Roman Catholic - 77%; Protestant - 20%; Orthodox - 2%; other - 1%.

LANGUAGE: Czech and Slovak are the official and predominant languages.

EDUCATION: Illiteracy: 1%. In 1984/85, there were 6,398 primary schools with 2,037,121 students; 2,269 secondary schools with 552,158 students; and 36 schools of higher learning with 174,304 students.

ECONOMIC DATA

Expenditures by Function [as % of total]: (not available)
GDP per capita: (not available)

TRAVEL NOTES

Climate: Czechoslovakia has a continental climate, with warm summers and cold winters. The average annual temperature is 49°F and the annual rainfall averages 30 inches.
Health Precautions: Health conditions are generally good; however, visitors coming from areas where smallpox, yellow fever or cholera are endemic must have the proper inoculations.
Miscellaneous: Czechoslovakia has beautiful scenery, numerous historic cities and many famous castles and cathedrals. Winter sports are a big attraction, as are the country's 57 spas with natural mineral springs.

GOVERNMENT

Czechoslovakia (Ceskoslovenska Socialisticka Republika—Czechoslovak Socialist Republic) is a highly-centralized federal state composed of the Czech and Slovak nations, each of which has equal rights and its own government. Effective political power rests with the Communist Party of Czechoslovakia. Attempts by the Communist Party leadership, under Alexander Dubcek, to liberalize the social, economic and political structure resulted in the invasion of the country by the Soviet Union and Warsaw Treaty forces on Aug 20, 1968. Soviet military forces continue to be stationed in the country. In 1987, then-Communist Party of Czechoslovakia General Secretary Gustav Husak formally embraced the economic reform policies encouraged by Soviet leader Mikhail Gorbachev, however, the Communist Party of Czechoslovakia has been reluctant to implement reforms.

Constitution: Proclaimed in July 1960, the Czechoslovak Constitution was amended on Oct 27, 1968, to establish a federal republic with a socialist economic society. The Constitution emphasizes the role of the citizen in government and the duty of each person to work in the interest of society. The Communist Party of Czechoslovakia is the guiding force in society and in the state political apparatus. The principle administrative division is between the federal government and the two national governments. The bicameral Federal Assembly is the nominally supreme organ of the federal government, while the two national governments, the Czech Socialist Republic and the Slovak Socialist Republic, each have their own executive (Prime Minister) and legislature (National Council) operating concurrently with the central state organs. The federal government has exclusive jurisdiction over foreign affairs, defense, trade, transport and communications. In theory, it shares authority with the national governments in other areas, but in practice, the Czech and Slovak Socialist Republics take their cue from the federal government.

DENMARK
Kingdom of Denmark

LOCATION: Denmark is located in northwest Europe, bounded on the south by West Germany, on the east by the Baltic Sea and on the west by the North Sea. The country consists of the mainland of Jutland, 5 major islands—Bornholm, lster, Funen, Lolland and Zealand—and 480 smaller islands. There are also two self-governing provinces within the Kingdom of Denmark: the Faroe Islands, which are located in the north Atlantic Ocean, and Greenland.

AREA: 16,638 sq. miles (Faroe Islands: 540)

Land Use: 62.00% cropland; 5.57% permanent pasture; 11.64% forests and woodland; 20.79% other.
Arable Land: 62% (Faroe Islands: 2%)
Arable Land per capita: 1.29 acres (Faroe Islands: 0.17 acres)

POPULATION: 5,082,000 (Faroe Islands: 46,000) (1988 estimate)

Population Density: 205 inhabs. per sq. mile (Faroe Islands: 85) (1988 estimate)
Population Distribution: 85.94% urban (1985)
Population Growth Rate: -0.20% (Faroe Islands: 0.70%) (1988 estimate)

VITAL STATISTICS

Average Life Expectancy: 75.10 years (1985-90 projection)
Male: 72.10 years (1985-90 projection)
Female: 78.30 years (1985-90 projection)
Age Distribution: (1985)
0-14 . . . . 18.68%
15-64 . . . . 66.40%
65+ 14.92%
Median Age: 35.90 years (1985)
Maternal Mortality: 7.70 per 100,000 live births (1984)
Infant Mortality: 8 per 1,000 live births (Faroe Islands: 11) (1985)

HEALTH CARE

Hospital Beds: 71 per 10,000 population (1985) (Faroe Islands: 88—1984)
Doctors: 25 per 10,000 population (1985) (Faroe Islands: 19—1984)

ETHNIC COMPOSITION: The vast majority of the population is ethnic Danish, although there is a small German minority. The Faroe Islands are inhabited by Faroese peoples.

RELIGION: Evangelical Lutheran - 97%; Roman Catholic and other Protestant - 2%; other - 1%.

LANGUAGE: Danish is the official language. Faroese is spoken in the Faroe Islands.

EDUCATION: Illiteracy: 1% (including Faroe Islands and Greenland—1987). In 1986/87, there were 2,421 primary and secondary schools with a combined enrollment of 782,100 students and 5 universities with 55,633 students in Denmark.

ECONOMIC DATA

Expenditures by Function [as % of total]: (1984)
General public services 7.51%
Defense 5.38%
Education 9.57%
Health 1.07%
Social security and welfare 37.98%
Housing and community amenities 2.04%
Other community and social services 1.67%
Economic services 7.04%
Agriculture, forestry, fishing and hunting . .0.95%
Roads 0.77%
Other transportation and communication . . .2.11%
Other purposes 27.74%
GDP per capita: $17,693 (1986) (Faroe Islands: $8,800—1980)

TRAVEL NOTES

Climate: The Danish climate is moderate, with cold summers and wet winters. Temperatures range from an average of 61°F in July to 32°F in February. The wettest season lasts from August to October, and annual rainfall averages 24 inches.
Health Precautions: None
Miscellaneous: Visitors are attracted to Denmark's beautiful coastline with its fjords and majestic cliffs, Copenhagen with its 18th century palaces and beautiful canals, and the friendliness and hospitality of the Danish people.

GOVERNMENT

Denmark (Kongeriget Danmark—Kingdom of Denmark) is a limited or constitutional monarchy. In April 1988, a Parliamentary crisis over a ban on North Atlantic Treaty Organization (NATO) ships carrying nuclear weapons in Danish waters prompted Prime Minister Poul Schluter to call for new elections. The election results forced Schluter to resign as head of a 4-party coalition Government, yet he was subsequently called upon to form a new Government after other attempts at assembling a coalition failed.

Constitution: The revised Constitution (Grundlov), dated Jun 5, 1953, changed the succession law, allowing the female line to succeed to the throne of Denmark in the absence of male heirs. It abolished the upper house and introduced a unicameral Parliament. The 1953 Constitution also made Greenland an integral part of Denmark.

DJIBOUTI
Republic of Djibouti

LOCATION: Situated in the Horn of Africa at the southern end, Djibouti has borders with Ethiopia on the north, west and southwest and with Somalia on the southeast.

AREA: 8,958 sq. miles

Land Use: 0% cropland; 9.10% permanent pasture; 0.27% forests and woodland; 90.63% other (mostly desert).
Arable Land: 1%
Arable Land per capita: 0.12 acres

POPULATION: 460,000 (1986)

Population Density: 51 inhabs. per sq. mile (1986)
Population Distribution: 50% urban (1978)
Population Growth Rate: 2.50% per year (1986)

VITAL STATISTICS

Average Life Expectancy: 50 years (1985)
Male: (not available)
Female: (not available)
Age Distribution: (not available)
Median Age: (not available)

Maternal Mortality: (not available)
Infant Mortality: (not available)

HEALTH CARE

Hospital Beds: 30 per 10,000 population (1985)
Doctors: 1.60 per 10,000 population (1985)

ETHNIC COMPOSITION: Somali (Issa) - 60%; Afar - 35%; French, Arab, Ethiopian and Italian - 5%.

RELIGION: Moslem - 94%; Christian - 6%.

LANGUAGE: French is the official language; Somali and Afar are widely spoken.

EDUCATION: Illiteracy: 83%. In 1985/86, there were 25,212 primary school students; and 6,934 secondary and technical school students.

ECONOMIC DATA

Expenditures by Function [as % of total]: (1979)
General public services 19.33%
Defense 27.99%
Education 6.73%
Health 5.85%
Social security and welfare 9.21%
Housing and community amenities 4.02%
Other community and social services 1.26%
Economic services 14.59%
Agriculture, forestry, fishing and hunting . .1.10%
Roads 3.59%
Other transportation and communication . . .2.26%
Other purposes 5.21%
GDP per capita: $827 (1984)

TRAVEL NOTES

Climate: The Djiboutian climate is very hot and arid.
Health Precautions: Water is generally brackish. Care should be taken to compensate for the intense heat. Visitors from temperate climates should get extra rest, fluids and salt.
Miscellaneous: The Government is making efforts to encourage tourism, with the main attractions being scenery in the desert and a potential for underwater sports along the coast.

GOVERNMENT

Djibouti (Republique de Djibouti—Jumhuriyah Djibouti—Republic of Djibouti), formerly the French Territory of the Afars and the Issas

(French Somalia), became an independent state on Jun 27, 1977. The political scene is strongly influenced by rivalry between the two main tribal groups, Afars and Issas, who roughly split the bulk of the population between them, with the Issas in a slight majority. Under agreements concluded at independence, France maintains an armed force in Djibouti of about 4,000 men, at the disposal of the Government, and is responsible for its defense. France also has agreed to provide substantial long-term economic aid to the country.

Constitution: There is no formal Constitution, but in 1981 the National Assembly approved constitutional laws controlling the election of the President and deputies. A law approving the establishment of a single-party system was passed in October 1981.

DOMINICAN REPUBLIC

LOCATION: The Dominican Republic is situated on the eastern part of Hispaniola island, in the Caribbean Sea between Puerto Rico and Cuba. Haiti lies to the west.

AREA: 18,696 sq. miles

Land Use: 30% cropland; 43% permanent pasture; 13% forests and woodland; 14% other.
Arable Land: 30%
Arable Land per capita: 0.43 acres

POPULATION: 6,531,000 (1987 projection)

Population Density: 349 inhabs. per sq. mile (1987)
Population Distribution: 55.70% urban (1985)
Population Growth Rate: 2.21% per year (1985-90 projection)

VITAL STATISTICS

Average Life Expectancy: 64.60 years (1985-90 projection)
Male: 62.70 years (1985-90 projection)
Female: 66.70 years (1985-90 projection)
Age Distribution: (1985)
0-14 .... 40.70%
15-64 .... 56.30%
65+ 3.00%
Median Age: 18.90 years (1985)

Maternal Mortality: (not available)
Infant Mortality: 65 per 1,000 live births (1985-90 projection)

HEALTH CARE

Hospital Beds: 16 per 10,000 population (1980)
Doctors: 4 per 10,000 population (1980)

ETHNIC COMPOSITION: Mixed (mestizos and mulattoes) - 73%; white - 16%; black - 11%.

RELIGION: Roman Catholic - 95%; other (Protestant and Jewish) - 5%.

LANGUAGE: Spanish is the official language.

EDUCATION: Illiteracy: 32%. Education is compulsory, where possible, for children between the ages of 7 and 14. In 1983/84, there were 5,864 primary schools with 1,039,405 students and 1,664 secondary schools with 384,091 students. In 1977/78 there were 5 universities and institutions of higher learning with 59,321 students.

ECONOMIC DATA

Expenditures by Function [as % of total]: (1983)
General public services 15.35%
Defense 8.74%
Education 15.31%
Health 10.55%
Social security and welfare 8.59%
Housing and community amenities 6.12%
Other community and social services 1.63%
Economic services 29.69%
Agriculture, forestry, fishing and hunting .12.93%
Roads 1.87%
Other transportation and communication ...8.82%
Other purposes 6.03%
GDP per capita: $789 (1985)

TRAVEL NOTES

Climate: The climate is subtropical. In the west and southwest, conditions are arid.
Health Precautions: Water should be boiled for 10 minutes.
Miscellaneous: Strenuous efforts were made during the mid-1980s to continue development of the tourist industry. There are many hotels, seaside resorts and casinos, as well as tours of Spanish colonial settlements. Passports are not required for nonofficial US visitors, but visitors should obtain a Dominican tourist card before leaving the US.

GOVERNMENT

Dominican Republic (Republica Dominicana) gained independence from Spain in 1821 and from Haiti in 1844. It was occupied by US troops from 1916 to 1924, and ruled by a dictator, Gen. Rafael Trujillo, from 1930 to 1961. It is presently a representative democracy with a strong President.

Constitution: The present Constitution, promulgated on Nov 28, 1966, provides for a civil, democratic and representative form of government. Government is divided into three independent powers: executive, legislative and judicial. Constitutional reform requires two-thirds majority in a special session of Congress.

EAST GERMANY
German Democratic Republic

LOCATION: Lying in Eastern Europe, East Germany is bordered on the west, southwest and south by West Germany, on the southeast by Czechoslovakia, on the east by Poland and on the north by the Baltic Sea.

AREA: 41,828 sq. miles

Land Use: 43% arable; 27% forest; 15% meadow and pasture; 15% other.
Arable Land: 43%
Arable Land per capita: 0.69 acres

POPULATION: 16,692,000 (1986)

Population Density: 399 inhabs. per sq. mile (1986)
Population Distribution: 76.60% urban (1984)
Population Growth Rate: 0% per year (1986)

VITAL STATISTICS

Average Life Expectancy: 72.44 years (1983)
Male: 69.46 years (1983)
Female: 75.42 years (1983)
Age Distribution: (1983)
0-14 .... 20.60%
15-59 .... 58.70%
60+ 20.70%
Median Age: 35.80 years (1980)
Maternal Mortality: 16.70 per 100,000 live births (1983)
Infant Mortality: 10 per 1,000 live births (1984)

HEALTH CARE

Hospital Beds: 102 per 10,000 population (1983)
Doctors: 21.66 per 10,000 population (1983)

ETHNIC COMPOSITION: German - 99.70%; Slavic and other - 0.30%.

RELIGION: Protestant - 47%; Roman Catholic - 7%; unaffiliated or other - 46%.

LANGUAGE: German is the official language. There is a Sorbian-speaking minority.

EDUCATION: Illiteracy: 1%. In 1983, there were 12,563 primary schools with 750,718 students; 5,397 polytechnic (general and extended) schools with 3,992,789 students; 240 technical colleges with 167,864 students; 969 vocational schools with 411,166 students; and 54 universities with 130,097 students.

ECONOMIC DATA

Expenditures by Function [as % of total]: (not available)
GDP per capita: $8,000 (1984 estimate)

TRAVEL NOTES

Climate: The climate is temperate, with a mean annual temperature of 47.30°F.
Health Precautions: None
Miscellaneous: The island of Ruegen off the Baltic coast attracts many tourists, while the mountains of Thuringia and the Erzgebirge are much visited in both summer and winter.

GOVERNMENT

East Germany (German Democratic Republic [GDR]—Deutsche Demokratische Republik [DDR]) is dominated by the Socialist Unity (Communist) Party of Germany.

Constitution: Following the proclamation of the Federal Republic of Germany (West Germany) in 1949, the provisional legislative organ (Volkskammer) in the Soviet-occupied zone of Germany enacted a Constitution for the German Democratic Republic. This Constitution was replaced on Apr 9, 1968 and amended in 1974; the amendment proclaimed the German Democratic Republic a "Socialist state of workers and farmers," linked the country "irrevocably and forever with the Soviet Union" and stated that the German Democratic

Republic is an "inseparable part of the Socialist community of states." A passage stating that East Germany had the responsibility to "point the way to peace and socialism for the whole German nation" was deleted from the Constitution in September 1973 after conclusion of a meeting with West Germany and the admission of the two Germanies to the United Nations as separate states.

ECUADOR
Republic of Ecuador

LOCATION: Located on the west coast of South America, Ecuador is bordered by the Pacific Ocean to the west, Peru to the south and east and Colombia to the north.

AREA: 104,500 sq. miles

Land Use: 9.00% cropland; 16.52% permanent pasture; 51.47% forests and woodland; 23.01% other.
Arable Land: 9%
Arable Land per capita: 0.68 acres

POPULATION: 10,204,000 (1988 estimate)

Population Density: 98 inhabs. per sq. mile (1988 estimate)
Population Distribution: 53.46% urban (1987)
Population Growth Rate: 2.80% per year (1988)

VITAL STATISTICS

Average Life Expectancy: 65.40 years (1985-90 projection)
Male: 63.40 years (1985-90 projection)
Female: 67.60 years (1985-90 projection)
Age Distribution: (1985)
0-14 . . . . 41.80%
15-64 . . . . 54.52%
65+ 3.68%
Median Age: 18.70 years (1985)
Maternal Mortality: 185.90 per 100,000 live births (1981)
Infant Mortality: 63 per 1,000 live births (1985-90 projection)

HEALTH CARE

Hospital Beds: 17 per 10,000 population (1984)
Doctors: 12 per 10,000 population (1984)

ETHNIC COMPOSITION: Mestizo - 55%; Indian - 25%; Spanish - 10%; black - 10%.

RELIGION: Roman Catholic - 95%; other - 5% (mainly Christian).

LANGUAGE: Spanish is the official language, but indigenous languages such as Quechan and Jivaroan are widely spoken.

EDUCATION: Illiteracy: 10% (1986). In 1983/84, there were 11,480 primary schools with 1,407,898 students and 1,099 middle schools with 477,829 students. In 1980, there were 12 higher schools with 227,233 students.

ECONOMIC DATA

Expenditures by Function [as % of total]: (1986)
General public services 24.39%
Defense . . . . (not available)
Education 23.71%
Health 6.63%
Social security and welfare 1.11%
Housing and community
amenities . . . . (not available)
Other community and social
services . . . . (not available)
Economic services 0.63%
Agriculture, forestry, fishing and hunting . .2.96%
Roads . . . . (not available)
Other transportation and communication . . .8.13%
Other purposes . . . . (not available)
GDP per capita: $967 (1986)

TRAVEL NOTES

Climate: Temperatures vary with altitude from the Andes Mountains to the tropical rain forests on the coast. The rainy season lasts from October to May, during which time an average of 43 inches of rain falls.
Health Precautions: Inoculations against typhoid, paratyphoid, yellow fever, tetanus and hepatitis are recommended. Tap water is not potable.
Miscellaneous: Ecuador is renowned for its rich archaeological history, for the natural beauty of the countryside and mountains and for the ecological preserves on the Galapagos Islands.

GOVERNMENT

Ecuador (Republica del Ecuador—Republic of Ecuador), was liberated from Spanish rule and became a part of Gran Colombia in 1822, finally becoming a separate independent republic in 1830. Its turbulent political history has been marked by many military coups. A civilian Government was installed on Aug 10, 1979, ending a military regime that began in 1972. The transition to civilian rule marked the 19th time in Ecuador's history that a military Government turned over authority to a civilian regime.

Constitution: The present Constitution, the country's 17th since its liberation from Spain, was approved in a referendum on Jan 15, 1978, and came into force on Aug 10, 1979. The Constitution provides for a democracy with a presidential form of government, guarantees social rights for all citizens and forbids religious discrimination.

EGYPT
Arab Republic of Egypt

LOCATION: Situated in the northeastern corner of Africa, Egypt is bounded to the west by Libya, to the south by Sudan and to the east by Israel and the Red Sea. The Mediterranean Sea provides Egypt's northern boundary.

AREA: 385,229 sq. miles

Land Use: 2.48% cropland; 0% permanent pasture; 0% forests and woodland; 97.52% other (mostly desert).
Arable Land: 2%
Arable Land per capita: 0.09 acres

POPULATION: 53,348,000 (1988 estimate)

Population Density: 138 inhabs. per sq. mile (1988 estimate)
Population Distribution: 48.80% urban (1985)
Population Growth Rate: 2.60% per year (1988 estimate)

VITAL STATISTICS

Average Life Expectancy: 60.60 years (1985-90 projection)
Male: 59.30 years (1985-90 projection)
Female: 62.00 years (1985-90 projection)
Age Distribution: (1985)
0-14 .... 39.60%
15-64 .... 56.40%
65+ 4.00%
Median Age: 20.10 years (1985)

Maternal Mortality: 93.10 per 100,000 live births (1980)
Infant Mortality: 105 per 1,000 live births (1985)

HEALTH CARE

Hospital Beds: 18 per 10,000 population (1984)
Doctors: 15 per 10,000 population (1984)

ETHNIC COMPOSITION: Eastern Hamitic - 90%; other - 10% (including Greek, Italian and Syro-Lebanese).

RELIGION: Moslem - 94% (mostly Sunni); Coptic Christian and other - 6%.

LANGUAGE: Arabic is the official language. English and French are also widely understood.

EDUCATION: Illiteracy: 60%. In 1984, there were 5,856,704 primary school students; 2,000,087 preparatory school students; 563,792 general secondary school students; 85,630 technical school students; 77,535 students in teacher training programs; and 682,348 students enrolled in 14 universities.

ECONOMIC DATA

Expenditures by Function [as %of total]: (1984)
General public services: 6.57%
Defense: 17.66%
Education: 10.82%
Health: 2.39%
Social security and welfare: 10.79%
Housing and community amenities: 4.13%
Other community and social services: 6.75%
Economic services: 9.32%
Agriculture, forestry, fishing and hunting: ..3.99%
Roads: 2.31%
Other transportation and communication: ..0.47%
Other purposes: 31.56%
GDP per capita: $1,211 (1987 estimate)

TRAVEL NOTES

Climate: Egypt's climate is generally warm and dry. Summer daytime temperatures can reach 110°F and the average temperature for a winter day is around 65°F. Coastal areas are an average of 8-10°F cooler than inland areas, and also receive more rain. While the Mediterranean coast has an average annual rainfall of 8 inches, much of the inland region is desert, receiving less than one inch of rainfall.

Health Precautions: Immunizations for typhoid, polio, measles, tetanus and diphtheria are strongly recommended. Tap water is not potable.

Miscellaneous: The pyramids and the great Sphinx at Giza have drawn tourists for centuries, as has the Nile river itself. Other points of interest include the Aswan High Dam—the largest man-made water barrier in the world—and the Suez Canal. Alexandria is widely known as a seaside resort.

GOVERNMENT

Egypt (Jumhuriyat Misr al-'Arabiya—Arab Republic of Egypt) is an independent republic with a strong President. British forces occupied this former province of the Ottoman Empire in 1882 and established a British Protectorate in 1914. Independence was nominally granted in 1914 when King Faud assumed the throne, but Great Britain's influence was evident until the withdrawal of British troops from the Suez Canal zone in 1956. In 1958, Egypt and Syria united to form the United Arab Republic, but Syria withdrew from the partnership in 1961, though Egypt retained the UAR name until 1971. In May 1967, Egypt occupied the southern tip of the Sinai peninsula and closed the Straits of Tiran to Israeli shipping. In retaliation, Israel mounted the devastating offensive known as the Six Day War, gaining control of the Sinai Peninsula and the Gaza Strip. In October 1977, President Anwar el-Sadat was assassinated by members of al-Jihad, an Islamic extremist group. Sadat was succeeded by his Vice President, Lt. Gen. Hosni Mubarak.

Constitution: The permanent Constitution was approved on Sep 11, 1971, and is based on an interim Constitution of 1964. The Constitution invests the executive branch with the power to appoint Vice Presidents and Government ministers, and provides for a 458-member People's Assembly. While Islam is designated as the state religion, freedom of religion is guaranteed to the individual, and equal social and political rights are guaranteed to men and women. Amendments passed in 1980 allowed the formation of multiple political parties, abolished the Arab Socialist Union and specified Islamic jurisprudence as the main foundation for the Egypian legal system. An addition to the Constitution provided for the formation of a Shura, or Consultative Council, comprising 140 elected members and 70 members appointed by the President.

EL SALVADOR
Republic of El Salvador

LOCATION: Located on the Pacific coast of Central America, El Salvador is bordered on the west by Guatemala and on the north and east by Honduras.

AREA: 8,260 sq. miles

Land Use: 32% cropland; 26% pasture; 11% forest; 31% other.
Arable Land: 35%
Arable Land per capita: 0.36 acres

POPULATION: 5,105,000 (1986)

Population Density: 618.04 inhabs. per sq. mile (1986)
Population Distribution: 39.20% urban (1982)
Population Growth Rate: 2.50% per year (1986)

VITAL STATISTICS

Average Life Expectancy: 64.45 years (1986)
Male: 62.60 years (1986)
Female: 66.30 years (1986)
Age Distribution: (1985)
0-14 ....45.30%
15-59 ....50.00%
60+ 4.70%
Median Age: 17.20 years (1980)
Maternal Mortality: 74.20 per 100,000 live births (1983)
Infant Mortality: 41 per 1,000 live births (1984)

HEALTH CARE

Hospital Beds: 18.04 per 10,000 population (1979)
Doctors: 3.31 per 10,000 population (1980)

ETHNIC COMPOSITION: Mestizo - 89%; Indian - 10%; Caucasian - 1%.

RELIGION: Probably about 80% of the population is Roman Catholic. Other Christian religions are practiced.

LANGUAGE: Spanish is the dominant language, though some Indians speak Nahuatl.

EDUCATION: Illiteracy: 35%. In 1984, there were 2,631 primary schools with 883,214 students; 329 secondary schools with 85,906 students; and 34 institutions of higher education with 74,113 students.

ECONOMIC DATA

Expenditures by Function [as % of total]: (1984)
General public services 14.61%
Defense 24.55%
Education 15.51%
Health 8.12%
Social security and welfare 3.67%
Housing and community amenities 1.05%
Other community and social services 1.07%
Economic services 18.45%
Agriculture, forestry, fishing and hunting .. 6.74%
Roads 7.71%
Other transportation and communication .. 0.82%
Other purposes 9.06%
GDP per capita: $1,163 (1985)

TRAVEL NOTES

Climate: Tropical on the coastal plain, but cooler in the mountainous regions inland. The average temperature for San Salvador is 73°F while the average temperature along the coast is 80°F.

Health Precautions: Good medical services are available in the capital. The most serious diseases include typhoid fever and amoebic and bacillary dysentery, which can be averted by careful handling of food. Influenza, malaria and hepatitis are problems as well. Tap water must be boiled.

Miscellaneous: The main tourist attractions include beaches, mountain scenery and ruins of Mayan temples and cities. The unstable political situation can affect tourists' plans.

GOVERNMENT

El Salvador (Republica de El Salvador—Republic of El Salvador) gained its independence from Spain in 1839. Violence, instability and frequent coups mark El Salvador's political history. In this century, the army has dominated political affairs. But since 1960, this domination has met with increased resistance. Legal and underground opposition groups have been growing, particularly since the presidential elections of 1972 and 1977, which critics charge were rigged by right-wing forces. This was accompanied by an escalation of violent conflict and terrorism by extremists on both the right and the left, which continues in the present. The first democratic change of power occurred following the 1989 elections, which, however, were marred by violence and boycotts by the left.

Constitution: A new Constitution, the 36th since independence, became effective on Dec 20, 1983. The Constitution provides for a republican, democratic and representative form of government with separation into executive, legislative and judicial powers. Presidential and congressional elections may not be held simultaneously.

ENGLAND
See Britain

EQUATORIAL GUINEA
Republic of Equatorial Guinea

LOCATION: Equatorial Guinea consists of a mainland territory and 5 islands. The mainland territory, Rio Muni, lies on the west coast of Africa bordered to the north by Cameroon and to the east and south by Gabon. The islands include Bioko (where the capital is located), Corisco, Pagalu, Small Elobey and Great Elobey.

AREA: 10,830 sq. miles

Land Use: 8.20% permanent crops; 3.71% permanent pasture; 46.17% forest; 41.92% other.
Arable Land: 8%
Arable Land per capita: 1.50 acres

POPULATION: 379,000 (1988 estimate)

Population Density: 35 inhabs. per sq. mile (1988 estimate)
Population Distribution: 59.69% urban (1985)
Population Growth Rate: 2.60% per year (1988 estimate)

VITAL STATISTICS

Average Life Expectancy: 46.00 years (1985-90 projection)
Male: 44.40 years (1985-90 projection)
Female: 47.60 years (1985-90 projection)
Age Distribution: (1985)
0-14 .... 41.43%

15-64 .... 54.48%
65+ 4.09%
Median Age: 19.40 years (1985)
Maternal Mortality: (not available)
Infant Mortality: 132 per 1,000 live births (1985)

HEALTH CARE

Hospital Beds: 86 per 10,000 population (1982)
Doctors: 0.16 per 10,000 population (1980)

ETHNIC COMPOSITION: The population is mainly of the Bantu subgroupings Bubi and Fang. Other tribal groups include the Fernandino, Kombe and Bujeba.

RELIGION: Roman Catholic - 80%; other - 20%.

LANGUAGE: Spanish is the official language; African dialects and pidgin English are also spoken.

EDUCATION: Illiteracy: 45%. In 1980/81, there were 511 primary schools with 40,110 students and 14 secondary and other schools with 3,013 students.

ECONOMIC DATA

Expenditures by Function [as % of total]: (not available)
GDP per capita: $278 (1986)

TRAVEL NOTES

Climate: The country experiences a wet, warm climate. Temperatures average above 80°F.
Health Precautions: Visitors should take precautions against malaria, whooping cough and hepatitis. Tap water is not potable.
Miscellaneous: Tourism in Equatorial Guinea has not been completely developed.

GOVERNMENT

Equatorial Guinea (Republica de Guinea Ecuatorial—Republic of Equatorial Guinea), formerly a Portuguese territory and later Spanish Guinea, became independent on Oct 12, 1968. From independence until August 1979, the politics and government of Equatorial Guinea were dominated by President Francisco Macias (Macie) Nguema, who established a regime often described as brutal and repressive. The Macias regime came to an end on Aug 3, 1979 as the result of a bloodless military coup led by Macias' nephew, Deputy Defense Minister Col. Teodoro Obiang Nguema Mbasogo. The armed forces subsequently announced the establishment of a Supreme Military Council to govern the country by decree. Since the coup, new moves have been made toward democracy, with the establishment of a new Constitution, the advent of an elected legislature and the end of a complete ban on political parties.

Constitution: An Aug 15, 1982 referendum approved a new Constitution, which establishes a parliamentary Government with a President as head of state and a Prime Minister as head of government. The new Constitution creates a consultative National Council for Economic and Social Development. The state is also given sole control of minerals and coal mines, posts and telecommunications, radio, television and utility supply.

ETHIOPIA
People's Democratic Republic of Ethiopia

LOCATION: Extending inland from the coast of eastern Africa, Ethiopia shares a long frontier with Somalia. Djibouti lies to the east, Sudan to the west and Kenya to the south.

AREA: 472,435 sq. miles

Land Use: 13% cropland; 41% permanent pasture; 25% forests and woodland; 21% other.
Arable Land: 14%
Arable Land per capita: 0.92 acres

POPULATION: 45,997,000 (1987)

Population Density: 97.36 inhabs. per sq. mile (1987)
Population Distribution: 11.60% urban (1985)
Population Growth Rate: 2.79% per year (1985-90)

VITAL STATISTICS

Average Life Expectancy: 41.90 years (1985-90)
Male: 40.30 years (1985-90)
Female: 43.50 years (1985-90)
Age Distribution: (1985)
0-14 ....44.80%
15-64 ....52.50%
65+ 2.60%
Median Age: 17.50 years (1985)

Maternal Mortality: (not available) (1983)
Infant Mortality: 149 per 1,000 live births (1985-90)

HEALTH CARE

Hospital Beds: 3.30 per 10,000 population (1980)
Doctors: 0.14 per 10,000 population (1980)

ETHNIC COMPOSITION: Oromo - 40%; Amhara and Tigrean - 32%; Sidamo - 9%; Shankella - 6%; Somali - 6%; Afar - 4%; Gurage - 2%; other - 1%.

RELIGION: Moslem - 45%; Ethiopian Orthodox - 35%; animist - 15%; other - 5%.

LANGUAGE: The official language is Amharic, but many other local languages are also spoken. English is also widely spoken.

EDUCATION: Illiteracy: 65%. In 1982, there were 2,511,050 primary school students; 535,152 secondary schools students; 10,512 university students; and 5,605 other higher education students.

ECONOMIC DATA

Expenditures by Function [as %of total]: (1980)
General public services . . . . (not available)
Defense . . . . (not available)
Education 9.28%
Health 3.45%
Social security and welfare 3.78%
Housing and community amenities 1.18%
Other community and social services 1.27%
Economic services 21.99%
Agriculture, forestry, fishing and hunting . . 6.36%
Roads 8.35%
Other transportation and communication . . 2.57%
Other purposes 41.77%
GDP per capita: $125 (1986)

TRAVEL NOTES

Climate: Because most of Ethiopia lies on a high plateau, the climate is temperate in most areas, with an average annual temperature of about 55°F. In most years rainfall is abundant, though the humidity is low.

Health Precautions: Immunizations for cholera and yellow fever are necessary for entry into Ethiopia, and care should be taken in handling food in order to avoid amoebic and bacillary dysentery. Other common diseases are malaria, trachoma, tuberculosis, hepatitis and schistosomiasis.

Miscellaneous: Tourist attractions include the early Christian churches and monuments and the ancient cities of Gondar and Axum. Ethiopia is also a popular place for hunting.

GOVERNMENT

Ethiopia (People's Democratic Republic of Ethiopia) is a democratic republic based on a traditional Marxist model. A new Constitution, drawn up by the nation's Marxist leaders, was approved by the people in February 1987. It closely resembles the Soviet constitution, but bestows more power on the head of state. Prior to this, the country was run by a provisional military regime that deposed Emperor Haile Selassie on Sep 12, 1974. The current regime has been troubled by internal feuds among the military rulers and beset by Arab-supported insurgency in Eritrea and Tigre and Somali-supported insurgency in the Ogaden region.

Constitution: The new Constitution, approved by the electorate in February 1987 and implemented on Sep 12 of the same year, describes Ethiopia as a socialist state that is "still in a transitional stage and is going through a process of national democratic revolution." The document enshrines the principles of a one-party orthodox Communist state, naming the Workers' Party of Ethiopia (WPE) as "the leading force of the state and society." The Constitution decrees that all candidates for the Assembly "must be nominated by organs of the Workers' Party of Ethiopia, mass organizations, military units and other bodies so entitled."

FEDERAL REPUBLIC OF GERMANY
See West Germany

FIJI

LOCATION: Comprising more than 300 islands, Fiji is situated in the Pacific Ocean, about 1,200 miles south of the equator. The 4 main islands are Viti Levu (on which almost 70% of the population lives), Vanua Levu, Tavenui and Kadavu.

AREA: 7,095 sq. miles

Land Use: 12.97% cropland; 3.28% permanent pasture; 64.86% forests and woodland; 18.88% other.
Arable Land: 30%
Arable Land per capita: 1.91 acres

POPULATION: 714,548 (1986 provisional)

Population Density: 101 inhabs. per sq. mile (1986)
Population Distribution: 21.90% urban (1985)
Population Growth Rate: 2.35% per year (1985-90 projection)

VITAL STATISTICS

Average Life Expectancy: 70.50 years (1985-90 projection)
Male: 68.20 years (1985-90 projection)
Female: 72.70 years (1985-90 projection)
Age Distribution: (1985)
0-14 .... 41.30%
15-64 .... 56.10%
65+ 2.60%
Median Age: 19 years (1985)
Maternal Mortality: 26 per 100,000 live births (1983)
Infant Mortality: 26 per 1,000 live births (1985-90)

HEALTH CARE

Hospital Beds: 273 per 10,000 population (1981)
Doctors: 45 per 10,000 population (1980)

ETHNIC COMPOSITION: Indian - 50%; Fijian - 45%; European and part European - 2.12%; Rotumans - 1.22%; Chinese - 0.68%; others - 0.08%.

RELIGION: Most Fijians are Christian; Indians are Hindu with a Moslem minority.

LANGUAGE: The official language is English; Fijian and Hindustani are also spoken.

EDUCATION: Illiteracy: 20%. In 1984, there were 672 primary schools, 139 secondary schools, 36 vocational and technical schools with 3,639 students, 3 teacher training schools with 181 students, and 1 medical school with 213 students; in 1985, there were 127,286 primary school students and 41,505 secondary school students.

ECONOMIC DATA

Expenditures by Function [as % of total]: (not available)
GDP per capita: $1,850 (1984)

TRAVEL NOTES

Climate: With temperatures ranging from 60-90°F and heavy rainfall on the windward side, conditions are tropical.
Health Precautions: Filariasis and dengue occur in the islands, and infectious hepatitis is common. Tap water is potable.
Miscellaneous: Tourism is an increasingly important industry. Scenery, climate and fishing attract visitors to the islands. A succession of cyclones in 1985 had a detrimental effect on tourism, but the industry is expected to recover rapidly.

GOVERNMENT

Fiji became an independent state within the Commonwealth of Nations on Oct 10, 1970. Until a coup in September 1987, it was a constitutional monarchy, with the British monarch as the nominal head of state and a parliamentary form of government. Constitutional rule was interrupted briefly in 1987, from May 14 to 22, when the military, led by Lt. Col. Sitiveni Rabuka, seized power, ostensibly to end violent ethnic clashes following the ouster of the Fijian-dominated Government in the Apr 4-12 elections. An interim Government held power until Sep 25, 1987, when Col. Rabuka staged a second coup, firing the Governor General and declaring the "indigenous Fiji race" as the rightful leaders of the new republic. After declaring Fiji an independent republic on Oct 7, 1987, the former army leader promoted himself to the rank of Brigadier-General in November. In December 1987, Rabuka named a new President and Prime Minister, who then appointed a mostly civilian Cabinet charged with framing a new constitution.

Constitution: The Constitution, promulgated on Oct 10, 1970 and suspended briefly during a military takeover on May 14, 1987, has once again been scrapped under Brig. Gen. Rabuka's new republic. The new Government is to propose constitutional changes, which will need the approval of an appointed Parliament. A new, elected Parliament will then be installed. Among the constitutional changes anticipated are guarantees of a Fijian majority in Parliament and a Fijian Prime Minister. The 1970 Constitution, based on the British Order of Council of Sep 23, 1966, was intended to provide political balance between the racial and ethnic communities in the country, particularly between Fijians and Indians, as Indians comprise 49% of the population. These provisions are uncertain following the September coup.

FINLAND
Republic of Finland

LOCATION: Finland lies in northern Europe, bounded by Norway to the north, Sweden to the northwest, the Soviet Union along the eastern frontier, and the Baltic Sea to the west and the south.

AREA: 130,559 sq. miles

  Land Use: 7.69% cropland; 0.46% permanent pasture; 76.35% forest and woodland; 15.50% other.

  Arable Land: 8%

  Arable Land per capita: 1.36 acres

POPULATION: 4,926,000 (1987)

  Population Density: 37.73 inhabs. per sq. mile (1987)

  Population Distribution: 64% urban (1985)

  Population Growth Rate: 0.30% per year (1985-90)

VITAL STATISTICS

  Average Life Expectancy: 74.60 years (1985-90)

  Male: 70.60 years (1985-90)

  Female: 78.70 years (1985-90)

  Age Distribution: (1985)

0-14	19.30%
15-64	68.50%
65+	12.30%

  Median Age: 34.60 years (1985)

  Maternal Mortality: 3 per 100,000 live births (1982)

  Infant Mortality: 6 per 1,000 live births (1985-90)

HEALTH CARE

  Hospital Beds: 155.42 per 10,000 population (1980)

  Doctors: 19.87 per 10,000 population (1981)

ETHNIC COMPOSITION: Finns - 94%; Swedes, Lapps, Gypsies, Tatars and others - 6%.

RELIGION: Evangelical Lutheran - 97.00%; Greek Orthodox - 1.20%; other - 1.80%.

LANGUAGE: There are two official languages, Finnish (spoken by 93.50% of the population) and Swedish (6.30%).

EDUCATION: Illiteracy: negligible. In 1983/84, there were 4,230 primary schools with 369,047 students; 1,082 secondary schools with 316,740 students; and 571 higher institutions with 119,982 students.

ECONOMIC DATA

  Expenditures by Function [as % of total]: (1983)

General public services	7.25%
Defense	5.53%
Education	13.81%
Health	10.55%
Social security and welfare	30.19%
Housing and community amenities	1.77%
Other community and social services	1.40%
Economic services	25.10%
Agriculture, forestry, fishing and hunting	11.63%
Roads	4.19%
Other transportation and communication	3.85%
Other purposes	4.39%

  GDP per capita: $12,640 (1985)

TRAVEL NOTES

  Climate: There are sharp variations in climate, with long, cold winters and short, warm summers.

  Health Precautions: Public health standards are high. Tap water is safe to drink.

  Miscellaneous: Most tourists are attracted to Finland for its vast forests, magnificent unspoiled scenery, the largest inland water system in Europe and the likelihood of holiday seclusion. The long winter sports season is also appealing.

GOVERNMENT

Finland (Suomen Tasavalta—Republiken Finland—Republic of Finland) is a constitutional democracy. Political power tends to be fractionalized among a wide variety of socioeconomic groups and political parties. Both domestic and foreign policy are necessarily strongly influenced by Finland's superpower neighbor, the Soviet Union.

Constitution: Under the Constitution of Jul 17, 1919, governmental power is divided between a unicameral Parliament and a President with strong independent powers. The Constitution may be amended by a special act of the legislature, which must have the approval of a specified majority of the members. A Constitutional Committee has been discussing possible reform since 1974. No major changes are expected in this decade.

FRANCE
French Republic

LOCATION: Located in western Europe, France is bounded by the English Channel to the north, Belgium and Luxembourg to the northeast, West Germany and Switzerland to the east, Italy to the southeast, the Mediterranean Sea and Spain to the south and the Atlantic Ocean to the west. The island of Corsica, which is considered part of metropolitan France, lies 160 miles southeast of Monaco, a principality located on the Mediterranean coast in southeastern France.

AREA: 210,026 sq. miles

Land Use: 34.37% cropland; 22.93% permanent pasture; 26.76% forests and woodland; 15.94% other.
Arable Land: 35%
Arable Land per capita: 0.83 acres

POPULATION: 55,625,000 (1988 estimate)

Population Density: 265 inhabs. per sq. mile (1988 estimate)
Population Distribution: 73.40% urban (1985)
Population Growth Rate: 0.30% per year (1988 estimate)

VITAL STATISTICS

Average Life Expectancy: 75.20 years (1985-90 projection)
Male: 71.30 years (1985-90 projection)
Female: 79.40 years (1985-90 projection)
Age Distribution: (1985)
0-14 . . . . 21.30%
15-64 . . . . 66.30%
65+ 12.40%
Median Age: 33.60 years (1985)

Maternal Mortality: 15.10 per 100,000 live births (1983)
Infant Mortality: 8 per 1,000 live births (1985)

HEALTH CARE

Hospital Beds: 91 per 10,000 population (1983)
Doctors: 22 per 10,000 population (1984)

ETHNIC COMPOSITION: The majority of the population has Celtic and Latin roots, with minor Teutonic, Slavic, North African, Indochinese and Basque influences.

RELIGION: Roman Catholic - 90%; Protestant - 2%; Jewish - 1%; Moslem - 1%; other - 6%.

LANGUAGE: French is the official language. A number of regional dialects are spoken, including Provencal, Breton, Germanic, Corsican, Catalan, Basque and Flemish.

EDUCATION: Illiteracy: 1%. In 1983/84, there were 49,356 primary schools with 4,233,400 students; 11,181 secondary schools with 5,453,400 students; and 1,124,900 university students.

ECONOMIC DATA

Expenditures by Function [as % of total]: (1983)
General public services 6.46%
Defense 7.35%
Education 8.13%
Health 14.50%
Social security and welfare 43.96%
Housing and community amenities 3.36%
Other community and social services 0.65%
Economic services 7.19%
Agriculture, forestry, fishing and hunting . . 1.11%
Roads 0.82%
Other transportation and communication . . . 1.28%
Other purposes 8.40%
GDP per capita: $9,274 (1985)

TRAVEL NOTES

Climate: The climate throughout France is temperate, with the southern part of the country having Mediterranean-type warm summers and mild winters.
Health Precautions: None
Miscellaneous: The most popular tourist attractions are the Atlantic and Mediterranean coasts and the French Alps. Other tourist spots include ancient towns, fishing villages, spas and places of pilgrimage, such as Lourdes and Vichy. Paris

is famous for its historic architecture, art works, boulevards, theaters, fashion houses, restaurants, night clubs and music halls.

GOVERNMENT

France (Republique Francaise—French Republic) has a republican form of government that has given rise to 5 different regimes since the Revolution of 1789. The current Fifth Republic was established by Gen. Charles de Gaulle in 1958 during a time of national crisis caused by the revolt of the French colony of Algeria. On May 14, 1988, newly-reelected President Francois Mitterrand dissolved the National Assembly after Socialist Prime Minister Michel Rocard failed to form a working alliance with the conservative-dominated Assembly. However, although Mitterrand's Socialist Party won more seats than any other party in the ensuing elections, the party failed to gain an absolute majority. The event marked the first time during the Fifth Republic that no party won an absolute majority in the Assembly.

Constitution: The Constitution of the Fifth Republic was approved by a national referendum and promulgated in 1958. It was intended to significantly increase the authority of the President within the mixed presidential-parliamentary form of government. The Constitution's preamble deals with the Rights of Man and its 92 articles specify the powers and limitations of the executive, the bicameral legislature and the judicial system.

GABON
Gabonese Republic

LOCATION: Lying on the western coast of central Africa, Gabon is bounded by Equatorial Guinea and Cameroon to the north, the Congo Republic to the east and south and the Atlantic Ocean to the west.

AREA: 103,347 sq. miles

Land Use: 1.75% cropland; 18.24% permanent pasture; 77.62% forests and woodland; 2.39% other.
Arable Land: 2%
Arable Land per capita: 1.04 miles

POPULATION: 1,110,000 (1989 estimate)

Population Density: 10.74 inhabs. per sq. mile (1989 estimate)
Population Distribution: 40.83% urban (1985)
Population Growth Rate: 2.01% per year (1985-90 projection)

VITAL STATISTICS

Average Life Expectancy: 51.00 years (1985-90 projection)
Male: 49.30 years (1985-90 projection)
Female: 52.70 years (1985-90 projection)
Age Distribution: (1985)
0-14 . . . . .34.58%
15-64 . . . . .59.25%
65+ 6.17%
Median Age: 24.00 years (1985)
Maternal Mortality: (not available)
Infant Mortality: 159 per 1,000 live births (1985)

HEALTH CARE

Hospital Beds: 52 per 10,000 population (1985)
Doctors: 3 per 10,000 population (1985)

ETHNIC COMPOSITION: Among the largest of Gabon's more than 40 tribes are the Fang (which represent about 25% of the population), Bapounou (about 10%), Eshira and Bateke.

RELIGION: About 60% of the population is Christian, with the majority of the remainder practicing animist beliefs.

LANGUAGE: French is the official language. The Fang language is spoken in northern Gabon, and Bantu dialects are prominent in the rest of the country.

EDUCATION: Illiteracy: 35%. In 1983, there were 929 primary schools with 172,201 students; 24,651 general secondary school students; 4,703 vocational secondary school students; 6,806 teacher training students; 1 university with 2,059 students; and 1,169 students in other institutions of higher learning.

ECONOMIC DATA

Expenditures by Function [as % of total]: (not available)
GDP per capita: $3,497 (1986)

TRAVEL NOTES

Climate: The climate is tropical. The average annual temperature nationwide is 79°F, the annual average rainfall 98 inches. The periods of heaviest rainfall occur during October and November, and from March through May.

Health Precautions: Inoculations against cholera and yellow fever are required; precautions are strongly recommended against typhoid, malaria, polio and tetanus. Tap water is not potable.

Miscellaneous: Dr. Albert Schweitzer founded his famous jungle hospital in Lambarene. Gabon also boasts national parks and beach resorts.

GOVERNMENT

Gabon (Republique Gabonaise—Gabonese Republic) is an independent republic with a strong President and a single legal political party. It became completely independent on Aug 17, 1960, after having been a part of French Equatorial Africa.

Constitution: The Constitution, adopted in February 1961 and amended 4 times since, provides for independent executive, legislative and judicial branches of government. It guarantees freedom of religion and provides for universal suffrage.

GAMBIA
Republic of the Gambia

LOCATION: Gambia consists of a narrow strip of land that runs from the western coast of Africa inland to the source of the River Gambia. With the exception of a short Atlantic coastline, the country is completely surrounded by Senegal.

AREA: 3,860 sq. miles

Land Use: 16.20% cropland; 0.90% permanent pasture; 19.80% forests and woodland; 55.00% other.
Arable Land: 16%
Arable Land per capita: 0.48 acres

POPULATION: 818,000 (1988 estimate)

Population Density: 212 inhabs. per sq. mile (1988 estimate)
Population Distribution: 20.10% urban (1985)

Population Growth Rate: 2.60% per year (1988 estimate)

VITAL STATISTICS

Average Life Expectancy: 37.00 years (1985-90 projection)
Male: 35.50 years (1985-90 projection)
Female: 38.60 years (1985-90 projection)
Age Distribution: (1985)
0-14 . . . . .42.46%
15-64 . . . . .54.43%
65+ 3.11%
Median Age: 18.80 years (1985)
Maternal Mortality: (not available)
Infant Mortality: 191 per 1,000 live births (1985)

HEALTH CARE

Hospital Beds: 11 per 10,000 population (1980)
Doctors: 1 per 10,000 population (1980)

ETHNIC COMPOSITION: Mandinka - 42%; Fula - 18%; Wolof - 16%; Jola - 10%; Serahuli - 9%; other - 5%.

RELIGION: Moslem - 90%; Christian - 9%; indigenous beliefs - 1%.

LANGUAGE: English is the official language. Mandinka, Fula, Wolof and other indigenous languages are also spoken.

EDUCATION: Illiteracy: 75%. In 1985, there were 189 primary schools with 66,257 students; 8 general secondary schools with 4,348 students; 16 secondary technical schools with 10,102 students; and 8 post-secondary schools with 1,489 students.

ECONOMIC DATA

Expenditures by Function [as % of total]: (1982)
General public services 35.96%
Defense 0%
Education 17.39%
Health 7.98%
Social security and welfare 3.61%
Housing and community amenities 3.32%
Other community and social services 2.31%
Economic services 25.03%
Agriculture, forestry, fishing and hunting .10.98%
Roads 10.75%
Other transportation and communication . . .0.26%
Other purposes 4.41%
GDP per capita: $172 (1986)

TRAVEL NOTES

Climate: Gambia's climate is subtropical, with temperatures ranging from a low in January of 48°F to a high in October of 110°F. Rainfall is heavier in the western part of the country, which averages 48 inches annually, while the inland regions receive an average of 34 inches of annual rainfall. Inland regions are also subject to periods of severe drought.

Health Precautions: Precautions should be taken against dysentery, hepatitis and malaria. The water is not potable.

Miscellaneous: The beautiful Gambian beaches attract many tourists each year. Gambia is also widely known as a bird refuge. Over 400 species of birds are known to inhabit the region.

GOVERNMENT

Gambia (Republic of The Gambia), formerly a British colony, became an independent member of the Commonwealth on Feb 18, 1965, with the British sovereign as the nominal head of state and Dr. Dawda Kairaba Jawara as Prime Minister. Following a referendum in 1970, a new Constitution was adopted that restructured the Parliamentary government to form a republic. Jawara continued to lead the country, serving as President under the new Constitution. In July 1981, left-wing rebel Kukoi Samba Sanyang seized power briefly while President Jawara was out of the country, but Senegalese troops entered Banjul and quickly restored the Jawara Government. On Feb 1, 1982, Gambia and Senegal formed the Confederation of Senegambia (La Confederation de Senegambie) headed by Senegalese President Abdou Diouf. The Confederation ensures cooperation between the two countries in economic and foreign policy matters and provides for their common defense, though full integration of the military forces was incomplete as of 1988.

Constitution: The present Constitution, promulgated on Apr 24, 1970, provides for independent executive, legislative and judicial branches of government.

GERMANY, EAST
See East Germany

GERMANY, WEST
See West Germany

GHANA
Republic of Ghana

LOCATION: Ghana, located just north of the equator on the west coast of Africa, is bordered by the Cote d'Ivoire to the west, Togo to the east and Burkina Faso to the north.

AREA: 92,100 sq. miles

Land Use: 12% cropland; 15% permanent pasture; 37% forests and woodland; 36% other (mostly scrubland).
Arable Land: 12%
Arable Land per capita: 0.48 acres

POPULATION: 14,786,000 (1989 estimate)

Population Density: 161 inhabs. per sq. mile (1989 estimate)
Population Distribution: 31.53% urban (1985)
Population Growth Rate: 3% per year (1989 estimate)

VITAL STATISTICS

Average Life Expectancy: 54.00 years (1985-90 projection)
Male: 52.20 years (1985-90 projection)
Female: 55.80 years (1985-90 projection)
Age Distribution: (1985)
0-14 . . . . .46.67%
15-64 . . . . .50.50%
65+ 2.83%
Median Age: 16.60 years (1985)
Maternal Mortality: (not available)
Infant Mortality: 75 per 1,000 live births (1985)

HEALTH CARE

Hospital Beds: (not available)
Doctors: 1 per 10,000 population (1984)

ETHNIC COMPOSITION: Akan - 44%; Moshi-Dagomba - 16%; Ewe - 13%; Ga - 8%; other - 19% (mainly African ethnic groups).

RELIGION: Indigenous beliefs - 38%; Moslem - 30%; Christian - 24%; other - 8%.

LANGUAGE: English is the official language. Over 50 native languages are also spoken, including Akan, Mole-Dagbani, Ewe and Ga.

EDUCATION: Illiteracy: 70%. In 1984/85, there were 8,965 primary schools with 1,464,424 students; 5,242 middle schools with 579,624 students; 229 secondary schools with 125,659 students; 22 technical colleges with 9,947 students; 39 teacher training colleges with 14,880 students; and 3 universities with 7,878 students.

ECONOMIC DATA

Expenditures by Function [as % of total]: (1986)
General public services 18.91%
Defense 6.52%
Education 23.92%
Health 8.28%
Social security and welfare 5.35%
Housing and community amenities 1.93%
Other community and social services 1.69%
Economic services 15.71%
Agriculture, forestry, fishing and hunting . . 4.53%
Roads 3.78%
Other transportation and communication . . 3.83%
Other purposes 17.69%
GDP per capita: $442 (1985)

TRAVEL NOTES

Climate: The climate is tropical, with temperatures ranging from 70°F to 90°F. Annual rainfall in the coastal zone averages 80 inches. Humidity in Accra is highest at dawn and falls from 94% to 66% at dusk.

Health Precautions: Inoculations against yellow fever and cholera are required. Strongly recommended are inoculations against polio, tetanus, diphtheria and typhoid. Gamma globulin and rabies shots are also advised. Tap water is not potable. Malaria risk is present in all areas throughout the year.

Miscellaneous: Tourist attractions include game reserves, fine beaches and old trading forts and castles.

GOVERNMENT

Ghana (Republic of Ghana) was formed by a merger of part of Togoland, a British administered UN Trust Territory, and the Gold Coast, a former British colony. Ghana became an independent state within the British Commonwealth on Mar 6, 1957, and on Jul 1, 1960, was declared a republic, with its first Premier, Kwame Nkrumah, as President. The armed forces have overthrown constitutional civilian governments on three occasions: on Feb 24, 1966, with the ousting of Nkrumah; on Jan 13, 1978, with the takeover of a restored parliamentary government; and on Dec 31, 1981, with a coup led by Flight Lt. Jerry Rawlings. A military government, led by Rawlings, is currently in power.

Constitution: The 1979 Constitution, which established a Parliament and an executive presidency, was suspended following the December 1981 coup.

GREAT BRITAIN
See Britain

GREECE
Hellenic Republic

LOCATION: Greece occupies the southern end of the Balkan Peninsula in southeastern Europe and includes several hundred offshore islands. It is bounded by Albania, Yugoslavia and Bulgaria to the north; Turkey to the northeast; the Aegean Sea to the east; the Mediterranean Sea to the south; and the Ionian Sea to the west.

AREA: 50,949 sq. miles

Land Use: 30.32% cropland; 40.18% permanent pasture; 20.03% forests and woodland; 9.47% other.
Arable Land: 30%
Arable Land per capita: 0.98 acres

POPULATION: 10,018,000 (1988 estimate)

Population Density: 197 inhabs. per sq. mile (1988 estimate)
Population Distribution: 60.10% urban (1985)

Population Growth Rate: 0.30% per year (1988 estimate)

VITAL STATISTICS

Average Life Expectancy: 74.80 years (1985-90 projection)
Male: 72.60 years (1985-90 projection)
Female: 77.00 years (1985-90 projection)
Age Distribution: (1984)

0-14	21.54%
15-64	65.32%
65+	13.14%

Median Age: 34.80 years (1985)
Maternal Mortality: 14.30 per 100,000 live births (1984)
Infant Mortality: 13.80 per 1,000 live births (1985)

HEALTH CARE

Hospital Beds: 58 per 10,000 population (1984)
Doctors: 28 per 10,000 population (1984)

ETHNIC COMPOSITION: Greek - 97.70%; Turkish - 1.30%; other - 1.00% (including Vlach, Slav, Albanian and Pomach).

RELIGION: Greek Orthodox - 98.00%; Moslem - 1.30%; other - 0.70%.

LANGUAGE: Greek is the official language, but English and French are also widely spoken.

EDUCATION: Illiteracy: 5%. In 1983/84, there were 9,234 primary schools with 896,339 students; 3,004 secondary schools with 790,366 students; and 107 institutions of higher learning with 148,515 students.

ECONOMIC DATA

Expenditures by Function [as %of total]: (1981)

General public services	11.70%
Defense	10.78%
Education	9.61%
Health	10.54%
Social security and welfare	30.63%
Housing and community amenities	2.50%
Other community and social services	1.96%
Economic services	17.11%
Agriculture, forestry, fishing and hunting	6.37%
Roads	3.63%
Other transportation and communication	1.72%
Other purposes	9.77%

GDP per capita: $4,029 (1986)

TRAVEL NOTES

Climate: Greece has a Mediterranean climate, with mild winters and hot summers. There is a substantial difference in temperatures between northern and southern Greece.
Health Precautions: The water is potable in most cities, but bottled water should be used in smaller villages.
Miscellaneous: Visitors are attracted to Greece by its warm climate, beautiful natural scenery and its great history and traditions. There are also numerous islands filled with ruins and other items of archaeological interest.

GOVERNMENT

Greece (Elliniki Demokratia—Hellenic Republic) was ruled by a constitutional monarchy from 1949 until 1967, when a right-wing military coup forced King Constantine into exile. Civilian control of the Government was reinstituted in July 1974, and a new Constitution providing for a parliamentary democracy was adopted on Jun 7, 1975.

Constitution: The 1975 Constitution established a parliamentary form of government with a strong presidency. The President was granted a wide range of powers, including the right to appoint and dismiss the Cabinet, to dissolve Parliament, to veto legislation and to declare a state of emergency. In March 1986, Parliament passed a series of constitutional amendments that effectively rescinded these rights and transferred executive authority to the Prime Minister and the Cabinet. The Constitution also provided for a number of individual and civil rights, including the full protection of life, honor and freedom, regardless of race, creed, nationality or political allegiance. Freedom of association, speech and press were also guaranteed.

GREENLAND

LOCATION: A self-governing province within the Kingdom of Denmark, Greenland is an island located in the north Atlantic Ocean. Northern Canada lies to the west, while Iceland is located to the southeast.

AREA: 840,000 sq. miles

Land Use: 0% cropland; 1% permanent pasture;
0% forests and woodland; 99% other (mainly
permanent snow and ice).
Arable Land: 0%
Arable Land per capita: 0 acres

POPULATION: 55,000 (1988 estimate)

Population Density: 0.07 inhabs. per sq. mile
(1988 estimate)
Population Distribution: (not available)
Population Growth Rate: 0.90% per year (1988
estimate)

VITAL STATISTICS

Average Life Expectancy: (not available)
Male: 59.70 years (1987)
Female: 67.30 years (1987)
Age Distribution: (not available)
Median Age: (not available)
Maternal Mortality: (not available)
Infant Mortality: 36 per 1,000 live births (1985)

HEALTH CARE

Hospital Beds: (not available)
Doctors: 12 per 10,000 population (1984)

ETHNIC COMPOSITION: Greenlander - 86%;
Danish - 14%.

RELIGION: The majority of Greenland's population is Evangelical Lutheran.

LANGUAGE: Greenlandic and Danish are the
primary languages.

EDUCATION: Illiteracy: 1%. In 1986/87, there
were approximately 100 primary and secondary
schools with 9,488 students.

ECONOMIC DATA

Expenditures by Function [as %of total]: (1985)
General public services: ....(not available)
Defense: ....(not available)
Education: 13.85%
Health: 9.70%
Social security and welfare: 14.37%
Housing and community amenities: 14.74%
Other community and
social services: ....(not available)
Economic services: ....(not available)

Agriculture, forestry, fishing and hunting: . 9.75%
Roads: ....(not available)
Other transportation and communication: . 7.66%
Other purposes: ....(not available)
GDP per capita: $8,572 (1983)

TRAVEL NOTES

Climate: Greenland's climate is very cold, with
most of the country permanently covered by ice
and snow.
Health Precautions: (not available)
Miscellaneous: Tourism is limited.

GOVERNMENT

Greenland (Kalaallit Nunaat—Gronland), first
colonized in the 10th century by Norsemen,
came under Danish control in 1380. In the 1953
revision of the Danish Constitution, Greenland
became an integral part of the Kingdom of
Denmark. It gained limited internal autonomy
on May 1, 1979, and has gradually increased its
jurisdiction over its internal affairs. A political
crisis struck in March 1987 concerning the
monitoring of the modernization of a North
Atlantic Treaty Organization radar system at a
US military base at Thule. This crisis forced
Prime Minister Jonathan Motzfeldt to call for
early elections, but Motzfeldt was returned to
power after re-forming a two-party coalition.

Constitution: A January 1979 referendum in
Greenland approved Danish jurisdiction in con-
stitutional matters, foreign affairs and defense,
and provided for Danish representation in
Greenland by a Rigsombudsmanden (High
Commissioner). Greenland is represented in the
Danish Folketing (Parliament) by two elected
representatives.

GRENADA
State of Grenada

LOCATION: The southernmost of the Windward
Islands in the eastern Caribbean Sea, the country
of Grenada consists of the main island and a number of smaller islands, including Carriacou and
Petit Martinique.

AREA: 133 sq. miles

Land Use: 41% cropland; 3% permanent pasture; 9% forests and woodland; 47% other.
Arable Land: 41%
Arable Land per capita: 0.30 acres

POPULATION: 126,000 (1988 estimate)

Population Density: 947 inhabs. per sq. mile (1988 estimate)
Population Distribution: (not available)
Population Growth Rate: 0.80% per year (1989 estimate)

VITAL STATISTICS

Average Life Expectancy: 69 years (1988)
Male: (not available)
Female: (not available)
Age Distribution: (not available)
Median Age: (not available)
Maternal Mortality: (not available)
Infant Mortality: 22 per 1,000 live births (1985)

HEALTH CARE

Hospital Beds: 33 per 10,000 population (1984)
Doctors: 3 per 10,000 population (1984)

ETHNIC COMPOSITION: A large majority of the population is of black African descent.

RELIGION: Roman Catholicism is the predominant religion, with Anglicanism and other Protestant denominations constituting a substantial minority.

LANGUAGE: English is the official and most used language; French patois is also spoken.

EDUCATION: Illiteracy: 15%. In 1984, there were 58 primary schools with 19,736 students and 20 secondary schools with 6,686 students. There were 519 students of higher education in 1982.

ECONOMIC DATA

Expenditures by Function [as % of total]: (1977)
General public services 6.13%
Defense 15.62%
Education 18.29%
Health 15.56%
Social security and welfare 5.03%
Housing and community amenities 1.24%
Other community and social services 0.66%
Economic services 33.99%

Agriculture, forestry, fishing and hunting . . 5.00%
Roads 8.80%
Other transportation and
communication . . . . (not available)
Other purposes 3.48%
GDP per capita: $1,170 (1986)

TRAVEL NOTES

Climate: Grenada has a tropical climate, with an average annual temperature of 80°F. The dry season lasts from January to May, while the rainy season extends from June to December. Annual rainfall averages 60 inches in the coastal regions and between 150-200 inches in the mountainous areas.
Health Precautions: Precautions against hepatitis, dengue fever and gastroenteritis should be taken, along with inoculations against polio, tetanus, typhoid and yellow fever. The water is not potable.
Miscellaneous: The major tourist attractions are St. George's colonial architecture, superb yachting facilities and Grand Anse beach. Grenada is also a frequent stopping place for cruise ships.

GOVERNMENT

Grenada (State of Grenada) became an independent state within the Commonwealth of Nations on Feb 7, 1974, with a parliamentary form of government. On Mar 13, 1979, the Government, headed by Sir Eric M. Gairy, was overthrown in a coup led by Maurice Bishop of the New Jewel Movement, and the People's Revolutionary Government was formed. Bishop's regime was itself overthrown on Oct 13, 1983 and he was later executed. Following an invasion by US and Caribbean forces on Oct 25, 1983, an interim Government was named by the Governor General to prepare for elections, which were subsequently held on Dec 3, 1984.

Constitution: The 1967 Constitution was modified at independence in 1974. It was suspended on Mar 13, 1979 and restored on Nov 9, 1983. The Constitution names the British monarch as head of state, represented locally by a Governor General.

GUATEMALA
Republic of Guatemala

LOCATION: Guatemala is located in Central America, and is bounded by Mexico to the north and west; Belize, the Caribbean Sea and Honduras to the east; El Salvador to the south; and the Pacific Ocean to the southwest.

AREA: 42,040 sq. miles

Land Use: 16.65% cropland; 12.30% permanent pasture; 39.75% forests and woodland; 31.30% other.
Arable Land: 17%
Arable Land per capita: 0.61 acres

POPULATION: 9,133,000 (1988 estimate)

Population Density: 217 inhabs. per sq. mile (1988 estimate)
Population Distribution: 32.67% urban (1987)
Population Growth Rate: 3% per year (1988 estimate)

VITAL STATISTICS

Average Life Expectancy: 62.00 years (1985-90 projection)
Male: 59.70 years (1985-90 projection)
Female: 64.40 years (1985-90 projection)
Age Distribution: (1985)
0-14 .... 45.91%
15-64 .... 51.15%
65+ 2.94%
Median Age: 16.90 years (1985)
Maternal Mortality: 96.30 per 100,000 live births (1980)
Infant Mortality: 61 per 1,000 live births (1986)

HEALTH CARE

Hospital Beds: (not available)
Doctors: 5 per 10,000 pop. (1984)

ETHNIC COMPOSITION: Ladino (westernized Indian and mestizo) - 56%; Indian - 44%.

RELIGION: The majority of the population is Roman Catholic, with another large group being Protestant. Some of the population practices indigenous beliefs.

LANGUAGE: Spanish is the official language, but a large percentage of the population speaks at least one of the more than 20 dialects—such as Caribe, Chol, Mam, Maya, Pocomam and Quiche—that are derived from ancient Mayan languages.

EDUCATION: Illiteracy: 50%. In 1986, there were 7,979 primary schools with 1,073,756 students; 1,390 secondary schools with 223,473 students; and 5 universities.

ECONOMIC DATA

Expenditures by Function [as % of total]: (1985)
General public services: .... (not available)
Defense 16.57%
Education 11.61%
Health 6.64%
Social security and welfare .... (not available)
Housing and community amenities   (not available)
Other community and social
 services .... (not available)
Economic services .... (not available)
Agriculture 2.85%
Roads and transportation 6.13%
Other transportation and communication ...6.52%
Other purposes .... (not available)
GDP per capita: $734 (1986)

TRAVEL NOTES

Climate: The Guatemalan climate is moderate in the mountain regions and tropical in the lowlands. During the rainy season, which lasts from June to October, rainfall averages 52 inches. The average temperatures in January range from a low of 53°F to a high of 73°F.
Health Precautions: Precautions should be taken against hepatitis, tetanus, typhus, paratyphoid and typhoid fever. Tap water is not potable.
Miscellaneous: Tourists are attracted by Mayan ruins—such as those at El Mirador, Nakum, Tikal and Yaxha—as well as the country's many volcanos, lakes and numerous tiny villages.

GOVERNMENT

Guatemala (Republica de Guatemala—Republic of Guatemala) gained independence from Spain in 1821, and was a member of the United Provinces of Central America from 1824 to 1838. It became a separate state in 1839. Since that time the country's history has been marked by a series of dictatorships alternating with short periods of representative government. A 1954 military coup, sponsored by the US Central Intelligence Agency (CIA), overthrew the civilian Government of President Jacobo Arbenz Guzman. Following a bloodless coup on Mar 23, 1982, a junta of three military officers suspended the Constitution and banned all political parties. On Jun 9, 1982, the leader of the junta, Gen. Efrain Rios Montt, declared himself President. He in turn was ousted on Aug 8, 1983 by a group led by Brig. Gen. Oscar Mejia Victores, who instituted reforms leading to the return of democratic rule. On Jan 14, 1986, Marco Vinicio Cerezo Arevalo was installed as the country's first civilian President in 15 years.

Constitution: A new Constitution was adopted on May 31, 1985, and came into force on Jan 14, 1986. It provides for a representative democracy to be headed by a civilian President and a National Congress. The Constitution prohibits racial and sexual discrimination, and designates the military as a non-political body.

GUINEA
People's Revolutionary Republic of Guinea

LOCATION: Guinea is located on the west coast of Africa, bounded by Guinea-Bissau on the northwest, Senegal on the north, Mali on the northeast, Cote d'Ivoire on the southeast, Liberia on the south and Sierra Leone on the southwest.

AREA: 94,939 sq. miles

Land Use: 15% cultivated; 10% forest; 75% unused.
Arable Land: 7%
Arable Land per capita: 0.74 acres

POPULATION: 5,734,000 (1986)

Population Density: 61 inhabs. per sq. mile (1986)
Population Distribution: 19.10% urban (1980)
Population Growth Rate: 2.40% per year (1986)

VITAL STATISTICS

Average Life Expectancy: 40.25 years (1985)
Male: 38.70 years (1985)
Female: 41.80 years (1985)
Age Distribution: (1980)
0-14 .... 43.80%
15-64 .... 53.20%
65+.............................. 3.00%
Median Age: 17.70 years (1980)

Maternal Mortality: (not available)
Infant Mortality: 172 per 1,000 live births (1980)

HEALTH CARE

Hospital Beds: 15.80 per 10,000 population (1977)
Doctors: 1.23 per 10,000 population (1981)

ETHNIC COMPOSITION: The majority of the population is African, with the most important tribes being Fulani, Malinke and the Susa.

RELIGION: Moslems - 75%; animists - 24%; Christian - 1%.

LANGUAGE: French is the official language.

EDUCATION: Illiteracy: 1%. In 1980, there were 2,555 primary schools with 257,547 students; 346 secondary schools with 89,900 students; and 45 higher education institutions with 18,270 students.

ECONOMIC DATA

Expenditures by Function [as % of total]: (not available)
GDP per capita: $300 (1984)

TRAVEL NOTES

Climate: The coastal area is hot and moist with temperatures ranging from about 62°F in the dry season to about 86°F in the wet season. The interior is higher and cooler.
Health Precautions: Smallpox and yellow fever vaccinations are required. Tap water is not potable. Tetanus, typhoid and typhus shots are recommended.
Miscellaneous: Tourists are attracted by the beauty of the mountain scenery.

GOVERNMENT

Guinea (Republique de Guinee—Republic of Guinea) gained independence from France on Oct 2, 1958. Middle-ranking officers of the army staged a coup on Apr 3, 1984, a week after the death of President Ahmed Sekou Toure. An attempted coup led by former Prime Minister and Education Minister Col. Diarra Traore was quelled on Jul 5, 1985.

Constitution: The Constitution of 1982, which provided for a democratically elected National Assembly, was suspended on Apr 3, 1984.

GUINEA-BISSAU
Republic of Guinea-Bissau

LOCATION: Guinea-Bissau lies on the west coast of northern Africa, bordered by Senegal to the north, Guinea to the southeast and the Atlantic Ocean to the west.

AREA: 13,948 sq. miles

Land Use: 10.29% cropland; 45.71% permanent pasture; 38.21% forests and woodland; 5.79% other.
Arable Land: 10%
Arable Land per capita: 1.07 acres

POPULATION: 929,000 (1989 estimate)

Population Density: 67 inhabs. per sq. mile (1989 estimate)
Population Distribution: 27.11% urban (1985)
Population Growth Rate: 2.10% per year (1989 estimate)

VITAL STATISTICS

Average Life Expectancy: 45.00 years (1985-90 projection)
Male: 43.40 years (1985-90 projection)
Female: 46.60 years (1985-90 projection)
Age Distribution: (1985)
0-14 .... 40.72%
15-64 .... 55.01%
65+ 4.27%
Median Age: 19.90 years (1985)
Maternal Mortality: (not available)
Infant Mortality: 137 per 1,000 live births (1985)

HEALTH CARE

Hospital Beds: 18 per 10,000 population (1981)
Doctors: 1 per 10,000 population (1980)

ETHNIC COMPOSITION: Balanta - 30%; Fula - 20%; Manjaca - 14%; Mandinga - 13%; Papel - 7%; other African - 15%; European and mulatto - 1%.

RELIGION: Animist - 65%; Moslem - 30%; Christian - 5%.

LANGUAGE: Portuguese is the official language. Criolo and several African dialects are also spoken.

EDUCATION: Illiteracy: 91%. In 1984/85, there were 640 first cycle schools with 67,818 students; 28 second cycle schools with 13,626 students; 12 secondary schools with 11,710 students; 2 technical colleges with 433 students; and 2 teacher training schools with 594 students.

ECONOMIC DATA

Expenditures by Function [as % of total]: (1985)
General public services 10.60%
Defense 5.08%
Education 10.16%
Health 5.19%
Social security and welfare 1.10%
Housing and community amenities 2.32%
Other community and social services 5.08%
Economic services 54.15%
Agriculture, forestry, fishing
and hunting .... (not available)
Roads .... (not available)
Other transportation and
communication .... (not available)
Other purposes 9.50%

GDP per capita: $180 (1984)

TRAVEL NOTES

Climate: The climate is tropical, with a rainy season lasting from June to November, during which rainfall averages between 49 and 80 inches. The average temperature is 68°F, although the temperature generally ranges from 75°F to 90°F.
Health Precautions: Inoculations against indigenous diseases are recommended, as are gamma globulin injections and malaria suppressants. Tap water is not potable.
Miscellaneous: Beaches and resorts include Varela and the island of Bubaque.

GOVERNMENT

Guinea-Bissau (Republica da Guine-Bissau— Republic of Guinea-Bissau) was granted independence by Portugal on Sep 10, 1974, following a protracted guerrilla battle led by the Partido Africano da Independencia da Guine e Cabo Verde (PAIGC—African Party for the Independence of Guinea and Cape Verde). Guinea-Bissau and the Cape Verde Islands had been administered together as Portuguese Guinea, and were granted separate independence with the as-yet unfulfilled expectation that they would eventually unify. Effective political power rests with the PAIGC and its leader, Brig. Gen. Joao Bernardo Vieira, who seized control of the country in a November 1980 coup.

Constitution: The Constitution of May 16, 1984 deems the PAIGC to be the leading political force. The economy is to be controlled by the state. Amendments to the Constitution may be made by the National People's Assembly.

GUYANA
Cooperative Republic of Guyana

LOCATION: Guyana is located on the northeastern coast of South America and is bordered by Venezuela to the west, Suriname to the east and Brazil to the south.

AREA: 83,322 sq. miles

Land Use: 2.51% cropland; 6.23% permanent pasture; 83.15% forest and woodland; 8.11% other.
Arable Land: 3%
Arable Land per capita: 1.74 acres

POPULATION: 779,000 (1989 estimate)

Population Density: 9.35 inhabs. per sq. mile (1989 estimate)
Population Distribution: 32.21% urban (1985)
Population Growth Rate: 0.40% per year (1989)

VITAL STATISTICS

Average Life Expectancy: 69.80 years (1985-90 projection)
Male: 67.30 years (1985-90 projection)
Female: 72.50 years (1985-90 projection)
Age Distribution: (1985)
0-14 . . . . 36.94%
15-64 . . . . 59.18%
65+ 3.88%
Median Age: 20.90 years (1985)
Maternal Mortality: 104.30 per 100,000 live births (1977)
Infant Mortality: 32 per 1,000 live births (1985)

HEALTH CARE

Hospital Beds: 47 per 10,000 population (1977)
Doctors: 3 per 10,000 population (1982)

ETHNIC COMPOSITION: East Indian - 51%; Black African - 43%; Amerindian - 4%; European and Chinese - 2%.

RELIGION: Christian - 57%; Hindu - 33%; Moslem - 9%; other - 1%.

LANGUAGE: English is the official language. Hindi, Urdu and a variety of Amerindian dialects are also spoken.

EDUCATION: Illiteracy: 15%. In 1981, there were 423 primary schools with 130,003 students and an undetermined number of secondary schools with 73,762 students. In 1983, 15 institutions of higher education (including the University of Guyana) enrolled 2,111 students.

ECONOMIC DATA

Expenditures by Function [as % of total]: (not available)
GDP per capita: $339 (1987)

TRAVEL NOTES

Climate: Guyana has a tropical climate, with a mean temperature at Georgetown of 80°F and an average annual rainfall of 92 inches. Two wet seasons, one from May to August and the other from November to January, occur in the coastal regions.
Health Precautions: Immunizations against typhoid, yellow fever, tetanus and polio, as well as gamma globulin shots, are required for entry. Tap water is not potable.
Miscellaneous: Kaieteur Falls, located deep in the interior of the country, is 4 times as high as Niagara Falls.

GOVERNMENT

Guyana (Cooperative Republic of Guyana), the former British colony of British Guiana, has been independent since May 26, 1962, and became a republic within the Commonwealth on Feb 23, 1970.

Constitution: On Oct 6, 1980, a new Constitution went into effect that reinforced the country's commitment to cooperative socialism.

HAITI
Republic of Haiti

LOCATION: Haiti occupies the western third of the Caribbean island of Hispaniola (with the Dominican Republic making up the remaining two-thirds), and includes several smaller islands off-shore. The Bahamas lie to the north and northwest, while Cuba and Jamaica are located to the west.

AREA: 10,714 sq. miles

Land Use: 32.66% cropland; 18.21% permanent pasture; 2.00% forests and woodland; 47.13% other.
Arable Land: 33%
Arable Land per capita: 0.37 acres

POPULATION: 6,096,000 (1988 estimate)

Population Density: 569 inhabs. per sq. mile (1988 estimate)
Population Distribution: 26.67% urban (1987)
Population Growth Rate: 1.90% per year (1988 estimate)

VITAL STATISTICS

Average Life Expectancy: 54.70 years (1985-90 projection)
Male: 53.10 years (1985-90 projection)
Female: 56.40 years (1985-90 projection)
Age Distribution: (1984)
0-14 .... 43.57%
15-64 .... 52.98%
65+ 3.45%
Median Age: 18 years (1985)
Maternal Mortality: (not available)
Infant Mortality: 107 per 1,000 live births (1985)

HEALTH CARE

Hospital Beds: 8 per 10,000 population (1980)
Doctors: 2 per 10,000 population (1984)

ETHNIC COMPOSITION: Black - 95%; mulatto and European - 5%.

RELIGION: Roman Catholic - 80%; Protestant - 10%; other - 10%. A substantial portion of the population practices voodoo, a religion derived from African ancestor worship.

LANGUAGE: French and Creole are the official languages.

EDUCATION: Illiteracy: 77%. In 1981/82, there were 3,321 primary schools with 658,102 students. There were 98,562 general secondary students, 2,124 vocational students and 833 teacher-training students. In 1985, 4,500 students were enrolled at the University of Haiti.

ECONOMIC DATA

Expenditures by Function [as %of total]: (1982)
General public services 14.49%
Defense 9.86%
Education 7.33%
Health 7.39%
Social security and welfare 5.39%
Housing and community amenities 0.17%
Other community and social services 4.00%
Economics services 19.55%
Agriculture, forestry, fishing and hunting ..4.71%
Roads 7.05%
Other transportation and communication ...0.51%
Other purposes 31.82%
GDP per capita: $382 (1986)

TRAVEL NOTES

Climate: Haiti has a tropical climate with little variation in seasonal temperatures. The year-round average temperature ranges from 70° to 90°F. The rainy season lasts from May to November.
Health Precautions: Inoculations against diphtheria, hepatitis, polio, tetanus and typhoid are recommended.
Miscellaneous: Haiti has numerous tourist attractions, including beautiful bays, beaches, mountains and the spectacular 19th-century fortress of King Henri Christophe. The country is also known for its distinctive folklore and primitive art.

GOVERNMENT

Haiti (Republique d' Haiti—Republic of Haiti) became Latin America's first independent republic in 1804. For over a century, Haiti's political life was characterized by violence and instability as the country's blacks and mulattoes engaged in a struggle for dominance. Francois Duvalier was elected president in 1957, and through the use of his own personal army, the Tontons Macoute, his rule quickly degenerated into a dictatorship. In May 1964, he had himself designated president-for-life and amended the Constitution in January 1971 so that he could designate his son as his successor. Jean-Claude assumed the presidency following his father's death on Apr 21, 1971. The younger Duvalier also made use of the Tontons Macoute as he wielded dictatorial power until February 1986, when increasing domestic and foreign pressure forced him to leave Haiti for exile in France. A provisional Government, headed by Lt. Gen. Henri Namphy and controlled by the military, immediately assumed power, and a new Constitution was drawn up. Presidential elections, originally set for November 1987, were called off after only a few hours of voting because of widespread violence, and rescheduled for Jan 17, 1988. In balloting that was boycotted by leading opposition candidates amid widespread charges of electoral fraud, Leslie Manigat was elected President, but in June 1988 was overthrown in a military coup, and Gen. Namphy was reinstalled. Gen. Namphy suspended the Constitution soon afterward, and in turn was overthrown in a new coup the following September, when Lt. Gen. Prosper Avril, promising democratic reform, was installed as the country's leader.

Constitution: The suspended Constitution, originally approved by 99% of the electorate on Mar 29, 1987, provided for a balanced government with power being shared by a president, a prime minister and a bicameral legislature. Former associates and supporters of Jean-Claude Duvalier were prohibited from holding political office for 10 years, although this provision was ignored. The Constitution also designated Creole as an official language along with French, and eliminated official, but generally ignored, restrictions against the practice of voodoo. A number of basic civil rights were also provided for, including free education, fair wages, decent housing and other welfare services.

HONDURAS
Republic of Honduras

LOCATION: Honduras is located in Central America, with a long Caribbean coastline in the north, Guatemala to the west, El Salvador and a small outlet to the Pacific Ocean to the southwest, and Nicaragua to the southeast.

AREA: 43,277 sq. miles

Land Use: 36% waste and urban, 30% pasture, 27% forest, 7% cropland.
Arable Land: 16%
Arable Land per capita: 0.95 acres

POPULATION: 4,648,000 (1986)

Population Density: 107 inhabs. per sq. mile (1986)
Population Distribution: 37% urban (1983)
Population Growth Rate: 3.30% per year (1986)

VITAL STATISTICS

Average Life Expectancy: 58.70 years (1984)
Male: 53.38 (1975)
Female: 56.93 (1975)
Age Distribution: (1985)
0-14 . . . . .48.10%
15-59 . . . . .47.50%
60+ 4.50%
Median Age: 16.40 years (1985)
Maternal Mortality: (not available)
Infant Mortality: 78 per 1,000 live births (1984)

HEALTH CARE

Hospital Beds: 13 per 10,000 population (1980)
Doctors: 3 per 10,000 population (1980)

ETHNIC COMPOSITION: Mestizo - 90%; Indian - 7%; black - 2%; Caucasians - 1%.

RELIGION: An overwhelming majority of the population is Catholic, while there is a small Protestant minority.

LANGUAGE: Spanish is the national language, though some Indian dialects are spoken.

EDUCATION: Illiteracy: 44%. In 1984, there were 6,308 primary schools with 737,093 students; 393 secondary schools with 123,231 students; 1 teacher training college with 1,752 students; and 2 universities with 29,786 students.

ECONOMIC DATA

Expenditures by Function [as % of total]: (1976)
General public services 27.72%
Defense 10.49%
Education 20.69%
Health 14.69%
Social security and welfare 4.73%
Housing and community amenities 2.57%

Other community and social services 0.93%
Economic services 18.76%
Agriculture, forestry, fishing and hunting . . 3.10%
Roads 12.35%
Other transportation and communication 0%
Other purposes 0%
GDP per capita: $765 (1985)

TRAVEL NOTES

Climate: The Honduran climate is temperate in
the mountain regions and tropical along the
coast, with the rainy season lasting from May to
November.

Health Precautions: Water is highly contaminated so drinking and cooking water should
be boiled for 20 minutes before use. Fruits and
vegetables should be soaked in disinfectant and
meats should be thoroughly cooked. Rabies can
be a threat to children, and malaria is prevalent
in some outlying areas. Intestinal diseases of
bacterial, viral and parasitic origin are endemic.

Miscellaneous: The tourist attractions of
Honduras include the ruins of the ancient
Mayan city of Copan, Lake Yojoa and Trujillo
Bay, which are popular fishing and boating
spots, and the beaches of the Bay Islands and
the northern coast.

GOVERNMENT

*Honduras (Republica de Honduras—Republic of
Honduras)* is an independent republic. Presidential and congressional elections on Nov 29,
1981 ended 18 years of predominantly military
rule. The inauguration of President Azcona on
Jan 27, 1986 marked the first time in over 50
years that one elected civilian President relinquished power to another in Honduras.

Constitution: A Constituent Assembly elected on
Apr 20, 1980 drafted a new Constitution which
provided for the return of civilian rule, and was
subsequently promulgated on Jan 20, 1982. The
Constitution declares the right to life inviolable
and recognizes the rights of free thought,
opinion, expression, circulation of information
and peaceful assembly, as well as freedom of
religion and education.

HONG KONG

LOCATION: Hong Kong, which consists of
territory on the southern Chinese mainland and
several islands off the coast, lies due west of the
southern tip of Taiwan and northwest of the offshore island of Hainan.

AREA: 413 sq. miles

Land Use: 8% cropland; 1% permanent pasture;
12% forests and woodland; 79% other.
Arable Land: 8%
Arable Land per capita: 0.01 acres

POPULATION: 5,611,000 (1989 estimate)

Population Density: 13,586 inhabs. per sq. mile
(1989 estimate)
Population Distribution: 92.45% urban (1985)
Population Growth Rate: 0.80% per year (1989
estimate)

VITAL STATISTICS

Average Life Expectancy: 75.70 years (1985-90
projection)
Male: 73.00 years (1985-90 projection)
Female: 78.50 years (1985-90 projection)
Age Distribution: (1985)
0-14 . . . . .23.67%
15-64 . . . . .68.78%
65+ 7.55%
Median Age: 28.30 years (1985)
Maternal Mortality: 6.40 per 100,000 live births
(1984)
Infant Mortality: 10 per 1,000 live births (1985)

HEALTH CARE

Hospital Beds: 43 per 10,000 population (1983)
Doctors: 7 per 10,000 population (1982)

ETHNIC COMPOSITION: Chinese - 98%; British
and other - 2%.

RELIGION: Buddhism is the main religion,
although Confucianism, Taoism, Islam and Christianity are also practiced.

LANGUAGE: English and Cantonese are the
official languages.

QUALITY OF LIFE INDICATORS

EDUCATION: Illiteracy: 25%. In 1987, there were 535,859 primary students, 485,488 secondary students, 10,416 full-time technical students and 2 universities with 12,890 full-time students.

ECONOMIC DATA

Expenditures by Function [as % of total]: (not available)
GDP per capita: $8,495 (1987 estimate)

TRAVEL NOTES

Climate: The hot humid monsoon season lasts from May to October, when the temperature averages 86°F. The months from November to February are mild and pleasant.
Health Precautions: Vaccinations against typhoid and cholera are required of travelers arriving from infected areas.
Miscellaneous: Hong Kong is known for its cosmopolitan capital, which offers shopping and cultural events.

GOVERNMENT

Hong Kong is a British Crown Colony until Jun 30, 1997, when, under the terms of an accord initialed in draft form on Sep 26 and formally signed Dec 19, 1984, China will resume sovereignty over Hong Kong, to be known as a Special Administrative Region (SAR) of China "with a high degree of autonomy." The agreement provides for a continuation of Hong Kong's legal, economic and other systems for 50 years after 1997, with a large measure of self-rule for Hong Kong's citizens. The SAR Government will have legislative, executive and judicial power, but China will control defense and foreign affairs.

HUNGARY
Hungarian People's Republic

LOCATION: Located in eastern Europe, Hungary is a landlocked country bounded to the north by Czechoslovakia, to the northeast by the Soviet Union, to the east by Rumania, to the south by Yugoslavia and to the west by Austria.

AREA: 35,920 sq. miles

Land Use: 57.34% cropland; 13.74% permanent pasture; 17.72% forests and woodland; 11.20% other.
Arable Land: 57.34%
Arable Land per capita: 1.24 acres

POPULATION: 10,671,000 (1988 estimate)

Population Density: 297 inhabs. per sq. mile (1988 estimate)
Population Distribution: 56.20% urban (1985)
Population Growth Rate: -0.07% per year (1985-90 projection)

VITAL STATISTICS

Average Life Expectancy: 71.30 years (1985-90 projection)
Male: 67.70 years (1985-90 projection)
Female: 75.10 years (1985-90 projection)
Age Distribution: (1985)
0-14 . . . . .21.60%
15-64 . . . . .65.94%
65+ 12.46%
Median Age: 35.00 years (1985)
Maternal Mortality: 14.60 per 100,000 live births (1984)
Infant Mortality: 17.00 per 1,000 live births (1985-90 projection)

HEALTH CARE

Hospital Beds: 96 per 10,000 population (1985)
Doctors: 33 per 10,000 population (1985)

ETHNIC COMPOSITION: Hungarian - 96.60%; German - 1.60%; Slovak - 1.10%; Southern Slav - 0.30%; Rumanian - 0.20%; other - 0.20%.

RELIGION: Roman Catholic - 67.50%; Calvinist - 20.00%; Lutheran - 5.00%; other - 7.50%.

LANGUAGE: Hungarian (Magyar) is the principal language.

EDUCATION: Illiteracy is about 1.10%. In 1985/86, there were 3,546 primary schools with 1,297,818 students; 561 secondary schools with 320,708 students; and 58 institutions of higher learning with 99,344 students.

ECONOMIC DATA

Expenditures by Function [as % of total]: (not available)

GDP per capita: $2,050 (1985)

TRAVEL NOTES

Climate: Hungary has a continental climate, with long, dry summers and cold, damp winters. The average annual temperature ranges from 27°F to 82°F. The yearly rainfall average is 25 inches, with the rainy season lasting from November to January.

Health Precautions: Health conditions are generally good and the tap water is potable.

Miscellaneous: The primary tourist attraction is Lake Balaton, which offers boating, fishing and bathing. Budapest has numerous hot springs and the annual Budapest Spring Festival is held in March.

GOVERNMENT

Hungary (Magyar Nepkoztarsasag—Hungarian People's Republic) was proclaimed a People's Republic on Aug 20, 1949. Spurred by a popular revolutionary movement, Hungary declared on Nov 1, 1956 that it was withdrawing from the Warsaw Pact. This revolt was crushed by Soviet troops that were stationed in Hungary, and a pro-Soviet regime was installed on Nov 4, 1956. Hungary has an authoritarian form of government based upon a one-party system, with effective political power resting in the hands of the Hungarian Socialist Workers' Party and its General Secretary.

Constitution: The 1949 Constitution, which was amended in April 1972 and again in December 1983, provides for a socialist economy with central planning, and declares Hungary to be a state in which all power is held by the working people and most of the means of production is publicly owned. The highest organ of state power, according to the Constitution, is the unicameral National Assembly, but in practice, political authority is exercised at all levels of Government by the Hungarian Socialist Workers' Party, either directly or through the Communist-controlled People's Patriotic Front.

ICELAND
Republic of Iceland

LOCATION: A small island in the North Atlantic, Iceland is situated approximately 190 miles southeast of Greenland and 620 miles west of Norway.

AREA: 39,769 sq. miles

Land Use: 0.08% cropland; 22.68% permanent pasture; 1.19% forest and woodland; 76.05% other.

Arable Land: 0%

Arable Land per capita: 0 acres

POPULATION: 249,000 (1988 estimate)

Population Density: 6 inhabs. per sq. mile (1988 estimate)

Population Distribution: 85% urban (1986)

Population Growth Rate: 0.90% per year (1988 estimate)

VITAL STATISTICS

Average Life Expectancy: 77.10 years (1985-90 projection)

Male: 73.90 years (1985-90 projection)

Female: 80.50 years (1985-90 projection)

Age Distribution: (1985)

0-14 . . . . .26.75%
15-64 . . . . .63.37%
65+ 9.88%

Median Age: 26.10 years (1985)

Maternal Mortality: 22.80 per 100,000 live births (1975)

Infant Mortality: 6 per 1,000 live births (1985)

HEALTH CARE

Hospital Beds: 110 per 10,000 population (1986)

Doctors: 24 per 10,000 population (1985)

ETHNIC COMPOSITION: Icelandic (descendants of Celts and Norwegians) - 99%; other - 1%.

RELIGION: Evangelical Lutheran - 97%; other (mostly other Christian denominations) - 3%.

LANGUAGE: Icelandic is the official language.

EDUCATION: Illiteracy: 0%. In 1982, there were 216 primary schools with 25,018 students; 115

secondary schools with 28,700 students; and 3 colleges and universities with 4,600 students.

ECONOMIC DATA

Expenditures by Function [as % of total]: (1984)
General public services 9.16%
Defense 0%
Education 11.99%
Health 23.02%
Social security and welfare 16.19%
Housing and community amenities 2.26%
Other community and social services 1.75%
Economic services 25.23%
Agriculture, forestry, fishing and hunting . . 9.11%
Roads 6.86%
Other transportation and communication . . 1.67%
Other purposes 10.41%
GDP per capita: $16,184 (1986)

TRAVEL NOTES

Climate: The effect of Iceland's northern location on the weather is offset somewhat by the Gulf Stream. The annual mean temperature is 41°F, with surprisingly little variation between summer and winter. Winter temperatures rarely drop below 20°F and summer highs rarely exceed 60°F. Reykjavik receives an average annual rainfall of 50 inches.

Health Precautions: No special health precautions are necessary for travel in Iceland. The water is potable.

Miscellaneous: Iceland's volcanic landscape offers tourists a stark beauty with such features as glaciers, geysers and hot springs.

GOVERNMENT

Iceland (Lythveldith Island—Republic of Iceland), after some 500 years under Danish rule, achieved internal self-government in 1918 with the Danish monarch as head of state. The country assumed fully independent status on Jun 17, 1944, when it adopted a new Constitution establishing a republic with a parliamentary form of government and a President as head of state. On Jun 29, 1980, Vigdis Finnbogadottir was elected President, becoming the world's first popularly elected female head of state.

Constitution: The Constitution, which was approved by a popular referendum, took effect on Jun 17, 1944. Amendments may be proposed by the Legislature, but must be approved in a referendum.

INDIA
Republic of India

LOCATION: India forms its own subcontinent in South Asia and is surrounded by Pakistan to the northwest; China, Nepal and Bhutan to the north; Bangladesh to the northeast; the Bay of Bengal to the east; the Indian Ocean to the south; and the Arabian Sea to the east.

AREA: 1,269,219 sq. miles (area includes Sikkim and the areas of Jammu and Kashmir that India holds)

Land Use: 56.62% cropland; 4.02% permanent pasture; 22.68% forests and woodland; 16.68% other.
Arable Land: 57%
Arable Land per capita: 0.64 acres

POPULATION: 816,828,000 (1988 estimate)

Population Density: 644 inhabs. per sq. mile (1988 estimate)
Population Distribution: 25.51% urban (1985)
Population Growth Rate: 2% per year (1988 estimate)

VITAL STATISTICS

Average Life Expectancy: 57.80 years (1985-90 projection)
Male: 57.90 years (1985-90 projection)
Female: 57.90 years (1985-90 projection)
Age Distribution: (1985)
0-14 . . . . 36.81%
15-64 . . . . 58.88%
65+ 4.31%
Median Age: 21.50 years (1985)
Maternal Mortality: (not available)
Infant Mortality: 101 per 1,000 live births (1985)

HEALTH CARE

Hospital Beds: 15 per 10,000 population (1981)
Doctors: 4 per 10,000 population (1984)

ETHNIC COMPOSITION: Indo-Aryan - 72%; Dravidian - 25%; Mongoloid and other - 3%.

RELIGION: Hindu - 83.50%; Moslem - 11.00%; Christian - 2.60%; Sikh - 2.00%; Buddhist - 0.70%; other - 0.20%.

LANGUAGE: Hindi is the official national language and is spoken by about 30% of the people. English is an associate language and is used for many official purposes, while there are 16 regional languages recognized by the Constitution, including Telugu, Bengali, Tamil, Gujarat, Urdu and Marathi. Many other local languages and dialects are spoken.

EDUCATION: Illiteracy: 64%. In 1985/86, there were 528,079 primary schools with 86,465,189 students; 49,594 secondary schools with 11,617,262 students; 4,511 higher secondary schools (old course) with 1,618,917 students; and 7,209 higher secondary schools (new pattern) with 1,869,755 students.

ECONOMIC DATA

Expenditures by Function [as % of total]: (1986)
General public services 5.76%
Defense 18.39%
Education 2.05%
Health 2.09%
Social security and welfare . . . . (not available)
Housing and community amenities . (not available)
Other community and
    social services . . . . (not available)
Economic services 23.37%
Agriculture, forestry, fishing and hunting . 8.02%
Roads . . . . (not available)
Other transportation and
    communication: . . . . (not available)
Other purposes 42.75%
GDP per capita: $283 (1986)

TRAVEL NOTES

Climate: The climate ranges from tropical in the south to near-Arctic cold in the Rajasthan Desert in the northwest. Rainfall varies greatly, although the summer monsoon brings heavy rain to much of the country.

Health Precautions: Precautions should be taken against gastrointestinal diseases, malaria, dengue fever, hepatitis and typhoid fever. The water is not potable.

Miscellaneous: Tourist attractions include the scenic countryside, abundant wildlife and many relics of the past, including forts, palaces and temples, as well as paintings in the mountain caves of Ajanta.

GOVERNMENT

India (Bharat—Republic of India), formerly part of the British Indian Empire, became an independent state on Aug 15, 1947, with the British monarch as the titular head of state. On Jan 26, 1950, it was proclaimed a republic within the Commonwealth of Nations. The country's history has been marked by separatist and religious violence, including the Oct 31, 1984 assassination of Prime Minister Indira Gandhi by two militant Sikh members of her personal bodyguard. India is a parliamentary democracy in which effective political authority rests with the Prime Minister and a Cabinet, who are responsible to Parliament.

Constitution: The present Constitution establishing the Indian Republic entered into effect on Jan 26, 1950. It is a comprehensive document with almost 400 articles, to which are annexed 9 schedules that outline in detail the principles and processes of the constitutional system. The Constitution establishes a federal system with parliamentary forms of government (patterned largely on the British system) at both state and national levels. The Constitution also bans the caste system, as well as the premise of untouchability, although some of these traditions are still practiced. The Constitution may be amended by a law passed by both houses of the federal Parliament and ratified by at least one-half of the 22 state legislatures. The ease of this process has led to frequent amendments.

INDONESIA
Republic of Indonesia

LOCATION: Indonesia consists of some 13,700 islands in the Malay archipelago. The country's only land borders are with Malaysia on the northern part of the island of Borneo and with Papua New Guinea on the island of New Guinea. The Philippines are located to the northeast, Australia lies to the southeast and the Indian Ocean lies to the southwest.

AREA: 735,358 sq. miles

Land Use: 11.18% cropland; 6.57% permanent pasture; 67.23% forests and woodland; 15.02% other.

Arable Land: 11%
Arable Land per capita: 0.33 acres

POPULATION: 184,082,000 (1988 estimate)

Population Density: 250 inhabs. per sq. mile (1988 estimate)
Population Distribution: 25.30% urban (1985)
Population Growth Rate: 2.00% per year (1988 estimate)

VITAL STATISTICS

Average Life Expectancy: 56.00 years (1985-90 projection)
Male: 54.60 years (1985-90 projection)
Female: 57.40 years (1985-90 projection)
Age Distribution: (1985)
0-14 .... 38.74%
15-64 .... 57.71%
65+ 3.55%
Median Age: 20.20 years (1985)
Maternal Mortality: (not available)
Infant Mortality: 88 per 1,000 live births (1985)

HEALTH CARE

Hospital Beds: 6 per 10,000 population (1985)
Doctors: 1 per 10,000 population (1985)

ETHNIC COMPOSITION: Javanese - 45%; Sudanese - 14%; Madurese - 8%; coastal Malay - 7%; other - 26%.

RELIGION: Moslem - 88%; Protestant - 6%; Catholic - 3%; Hindu - 2%; other - 1%.

LANGUAGE: Bahasa Indonesia (based primarily on Malay) is the official language. English and Dutch are the most widely spoken European languages.

EDUCATION: Illiteracy: 38% (1987). In 1984 there were 139,511 primary schools with 26,550,915 students; 24,962 general secondary schools with 8,801,235 students; 956 technical schools with 377,300 students; and 1,023,000 students enrolled in institutes of higher education. In 1987, Indonesia had 46 state universities and teacher colleges and 25 private universities.

ECONOMIC DATA

Expenditures by Function [as % of total]: (1986)
General public services 32.36%
Defense 9.32%
Education 8.51%
Health 1.87%
Social security and welfare .... (not available)
Housing and community amenities 1.37%
Other community and social services 0.69%
Economic services 19.30%
Agriculture, forestry, fishing and hunting ..4.55%
Roads 2.70%
Other transportation and communication ...2.22%
Other purposes 26.58%
GDP per capita: $333 (1986)

TRAVEL NOTES

Climate: The Indonesian climate is hot and humid, with an average annual temperature of 79°F. Temperatures are cooler at higher elevations, and in central West Irian there are several peaks covered with snow year-round. Rainfall is heavy during the monsoon season (November to March).
Health Precautions: Vaccinations for cholera, typhoid, yellow fever, polio, tetanus and hepatitis are recommended. Precautions against malaria should be taken when traveling outside the major urban areas. The water is not potable.
Miscellaneous: Beautiful beaches and rugged volcanic mountains as well as Buddhist and Hindu temples make Java attractive to tourists. Bali is noted for traditional Hindu dancing and religious festivals.

GOVERNMENT

Indonesia (Republik Indonesia—Republic of Indonesia) proclaimed its independence from the Netherlands on Aug 17, 1945, although the Netherlands did not formally transfer its sovereignty to the new state until Dec 27, 1949. Dr. Sukarno, a leader in the struggle for independence, was elected president and served in that role until March 1967. In August 1962, the Netherlands relinquished control of Irian Java (West Irian, the western part of the island of New Guinea) to Indonesia. On Jul 17, 1976, East Timor, a Portuguese possession for some 400 years, was incorporated into Indonesia and became the country's 27th province. However, resistance to Indonesian rule by rebel guerrilla groups has resulted in continued fighting between Government and insurgent forces on the island. Gen. Suharto, Indonesia's current leader, assumed key political and military powers in March 1966, and was elected President a year later. Effective political power rests with the military establishment aided by Golkar, a Government-sponsored coalition of "non-party" functional groups.

Constitution: On Jul 5, 1959, a presidential decree restored the original Indonesian Constitution of August 1945, which had been replaced by provisional Constitutions in February and August 1950. The 1945 Constitution establishes a strong presidential form of government with a highly centralized administrative structure. The preamble enshrines the "Pancasila," or guiding principles of Indonesian government: monotheism, humanitarianism, national unity, democracy by representative consensus and social justice.

IRAN
Islamic Republic of Iran

LOCATION: Iran is located on the Persian Gulf between the Middle East and South Asia. It is bordered to the north by the Soviet Union, to the east by Afghanistan and Pakistan, to the south by the Persian Gulf and the Gulf of Oman and to the west by Iraq and Turkey.

AREA: 636,296 sq. miles

Land Use: 9.07% cropland; 26.89% permanent pasture; 11.01% forest and woodland; 53.03% other.
Arable Land: 9%
Arable Land per capita: 0.83 acres

POPULATION: 51,005,000 (1989 estimate)

Population Density: 80 inhabs. per sq. mile (1989 estimate)
Population Distribution: 51.90% urban (1985)
Population Growth Rate: 2.90% per year (1989)

VITAL STATISTICS

Average Life Expectancy: 59.00 years (1985-90 projection)
Male: 58.70 years (1985-90 projection)
Female: 59.20 years (1985-90 projection)
Age Distribution: (1985)
0-14 .... 42.70%
15-64 .... 53.95%
65+ 3.35%
Median Age: 18.40 years (1985)

Maternal Mortality: (not available)
Infant Mortality: 112 per 1,000 live births (1985)

HEALTH CARE

Hospital Beds: 15 per 10,000 population (1984)
Doctors: 4 per 10,000 population (1983)

ETHNIC COMPOSITION: Persian - 63%; Turkish - 18%, other Iranian - 13%; Kurdish - 3%; Semitic - 3%.

RELIGION: Shiite Moslem - 93%; Sunni Moslem - 2%; other (Christian, Jewish, Zoroastrian) - 5%.

LANGUAGE: Farsi is the official language. Turkish, Kurdish and Arabic are spoken by the various ethnic groups.

EDUCATION: Illiteracy: 38%. In 1983/84, there were 5,994,000 primary school students, 2,685,000 secondary school students, and 148,000 technical college students; in 1984/85 there were 146,000 college and university students.

ECONOMIC DATA

Expenditures by Function [as % of total]: (1985)
General public services 7.20%
Defense 13.40%
Education 16.90%
Health 8.12%
Social security and welfare 11.53%
Housing and community amenities 2.12%
Other community and social services 1.39%
Economic services 20.36%
Agriculture, forestry, fishing and hunting ..2.79%
Roads 2.25%
Other transportation and communication ...2.36%
Other purposes 17.74%
GDP per capita: $3,800 (1985)

TRAVEL NOTES

Climate: Iran has a desert climate with unusual extremes in temperature. Summer temperatures exceeding 130°F have been recorded, while in the winter the higher elevations may experience temperatures as low as 0°F.
Health Precautions: Immunizations against cholera, typhoid, tetanus and polio are recommended, as are gamma globulin injections. The dry and dusty air may aggravate respiratory problems. Tap water in large cities is potable.
Miscellaneous: Iran is the home of many important ancient historical sites, such as Persepolis,

Tabriz and Isfahan. The rugs woven in Iran are widely admired as some of the finest textiles ever produced.

GOVERNMENT

Iran (Jomhori-e-Islami-e-Iran—Islamic Republic of Iran) became a republic on Apr 1, 1979, after a long-smoldering Islamic revolutionary movement led by the Ayatollah Ruhollah Khomeini caused the downfall of Shah Reza Pahlavi earlier in the year.

Constitution: A December 1979 referendum gave overwhelming approval to a new Constitution that establishes an Islamic Republic and "leadership by the clergy." The Constitution empowers the clergy to prevent deviations by Government officials from their "true Islamic functions and obligations."

IRAQ
Republic of Iraq

LOCATION: Located in southwest Asia, Iraq is surrounded by Syria and Jordan to the west, Turkey to the north, Iran to the east, the Persian Gulf and Kuwait to the southeast and Saudi Arabia to the south.

AREA: 169,235 sq. miles (includes territorial waters but excludes a 1,360 sq. mile Neutral Zone shared with Saudi Arabia)

Land Use: 12.56% cropland; 9.22% permanent pasture; 4.39% forests and woodland; 73.83% other (mostly desert).
Arable Land: 13%
Arable Land per capita: 0.95 acres

POPULATION: 17,069,000 (1988 estimate)

Population Density: 101 inhabs. per sq. mile (1988 estimate)
Population Distribution: 70.63% urban (1985)
Population Growth Rate: 3.10% per year (1988 estimate)

VITAL STATISTICS

Average Life Expectancy: 63.90 years (1985-90 projection)
Male: 63.00 years (1985-90 projection)
Female: 64.80 years (1985-90 projection)

Age Distribution: (1985)
0-14 . . . . .46.94%
15-64 . . . . .50.41%
65+ 2.65%
Median Age: 16.50 years (1985)
Maternal Mortality: (not available)
Infant Mortality: 80 per 1,000 live births (1985)

HEALTH CARE

Hospital Beds: 20 per 10,000 population (1986)
Doctors: 4 per 10,000 population (1986)

ETHNIC COMPOSITION: Arab - 75%; Kurdish - 20%; other - 5% (mainly Turkish).

RELIGION: Moslem - 97% (mainly Shiite); other - 3%.

LANGUAGE: Arabic is the official language, although a substantial minority speaks Kurdish. Turkish, Assyrian, Armenian and English are also spoken.

EDUCATION: Illiteracy: 45%. In 1986/87 there were 8,210 primary schools with 2,917,474 students; 2,315 secondary schools with 1,012,426 students; 245 vocational schools with 133,568 students; 43 teacher training institutes with 28,164 students; 6 universities with 110,173 students; and 19 technical institutes with 32,322 students.

ECONOMIC DATA

Expenditures by Function [as % of total]: (not available)
GDP per capita: $1,104 (1986)

TRAVEL NOTES

Climate: The climate fluctuates extremely between seasons, with hot, dry summers (temperatures rising to more than 120°F) and cold winters. Most of Iraq's scant rainfall occurs from December through April.
Health Precautions: Cholera, tetanus, polio, typhoid and gamma globulin inoculations are recommended. Tap water is potable in the larger cities.
Miscellaneous: Visitors enjoy visiting ruins of ancient civilizations. Remnants from the Sumerian, Akkadian, Babylonian, Assyrian, Chaldean, Persian, Greek, Parthian, Ottoman and Islamic empires are still evident in Iraq.

GOVERNMENT

Iraq (al Jumhouriya al 'Iraqia—Republic of Iraq) became an independent sovereign state on Oct 3, 1932, when the League of Nations formally ended a British mandate installed in the territory following the dissolution of the Turkish Ottoman Empire after World War I. Iraq was proclaimed a republic on Jul 14, 1958, after a bloody military coup overthrew the Hashemite monarchy established under the British mandate. The republic has been plagued by a series of military coups, the latest occurring on Jul 17, 1968, when the Arab Baath Socialist Party came to power. Iraq has also been plagued with separatist pressure and violence from the country's ethnic Kurdish minority. Another recent problem was a war with neighboring Iran, which lasted from 1980 until an August 1988 cease-fire. Effective political authority in Iraq rests with the Revolutionary Command Council, which rules with the aid of the Baath Party and a National Assembly.

Constitution: A Provisional Constitution was proclaimed on Sep 22, 1968. It provides for a socialist republic with Islam as the official religion, but bans discrimination based on religion, race or language, and guarantees freedom of the press and the right to association in conformity with the law. It acknowledges that the population consists of two main nationalities, Arab and Kurdish, and provides for the rights of the Kurds and other minorities.

IRELAND
Republic of Ireland

LOCATION: Covering the greater part of the island of Ireland, the republic lies in the Atlantic Ocean about 50 miles west of Britain.

AREA: 27,136 sq. miles

Land Use: 14.11% cropland; 70.52% permanent pasture; 4.86% forest and woodland; 10.51% other.
Arable Land: 14.11%
Arable Land per capita: 0.66 acres

POPULATION: 3,700,000 (1987 estimate)

Population Density: 136 inhabs. per sq. mile (1987 estimate)

Population Distribution: 57% urban (1985)
Population Growth Rate: 1.26% per year (1985-90 projection)

VITAL STATISTICS

Average Life Expectancy: 73.80 years (1985-90 projection)
Male: 71.10 years (1985-90 projection)
Female: 76.70 years (1985-90 projection)
Age Distribution: (1985)
0-14 ....29.60%
15-64 ....60.00%
65+ 10.40%
Median Age: 26.40 years
Maternal Mortality: 5 per 100,000 live births (1980)
Infant Mortality: 9 per 1,000 live births (1985-90 projection)

HEALTH CARE

Hospital Beds: 97.14 per 10,000 population (1980)
Doctors: 12.92 per 10,000 population (1981)

ETHNIC COMPOSITION: Celtic, with an English minority.

RELIGION: Roman Catholic - 94%; Anglican - 4%; other - 2%.

LANGUAGE: Irish is the official first language, but English is also used on official documents, and is universally spoken.

EDUCATION: Illiteracy: 1%. In 1984/85, there were 3,387 primary schools with 566,289 students; 507 secondary schools with 212,342 students; 250 vocational colleges with 79,930 students; 6 teacher training colleges with 1,957 students; and 7 universities and institutes with 31,425 students.

ECONOMIC DATA

Expenditures by Function [as % of total]: (1985)
General public services 7.26%
Defense 3.14%
Education 11.71%
Health 13.15%
Social security and welfare 25.47%
Housing and community amenities 4.62%
Other community and social services 0.31%
Economic services 14.98%
Agriculture, forestry, fishing and hunting ..6.04%
Roads...............................1.69%
Other transportation and communication ...1.84%

Other purposes 19.36%
GDP per capita: $7,211 (1986)

TRAVEL NOTES

Climate: The climate is mild and equable, with temperatures ranging from 32°F to 70°F.
Health Precautions: None.
Miscellaneous: Among the numerous scenic spots in Ireland are the Killarney Lakes and the Irish west coats.

GOVERNMENT

Ireland (Irish Republic—Eire) is a sovereign, independent, democratic state with a parliamentary form of government. Following an insurrection against British rule, a National Parliament was elected in December 1918.

Constitution: The first Constitution of the Irish Republic came into force on Dec 6, 1922. On Jun 14, 1937 a new Constitution was approved by the National Parliament. It was enacted by a plebiscite on Jul 1, 1937 and came into force on Dec 29, 1937. The Constitution applies to the whole of Ireland, including the 6 counties of Northern Ireland which are part of Britain but, pending their reintegration, laws enacted in the National Parliament apply to the Irish Republic only. (In November 1985, Parliament signed an agreement with Britain's Parliament, called the Anglo-Irish Agreement, which gives Dublin a consultative role in the governing of Northern Ireland for the first time.) The 1948 Republic of Ireland Bill severed the last ties with Britain. Amendments to the Constitution can be effected only by popular referendum.

ISRAEL
State of Israel

LOCATION: Israel is located in western Asia, and lies on the eastern edge of the Mediterranean Sea. It is bordered by Lebanon to the north, Syria to the northeast, Jordan to the east and Egypt to the west.

AREA: 8,473 sq. miles (includes East Jerusalem)

Land Use: 21.50% cropland; 40.24% permanent pasture; 5.71% forest and woodland; 32.56% other (mostly desert).
Arable Land: 21.50%
Arable Land per capita: 0.28 acres

POPULATION: 4,399,000 (1987 estimate)

Population Density: 519 inhabs. per sq. mile (1987)
Population Distribution: 90.30% urban (1985)
Population Growth Rate: 1.83% per year (1987)

VITAL STATISTICS

Average Life Expectancy: 75.10 years (1985-90 projection)
Male: 73.10 years (1985-90 projection)
Female: 77.20 years (1985-90 projection)
Age Distribution: (1985)
0-14 . . . . .31.70%
15-64 . . . . .59.40%
65+ 8.90%
Median Age: 25.60 years (1985)
Maternal Mortality: 2.00 per 100,000 live births (includes East Jerusalem and certain occupied territories) (1983)
Infant Mortality: 13 per 1,000 live births (1985)

HEALTH CARE

Hospital Beds: 65.01 per 10,000 population (1985)
Doctors: 28.97 per 10,000 population (1983)

ETHNIC COMPOSITION: Jewish - 83%; non-Jewish - 17% (mainly Arab).

RELIGION: Jewish - 83%; Moslem (mostly Sunni) - 12%; Christian - 2%; Druze - 1%.

LANGUAGE: Hebrew is the official language. Arabic and English are also common.

EDUCATION: Illiteracy: 30% Arabs, 12% Jews. In 1985/86 there were 1,307 Jewish primary schools with 470,746 students (314 Arab primary schools with 138,325 students); 283 Jewish intermediate schools with 107,624 students (55 Arab intermediate schools with 22,357 students); 519 Jewish secondary schools with 184,744 students (79 Arab secondary schools with 33,537 students); 305 Jewish vocational schools with 89,132 students (36 Arab vocational schools with 5,444 students); 26 Jewish agricultural schools with 4,924 students (2 Arab agricultural schools with 420 students); and 33 Jewish teacher training schools with 11,601 students (2 Arab teacher training schools with 420 students).

ECONOMIC DATA

Expenditures by Function [as % of total]: (1984)
General public services 3.29%
Defense 27.79%
Education 7.05%
Health 3.45%
Social security and welfare 20.17%
Housing and community amenities 0.11%
Other community and social services 0.67%
Economic services 5.38%
Agriculture, forestry, fishing and hunting . . 0.60%
Roads 0.13%
Other transportation and communication . . 0.79%
Other purposes 32.65%
GDP per capita: $6,313 (1983)

TRAVEL NOTES

Climate: The climate is Mediterranean, with hot, dry summers and mild, rainy winters.
Health Precautions: Tetanus, typhoid and gamma globulin shots are recommended.
Miscellaneous: Sightseeing places include religious holy sites, the Walled City of Jerusalem and "Kibbutzim."

GOVERNMENT

Israel (Medinat Yisrael—Dawlat Israil—State of Israel) is an independent republic with a parliamentary form of government based on a multiparty system. It was created in 1948, and has occupied additional territory, including the West Bank (Judea and Samaria) and the Gaza Strip, since the 1967 6-Day War.

Constitution: Israel does not have a formal written Constitution, but instead relies on a number of basic laws, which taken together constitute the fundamental law. The Knesset (Parliament) resolution (Jun 13, 1950) that established this approach foresees the possibility of one day consolidating the basic laws into a single constitutional document. Over the years, several laws have been passed dealing with the fundamental institutions of the Government (the legal system, Parliament, the Presidency, the Cabinet, the Judiciary, the electoral system and the administrative structure). Others deal with such varied topics as the right of all Jews to immigrate to Israel, civil liberties, equality of women, social security and other economic benefits and the right to education.

ITALY
Italian Republic

LOCATION: Italy is composed of a peninsula extending from southern Europe into the Mediterranean Sea and a number of small adjacent islands. It is bounded by Switzerland and Austria to the north, France to the northwest and Yugoslavia to the northeast. The two main islands are Sicily to the southwest and Sardinia to the west.

AREA: 116,324 sq. miles

Land Use: 41.84% cropland; 17.05% permanent pasture; 21.73% forests and woodland; 19.38% other.
Arable Land: 42%
Arable Land per capita: 0.55 acres

POPULATION: 57,373,000 (1988 estimate)

Population Density: 493 inhabs. per sq. mile (1988 estimate)
Population Distribution: 67.40% urban (1985)
Population Growth Rate: 0.10% per year (1988 estimate)

VITAL STATISTICS

Average Life Expectancy: 75.20 years (1985-90 projection)
Male: 71.90 years (1985-90 projection)
Female: 78.70 years (1985-90 projection)
Age Distribution: (1985)
0-14 . . . . .19.40%
15-64 . . . . .67.61%
65+ 12.99%
Median Age: 35.50 years (1985)
Maternal Mortality: 13.20 per 100,000 live births (1981)
Infant Mortality: 12 per 1,000 live births (1985)

HEALTH CARE

Hospital Beds: 88 per 10,000 population (1983)
Doctors: 17 per 10,000 population (1981)

ETHNIC COMPOSITION: Italians form the majority of the population. There are small minorities of Germans, Slovenes, Albanians, French, Ladins and Greeks.

RELIGION: Nearly 100% of the population professes Roman Catholicism.

LANGUAGE: The principal language is Italian, with German, French and Slovene being spoken in selected regions.

EDUCATION: Illiteracy: 7% (1987). In 1984/85, there were 28,244 primary schools with 3,904,143 students; 25,187 secondary schools with 7,888,878 students; and 839 higher schools with 766,243 students.

ECONOMIC DATA

Expenditures by Function [as % of total]: (1986)
General public services 7.16%
Defense 3.15%
Education 7.25%
Health 9.89%
Social security and welfare 29.05%
Housing and community amenities 0.95%
Other community and social services 0.76%
Economic services 13.19%
Agriculture, forestry, fishing and hunting .. 1.16%
Roads 1.83%
Other transportation and communication .. 4.37%
Other purposes 26.06%
GDP per capita: $11,508 (1986)

TRAVEL NOTES

Climate: The climate is temperate in the north and Mediterranean in the south. Winters are mild, while summers tend to be long and dry. Temperatures in Rome average 45°F in January and 78°F in July.

Health Precautions: Health conditions are generally good, but inoculations against hepatitis and influenza are recommended. The water is potable.

Miscellaneous: Besides its Roman buildings, medieval and Baroque churches, Renaissance towns and palaces, paintings, sculptures and famous opera houses, Italy has Alpine and Mediterranean scenery combined with a sunny climate to attract visitors.

GOVERNMENT

Italy (Repubblica Italiana—Italian Republic) is a parliamentary republic. The ruling Christian Democratic Party, which pursues a broadly centrist and anti-Communist policy, has controlled the Government either alone or in coalition with smaller democratic parties since 1945. The Government collapsed Mar 11, 1988, when Prime Minister Giovanni Goria resigned in a political dispute over the construction of a new nuclear power plant. On Mar 16, President Francesco Cossiga selected Ciriaco De Mita as the Prime Minister-designate. De Mita announced his new Cabinet and the formation of Italy's 48th postwar Government on Apr 13. De Mita resigned May 19, 1989, and former Prime Minister Giulio Andreotti has been asked to form the 49th Government.

Constitution: Italy has been a democratic republic since 1946, when the monarchy was abolished by popular referendum. The Constitution, which came into force on Jan 1, 1948, provides for an executive branch composed of a President of the Republic and a Cabinet, which is headed by a Prime Minister. The Constitution also establishes a bicameral Parliament, with specifications concerning the size and composition of each house, and provides for a separate judiciary.

JAMAICA

LOCATION: Jamaica is located in the Caribbean Sea, 90 miles south of Cuba.

AREA: 4,260 sq. miles

Land Use: 23% meadow and pasture; 19% forest; 58% waste, urban and other.
Arable Land: 21%
Arable Land per capita: 0.23 acres

POPULATION: 2,428,000 (1985)

Population Density: 570 inhabs. per sq. mile (1985)
Population Distribution: 41.90% urban (1981)
Population Growth Rate: 1.60% per year (1985)

VITAL STATISTICS

Average Life Expectancy: 65 years (1984)
Male: (not available)
Female: (not available)
Age Distribution: (1984)
0-14 ....36.70%
15-59 ....52.80%
60+ 8.50%
Median Age: 18.50 years (1980)
Maternal Mortality: 128.30 per 100,000 live births (1971)

Infant Mortality: 16.80 per 1,000 live births (1984)

HEALTH CARE

Hospital Beds: 28.52 per 10,000 population (1980)
Doctors: 3.02 per 10,000 population (1980)

ETHNIC COMPOSITION: 76.00% African; 15.00% Afro-European; 1.20% Chinese and Afro-Chinese; 3.40% East Indian and Afro-East Indian; 3.20% white.

RELIGION: Protestant - 75%; Roman Catholic - 8%; other - 17%.

LANGUAGE: English, Creole.

EDUCATION: Illiteracy rate: 14%. In fiscal year 1980/81, about 12% of the national budget was allotted to education and social welfare. In 1980, there were 849 primary schools with an enrollment of 359,488; 204 secondary schools with an enrollment of 248,001; and 11 teacher training schools with an enrollment of 9,451. There was one university with an enrollment of 4,548.

ECONOMIC DATA

Expenditures by Function [as % of total]: (1977)
General public services 13.20%
Defense 2.80%
Education 19.57%
Health 8.35%
Social security and welfare 3.51%
Housing and community amenities 6.22%
Other community and social services 3.13%
Economic services 24.27%
Agriculture, forestry, fishing and hunting . . 7.15%
Roads 3.96%
Other transportation and communication . . 2.70%
Other purposes 25.37%
GDP per capita: $815 (1984)

TRAVEL NOTES

Climate: Mountains cover about 80% of the country. Jamaica has a tropical, humid climate most of the year; from November to March, however, temperatures are cooler, particularly along the north shore, where the range is between 70°F and 80°F. Rainfall is seasonal, with striking regional variations. Some northern regions get up to 200 inches a year while the southern and southwestern plains receive almost no rain at all. Summer clothes are suitable year round. The evenings, especially in the winter months, can be chilly and light wraps or sweaters are recommended.

Health Precautions: Municipal water supplies are safe, as are fruits and vegetables.

Miscellaneous: Local buses are overcrowded but provide fairly regular service. Taxis are available. Main roads are nearly all paved, but since Jamaica is largely mountainous, they are often narrow and winding, with uneven surfaces.

GOVERNMENT

Jamaica has been an independent member of the Commonwealth of Nations since Aug 6, 1962. It recognizes the British monarch as head of state.

Constitution: The new Constitution, enacted at independence in August 1962, recognized the British monarch as head of state and established a parliamentary form of government. A 6-member Privy Council, appointed by the Governor General (who represents the British monarch) on the advice of the Prime Minister, advises the Governor General on the exercise of the Royal Prerogative of Mercy and on appeals on disciplinary matters from Service Commissions.

JAPAN

LOCATION: Japan, located off the northeastern coast of Asia, is an archipelago consisting of more than 3,000 islands. Four large islands—Hokkaido, Honshu, Shikoku, Kyushu—comprise about 98% of the land area. The Sea of Japan separates the country from the Soviet Union to the northwest, the Korean peninsula to the west and China to the southwest.

AREA: 145,869 sq. miles

Land Use: 12.95% cropland; 1.63% permanent pasture; 67.91% forests and woodland; 17.51% other.
Arable Land: 12.95%
Arable Land per capita: 0.10 acres

POPULATION: 122,053,000 (1987 estimate)

Population Density: 837 inhabs. per sq. mile (1987 estimate)
Population Distribution: 76.50% urban (1985)

Population Growth Rate: 0.51% per year (1985-90 projection)

VITAL STATISTICS

Average Life Expectancy: 77.20 years (1985-90 projection)
Male: 74.50 years (1985-90 projection)
Female: 80.10 years (1985-90 projection)
Age Distribution: (1985)
0-14 .... 21.80%
15-64 .... 68.20%
65+ 10.00%
Median Age: 35.00 years (1985)
Maternal Mortality: 15.30 per 100,000 live births (1984)
Infant Mortality: 6.00 per 1,000 live births (1985-90 projection)

HEALTH CARE

Hospital Beds: 118.36 per 10,000 population (1982)
Doctors: 13.61 per 10,000 population (1982)

ETHNIC COMPOSITION: Japanese - 99.40%; other - 0.60% (mostly Korean).

RELIGION: Buddhism and Shintoism are the major religions, with various other faiths practiced by 16% of the population.

LANGUAGE: The official language is Japanese.

EDUCATION: Illiteracy: 1%. In 1985, there were 25,040 primary schools with 11,095,372 students; 11,131 secondary schools with 5,990,183 students; 5,453 high schools with 5,177,681 students; 62 technical colleges with 48,288 students; 543 junior colleges with 371,095 students; and 460 graduate schools and universities with 1,848,698 students.

ECONOMIC DATA

Expenditures by Function [as % of total]: (not available)
GDP per capita: $12,977 (1985)

TRAVEL NOTES

Climate: Japan has a temperate climate throughout the year, with the average annual temperature ranging from 41°F to 96°F. January and February are the coldest months, and June and September the hottest. Typhoons and heavy rains occur frequently during the summer.

Health Precautions: None.
Miscellaneous: Among the numerous tourist attractions in Japan are the pagodas and temples, and the traditional festivals and classical Kabuki theater.

GOVERNMENT

Japan (Nihon or Nippon) signed the armistice ending World War II on Sep 2, 1945. Under the terms of the surrender, Allied military forces began an occupation of Japan that officially lasted until a formal peace treaty went into effect on Apr 28, 1952. A new democratic Constitution, renouncing war and rejecting the Emperor's divinity, was promulgated in November 1946, and became effective May 3, 1947. The Liberal Democratic Party, formed in 1955 with the merger of rival conservative political parties, dominated the first elections held under the new Constitution and has remained the ruling party ever since.

Constitution: The Constitution of 1946 established a constitutional monarchy, with the Emperor stripped of all governing power and granted the ceremonial title of head of state. The Cabinet, headed by a Prime Minister, who is the leader of the majority party, wields executive power. Legislative authority is vested in the bicameral Diet, which consists of a House of Councillors and a House of Representatives. War as a means of settling international disputes is renounced in Article 9 of the Constitution, along with the maintenance of armed forces (although a "Self Defense Force" consisting of about 250,000 people has since been formed). In addition, the Constitution provides for numerous civil rights, including freedom of thought and conscience, and freedom of the press. On Jul 3, 1964, the Japanese Commission on the Constitution, established to consider a possible revision, stated in its report that "the post-war Constitution was forced on the country by the occupation authorities" and recommended that it "be replaced by a document based on the free will of the people." However, no changes have been made yet due to the political difficulty of making such an amendment.

JORDAN
Hashemite Kingdom of Jordan

LOCATION: Jordan is a nearly landlocked country in western Asia, with the port of Aqaba in the south giving it a narrow outlet to the Red Sea. Located in the Middle East, Jordan is bounded by Syria to the north, Iraq to the northeast, Saudi Arabia to the east and south and Israel to the west.

AREA: 37,738 sq. miles (includes Israeli-occupied West Bank)

Land Use: 4.27% cropland; 1.03% permanent pasture; 0.42% forests and woodland; 94.28% other (mostly desert).
Arable Land: 4.27%
Arable Land per capita: 0.26 acres

POPULATION: 3,958,000 (1988 estimate)

Population Density: 105 inhabs. per sq. mile (1988 estimate)
Population Distribution: 64.40% urban (1985)
Population Growth Rate: 3.99% (1985-90 projection)

VITAL STATISTICS

Average Life Expectancy: 66.00 years (1985-90 projection)
Male: 64.10 years (1985-90 projection)
Female: 68.00 years (1985-90 projection)
Age Distribution: (1985)
0-14 .... 48.20%
15-64 .... 49.10%
65+ 2.70%
Median Age: 15.80 years (1985)
Maternal Mortality: (not available)
Infant Mortality: 44 per 1,000 live births (1985-90 projection)

HEALTH CARE

Hospital Beds: 10 per 10,000 population (1985)
Doctors: 7 per 10,000 population (1985)

ETHNIC COMPOSITION: East Bank: Arab - 98%; Circassian - 1%; Armenian - 1%. West Bank: Arab - 88%; Jewish - 12%.

RELIGION: East Bank: Sunni Moslem - 95%; Christian - 5%. West Bank: Moslem (mainly Sunni) - 80%; Jewish - 12%; other - 8% (mainly Christian).

LANGUAGE: Arabic is the official language.

EDUCATION: Illiteracy is about 29%. In 1984/85, there were 3,065 schools with 34,119 teachers and 863,892 students.

ECONOMIC DATA

Expenditures by Function [as % of total]: (1985)
General public services 12.20%
Defense 26.71%
Education 12.23%
Health 3.82%
Social security and welfare 7.75%
Housing and community amenities 0.80%
Other community and social services 2.45%
Economic services 22.46%
Agriculture, forestry, fishing and hunting ..1.70%
Roads 0.49%
Other transportation and communication ...0.30%
Other purposes 7.78%
GDP per capita: $1,281 (1986)

TRAVEL NOTES

Climate: Jordan's climate is hot and dry, with an average annual temperature of 60°F. The rainy season lasts from November to April, but inadequate rainfall is a recurring problem.
Health Precautions: No vaccinations are required, but immunizations against cholera, tetanus, typhoid fever and polio are recommended. Precautions against hepatitis and malaria are also suggested.
Miscellaneous: Popular tourist attractions include the ancient cities of Jerash and Petra, and the archaeological remains of Roman palaces and theaters, Moslem shrines and Medieval castles.

GOVERNMENT

Jordan (al-Mamlakah al-Urduniyah al-Hashimiyah—Hashemite Kingdom of Jordan), formerly a part of the Ottoman Empire, was placed under British administration by a League of Nations mandate in 1920. Jordan became an independent state on May 25, 1946, and a constitutional monarchy was established, with effective political power being held by the King. The Arab-Israeli War in 1967 resulted in the loss to Israel of all territory west of the Jordan River.

Constitution: The Constitution, adopted on Jan 8, 1952, established a constitutional monarchy, which provided for the sharing of authority between the King and the legislature. In theory, executive power is vested in the King, who is assisted by an appointed Council of Ministers, with the King and a bicameral National Assembly wielding legislative power. In fact, however, the King exercises complete authority, serving as commander-in-chief of the armed forces, possessing the authority to appoint a Cabinet, order elections, convene and dissolve the Assembly and approve and implement laws.

KENYA
Republic of Kenya

LOCATION: Lying in east Africa, Kenya is bordered by Tanzania to the south, Uganda to the west, Ethiopia and Sudan to the north and Somalia and the Indian Ocean to the east.

AREA: 224,100 sq. miles

Land Use: 4.07% cropland; 6.59% permanent pasture; 6.62% forests and woodland; 82.72% other (mainly desert).
Arable Land: 4%
Arable Land per capita: 0.31 acres

POPULATION: 22,810,000 (1988 estimate)

Population Density: 102 inhabs. per sq. mile (1988 estimate)
Population Distribution: 19.67% urban (1985)
Population Growth Rate: 3.90% per year (1988 estimate)

VITAL STATISTICS

Average Life Expectancy: 55.30 years (1985-90 projection)
Male: 53.50 years (1985-90 projection)
Female: 57.10 years (1985-90 projection)
Age Distribution: (1985)
0-14 .... 52.53%
15-64 .... 45.67%
65+ 1.80%
Median Age: 14.10 years (1985)
Maternal Mortality: (not available)
Infant Mortality: 59 per 1,000 live births (1985)

HEALTH CARE

Hospital Beds: 15 per 10,000 population (1984)
Doctors: 1 per 10,000 population (1984)

ETHNIC COMPOSITION: Kikuyu - 21%; Luhya - 14%; Luo - 13%; Kamba - 11%; Kalenjin - 11%; Meru - 6%; Kisii - 6%; other - 18%.

RELIGION: Protestant - 38%; Catholic - 28%; traditional beliefs - 26%; Moslem - 6%; other - 2%.

LANGUAGE: Kiswahili is the official language. English, Kikuyu, Somali and Luo are also widely spoken.

EDUCATION: Illiteracy: 53% (1987). In 1985, there were 12,936 primary schools with 4,702,414 students; 2,413 secondary schools with approximately 500,000 students; 34 technical schools with 12,138 students; 24 polytechnic and teacher-training institutions with 17,258 students; and 3 universities with approximately 10,000 students.

ECONOMIC DATA

Expenditures by Function [as % of total]: (1985)
General public services 16.09%
Defense 8.72%
Education 19.75%
Health 6.43%
Social security and welfare 0.12%
Housing and community amenities 0.37%
Other community and social services 3.81%
Economic services 27.65%
Agriculture, forestry, fishing and hunting 10.40%
Roads 4.60%
Other transportation and communication . . .0.40%
Other purposes 17.05%
GDP per capita: $333 (1986)

TRAVEL NOTES

Climate: The coastal zone is hot and humid, with average temperatures ranging between 69°F and 90°F. In the interior highland areas, temperatures average from 45°F to 80°F. While the highlands and western areas receive ample rainfall, most northern parts are arid. The rainy season lasts from April to May, while June through September is cool and dry, October and November experience some amounts of rain and December through March is hot and sunny.
Health Precautions: A yellow fever certificate is required for entry to Kenya. Outside of Nairobi, where the water is not potable, precautions should be taken against malaria.
Miscellaneous: Kenya boasts 15 National Parks and 23 public game reserves. Tourists also

enjoy Kenya's excellent climate and coastal area.

GOVERNMENT

Kenya (Djumhuri ya Kenya—Republic of Kenya) became an independent state within the Commonwealth on Dec 12, 1963, with the British monarch as nominal head of state. On Dec 12, 1964, it became a republic. Kenya is a one-party state with effective political authority resting with the Kenya African National Union (KANU), led by President Daniel arap Moi. However, the political system has undergone periodic crises stemming from tribal rivalries and recent accusations of Government human rights violations.

Constitution: The republican Constitution of Dec 12, 1964, established a strong central government, and subsequent amendments have increased the power of the central authorities at the expense of regional and local governments, which had enjoyed substantial powers prior to independence. The Constitution provides guarantees of individual rights (including freedom of speech and assembly, privacy and compensation for confiscated property). In certain matters (e.g., human rights, land-holding), the Constitution may be amended only by a majority vote of 65% of the National Assembly. In other matters, failing the 65% majority, amendments may be adopted by a two-thirds vote in a national referendum. In practice, however, the dominance of KANU in the National Assembly is such that government-sponsored amendments can easily receive the required majority.

KIRIBATI
Republic of Kiribati

LOCATION: Kiribati is composed of three principal groups of islands, containing 33 atolls, scattered over 2,000,000 square miles in the mid-Pacific Ocean. Located near where the equator meets the international dateline, Kiribati lies to the north of Tuvalu and Tokelau, and to the east of Nauru.

AREA: 277 sq. miles

Land Use: (not available)
Arable Land: 0%
Arable Land per capita: 0 acres

POPULATION: 65,000 (1988 estimate)

Population Density: 235 inhabs. per sq. mile (1988 estimate)
Population Distribution: (not available)
Population Growth Rate: 1.10% (1988 estimate)

VITAL STATISTICS

Average Life Expectancy: (not available)
Male: (not available)
Female: (not available)
Age Distribution: (not available)
Maternal Mortality: (not available)
Infant Mortality: 68 per 1,000 live births (1985 estimate)

HEALTH CARE

Hospital Beds: 45 per 10,000 population (1982)
Doctors: 3 per 10,000 population (1982)

ETHNIC COMPOSITION: Kiribatians are mostly Micronesian, although some are Polynesian.

RELIGION: Roman Catholic - 48%; Protestant - 45%; other - 7%.

LANGUAGE: The main languages are I-Kiribati (Gilbertese) and English.

EDUCATION: Illiteracy: 10% (1988). In 1986, there were 112 primary schools with 13,440 students and 6 secondary schools with 1,567 students. In 1983 there were 799 vocational school students and one teacher training school with 80 students.

ECONOMIC DATA

Expenditures by Function [as % of total]: (not available)
GDP per capita: $323 (1985 estimate)

TRAVEL NOTES

Climate: Kiribati experiences a tropical climate, with daytime temperatures ranging from 79°F to 90°F. Annual rainfall averages vary from 118 inches to 28 inches.
Health Precautions: (not available)
Miscellaneous: Although the number of tourists

visiting Kiribati is small due to the remoteness of the islands, some tourists are attracted by the islands' historical significance; the islands of Kiribati were the site of some of the bloodiest battles during World War II.

GOVERNMENT

Kiribati (Republic of Kiribati) was formerly known as the Gilbert Islands. Kiribati (pronounced "Kiribass") first became a British protectorate in 1892, finally becoming an independent republic within the Commonwealth on Jul 12, 1979. Ieremia Tabai became President upon independence, but his Government fell during a Parliamentary crisis in December 1982 and an interim three-member Council of State assumed governing responsibilities. Tabia, however, regained the Presidency in elections held the following February.

Constitution: The Constitution states that Kiribati is a "sovereign democratic Republic" and that the Constitution is the supreme law. It makes provision for finance and a public service, and contains a special provision for the island of Banaba, site of the nation's once lucrative phosphate mines.
BANABA. A chapter of the Constitution states that one seat in the Assembly is reserved for a nominated member of the Banaban community. The Constitution guarantees the Banabans' inalienable right to enter and reside in Banaba which, due to environmental factors stemming from open-pit mining for phosphate, has been virtually evacuated by its original inhabitants, most of whom reside on Rabi Island, some 1,560 miles away in the Fiji group. The Constitution ensures that any land rights usurped by the state for phosphate mining will revert to the original landowners or their heirs upon completion of mining operations. The Constitution also provides for a Banaba Island Council and the creation of an independent Commission of Inquiry to review the operation of the Constitution's special provisions for Banabans and to make "such recommendations as it thinks fit" to the Assembly.

KOREA, NORTH
See North Korea

KOREA, SOUTH
See South Korea

KUWAIT
State of Kuwait

LOCATION: Lying at the northwestern end of the Persian (Arabian) Gulf, Kuwait is bordered to the northwest by Iraq and to the south by Saudi Arabia.

AREA: 6,880 sq. miles

Land Use: 99% desert, waste or urban; 1% forest and cultivated.
Arable Land: 1%
Arable Land per capita: 2.49 acres

POPULATION: 1,771,000 (1986)

Population Density: 257 inhabs. per sq. mile (1986)
Population Distribution: 84% urban (1975)
Population Growth Rate: 3.50% per year (1986)

VITAL STATISTICS

Average Life Expectancy: 68.95 years (1984)
Male: 66.40 years (1984)
Female: 71.50 years (1984)
Age Distribution: (1983)
0-14 . . . . .40.20%
15-59 . . . . .57.60%
60+ 2.30%
Median Age: (not available)
Maternal Mortality: (not available)
Infant Mortality: 26.10 per 1,000 live births (1985)

HEALTH CARE

Hospital Beds: 44.56 per 10,000 population (1983)
Doctors: 17.48 per 10,000 population (1983)

ETHNIC COMPOSITION: Kuwaiti - 39%; other Arab - 39%; South Asian - 9%; Iranian - 4%; other - 9%.

RELIGION: Moslem - 85%; Christian, Hindu, Parsi and other - 15%.

LANGUAGE: Arabic is the official language. English is also widely spoken.

EDUCATION: Illiteracy: 29%. In 1985, there were 183 primary schools with 126,441 students; 164 intermediate schools with 119,037 students; 102 secondary schools with 77,626 students; 4 religious institutes with 1,175 students; and 29 special training institutes with 1,928 students.

ECONOMIC DATA

Expenditures by Function [as % of total]: (1984)

General public services	15.23%
Defense	13.78%
Education	10.70%
Health	6.27%
Social security and welfare	8.93%
Housing and community amenities	8.47%
Other community and social services	1.71%
Economic services	26.39%
Agriculture, forestry, fishing and hunting	0.26%
Roads	2.86%
Other transportation and communication	2.03%
Other purposes	8.53%

GDP per capita: $12,025 (1985)

TRAVEL NOTES

Climate: The climate is hot and humid, and summer temperatures may exceed 122°F; winter temperatures drop as low as 27°F. Most of the country is arid desert. Annual rainfall ranges from 0.40 inches to 14.60 inches.

Health Precautions: Health service is among the finest in the world. Fruits and vegetables must be treated and meat should be well-cooked.

Miscellaneous: Travelers to Kuwait should have Kuwaiti visas, and passports should be free of any Israeli stamp. Women are required to dress conservatively in public places.

GOVERNMENT

Kuwait (Dawlat al-Kuwayt—State of Kuwait) was a British protectorate from 1899 until Jun 19, 1961 when it assumed full control over its internal and external affairs. Kuwait is a constitutional monarchy, with effective political authority resting with the ruling dynasty and its traditional supporters. The continuing dominance of the traditional authorities is explained by the systematic exclusion of all foreigners from the political process and government office, despite the fact that native Kuwaitis are in a minority. On Jul 3, 1986 the National Assembly was dissolved, parts of the Constitution suspended and press censorship imposed. A new Government was formed Jul 13, 1986.

Constitution: The present Constitution, promulgated on Nov 16, 1962, concentrates political authority in the monarch, the Emir, who rules with the assistance of an elected legislature and appointed cabinet. The Constitution proclaims Islam as the state religion, but also guarantees freedom of worship. It declares all Kuwaitis to be equal before the law in status and in rights and duties, and provides constitutional guarantees of freedom of opinion and other civil liberties. The Constitution prohibits offensive war. The Emir partially suspended the Constitution on Jul 3, 1986.

LAOS
Lao People's Democratic Republic

LOCATION: Laos is a landlocked country in Southeast Asia, bounded by China to the north, Vietnam to the east, Cambodia to the south, Thailand to the west and Burma to the northwest.

AREA: 91,400 sq. miles

Land Use: 3.86% cropland; 3.47% permanent pasture; 58.06% forests and woodland; 34.61% other.

Arable Land: 4%

Arable Land per capita: 0.54 acres

POPULATION: 4,322,000 (1987 estimate)

Population Density: 47 inhabs. per sq. mile (1987 estimate)

Population Distribution: 15.90% urban (1985)

Population Growth Rate: 2.43% per year (1985-90 projection)

VITAL STATISTICS

Average Life Expectancy: 52.00 years (1985-90 projection)

Male: 50.50 years (1985-90 projection)

Female: 53.50 years (1985-90 projection)

Age Distribution: (1985)

0-14 .... 42.50%

15-64 .... 54.40%

65+ 3.10%

Median Age: 18.50 years (1985)

Maternal Mortality: (not available)

Infant Mortality: 110 per 1,000 live births (1985-90 projection)

HEALTH CARE

Hospital Beds: 23.82 per 10,000 population (1985)

Doctors: 1.35 per 10,000 population (1985)

ETHNIC COMPOSITION: Lao - 48%; Phoutheung (Kha) - 25%; Tai - 14%; other - 13% (mainly Meo and Yao).

RELIGION: Buddhist - 50%; other - 50% (mainly animist).

LANGUAGE: Lao is the official language. French, English and numerous tribal languages, including Meo, are also widely spoken.

EDUCATION: Illiteracy: 15%. In 1982/83, there were 6,525 first level schools with 480,871 students; 419 second level schools with 64,500 students; 60 third level schools with 17,492 students; and 55 vocational institutions with 13,132 students.

ECONOMIC DATA

Expenditures by Function [as % of total]: (not available)

GDP per capita: $136 (1983)

TRAVEL NOTES

Climate: Laos has a tropical climate, with a rainy season lasting from May to September. The coolest temperatures during the year occur from October to January, while March and April are the hottest months. There is high humidity year-round.

Health Precautions: A cholera inoculation is required and immunizations against hepatitis, yellow fever, typhoid, typhus, poliomyelitis and tetanus are strongly recommended. The water is not potable.

Miscellaneous: The country's main attractions are its dense jungles, rugged mountains and the Mekong, one of the world's largest rivers. Laos has a wide and fascinating variety of insects, reptiles and colorful tropical flowers.

GOVERNMENT

Laos (Sathalanalat Paxathipatai Paxaxon Lao—Lao People's Democratic Republic) became a French protectorate in 1893 and gained limited self-government as a member of the French Union on Jun 19, 1949. The last French ties to Laos were severed in December 1954 under the Geneva accords. The Communists seized control of the Government in the summer of 1975, following the fall of neighboring Cambodia and South Vietnam to communist insurgents. On Dec 2, a National Congress of People's Representatives abolished the monarchy and established the People's Democratic Republic. Laos became a one-party state, with effective political authority held by the Lao People's Revolutionary Party. Since 1975, Laos has been heavily dependent on Vietnam for economic and military aid; there are an estimated 50,000 Vietnamese troops stationed in the country.

Constitution: A 264-member National Congress of People's Representatives was elected in 1975 by local government officials. The Congress appointed a 45-member Supreme People's Assembly, which was charged with drafting a new constitution, but the document has yet to be drawn up.

LEBANON
Republic of Lebanon

LOCATION: Lebanon is located in western Asia on the eastern edge of the Mediterranean Sea and is bordered by Syria to the east and north, and Israel to the south.

AREA: 4,036 sq. miles

Land Use: 29.13% cropland; 0.98% permanent pasture; 8.11% forests and woodland; 61.78% other (mostly desert).

Arable Land: 29.13%

Arable Land per capita: 0.29 acres

POPULATION: 2,762,000 (1987)

Population Density: 684 inhabs. per sq. mile (1987)

Population Distribution: 80.10% urban (1985)

Population Growth Rate: 2.13% per year (1985-90 projection)

VITAL STATISTICS

Average Life Expectancy: 67.20 years (1985-90 projection)
Male: 65.10 years (1985-90 projection)
Female: 69.50 years (1985-90 projection)
Age Distribution: (1985)
0-14 .... 37.50%
15-64 .... 57.40%
65+ 5.10%
Median Age: 20.20 years (1985)
Maternal Mortality: (not available)
Infant Mortality: 39 per 1,000 live births (1985-90 projection)

HEALTH CARE

Hospital Beds: 43 per 10,000 population (1982)
Doctors: 11 per 10,000 population (1982)

ETHNIC COMPOSITION: Lebanese - 82%; Palestinian - 9%; Armenian - 5%; other - 4%.

RELIGION: Moslem and Druze - 57%; Christian (mostly Maronite and Greek Orthodox) - 42%; other - 1%.

LANGUAGE: Arabic is the official language, while French is a common second language, and Kurdish, English and Armenian are spoken by some.

EDUCATION: Illiteracy: 25%. In 1982, there were 382,500 primary school students, 258,353 secondary school students, 39,933 vocational school students and 73,052 students in institutions of higher learning. In 1980 there were 1,663 students in teacher training schools.

ECONOMIC DATA

Expenditures by Function [as % of total]: (1985)
General public services .... (not available)
Defense 21.52%
Education 14.41%
Health 3.17%
Social security and welfare .... (not available)
Housing and community amenities 0.46%
Other community and
    social services .... (not available)
Economic services 1.41%
Agriculture, forestry, fishing and hunting .. 1.08%
Roads .... (not available)
Other transportation and communication .. 6.93%
Other purposes .... (not available)
GDP per capita: $412 (1985)

TRAVEL NOTES

Climate: The climate varies with altitude. The lowlands on the coast are hot and humid in the summer and mild and damp in the winter. Weather in the mountains is cool in the summer with heavy snowfall in the winter.
Health Precautions: (not available)
Miscellaneous: Before the beginning of the civil war in 1975, Lebanon was a major tourist center because of its natural beauty and such historic sites as Baalbek and Byblos.

GOVERNMENT

Lebanon (al-Jumhuriyah al-Lubnaniyah— Republic of Lebanon) is a republic with a parliamentary form of government. Independence was declared on Nov 26, 1941; full autonomy was achieved in December 1946 after the withdrawal of French troops, which had been in the country under a League of Nations mandate since 1920. The Lebanese Government has been virtually irrelevant for over a decade due to a civil war that began in 1975. The country is now effectively divided into spheres of influence by various religious and ethnic factions.

Constitution: The Constitution was promulgated on May 23, 1926, and has been amended several times. It established a unicameral legislature and an independent judiciary. The head of state is elected by the legislature. The National Pact of 1943 provided for the allocation of Government offices among various religious and ethnic groups. In April 1984 the National Pact was amended somewhat to enhance the representation of various Moslem factions in the executive and legislative branches.

LESOTHO
Kingdom of Lesotho

LOCATION: Located in southern Africa, Lesotho is a landlocked country completely surrounded by the Republic of South Africa.

AREA: 11,720 sq. miles

Land Use: 9.82% cropland; 65.90% permanent pasture; 0% forests and woodland; 24.28% other.
Arable Land: 10%
Arable Land per capita: 0.51 acres

POPULATION: 1,637,000 (1988 estimate)

Population Density: 140 inhabs. per sq. mile (1988 estimate)

Population Distribution: 16.72% urban (1985)

Population Growth Rate: 2.70% per year (1988 estimate)

VITAL STATISTICS

Average Life Expectancy: 51.30 years (1985-90 projection)

Male: 48.30 years (1985-90 projection)

Female: 54.30 years (1985-90 projection)

Age Distribution: (1985)

0-14 .... 42.33%
15-64 .... 54.11%
65+ 3.56%

Median Age: 18.80 years (1985)

Maternal Mortality: (not available)

Infant Mortality: 98 per 1,000 live births (1985)

HEALTH CARE

Hospital Beds: 16 per 10,000 population (1982)

Doctors: 1 per 10,000 population (1984)

ETHNIC COMPOSITION: Basotho - 99.70%; other - 0.30% (mainly European and Asian).

RELIGION: Christian - 80%; other - 20% (mainly indigenous beliefs).

LANGUAGE: English and Sesotho are the official languages. Xhosa and Zulu are also spoken.

EDUCATION: Illiteracy: 35% (1987). In 1984, there were 1,170 university students. In 1983, there were 1,152 primary schools with 289,590 students; 31,422 secondary school students; and 1,197 vocational students. In 1982, there were 108 secondary schools; 1 teacher-training college with 1,136 students; 11 technical and vocational schools; and 1 university.

ECONOMIC DATA

Expenditures by Function [as % of total]: (1985)

General public services 28.11%
Defense 9.62%
Education 15.49%
Health 6.87%
Social security and welfare 1.01%
Housing and community amenities 0.46%
Other community and social services 0.63%
Economic services 25.50%

Agriculture, forestry, fishing and hunting ..8.04%
Roads 8.12%
Other transportation and communication 2.54%
Other purposes 12.31%

GDP per capita: $236 (1987)

TRAVEL NOTES

Climate: The climate is generally mild, although it is somewhat cooler in the highlands than in the lowlands. Rainfall averages about 28 inches per year, with the rainy season occurring between October and April. Lowland temperatures average around 80°F in the summer and 40°F in the winter; highlands temperatures can be cooler.

Health Precautions: Yellow fever vaccinations are required; immunizations against cholera, polio and typhoid are recommended. Tap water is potable in Maseru.

Miscellaneous: Tourists are attracted by the country's scenic beauty, including beautiful mountains, picturesque villages, spectacular waterfalls and the national park at Sehlabathebe.

GOVERNMENT

Lesotho (Kingdom of Lesotho), formerly the British colony of Basutoland, became an independent sovereign state within the Commonwealth of Nations on Oct 4, 1966. Effective political authority rested with Prime Minister Leabua Jonathan, who ruled with the aid of his Basotho National Party (BNP) and the security forces, until a Jan 20, 1986 military coup. The coup followed the dissolution of the National Assembly by the King on Jan 1, 1985 and several unfulfilled promises of general elections, and came amid a growing national crisis created by a blockade of the country by South Africa, which deprived Lesotho of essential supplies. The new ruler, Maj. Gen. Justin Lekhanya, has created a Military Council to govern in the name of the King.

Constitution: The 1966 independence Constitution (suspended since Jan 31, 1970) provided for a constitutional monarchy with a parliamentary form of government patterned on that of Britain. In May 1983 Prime Minister Leabua Jonathan repealed the emergency order suspending the Constitution and established a framework to serve as a Constitution. This framework, however, was repealed by Maj. Gen. Lekhanya following the 1986 coup, and a system was established with executive and legislative power held by the King, to be aided by a Military Council and a Council of Ministers.

LIBERIA
Republic of Liberia

LOCATION: Liberia is situated on the west coast of Africa, with Sierra Leone and Guinea on the north and the Cote d'Ivoire on the east.

AREA: 37,743 sq. miles

Land Use: 3.85% cropland; 2.49% permanent pasture; 39.04% forests and woodlands; 54.62% other (mostly jungle and swamp).
Arable Land: 4%
Arable Land per capita: 0.44 acres

POPULATION: 2,336,000 (1987 projection)

Population Density: 59 inhabs. per sq. mile (1986)
Population Distribution: 39.50% urban (1985)
Population Growth Rate: 3.25% per year (1985-90 projection)

VITAL STATISTICS

Average Life Expectancy: 51.00 years (1985-90 projection)
Male: 49.30 years (1985-90 projection)
Female: 52.70 years (1985-90 projection)
Age Distribution: (1985)
0-14 .... 46.80%
15-64 .... 50.20%
65+ 3.00%
Median Age: 16.60 years (1985)
Maternal Mortality: (not available)
Infant Mortality: 122 per 1,000 live births (1985-90 projection)

HEALTH CARE

Hospital Beds: (not available)
Doctors: 0.90 per 10,000 population (1980)

ETHNIC COMPOSITION: Indigenous Africans (including Kpelle, Bassa, Gio, Kru, Grebo, Mano, Krahn, Gola, Gbandi, Loma, Kissi, Vai and Bella) - 95%; Americo-Liberians (descendants of black American settlers) - 5%.

RELIGION: Liberia is officially a Christian state. Indigenous beliefs - 70%; Islam - 20%; Christianity - 10%.

LANGUAGE: English is the official language. There are about 20 local dialects based on the Niger-Congo language; English is used by about 20% of the population.

EDUCATION: Illiteracy: 76%. In 1981 there were 1,635 primary and secondary schools with 303,168 pupils; in 1985, there was one university in Monrovia with 3,317 pupils. There are three other institutions of higher learning.

ECONOMIC DATA

Expenditures by Function [as % of total]: (1984)
General public services 19.44%
Defense 7.57%
Education 14.64%
Health 6.20%
Social security and welfare 0.80%
Housing and community amenities 0.74%
Other community and social services 2.61%
Economic services 26.71%
Agriculture, forestry, fishing and hunting ..5.63%
Roads................................7.71%
Other transportation and communication ...1.07%
Other purposes 21.28%
GDP per capita: $327 (1985)

TRAVEL NOTES

Climate: Liberia's climate is one-season tropical. There is a rainy period from April to November, which is characterized by frequent, prolonged and often torrential rainfalls. The humidity is very high, normally between 70% and 90%.
Health Precautions: Malaria is endemic nationwide, as is schistosomiasis in the interior of the country. Malaria suppressants should be taken regularly. All drinking water should be boiled and filtered and locally purchased meat thoroughly cooked. It is advisable to stay out of fresh water, particularly in the interior.
Miscellaneous: There are numerous beautiful beaches in Monrovia. The rivers and ocean provide excellent fishing, and there are various locations across the country for hunting. Erosion and mud make unpaved roads difficult to travel or unpassable during the rainy season, while long drives are dusty in the dry season.

GOVERNMENT

Liberia (Republic of Liberia) has its origins in the efforts of US philanthropic societies to establish colonies of freed American slaves on the west African coast in the 1820s. On Jul 26, 1847, the state was constituted as the Free and Independent Republic of Liberia. The US influence in the founding of Liberia was strongly reflected in the 1847 Constitution, which was modeled on the US Constitution of 1787. It established a government with a strong President and a system of separation of powers. In January 1986, Liberia returned to civilian rule after 4 years under a People's Redemption Council set up by Gen. Samuel K. Doe, who took power in a coup in 1980. Elections preceding the return to civilian rule were rigged, according to opposition politicians, and a subsequent aborted coup was reportedly widely celebrated by civilians who at first believed it to have been successful. Partial elections in December 1986 were boycotted by the 4 major opposition parties, who accused the electoral commission of illegal procedures. President Doe's National Democratic Party of Liberia swept all 6 seats in the National Legislature and won 24 of the 29 municipal posts.

Constitution: In anticipation of the 1986 return to civilian rule, the People's Redemption Council presented a draft constitution, which was accepted by 78.3% of the registered voters in a public referendum on Jul 3, 1984. The Constitution, which went into effect on Jan 6, 1987, provides for the division of government into the independent branches of legislature, executive and judiciary, and for a multi-party system of government.

LIBYA
Socialist People's Libyan Arab Jamahiriya

LOCATION: Libya is located in North Africa and is bordered by Egypt to the east, Sudan to the southeast, Chad and Niger to the south and Algeria and Tunisia to the west. The Mediterranean Sea lies to the north.

AREA: 685,524 sq. miles

Land Use: 1.20% cropland; 7.54% permanent pasture; 0.36% forests and woodland; 90.90% other (mostly desert).
Arable Land: 1.20%
Arable Land per capita: 1.52 acres

POPULATION: 3,883,000 (1987 estimate)

Population Density: 5.66 inhabs. per sq. mile (1987)
Population Distribution: 64.50% urban (1985)
Population Growth Rate: 3.67% pcr ycar (1985-90 projection)

VITAL STATISTICS

Average Life Expectancy: 60.80 years (1985-90 projection)
Male: 59.10 years (1985-90 projection)
Female: 62.50 years (1985-90 projection)
Age Distribution: (1985)
0-14 . . . . .46.40%
15-64 . . . . .51.30%
65+ 2.30%
Median Age: 16.80 years (1985)
Maternal Mortality: (not available)
Infant Mortality: 82 per 1,000 live births (1985-90 projection)

HEALTH CARE

Hospital Beds: 48.23 per 10,000 population (1982)
Doctors: 15.65 per 10,000 population (1982)

ETHNIC COMPOSITION: Berber and Arab - 97%; other - 3%.

RELIGION: Sunni Moslem - 97%; other - 3%.

LANGUAGE: Arabic is the official language. English and Italian are also spoken in the major cities.

EDUCATION: Illiteracy: 33.10% (1985 estimate). In 1982/83, there were 2,744 primary schools with 741,502 students; 1,350 preparatory schools with 239,679 students; 205 secondary schools with 61,736 students; 117 teacher training schools with 30,002 students and 78 technical schools with 20,361 students.

ECONOMIC DATA

Expenditures by Function [as % of total]: (not available)
GDP per capita: $5,345 (1986 estimate)

TRAVEL NOTES

Climate: The climate is hot and arid, although the coastal areas are cooler than the interior. Average temperature ranges are from 55°F to 100°F.

Health Precautions: Smallpox, typhoid, tetanus, cholera and polio inoculations are recommended.

Miscellaneous: Tourist attractions include the beaches and clubs of Tripoli, the Roman provincial cities of Leptis Magna, Sabratha and Cyrene, as well as the historic oases of Mizda and Ghadames.

GOVERNMENT

Libya (al-Jamahiriya al-'Arabiyah al-Libiya al-Sha'biya al-Ishtirakiya—The Great Socialist People's Libyan Arab Jamahiriya) was under Ottoman Turkish rule from the middle of the 16th century to the beginning of the 20th century. It was then successively controlled by Italy, Britain and France, until finally receiving its independence on Dec 24, 1951, as the United Kingdom of Libya. The monarchy was overthrown on Sep 1, 1969, in a bloodless military coup by a group of young officers under Col. Muammar Ghaddafi. The officers established a Revolutionary Command Council (RCC), with Ghaddafi as Chairman, and proclaimed the Libyan Arab Republic. In March 1977, the word "republic" was dropped from the official name of the country and a newly coined Arab word, Jamahiriya, was substituted. It may be loosely translated as "a state of the public" or "state of the masses," and signifies the idea of the people governing themselves. At this time, Ghaddafi further solidified his base of authority within the new Government and assumed the title of Revolutionary Leader. He continues to be the dominant political figure in Libya.

Constitution: "The Declaration on the Establishment of the Authority of the People" (presented to the General People's Congress, meeting in special session on Feb 28-Mar 2, 1977) serves as the country's basic law. It provides for a government based on the Koran and Islamic law and direct popular authority through People's Committees, Trade Unions, Vocational Syndicates and People's Congresses. It also bans "all types of traditional means for ruling society including [rule by] individuals, family, tribe, religion, faction, party and groups of parties."

LIECHTENSTEIN
Principality of Liechtenstein

LOCATION: Liechtenstein is located in Western Europe, and is bordered by Switzerland on the south and west, and Austria on the northeast.

AREA: 62 sq. miles

Land Use: 25% cropland; 38% permanent pasture; 19% forests and woodland; 18% other.
Arable Land: 25%
Arable Land per capita: 0.33 acres

POPULATION: 30,000 (1989 estimate)

Population Density: 484 inhabs. per sq. mile (1989 estimate)
Population Distribution: (not available)
Population Growth Rate: 1.60% per year (1989)

VITAL STATISTICS

Average Life Expectancy: 72 years (1982)
Male: 65 years (1987)
Female: 74 years (1987)
Age Distribution: (not available)
Median Age: (not available)
Maternal Mortality: (not available)
Infant Mortality: 9 per 1,000 live births (1985)

HEALTH CARE

Hospital Beds: (not available)
Doctors: (not available)

ETHNIC COMPOSITION: Allemanic - 95%; Italian - 5%.

RELIGION: Roman Catholic - 83%; Protestant - 7%; other - 10%.

LANGUAGE: German is the official language; a German dialect, Allemanish, is most widely spoken.

EDUCATION: Illiteracy: 0%. In 1987/88, there were 14 primary schools with 1,754 students; 3 lower secondary schools with 447 students; 5 secondary schools with 786 students; and 1 grammar school with 474 students. There is 1 technical school.

ECONOMIC DATA

Expenditures by Function [as % of total]: (not available)

TRAVEL NOTES

Climate: Liechtenstein's climate is described as Alpine. In winter, the temperature rarely falls below 5°F while summer temperatures average between 68°F and 82°F.
Health Precautions: None
Miscellaneous: Attractions include skiing and the scenery of the Alps, and several notable museums in the capital.

GOVERNMENT

Liechtenstein (Fuerstentum Liechtenstein—Principality of Liechtenstein) is a constitutional monarchy that is hereditary in the male line. It has been a constituted independent state since 1719. In a series of treaties concluded after World War I, Switzerland assumed responsibility for the defense and routine diplomatic relations of Liechtenstein. Liechtenstein is incorporated in Swiss customs territory, and uses Swiss currency and postal services. On Aug 26, 1984, Prince Franz Josef II officially handed over executive authority to his heir, Crown Prince Hans Adam, but retained his official title and certain constitutional prerogatives.

Constitution: The Constitution, adopted on Oct 5, 1921, provides for a hereditary principality with a parliamentary system of government.

LUXEMBOURG
Grand Duchy of Luxembourg

LOCATION: Located in northwest Europe, Luxembourg is bordered by West Germany to the east, France to the south and Belgium to the northwest.

AREA: 999 sq. miles

Land Use: 25% cropland; 20% permanent pasture; 21% forests and woodland; 34% other.
Arable Land: 25%

Arable Land per capita: 0.43 acres

POPULATION: 369,000 (1989 estimate)

Population Density: 369 inhabs. per sq. mile (1989 estimate)
Population Distribution: 80.90% urban (1985)
Population Growth Rate: 0.20% per year (1989 estimate)

VITAL STATISTICS

Average Life Expectancy: 72.90 years (1985-90 projection)
Male: 68.90 years (1985-90 projection)
Female: 75.10 years (1985-90 projection)
Age Distribution: (1985)
0-14 . . . . .17.60%
15-64 . . . . .69.70%
65+ 12.70%
Median Age: 35.90 years (1985)
Maternal Mortality: 25 per 100,000 live births (1979)
Infant Mortality: 10 per 1,000 live births (1985)

HEALTH CARE

Hospital Beds: 125 per 10,000 population (1985)
Doctors: 18 per 10,000 population (1985)

ETHNIC COMPOSITION: The ethnic composition of the people of Luxembourg is a mix of German and French.

RELIGION: Roman Catholic - 97%; Protestant - 1%; other - 2%.

LANGUAGE: French and German are the official languages.

EDUCATION: Illiteracy: 0%. In 1986/87, there were 24,695 primary students, 7,951 secondary students, 15,562 technical students, 145 teacher training students and 3,034 university students.

ECONOMIC DATA

Expenditures by Function [as % of total]: (1984)
General public services 10.30%
Defense 2.18%
Education 8.33%
Health 2.23%
Social security and welfare 49.16%
Housing and community amenities 1.36%
Other community and social services 1.11%
Economic services 18.21%
Agriculture, forestry, fishing and hunting . .1.91%
Roads 5.00%

Other transportation and
communication 7.45%
Other purposes 7.12%
GDP per capita: $17,584 (1986)

TRAVEL NOTES

Climate: The climate is temperate with cool summers and rain and overcast conditions prevailing during the winter. The annual mean temperature is 49°F.

Health Precautions: None.

Miscellaneous: Luxembourg, known for its scenic beauty, offers visitors hiking trails and footpaths through the Ardennes Forest and tourist resorts surrounding medieval castles.

GOVERNMENT

Luxembourg (Grand-Duche de Luxembourg— Grossherzogtum Luxemburg—Grand Duchy of Luxembourg) was recognized as an independent sovereign state by the Treaty of London of 1867, but had previously enjoyed internal self-government since 1839, which the country considers its year of independence. Luxembourg is a constitutional monarchy with a parliamentary form of government.

Constitution: Luxembourg's Constitution was promulgated on Oct 17, 1868, but has been extensively revised since then. The Constituent Assembly of 1919 introduced democratic reforms that severely limited the independent authority of the monarch and shifted political power decisively to Parliament. The Constitution may be amended by special acts of Parliament.

MACAO

LOCATION: Located on the southern coast of the People's Republic of China at the mouth of the Canton River, Macao consists of a small peninsula and the islands of Taipa and Colaon.

AREA: 7 sq. miles

Land Use: 0% cropland; 0% permanent pasture; 0% forest and woodland; 100% other (urban).
Arable Land: 0%
Arable Land per capita: 0 acres

POPULATION: 429,000 (1989 estimate)

Population Density: 61,286 inhabs. per sq. mile (1989 estimate)
Population Distribution: 99% urban (1985)
Population Growth Rate: 1.70% per year (1989 estimate)

VITAL STATISTICS

Average Life Expectancy: (not available)
Male: (not available)
Female: (not available)
Age Distribution: (1970)
0-14 . . . . .37.50%
15-59 . . . . .55.10%
60+ 11.70%
Median Age: (not available)
Maternal Mortality: (not available)
Infant Mortality: 12 per 1,000 live births (1985)

HEALTH CARE

Hospital Beds: 61.20 per 10,000 population (1977)
Doctors: 10 per 10,000 population (1981)

ETHNIC COMPOSITION: Chinese - 95%; Portuguese - 3%; other - 2%.

RELIGION: Chinese Buddhist - 96%; Roman Catholic - 4%.

LANGUAGE: Portuguese is the official language, but Cantonese is the language most commonly used.

EDUCATION: Illiteracy: 1%. In 1985/86, there were 74 primary schools with 31,669 students; 31 secondary schools with 13,849 students; and 7 institutions of higher learning with 5,892 students. The University of East Asia had 1,000 students in 1987/88.

ECONOMIC DATA

Expenditures by Function [as % of total]: (not available)
GDP per capita: $4,831 (1987 estimate)

TRAVEL NOTES

Climate: Macao has mild winters and warm, tropical summers.
Health Precautions: Smallpox and yellow fever vaccinations are required.

Miscellaneous: Macao is becoming increasingly popular with tourists because of its fine hotels, casinos and dog tracks.

GOVERNMENT

Macao is a Chinese territory under the administration of Portugal. First used by the Portuguese as a trading port in 1557, Portugal formalized its administration over Macao by declaring it a Portuguese Overseas Possession in 1951. After Portugal's 1974 coup, the new Government tried to transfer Macao to the People's Republic of China, but the Chinese Government preferred to have the Portuguese maintain administrative control. On Mar 26, 1987, at the close of a 4th round of negotiations concerning Macao's future, China and Portugal signed an agreement under which the territory will become a "special administrative region" under the jurisdiction of the People's Republic of China in 1999. However, the Macanese Government will retain control over most internal matters, and China has agreed not to interfere with the capitalist economic system of the enclave for 50 years.

Constitution: In January 1976, Portugal approved a statute increasing Macao's autonomy over political and economic matters and upgrading its status to that of "Special Territory." Under the terms of the statute, Macao is ruled by a Governor who is appointed by Portugal's President after a conference with the legislative assembly of Macao.

MADAGASCAR
Democratic Republic of Madagascar

LOCATION: Madagascar comprises one large island (the world's 4th largest) and many smaller ones in the Indian Ocean about 300 miles off the southeast coast of Africa.

AREA: 226,658 sq. miles

Land Use: 5.18% cropland; 58.47% permanent pasture; 26.45% forests and woodland; 9.90% other.
Arable Land: 5%
Arable Land per capita: 0.77 acres

POPULATION: 11,148,000 (1989 estimate)

Population Density: 49 inhabs. per sq. mile (1989 estimate)
Population Distribution: 21.76% urban (1985)
Population Growth Rate: 2.90% per year (1989 estimate)

VITAL STATISTICS

Average Life Expectancy: 51.50 years (1985-90 projection)
Male: 50.80 years (1985-90 projection)
Female: 52.30 years (1985-90 projection)
Age Distribution: (1985)
0-14 . . . . .44.17%
15-64 . . . . .52.41%
65+ 3.42%
Median Age: 17.90 years (1985)
Maternal Mortality: (not available)
Infant Mortality: 101 per 1,000 live births (1985)

HEALTH CARE

Hospital Beds: 23 per 10,000 population (1982)
Doctors: 1 per 10,000 population (1982)

ETHNIC COMPOSITION: There are 18 ethnic groups, with Merina and Betsileo (Malayan-Indonesian groups) living in the highlands and Arab and African groups, collectively known as Cotiers, living along the coast. There is also a minority of European French, Indian French and Creoles.

RELIGION: Animist - 52%; Christian - 41%; Moslem - 7%.

LANGUAGE: French and Malagasy are the official languages, although many dialects, notably Hova, are also spoken.

EDUCATION: Illiteracy: 47%. In 1984, there were 13,973 primary schools with 1,625,216 students; 288,543 students at public general secondary schools; 9,204 students at public vocational secondary schools; and 37,746 students at institutes of higher learning. In 1983, there were 1,837 teacher training students at public schools.

ECONOMIC DATA

Expenditures by Function [as % of total]: (not available)
GDP per capita: $230 (1986)

TRAVEL NOTES

Climate: The climate is tropical, with a daily average maximum temperature of 90°F along the coast. Inland it is cooler. In the north, monsoons occur between December and April, but the rest of the island is generally dry. Cyclones also appear from time to time. Winter occurs from May to August, while summer lasts from December to February.

Health Precautions: Immunizations against yellow fever, typhoid, polio, diphtheria, tetanus and polio are recommended, as are regular gamma globulin injections and malaria suppressants. Tap water is not potable.

Miscellaneous: Tourist attractions include Madagascar's unique plant and animal wildlife, one of the world's best natural harbors and beautiful beaches.

GOVERNMENT

Madagascar (Repoblika Demokratika n'i Madagaskar—Republique Democratique de Madagascar—Democratic Republic of Madagascar), formerly a colony of France, was established as the Malagasy Republic within the French Community in 1958, gained independence in 1960 and has been under military rule since 1972. The country's name was changed from the Malagasy Republic to the Democratic Republic of Madagascar in a Dec 21, 1975 referendum.

Constitution: A new Constitution legitimizing the "Malagasy Socialist Revolution" was approved on Dec 21, 1975. The new Constitution provides for a President, a Supreme Revolutionary Council, a Cabinet headed by a Prime Minister, a National People's Assembly, a Military Development Committee and a Constitutional High Court.

MALAWI
Republic of Malawi

LOCATION: A landlocked country in east-central Africa, Malawi is bounded by Zambia to the west, Tanzania to the north and Mozambique to the south and east. Lake Malawi forms much of the eastern border.

AREA: 45,747 sq. miles

Land Use: 24.88% cropland; 19.56% permanent pasture; 50.40% forest and woodland; 5.16% other.
Arable Land: 25%
Arable Land per capita: 1.11 acres

POPULATION: 7,796,000 (1988 estimate)

Population Density: 170 inhabs. per sq. mile (1988 estimate)
Population Distribution: 12.04% urban (1985)
Population Growth Rate: 3.40% per year (1988 estimate)

VITAL STATISTICS

Average Life Expectancy: 47.00 years (1985-90 projection)
Male: 46.40 years (1985-90 projection)
Female: 47.70 years (1985-90 projection)
Age Distribution: (1985)
0-14 . . . . .45.98%
15-64 . . . . .51.45%
65+ 2.57%
Median Age: 16.90 years (1985)
Maternal Mortality: (not available)
Infant Mortality: 158 per 1,000 live births (1985)

HEALTH CARE

Hospital Beds: 19 per 10,000 population (1980)
Doctors: 0.20 per 10,000 population (1981)

ETHNIC COMPOSITION: Chewa - 90%; other (includes Nyanja, Lomwe and other Bantu tribes) - 10%.

RELIGION: Protestant - 55%; Roman Catholic - 20%, Moslem - 20%; other - 5%. Some members of all these groups also combine traditional beliefs and practices.

LANGUAGE: Chichewa and English are the official languages. Tombuka is also widely spoken.

EDUCATION: Illiteracy: 75%. In 1985/86, there were 924,539 primary school students; 25,177 secondary school students; 560 technical college students; and 1 university with 1,974 students.

ECONOMIC DATA

Expenditures by Function [as % of total]: (1985)
General public services 19.08%
Defense 5.99%

Education 11.03%
Health 6.87%
Social security and welfare 0.82%
Housing and community amenities 1.09%
Other community and social services 0.52%
Economic services 30.54%
Agriculture, forestry, fishing and hunting . . 8.44%
Roads 9.28%
Other transportation and communication . . 4.26%
Other purposes 20.46%
GDP per capita: $188 (1987)

TRAVEL NOTES

Climate: On the central plateau, the mean annual temperature is 67°F, and even during the warmest months nighttime temperatures are pleasantly cool. High winds and dust storms are common during the dry months of September and October.

Health Precautions: Recommended immunizations include cholera, typhus, yellow fever and gamma globulin. Precautions should be taken against malaria and schistosomiasis. The water is not potable.

Miscellaneous: The remote Nyika Park features beautiful scenery and a wide variety of wildlife. Steamer cruises on Lake Malawi are also very popular.

GOVERNMENT

Malawi (Republic of Malawi), the former British protectorate of Nyasaland, became an independent state within the Commonwealth of Nations on Jul 6, 1964, with the British monarch as the nominal head of state. On Jul 6, 1966, Malawi was proclaimed a republic and Hastings Kamuzu Banda was named as its President. Malawi is a one-party state with a strong presidential form of government. Effective political power rests with the Malawi Congress Party (MCP), led by President Banda.

Constitution: The Republican Constitution of Jul 6, 1966 enshrines the MCP as the only legal political party. Supreme state authority is vested in the President and the National Assembly. The Constitution may be amended by a two-thirds vote of the National Assembly.

MALAYSIA

LOCATION: Malaysia occupies two land masses in Southeast Asia. Peninsular Malaysia occupies the southern end of the Kra Peninsula, with the island of Singapore to the south, the Indonesian island of Sumatra to the south and southwest and Thailand bordering to the north.

AREA: 127,316 sq. miles

Land Use: 13.22% cropland; 0.08% permanent pasture; 62.52% forests and woodland; 24.19% other.
Arable Land: 13%
Arable Land per capita: 0.65 acres

POPULATION: 16,539,000 (1988 estimate)

Population Density: 130 inhabs. per sq. mile (1988 estimate)
Population Distribution: 38.20% urban (1985)
Population Growth Rate: 2.20% per year (1988 estimate)

VITAL STATISTICS

Average Life Expectancy: 68.60 years (1985-90 projection)
Male: 66.50 years (1985-90 projection)
Female: 70.80 years (1985-90 projection)
Age Distribution: (1985)
0-14 . . . . .37.80%
15-64 . . . . .58.40%
65+ 3.80%
Median Age: 20.70 years (1985)
Maternal Mortality: (not available)
Infant Mortality: 21 per 1,000 live births (1985)

HEALTH CARE

Hospital Beds: 23 per 10,000 population (1985)
Doctors: 3 per 10,000 population (1985)

ETHNIC COMPOSITION: Malay - 46%; Chinese - 32%; non-Malay indigenous peoples - 12%; Indian and Pakistani - 8%; other - 2%.

RELIGION: Islam is the state religion, but the Constitution guarantees the freedom to practice other religions. On Peninsular Malaysia, most Malays are Moslem, most Chinese are Buddhists and most Indians Hindus. In Sabah, percentages are as follows: Moslem - 38%; Christian - 17%; other (including animist) - 45%. Sarawak has the following breakdown: traditional beliefs - 35%; Buddhist and Confucian - 24%; Moslem - 20%; Christian - 16%; other - 5%.

LANGUAGE: Bahasa Malaysia, based on Malay, is the official language, but English is widely used. Tamil, Iban, Chinese dialects and tribal dialects are also spoken.

EDUCATION: Illiteracy: 35%. In 1986, there were 6,652 primary schools with 98,061 students; 1,162 general secondary schools with 58,223 students; 45 vocational secondary schools with 1,546 students; and 9 technical secondary schools with 363 students. In 1985, there were 27 teacher-training colleges with 1,701 students and 12 universities with 5,940 students.

ECONOMIC DATA

Expenditures by Function [as %of total]: (1986 estimate)
General public services . . . . (not available)
Defense 10.81%
Education 18.30%
Health 5.39%
Social security and welfare . . . . (not available)
Housing and community amenities . (not available)
Other community and social
 services . . . . (not available)
Economic services . . . . (not available)
Agriculture, forestry,
 fishing and hunting . . . . (not available)
Roads . . . . (not available)
Other transportation and
 communication . . . . (not available)
Other purposes . . . . (not available)
GDP per capita: $1,728 (1986)

TRAVEL NOTES

Climate: The climate is tropical, and temperatures fall between 72°F and 92°F year-round with little variation. Rain is common in all seasons, and the average annual rainfall of 100 inches creates high humidity.

Health Precautions: Health authorities recommend that visitors be inoculated against cholera, hepatitis, tetanus and typhoid, and that children and young adults receive in addition diphtheria and polio inoculations. Those who travel outside Kuala Lumpur should take precautions against malaria. Tap water is not potable.

Miscellaneous: In addition to the cultural diversity of its many ethnic groups, Malaysia's attractions include uncrowded beaches, jungle touring, island hopping and hilltop resorts.

GOVERNMENT

Malaysia has its origins in the 11 states of what is now west or Peninsular Malaysia, which united as the Federation of Malaysia in 1948, and on Aug 31, 1957 left British protection to become independent within the Commonwealth. On Sep 16, 1963, the Federation of Malaya (renamed the States of Malaya), the former British colonies of Sabah and Sarawak (now collectively known as east Malaysia) and the self-governing state of Singapore merged to form Malaysia; Singapore left the federation in August 1965. Malaysia is an elective constitutional monarchy, organized on a federal pattern, with parliamentary governments at both the federal and state levels. Malaysian political life has been troubled by tensions between its ethnic communities, particularly the Malays and the Chinese. Malays dominate the political structure.

Constitution: Malaysia's Constitution is based on that of the Federation of Malaya, amended to reflect the interests of Sabah and Sarawak, which joined in 1963. It dictates that the Yang di-Pertuan Agong (King or Supreme Sovereign) is the supreme head of state, and establishes a Majlis Raja Raja (Conference of Rulers), composed of the heads of Malacca, Penang, Sabah and Sarawak and of the leaders of Malaysia's other 9 states, who are hereditary rulers. The Conference of Rulers must be consulted on judicial and quasi-judicial appointments, proposed alterations of state boundaries, laws affecting the Islamic religion and proposed Constitutional amendments.

MALDIVES
Republic of Maldives

LOCATION: Lying in the Indian Ocean about 400 miles southwest of Sri Lanka, Maldives consists of over 2,000 islands (220 of which are inhabited) grouped into 19 atolls.

AREA: 115 sq. miles

Land Use: 10% cropland; 3% permanent pasture; 3% forests and woodland; 84% other (mostly tropical vegetation).
Arable Land: 10%
Arable Land per capita: 0.01 acres

POPULATION: 202,000 (1989 estimate)

Population Density: 1,756 inhabs. per sq. mile (1989 estimate)
Population Distribution: 26% urban (1985)
Population Growth Rate: 3% per year (1989 estimate)

VITAL STATISTICS

Average Life Expectancy: 46 years (1988)
Male: (not available)
Female: (not available)
Age Distribution: (1988)
0-14 . . . . 44.40%
15-59 . . . . 51.70%
60+ 3.90%
Median Age: (not available)
Maternal Mortality: (not available)
Infant Mortality: 81 per 1,000 live births (1985)

HEALTH CARE

Hospital Beds: (not available)
Doctors: 0.50 per 10,000 population (1981)

ETHNIC COMPOSITION: Maldivian ethnic groups include a mixture of Sinhalese, Dravidian, Arab and black.

RELIGION: The state religion is Islam, and most of the population is Sunni Moslem.

LANGUAGE: Dhivehi, which is related to Sinhala, is the official language. English is spoken by a small minority.

EDUCATION: Illiteracy: 64%. In 1986, there were 243 primary schools with 41,812 students; 9 secondary schools with 3,581 students; and 11 vocational schools with 544 students.

ECONOMIC DATA

Expenditures by Function [as % of total]: (1985)
General public services 37.81%
Defense 0%
Education 11.98%
Health 5.78%
Social security and welfare 3.69%
Housing and community amenities 19.57%
Other community and social services 0%
Economic services 16.20%
Agriculture, forestry, fishing and hunting . . 6.90%
Roads 0%
Other transportation and communication . . . 8.13%
Other purposes 4.97%
GDP per capita: $467 (1985)

TRAVEL NOTES

Climate: The average annual temperature is 80°F and yearly rainfall ranges between 100 and 150 inches.
Health Precautions: (not available)
Miscellaneous: Tourist attractions include white sandy beaches and colorful coral formations.

GOVERNMENT

Maldives (Dhivehi Jumhuriyah—Republic of Maldives), formerly an internally self-governing British protectorate, became an independent elective sultanate on Jul 26, 1965. On Nov 11, 1968, a republic was established in place of the sultanate and in 1969 the name of the country was changed from the Maldives Islands to Maldives. The Government is dominated by a small hereditary elite, the Didi clan, which has held power for the past 8 centuries.

Constitution: The 1968 Constitution provides for a President (head of state), a Cabinet and a unicameral legislature. It also guarantees freedom of "life movement," speech and development as basic rights within the provisions of Islam.

MALI
Republic of Mali

LOCATION: Mali is located in West Africa and is landlocked; it is bordered by Algeria on the north, Mauritania and Senegal on the west, the Cote d'Ivoire and Guinea on the south and Niger and Burkina Faso on the east.

AREA: 478,767 sq. miles

Land Use: 1.68% cropland; 24.60% permanent pasture; 7.11% forests and woodland; 66.78% other (mostly desert, includes a negligible amount of irrigated land).

Arable Land: 2%
Arable Land per capita: 0.72 acres

POPULATION: 8,569,000 (1987 projection)

Population Density: 17.90 inhabs. per sq. mile (1987)
Population Distribution: 18.00% urban (1985)
Population Growth Rate: 2.94% per year (1985-90 projection)

VITAL STATISTICS

Average Life Expectancy: 44.00 years (1985-90 projection)
Male: 42.40 years (1985-90 projection)
Female: 45.60 years (1985-90 projection)
Age Distribution: (1985)
0-14 .... 46.30%
15-64 .... 51.00%
65+ 2.70%
Median Age: 16.80 years (1985)
Maternal Mortality: (not available)
Infant Mortality: 169 per 1,000 live births (1985-90 projection)

HEALTH CARE

Hospital Beds: 5.24 per 10,000 population (1977)
Doctors: 0.38 per 10,000 population (1980)

ETHNIC COMPOSITION: Mande (includes Bambara, Malinke, Sarakole) - 50%; Peul - 17%; Voltaic - 12%; Songhai - 6%; Turaeg and Moor - 5%; other - 10%.

RELIGION: Moslem - 90%; indigenous beliefs - 9%; Christian - 1%.

LANGUAGE: The official language is French, though Bambara is spoken by 80% of the population. Local tribes have their own non-written alphabet, while the Turaeg have their own alphabet.

EDUCATION: Illiteracy: 90%. Education is officially compulsory and free between the ages of 6 and 15 years. In 1982, there were 1,301 primary schools with 296,301 students; 64,148 secondary school students; 2,444 students enrolled in teaching training institutes; 3,162 students enrolled in vocational schools; and 5,792 students enrolled in institutes of higher learning.

ECONOMIC DATA

Expenditures by Function [as % of total]: (1982)
General public services .... (not available)
Defense 21.19%
Education 22.33%
Health 5.42%
Social security and welfare .... (not available)
Housing and community amenities (not available)
Other community and
  social services .... (not available)
Economic services .... (not available)
Agriculture, forestry, fishing and
  hunting .... (not available)
Roads and other transport and
  communication 1.86%
Other purposes 49.20%
GDP per capita: $140 (1983)

TRAVEL NOTES

Climate: It is hot throughout Mali, very dry in the north (the Sahara Desert), and wetter in the south, where the rainy season lasts from June to October. The temperature in Bamako usually stays between 61°F and 103°F.
Health Precautions: Immunizations for various diseases are strongly recommended, including typhoid, cholera, yellow fever, tetanus, diphtheria, polio, infectious hepatitis and rabies. Malaria suppressants are also recommended and influenza, skin rashes and intestinal problems are prevalent. All water should be boiled and filtered.
Miscellaneous: Between November and February is the ideal time to visit as this is the cool season. Tourism continues to be developed based on hunting and fishing attractions.

MALTA
Republic of Malta

LOCATION: Positioned approximately 58 miles south of Sicily, Italy, and 180 miles north of Libya, Malta is an archipelago in the Mediterranean Sea consisting of three inhabited islands: Malta, Gozo and Comino.

AREA: 122 sq. miles

Land Use: 40.63% cropland; 0% permanent pasture; 0% forests and woodland; 59.37% other (urban or waste).

Arable Land: 41%
Arable Land per capita: 0.08 acres

POPULATION: 356,000 (1988 estimate)

Population Density: 2,918 inhabs. per sq. mile (1988 estimate)
Population Distribution: 85.38% urban (1985 estimate)
Population Growth Rate: 0.60% per year (1988 estimate)

VITAL STATISTICS

Average Life Expectancy: 72.70 years (1985-90 projection)
Male: 70.20 years (1985-90 projection)
Female: 75.40 years (1985-90 projection)
Age Distribution: (1985)
0-14 .... 23.98%
15-64 .... 66.58%
65+ 9.44%
Median Age: 31.30 years (1985)
Maternal Mortality: 32.90 per 100,000 live births (1982)
Infant Mortality: 11.00 per 1,000 live births (1985)

HEALTH CARE

Hospital Beds: 87 per 10,000 population (1982)
Doctors: 11 per 10,000 population (1982)

ETHNIC COMPOSITION: The population of Malta includes persons of Arab, Sicilian, Norman, Italian, Spanish and English descent.

RELIGION: Roman Catholic - 98%; other - 2%.

LANGUAGE: English and Maltese are the official languages. Italian is also widely spoken.

EDUCATION: Illiteracy: 15.90%. In 1984, there were 91 primary schools with 35,411 students; 21,759 general secondary school students; 6,140 vocational school students and 1 university with 1,474 students.

ECONOMIC DATA

Expenditures by Function [as % of total]: (1983)
General public services 8.81%
Defense 2.91%
Education 7.79%
Health 8.90%
Social security and welfare 35.89%
Housing and community amenities 3.27%
Other community and social services 0.52%
Economic services 27.04%
Agriculture, forestry, fishing and hunting ..1.55%
Roads 5.14%
Other transportation and communication ...1.25%
Other purposes 4.86%
GDP per capita: $4,783 (1986)

TRAVEL NOTES

Climate: Malta is hot and dry in the summer months; the winters are chilly and damp. Temperatures average 73°F in the summer and 57°F in winter. Average precipitation is 21 inches a year with virtually no rainfall from May to September.
Health Precautions: No special health hazards exist, but the usual immunizations for polio, whooping cough, diphtheria, tetanus and measles are recommended. Health care has recently been nationalized. Tap water is not potable.
Miscellaneous: Malta is a popular resort offering scenic beaches, examples of 17th century architecture and a government-licensed casino. Cars travel on the left-hand side of the road.

GOVERNMENT

Malta (Repubblika ta' Malta—Republic of Malta) gained full independence within the Commonwealth on Sep 21, 1964, having been part of the British Empire since 1814. Originally, Malta had a parliamentary system, with the British monarch as sovereign and a Governor General exercising executive authority on the sovereign's behalf. Malta became an independent republic on Dec 13, 1974, under a revised Constitution, with executive authority vested in the President. In May 1987, the conservative Nationalist Party, aided by a January 1987 Constitutional amendment that provided for the party with the majority of the popular vote to win the majority of the legislative seats, won the national election and ended 16 years of governing by the Socialist Malta Labor Party.

Constitution: The 1974 Constitution, an extensively revised version of the 1964 Constitution, guarantees fundamental rights and freedoms of the individual. It establishes Roman Catholicism as the official state religion, but guarantees freedom of worship to other religions. The Constitution also guarantees the rights of women workers and prohibits racial discrimination. Amendments in January 1987 guaranteed the neutrality of the country and changed the system of the allocation of legislative seats.

MAURITANIA
Islamic Republic of Mauritania

LOCATION: Mauritania is situated in northwestern Africa, and is bordered by the Western Sahara and Algeria to the north, Senegal to the south and Mali to the south and east. The Atlantic Ocean lies to the west.

AREA: 397,950 sq. miles (not including Western Sahara).

Land Use: 0.19% cropland; 38.09% permanent pasture; 14.56% forests and woodland; 47.16% other (mostly desert).
Arable Land: 0.19%
Arable Land per capita: 0.07 acres

POPULATION: 2,007,000 (1987 projection)

Population Density: 5.04 inhabs. per sq. mile (1987)
Population Distribution: 34.60% urban (1985)
Population Growth Rate: 3.08% per year (1985-90 projection)

VITAL STATISTICS

Average Life Expectancy: 46.00 years (1985-90 projection)
Male: 44.40 years (1985-90 projection)
Female: 47.60 years (1985-90 projection)
Age Distribution: (1985)
0-14 .... 46.40%
15-64 .... 50.80%
65+ 2.80%
Median Age: 16.80 years (1985)
Maternal Mortality: (not available)
Infant Mortality: 127 per 1,000 live births (1985-90 projection)

HEALTH CARE

Hospital Beds: 3.44 per 10,000 population (1980)
Doctors: 0.63 per 10,000 population (1980)

ETHNIC COMPOSITION: Mixed Arab-Berber (Moor) and black - 40%; Arab-Berber - 30%; black - 30%.

RELIGION: Moslem - nearly 100%.

LANGUAGE: Hassaniya Arabic is the national language and is spoken by about 80% of the people. French is the official language and is used in government and commerce. Several local languages are spoken by black Africans, including Tukulor, Fulani, Sarakole and Wolof.

EDUCATION: Illiteracy: 83%. In 1982, there were 637 primary schools with 107,390 students; 25,700 students in general secondary schools; and 1,027 students in teacher training secondary schools. In 1980, there were 1,004 students in vocational secondary schools.

ECONOMIC DATA

Expenditures by Function [as % of total]: (1979)
General public services 22.61%
Defense 29.40%
Education 10.41%
Health 2.81%
Social security and welfare 3.84%
Housing and community amenities 0.11%
Other community and social services 1.45%
Economic services 13.48%
Agriculture, forestry, fishing and hunting ..7.09%
Roads 2.37%
Other transportation and communication ...1.70%
Other purposes 5.69%
GDP per capita: $350 (1984)

TRAVEL NOTES

Climate: The climate is dry and hot, especially in the north, which is mainly desert. There is a cooler season between November and May.
Health Precautions: Vaccinations against yellow fever and cholera are required, and travelers should beware of tuberculosis, malaria, cholera, hepatitis, leprosy and typhoid fever. The dry air may increase respiratory problems and visitors should be cautious of dehydration.
Miscellaneous: The coast has ample sandy beaches that are excellent for camping, and the surf fishing is good throughout the year. Conservative summer apparel is suitable year-round.

GOVERNMENT

Mauritania (al-Jumhuriyah al-Muritaniyah—Republique Islamique de Mauritanie—Islamic Republic of Mauritania), formerly a part of French West Africa, became an independent nation on Nov 28, 1960. After independence, a one-party state was established under President Moktar Ould Daddah. The Government was overthrown on Jul 10, 1978, in a bloodless military coup led by Lt. Col. Moustapha Ould Mohamed Salek, who became Chairman of the ruling Military Committee for National Recovery (officially renamed in 1979 as the Military Committee for National Salvation). On Dec 12, 1984, the Government was overthrown again in a bloodless coup headed by former Prime Minister Muawiya Ould Sidi Ahmed Taya, who assumed the presidency and the posts of Prime Minister and Minister of Defense, as well as taking control of the Military Committee for National Salvation.

Constitution: The republican Constitution of 1961 was replaced in 1978 by a charter granting legislative and executive power to the Military Committee for National Salvation (CMSN). A draft Constitution providing for a return to civilian rule under a parliamentary form of government was published in December 1980, but the proposal has since been abandoned.

MAURITIUS

LOCATION: Mauritius consists of a group of islands located in the Indian Ocean some 500 miles east of Madagascar.

AREA: 788 sq. miles

Land Use: 57.84% cropland; 3.78% permanent pasture; 31.35% forest and woodland; 7.03% other.
Arable Land: 58%
Arable Land per capita: 0.30 acres

POPULATION: 1,047,000 (1989 estimate)

Population Density: 1,329 inhabs. per sq. mile (1989 estimate)
Population Distribution: 42.19% urban (1985)
Population Growth Rate: 0.80% per year (1989 estimate)

VITAL STATISTICS

Average Life Expectancy: 68.20 years (1985-90 projection)
Male: 65.80 years (1985-90 projection)
Female: 70.80 years (1985-90 projection)
Age Distribution: (1985)
0-14 . . . . 31.62%

15-64 . . . . .64.95%
65+ 3.43%
Median Age: 23.20 years (1985)
Maternal Mortality: 98.90 per 100,000 live births (1982)
Infant Mortality: 25 per 1,000 live births (1985)

HEALTH CARE

Hospital Beds: 28 per 10,000 population (1985)
Doctors: 7 per 10,000 population (1986)

ETHNIC COMPOSITION: Indo-Mauritian - 68%; Creole - 27%; Sino-Mauritian - 3%; Franco-Mauritian - 2%.

RELIGION: Hindu - 51%; Christian (mostly Roman Catholic) - 30%; Muslim - 17%; other - 2%.

LANGUAGE: English is the official language, but Creole is widely used in commerce. Other languages include Hindi and Bhojpuri.

EDUCATION: Illiteracy: 31%. In 1986, there were 273 primary schools with 138,765 students; 125 secondary schools with 68,604 students; 2 technical training centers with 203 students; 1 polytechnic institute with 346 students; and 1 university with 618 students.

ECONOMIC DATA

Expenditures by Function [as % of total]: (1985)
General public services 17.24%
Defense 0.84%
Education 13.80%
Health 7.56%
Social security and welfare . . . . (not available)
Housing and community amenities 1.34%
Other community and social services 1.03%
Economic services 12.84%
Agriculture, forestry, fishing and hunting . .7.03%
Roads 0.71%
Other transportation and communication . . .2.16%
Other purposes 29.86%
GDP per capita: $1,812 (1987)

TRAVEL NOTES

Climate: The Mauritian climate is sub-tropical, with hot, humid summers and warm, dry winters. The average annual temperature is 73°F on the coast and 66°F at higher elevations. The islands are subject to cyclones, which can be severe, between the months of September and May.

Health Precautions: Gamma globulin and tetanus inoculations are recommended. The water is not potable.

Miscellaneous: Mauritius is known for its beautiful beaches and rugged volcanic scenery. The islands offer an interesting mix of African, European, Indian and Chinese cultures.

GOVERNMENT

Mauritius was a British colony from 1814 until Mar 12, 1968, when it became an independent member of the Commonwealth. The British sovereign is the nominal head of state and is represented by an appointed Governor General.

Constitution: The Mauritius Independence Order of 1968, amended in 1969 by the Constitution of Mauritius Act, provides for a parliamentary system of government with a Council of Ministers appointed by the Governor General. the Constitution can be amended by an act of the Legislative Assembly.

MEXICO
United Mexican States

LOCATION: Mexico is located in southern North America, bordered on the north by the US and on the south by Guatemala and Belize. The Pacific Ocean lies to the west, and the Gulf of Mexico to the east and north.

AREA: 764,553 sq. miles

Land Use: 40% pasture; 12% cropland; 22% forest; 26% other.
Arable Land: 15%
Arable Land per capita: 0.89 acres

POPULATION: 81,709,000 (1986)

Population Density: 106.87 inhabs. per sq. mile (1986)
Population Distribution: 66% urban (1980)
Population Growth Rate: 2.50% per year (1986)

VITAL STATISTICS

Average Life Expectancy: 66.05 years (1985)
Male: 63.90 years (1985)
Female: 68.20 years (1985)

Age Distribution: (1984)
0-14 . . . . .42.90%
15-59 . . . . .52.30%
60+ 5.90%
Median Age: 17.10 years (1980)
Maternal Mortality: 91.80 per 100,000 live births (1981)
Infant Mortality: 53 per 1,000 live births (1985)

HEALTH CARE

Hospital Beds: 10.50 per 10,000 population (1978)
Doctors: 7.65 per 10,000 population (1980)

ETHNIC COMPOSITION: Mestizo - 60%; American Indian - 30%; Caucasian - 9%; other - 1%.

RELIGION: Roman Catholic - 97%; Protestant - 3%.

LANGUAGE: Spanish is the dominant language, while about 8% of the people speak indigenous languages.

EDUCATION: Illiteracy: 11.9%. In 1984, there were 79,202 primary schools with 15,376,153 students; 16,408 secondary schools with 4,277,606 students; 3,921 institutions of higher education with 1,786,658 students; and 75 normal schools with 140,093 students.

ECONOMIC DATA

Expenditures by Function [as % of total]: (1983)
General public services 7.37%
Defense 1.95%
Education 10.96%
Health 1.20%
Social security and welfare 10.24%
Housing and community amenities 2.25%
Other community and social services 0.65%
Economic services 26.21%
Agriculture, forestry, fishing and hunting . .4.77%
Roads 1.92%
Other transportation and communication . . .3.10%
Other purposes 40.76%
GDP per capita: $2,262 (1985)

TRAVEL NOTES

Climate: The climate is hot and wet in the coastal lowlands and the tropical southern regions, where the average temperature is about 64°F. The highlands of the central plateau are temperate, while desert covers much of the north and west.

Health Precautions: Raw vegetables and fruits should be carefully cleaned and treated before they are eaten. Tap water is generally not potable. Malaria is still a risk in some rural areas and immunization is recommended for typhoid, diphtheria, tetanus and yellow fever. Health facilities in the major cities are very good.

Miscellaneous: Among Mexico's tourist attractions are its coastal scenery, the Sierra Madre mountains, the ruins of Mayan and Aztec civilizations, and the well-developed tourist resorts, such as Acapulco and Zihuatanejo on the Pacific coast and Cancun on the Caribbean coast.

GOVERNMENT

Mexico (Estados Unidos Mexicanos—United Mexican States) is a federal republic composed of 31 states and a Federal District (Mexico City). Effective political power rests with the *Partido Revolucionario Institucional* (PRI— Institutional Revolutionary Party), which has dominated government and politics since its establishment in 1929.

Constitution: The present Constitution, Mexico's third, was proclaimed in 1917 and has remained continuously in force since then, although amended over 100 times. It provides for a system of division of powers between the states and the central Government, with the central Government having predominant power and extensive authority to intervene in state affairs. The Constitution also sets up a system of separation of powers between executive, legislative and judicial branches, but with executive powers far exceeding those of the other two branches. The Constitution also contains a number of social and economic provisions reflecting the outcome of the Mexican social revolution, and a list of civil rights guaranteed by the Mexican legal concept of "amparo" (protection of constitutional rights of an individual).

MONACO
Principality of Monaco

LOCATION: Situated on the Mediterranean coast of western Europe, Monaco is completely encircled by France except for a short coastline. The country lies about 10 miles east of the French city of Nice and 15 miles west of France's border with Italy.

AREA: 0.75 sq. miles

Land Use: 0% cropland; 0% permanent pasture; 0% forest and woodland; 100% other (urban).
Arable Land: 0%
Arable Land per capita: 0 acres

POPULATION: 29,000 (1988 estimate)

Population Density: 37,667 inhabs. per sq. mile (1988 estimate)
Population Distribution: 100% urban (1988)
Population Growth Rate: 0.90% per year (1988)

VITAL STATISTICS

Average Life Expectancy: (not available)
Male: (not available)
Female: (not available)
Age Distribution: (1987 estimate)
0-14 . . . . .12.70%
15-59 . . . . .56.30%
60+ 30.70%
Median Age: (not available)
Maternal Mortality: (not available)
Infant Mortality: 10 per 1,000 live births (1972)

HEALTH CARE

Hospital Beds: 135 per 10,000 population (1970)
Doctors: 22 per 10,000 population (1981)

ETHNIC COMPOSITION: French - 47%; Monegasque - 16%; Italian - 16%; other - 21%.

RELIGION: Roman Catholic - 95%; other (mostly Protestant) - 5%.

LANGUAGE: French is the official language, but Monegasque, English, Italian and other languages are widely spoken.

EDUCATION: Illiteracy: 1%. In 1986/87, there were 3,660 pupils enrolled in state schools, which included 525 pre-primary schools, 1,027 primary schools and 2,108 secondary schools.

ECONOMIC DATA

Expenditures by Function [as % of total]: (not available)
GDP per capita: (not available)

TRAVEL NOTES

Climate: Monaco enjoys a Mediterranean climate with hot, dry summers and mild, wet winters.
Health Precautions: No special health precautions are necessary. The water is potable.
Miscellaneous: Monaco is a favorite destination for tourists seeking luxury accommodation, gambling casinos and beautiful coastal scenery.

GOVERNMENT

Monaco (Principaute de Monaco—Principality of Monaco) has been ruled by the hereditary princes of the Grimaldi line since 1297. Placed under the protection of France in 1861, Monaco signed a treaty in 1918 that requires Monegasque policy to conform with the military and economic interests of France. A second treaty signed in 1919 provides for Monaco's integration with France should a reigning Monegasque prince die with no male heir.

Constitution: The 1962 Constitution promulgated by Prince Rainier specifies that any future amendments must be approved by the National Council. The Constitution guarantees Monegasque citizens the right of association, the right to form trade unions and the right to strike. Although it maintains the traditional hereditary monarchy, the Constitution renounces the principle of divine right.

MONGOLIA
Mongolian People's Republic

LOCATION: A landlocked country in Asia, Mongolia is bordered on the north by the Soviet Union and on the east, south and west by China.

AREA: 606,441 sq. miles

Land Use: 10% forest; 90% desert, waste and pasture.
Arable Land: 1%

Arable Land per capita: 1.99 acres

POPULATION: 1,942,000 (1986)

Population Density: 3 inhabs. per sq. mile (1986)
Population Distribution: 45% urban (1982)
Population Growth Rate: 2.60% per year (1986)

VITAL STATISTICS

Average Life Expectancy: 62.55 years (1980)
Male: 60.50 years (1980)
Female: 64.60 years (1980)
Age Distribution: (1980)
0-14 . . . . .43.10%
15-64 . . . . .53.70%
65+ 3.20%
Median Age: 18.30 years (1980)
Maternal Mortality: (not available)
Infant Mortality: 15 per 1,000 live births (1980)

HEALTH CARE

Hospital Beds: 109.30 per 10,000 population (1983)
Doctors: 23.30 per 10,000 population (1983)

ETHNIC COMPOSITION: Mongol - 90%; Kazakh - 4%; Chinese - 2%; Russian - 2%; other - 2%.

RELIGION: The population is predominantly Tibetan Buddhist with about 4% Moslem.

LANGUAGE: About 90% of the population speaks Khalkha Mongol. Other languages include Turkic, Russian and Chinese.

EDUCATION: Illiteracy: 20%. In 1985/86, there were 587 general schools with 412,600 students; 40 vocational-technical schools with 23,000 students; 25 special secondary schools with 23,000 students; and 8 higher education institutions with 24,500 students.

ECONOMIC DATA

Expenditures by Function [as % of total]: (not available)
GDP per capita: (not available)

TRAVEL NOTES

Climate: The climate is dry and extreme. Winter temperatures average well below freezing.
Health Precautions: (not available)

Miscellaneous: The main attractions for tourists are scenery, wildlife and historical relics.

GOVERNMENT

Mongolia (Bugd Nayramdah Mongol Ard Uls—Mongolian People's Republic), proclaimed an independent republic in November 1924, is based on the Soviet Communist model.

Constitution: The 1960 Constitution states that the nation is a sovereign democratic state of working people. Supreme state power is vested in a People's Assembly. In addition to state ownership of all natural resources, land, factories, transport and banking, the people have cooperative ownership of public enterprises. However, a limited degree of private ownership is permitted.

MOROCCO
Kingdom of Morocco

LOCATION: Located in northwest Africa, Morocco has a long western coastline on the Atlantic Ocean and a northern coastline on the Mediterranean Sea. Morocco is bordered on the east by Algeria and on the south by the disputed territory of Western Sahara, which is currently under Moroccan occupation.

AREA: 274,461 sq. miles (includes the disputed territory of Western Sahara).

Land Use: 18.60% cropland; 28.00% permanent pasture; 11.70% forests and woodland; 41.70% other (mostly desert).
Arable Land: 18%
Arable Land per capita: 0.80 acres

POPULATION: 23,014,000 (1987 projection)

Population Density: 84 inhabs. per sq. mile (1987)
Population Distribution: 44.80% urban (1985)
Population Growth Rate: 2.30% per year (1985-90 projection)

VITAL STATISTICS

Average Life Expectancy: 60.80 years (1985-90 projection)
Male: 59.10 years (1985-90 projection)
Female: 62.50 years (1985-90 projection)

Age Distribution: (1985)
0-14 ....41.00%
15-64 ....55.10%
65+ 3.90%
Median Age: 18.90 years (1985)
Maternal Mortality: (not available)
Infant Mortality: 82 per 1,000 live births (1985-90 projection)

HEALTH CARE

Hospital Beds: 12 per 10,000 population (1984)
Doctors: 2 per 10,000 population (1984)

ETHNIC COMPOSITION: Arab-Berber - 99.10%; non-Moroccan - 0.70%; Jewish - 0.20%.

RELIGION: Moslem - 98.70%; Christian - 1.10%; Jewish - 0.20%.

LANGUAGE: Arabic is the official language; several Berber dialects are also spoken, as is French.

EDUCATION: Illiteracy: 72%. In 1985/86, there were 2,279,887 primary school students; and 1,200,383 secondary school students; in 1984/85 there were 6 universities with 111,920 students.

ECONOMIC DATA

Expenditures by Function [as % of total]: (1983)
General public services 15.90%
Defense 14.59%
Education 18.60%
Health 2.93%
Social security and welfare 6.06%
Housing and community amenities 1.09%
Other community and social services 0.95%
Economic services 28.81%
Agriculture, forestry, fishing and hunting ..5.42%
Roads 1.71%
Other transportation and communication ...9.54%
Other purposes 11.08%
GDP per capita: $516 (1984)

TRAVEL NOTES

Climate: The climate is semitropical. The interior plains are intensely hot in summer, while the coast is warm and sunny.
Health Precautions: No vaccinations are required, though there is some risk of malaria in certain areas of Kenitra and Tata and the rural areas of Khemisset Province.

Miscellaneous: Morocco's desert and mountain scenery is spectacular. The coasts along the Atlantic and Mediterranean have numerous holiday resorts.

GOVERNMENT

Morocco (al-Mamlakah al-Maghribiyah—Kingdom of Morocco) is a constitutional monarchy, effective political authority being held by the Crown. From 1912 to 1956, the Sharifian Sultanate of Morocco was divided into a French protectorate and a Spanish protectorate. The French protectorate was terminated on Mar 2, 1956, following the restoration of the monarchy of Sultan Mohamed V, who had been deposed. Spain gave up its protectorate on Apr 7, 1956, and Tangier's international status was abolished on Oct 29, 1956. The Sultan was first designated King in August 1957. A 1962 Constitution formally established the monarchy.
Western Sahara. When Spain withdrew from the Spanish Sahara in 1976, the territory was partitioned between Morocco and Mauritania. In 1979, after a prolonged guerrilla war, Mauritania withdrew from its portion of the territory in favor of the Algerian-backed *Frente Popular para la Liberacion de Saguia el Hamra y Rio de Oro* (Polisario Front—Popular Front for the Liberation of Saguia el Hamra and Rio de Oro), which had declared a Saharan Arab Democratic Republic in 1976. Morocco moved its armed forces into the former Mauritanian sector and declared it to be Moroccan territory. The Polisario Front continues a guerrilla war against Morocco. Western Sahara is divided into 4 provinces: Essmara, Boujdour, Oued Eddahab and Laayoune.

Constitution: Morocco's third Constitution (promulgated on Mar 10, 1972) declares the country to be a "constitutional, democratic and social monarchy" with Islam as the official state religion. The Constitution provides for equality before the law and guarantees freedom of movement, speech, opinion and assembly. Amendments to the Constitution may be initiated by the King, but such initiatives require approval in a popular referendum.

MOZAMBIQUE
People's Republic of Mozambique

LOCATION: Located on the eastern coast of southern Africa, Mozambique is bounded on the south by Swaziland and South Africa, on the west by Zimbabwe, Zambia and Malawi and on the north by Tanzania, while Madagascar lies to the east across the Mozambique Channel of the Indian Ocean.

AREA: 308,640 sq. miles

Land Use: 3.93% cropland; 56.12% permanent pasture; 19.55% forests and woodland; 20.40% other.
Arable Land: 4%
Arable Land per capita: 0.60 acres

POPULATION: 14,832,000 (1988 estimate)

Population Density: 48 inhabs. per sq. mile (1988 estimate)
Population Distribution: 19.44% urban (1985)
Population Growth Rate: 2.80% per year (1985)

VITAL STATISTICS

Average Life Expectancy: 47.30 years (1985-90 projection)
Male: 46.40 years (1985-90 projection)
Female: 48.30 years (1985-90 projection)
Age Distribution: (1985)
0-14 . . . . .43.15%
15-64 . . . . .53.58%
65+ 3.27%
Median Age: 18.40 years (1985)
Maternal Mortality: 647.40 per 100,000 live births (1975)
Infant Mortality: 158 per 1,000 live births (1985)

HEALTH CARE

Hospital Beds: 9 per 10,000 population (1985)
Doctors: 0.23 per 10,000 population (1985)

ETHNIC COMPOSITION: The majority of the population consists of members of several dozen Bantu tribal groups.

RELIGION: Indigenous beliefs - 60%; Christian (mainly Roman Catholic) - 30%; Moslem - 10%.

LANGUAGE: Portuguese is the official language, although many Bantu dialects and indigenous languages are spoken as well, including Muchope, Ronga and Shangaan.

EDUCATION: Illiteracy: 86%. In 1986 there were 4,430 primary schools with 1,251,391 students; 171 secondary schools with 144,015 students; 34 technical schools with 10,485 students; 27 teacher training schools with 5,828 students; and 1 institution of higher learning with 1,569 students.

ECONOMIC DATA

Expenditures by Function [as % of total]: (not available)
GDP per capita: $152 (1984)

TRAVEL NOTES

Climate: Temperatures during the wet season (November to April) average from 79°F to 86°F, while during the dry season the temperature generally ranges from 64°F to 68°F.
Health Precautions: Vaccinations against typhoid, yellow fever, hepatitis and polio are strongly recommended, as are malaria suppressants. Tap water is not potable.
Miscellaneous: Travel may be limited because of an adverse security situation. Visitors enjoy the resort city of Beira and the 14th century cathedral in Tete.

GOVERNMENT

Mozambique (Republica Popular de Mocambique—People's Republic of Mozambique) was colonized by Portugal during the 1800s, and became an overseas province in the early 1950s. Following a protracted guerrilla battle, spearheaded by the *Frente de Libertacao de Mocambique* (Frelimo—Mozambique Liberation Front), Mozambique gained independence from Portugal on Jun 25, 1975. Mozambique is a one-party state, in which effective political power is exercised by Frelimo, the president of which is President of the Republic. After independence, Samora Machel became the country's first president. In October 1986, President Machel was killed in a plane crash, and was replaced by the country's current President, Joaquim Chissano.

Constitution: The Constitution, which entered into effect on Jun 25, 1975 and was revised in 1978, provides for a socialist state, with Frelimo acting as the "leading force." The Constitution provides for the separation of church and state, and for personal ownership of property. It bars discrimination based on race, religion or gender. The Constitution may be amended by an absolute majority vote of the People's Assembly.

NAMIBIA

LOCATION: Namibia, formerly known as South West Africa, is located on the west coast of Southern Africa. It is bounded to the north by Angola, to the east by Botswana and to the south and east by South Africa.

AREA: 318,252 sq. miles

Land Use: 1% cropland; 64% permanent pasture; 22% forest and woodland; 13% other.
Arable Land: 1%
Arable Land per capita: 1.39 acres

POPULATION: 1,319,000 (1989 estimate)

Population Density: 4 inhabs. per sq. mile (1989 estimate)
Population Distribution: 51.35% urban (1985)
Population Growth Rate: 4.10% per year (1989 projection)

VITAL STATISTICS

Average Life Expectancy: 50.20 years (1985-90 projection)
Male: 48.50 years (1985-90 projection)
Female: 51.90 years (1985-90 projection)
Age Distribution: (1985)
0-14 . . . . .44.32%
15-64 . . . . .52.45%
65+ 3.23%
Median Age: 17.80 years (1985)
Maternal Mortality: (not available)
Infant Mortality: 110 per 1,000 live births (1985)

HEALTH CARE

Hospital Beds: 76 per 10,000 population (1980)
Doctors: 2 per 10,000 population (1984)

ETHNIC COMPOSITION: Black - 85.60%; white - 7.50%; mixed - 6.90%.

RELIGION: About 90% of the population is nominally Christian, though most native inhabitants also practice indigenous beliefs.

LANGUAGE: Afrikaans and English are the official languages. German is also widely spoken. Several tribal languages are spoken by the native population.

EDUCATION: Illiteracy: 1% (whites); 84% (non-whites). In 1986, there were 1,071 primary and secondary schools with 344,889 students; 2 special schools with 191 students; 1 industrial school with 22 students; and 2 technical institutes with 154 students.

ECONOMIC DATA

Expenditures by Function [as % of total]: (1987-88)
General public services . . . . (not available)
Defense 10.12%
Education 5.24%
Health and welfare 4.21%
Housing and community amenities . (not available)
Other community and
    social services . . . . (not available)
Economic services 5.42%
Agriculture, forestry, fishing and hunting . . 2.59%
Roads 5.44%
Other transportation and communication . . 3.94%
Other purposes 63.04%
GDP per capita: $1,134 (1986)

TRAVEL NOTES

Climate: Namibia's climate is warm and very dry, with the average annual rainfall ranging from two inches in the Namib desert, which stretches along the coast, to 20 inches in the northern sections of the country. The easternmost part of Namibia extends into the Kalahari desert.

Health Precautions: Immunizations against yellow fever and cholera are recommended, and care should be taken to avoid swimming or wading in pools contaminated with bilharzia. The water is not potable.

Miscellaneous: Abundant wildlife and beautiful game reserves are Namibia's chief tourist attraction.

GOVERNMENT

Namibia (formerly South West Africa) is a disputed territory under de facto control of South Africa. An overseas territory of the German Empire from the 1880s until World War I, it became a League of Nations mandate administered by South Africa after the war. South Africa refused to allow South West Africa to be made a UN trust territory after World War II, and finally the UN General Assembly, after repeated requests to South Africa to negotiate an agreement to withdraw from the territory, terminated the mandate in 1966. A 1967 General Assembly resolution set up a UN Council for South West Africa, assisted by a commissioner, and a 1968 resolution changed the territory's name to Namibia. A 1973 General Assembly resolution recognized the black nationalist *South West Africa People's Organization of Namibia* (SWAPO) as the "authentic representative of the Namibian people." In 1978, the UN Security Council passed Resolution 435, which called for the withdrawal of South African troops and UN-supervised elections in Namibia. Despite all these actions, South Africa refused to relinquish its control over the region. In June 1985, amid international condemnation, South Africa installed the Transnational Government of National Unity composed of members drawn from 6 parties based inside the territory. The Transnational Government is responsible for internal affairs, but South Africa retains control of defense and foreign affairs. A diplomatic breakthrough was achieved in August 1988 at US-sponsored talks in Geneva between Angola, Cuba and South Africa. In these discussions, the situations in Namibia and neighboring Angola were considered jointly; the withdrawal of Cuban forces from Angola was linked to withdrawal of South African troops from Namibia, and to a halting of South African support for UNITA, a rebel group fighting the Angolan Government. Delegates from the three nations left having agreed upon a "de facto cessation of hostilities." However, neither UNITA nor SWAPO participated in the discussions. Negotiations continued in December 1988 at Brazzaville, Congo Republic, where a major agreement, known as the Brazzaville Protocol, was signed by Angola, Cuba and South Africa. Under the terms of the agreement, UN Security Council Resolution 435 is to be implemented in Namibia, and a provisional schedule for the withdrawal of South African troops and the holding of UN-supervised elections was agreed upon. South African troop strength in the territory is to be reduced from 60,000 to 1,500 by July 1989, and elections for an independent Namibian government are tentatively scheduled for November of that same year.

Constitution: The interim Transnational Government (see above) was charged with drawing up a new Constitution, and in 1985 a Constitutional Council was formed. In July 1987, the Council endorsed a draft constitution instituting a "one man, one vote democracy," but it was rejected by the South African Government, which instead proposed a constitution that protected "group rights" (i.e. provided special representation for the white minority).

NATIONALIST CHINA
See Taiwan

NAURU
Republic of Nauru

LOCATION: Nauru is an island in the central Pacific about 25 miles south of the Equator and 2,500 miles northeast of western Australia.

AREA: 8 sq. miles

Land Use: Mostly phosphate mining, the rest being wasteland.
Arable Land: 0%
Arable Land per capita: 0 acres

POPULATION: 8,000 (1986)

Population Density: 1,000 inhabs. per sq. mile (1986)
Population Distribution: 0% urban (1986)
Population Growth Rate: 1.3% per year (1986)

VITAL STATISTICS

Average Life Expectancy: (not available)
Male: (not available)
Female: (not available)
Age Distribution: (not available)
Median Age: (not available)
Maternal Mortality: (not available)
Infant Mortality: 31.2 per 1,000 live births (1981)

HEALTH CARE

Hospital Beds: 311 per 10,000 population (1984)
Doctors: 14.29 per 10,000 population (1971)

ETHNIC COMPOSITION: Nauruan - 58%; Other Pacific Islander - 26%; Chinese - 8%; European - 8%.

RELIGION: Protestant - 66%; Catholic - 33%; other - 1%.

LANGUAGE: Nauruan, a distinct Pacific Island language, is official. English is widely used.

EDUCATION: Illiteracy: 1%. In 1985, there were 4 infant schools with 383 students; 7 primary schools with 1,451 students; and 2 secondary schools with 465 students. In 1984, 88 Nauruans were studying at secondary and tertiary levels overseas.

ECONOMIC DATA

Expenditures by Function [as % of total]: (not available)
GDP per capita: $21,400 (1981)

TRAVEL NOTES

Climate: The climate is tropical, with a westerly monsoon season from November to February. Rainfall is extremely variable.
Health Precautions: None.
Miscellaneous: The island is linked by Air Nauru's flights to many of the other Pacific Islands, Australia, New Zealand, Japan and the Philippines.

GOVERNMENT

Nauru (Naoero—Republic of Nauru), a UN Trust Territory administered by Britain, Australia and New Zealand following World War II, became an independent state on Jan 31, 1968.

Constitution: Nauru's Constitution, adopted in 1968, establishes a parliamentary system of government.

NEPAL
Kingdom of Nepal

LOCATION: Located in central Asia, Nepal is a landlocked country bordered by China on the north and India on the west, south and east.

AREA: 54,362 sq. miles

Land Use: 16.94% cropland; 13.06% permanent pasture; 16.87% forests and woodland; 53.14% other.
Arable Land: 17%
Arable Land per capita: 0.32 acres

POPULATION: 18,760,000 (1989 estimate)

Population Density: 345 inhabs. per sq. mile (1989 estimate)
Population Distribution: 7.70% urban (1985)
Population Growth Rate: 2.50% per year (1989 estimate)

VITAL STATISTICS

Average Life Expectancy: 47.90 years (1985-90 projection)
Male: 48.60 years (1985-90 projection)
Female: 47.10 years (1985-90 projection)
Age Distribution: (1985)
0-14 .... 41.93%
15-64 .... 55.01%
65+ 3.06%
Median Age: 18.60 years (1985)
Maternal Mortality: (not available)
Infant Mortality: 106 per 1,000 live births (1985)

HEALTH CARE

Hospital Beds: 2 per 10,000 population (1982)
Doctors: 0.34 per 10,000 population (1986)

ETHNIC COMPOSITION: Ethnic groups include Newar, Indian, Tibetan, Gurung, Magar, Tamang, Bhotia, Rai, Limbu and Sherpa.

RELIGION: Hindu - 90% (official); Buddhism - 5.30%; Moslem - 2.70%; other - 2%.

LANGUAGE: Nepali is the official language. Other languages include Maithir and Bhojpuri.

EDUCATION: Illiteracy: 80%. In 1985, there were 11,946 primary schools with 1,818,688 students, 501,063 secondary school students and one university with 55,555 students.

ECONOMIC DATA

Expenditures by Function [as % of total]: (1985)
General public services 11.23%
Defense 6.19%
Education 12.07%
Health 4.97%
Social security and welfare 0.72%
Housing and community amenities 6.05%
Other community and social services 0.56%
Economic services 48.50%
Agriculture, forestry, fishing and hunting .22.04%
Roads 6.90%
Other transportation and communication ...7.12%
Other purposes 9.70%
GDP per capita: $152 (1987)

TRAVEL NOTES

Climate: The climate ranges from subtropical in the valleys to arctic at the peaks of the Himalayas. Temperatures in Kathmandu range between 35°F and 86°F.
Health Precautions: Immunizations against small pox, tetanus and diphtheria are recommended, as are malaria supressants and gamma globulin.
Miscellaneous: Tourist attractions include Limbini, Buddha's birthplace, and Mount Everest, the world's highest peak. Several tourist centers are being developed in the Kathmandu valley.

GOVERNMENT

Nepal (Nepal Alhirajya—Kingdom of Nepal) has been an independent monarchy since 1769. In 1962, a limited constitutional system was established, under which the monarch exercises strong powers.

Constitution: The Constitution, promulgated on Dec 16, 1962 and amended in 1967, 1976 and 1980, establishes a "partyless Panchayat democracy" (or a democracy based on village councils) in place of a parliamentary system. Amendments to the Constitution are made by the King, who may also declare a state of emergency and suspend the Constitution.

NETHERLANDS
Kingdom of the Netherlands

LOCATION: The Netherlands is located in Western Europe on the North Sea and is bordered on the east by West Germany and on the south by Belgium.

AREA: 13,103 sq. miles

Land Use: 70% cultivated; 8% forest; 8% inland water; 5% waste; 9% other.
Arable Land: 26%

Arable Land per capita: 0.18 acres

POPULATION: 14,536,000 (1986)

Population Density: 922 inhabs. per sq. mile (1986)
Population Distribution: 88.30% urban (1983)
Population Growth Rate: 0.40% per year (1986)

VITAL STATISTICS

Average Life Expectancy: 75 years (1984)
Male: 72 years (1984)
Female: 78 years (1984)
Age Distribution: (1985)
0-14 .... 20.40%
15-59 .... 63.10%
60+ 16.50%
Median Age: 31.30 years (1980)
Maternal Mortality: 5.30 per 100,000 live births (1983)
Infant Mortality: 8.30 per 1,000 live births (1984)

HEALTH CARE

Hospital Beds: 80 per 10,000 population (1980)
Doctors: 18.49 per 10,000 population (1979)

ETHNIC COMPOSITION: Dutch - 97%; Indonesian and other - 3%. (The Dutch are an ethnically homogeneous people descended from Frankish, Saxon and Frisian tribes with some Celtic admixture.)

RELIGION: Roman Catholic - 40%; Protestant - 30%; other - 30%.

LANGUAGE: Dutch is spoken.

EDUCATION: Illiteracy: 1%. In 1985, there were 8,059 preprimary schools with 397,000 students; 9,606 primary schools with 1,237,000 students; 1,471 secondary schools with 883,000 students; 1,892 vocational schools with 634,000 students; 380 further (nonuniversity) schools with 144,000 students; and 22 universities with 163,000 students.

ECONOMIC DATA

Expenditures by Function [as % of total]: (1984)
General public services 6.45%
Defense 5.24%
Education 10.68%
Health 10.97%
Social security and welfare 37.42%
Housing and community amenities 3.63%
Other community and social services 0.92%
Economic services 10.06%
Agriculture, forestry, fishing and hunting ..0.81%
Roads 1.12%
Other transportation and communication ...2.11%
Other purposes 14.63%
GDP per capita: $10,276 (1985)

TRAVEL NOTES

Climate: The climate is temperate, though summer temperatures rarely exceed 75°F. Winters are long and damp.
Health Precautions: None.
Miscellaneous: Tourist attractions in the Netherlands include historic towns, canals, art galleries, modern architecture and in the springtime, the fields of cultivated flowers.

GOVERNMENT

Netherlands (Koninkrijk der Nederlanden— Kingdom of the Netherlands) is a constitutional and hereditary monarchy that was established in 1814, toward the end of the Napoleonic Wars. Under the Constitution, 5 of the 6 islands of the Netherlands Antilles (Curacao, Bonaire, Saba, St. Eustatius and a part of St. Maarten) are integral parts of the Netherlands realm, but they are slated for independence. The island of Aruba became a separate, self-governing member of the Kingdom on Jan 1, 1986.

Constitution: The Constitution was first adopted in 1814 and subsequently amended. The present version of the Constitution came into force on Feb 17, 1983. Under it the Government is based on the principles of ministerial responsibility and parliamentary government common to most constitutional monarchies of Western Europe. The Government is composed of the Crown (Monarch, Council of Ministers, Council of State); the States-General (Parliament); and the Courts. Constitutional amendments must be made through a bill declaring that there is reason for such revision and containing the proposed revision. Approval of the bill is followed by the dissolution of both houses of Parliament and a second confirmation by the new States-General by two-thirds of the votes.

NETHERLANDS ANTILLES

LOCATION: The Netherlands Antilles comprise two groups of islands about 500 miles apart in the Caribbean Sea, north of Venezuela.

AREA: 706 sq. miles

Land Use: 5% cultivable; 95% waste, urban or other.
Arable Land: 5%
Arable Land per capita: 0.08 acres

POPULATION: 256,000 (1985)

Population Density: 363 inhabs. per sq. mile (1985)
Population Distribution: 32% (1960)
Population Growth Rate: 1.20% per year (1985)

VITAL STATISTICS

Average Life Expectancy: 62.30 years (1970)
Male: 58.90 years (1970)
Female: 65.70 years (1970)
Age Distribution:
0-14 .... 37.90%
15-59 .... 53.70%
60+ 8.20%
Median Age: (not available)
Maternal Mortality: (not available)
Infant Mortality: (not available)

HEALTH CARE

Hospital Beds: 85.20 per 10,000 population (1975)
Doctors: 4.40 per 10,000 population (1980)

ETHNIC COMPOSITION: Mixed black - 85%; Caribbean Indian - 14.50%; European and Asian - 0.50%.

RELIGION: Roman Catholicism is predominant. Protestants, Jews and Adventists are also represented.

LANGUAGE: Dutch is the official language. English, Spanish and Papiamento are also widely spoken.

EDUCATION: Illiteracy: 5%. Education is not compulsory. In 1974, there were 126 primary schools with 38,170 students; 34 junior high schools with 9,410 students; 4 senior high schools with 2,694 students; and 22 special schools with 1,715 students.

ECONOMIC DATA

Expenditures by Function [as % of total]: (1979)
General public services 34.37%
Defense 0.04%
Education 5.47%
Health 7.81%
Social security and welfare 11.32%
Housing and community amenities 1.05%
Other community and social services 1.64%
Economic services 11.52%
Agriculture, forestry, fishing and hunting . 0.31%
Roads 0.31%
Other transportation and communication . .4.76%
Other purposes 17.03%

TRAVEL NOTES

Climate: The climate is tropical and moderated by trade winds. Rainfall averages only 22 inches per year. Summer clothing is worn all year.
Health Precautions: Sea water is distilled for drinking, local water does not need to be chlorinated and food handling controls are adequate.
Miscellaneous: Tourism is a major industry with the white sandy beaches the major attraction.

GOVERNMENT

Netherlands Antilles (De Nederlandse Antillen), consisting of the two groups of Leeward and Windward Islands, is an autonomous part of the Kingdom of the Netherlands. Under an agreement with the Netherlands reached in March 1983, one of the Leeward Islands, Aruba, was given separate self-governing status on Jan 1, 1986 in anticipation of complete independence in 1996. The Union of the Netherlands Antilles and Aruba is a cooperative between all the islands on economic and monetary affairs.

Constitution: On Dec 29, 1954, the Charter of the Kingdom of the Netherlands came into force, establishing a parliamentary form of government for the islands. The Netherlands Antilles has complete domestic autonomy, including the right to amend or revise its own charter. Control over foreign policy and defense, on the other hand, is vested in the Council of Ministers at The Hague. The Antilles is represented in the Council by a Minister Plenipotentiary with full voting powers.

NEW ZEALAND

LOCATION: Consisting of North Island and South Island separated by the narrow Cook Strait, and several smaller islands, New Zealand is about 1,100 miles southeast of Australia in the South Pacific.

AREA: 103,883 sq. miles

Land Use: 1.75% cropland; 52.53% permanent pasture; 38.34% forests and woodland; 7.39% other.

Arable Land: 2%

Arable Land per capita: 0.39 acres

POPULATION: 3,378,000 (1987)

Population Density: 310.39 inhabs. per sq. mile (1987)

Population Distribution: 83.70% urban (1985)

Population Growth Rate: 0.86% per year (1985-90)

VITAL STATISTICS

Average Life Expectancy: 74.50 years (1985-90)

Male: 71.40 years (1985-90)

Female: 77.90 years (1985-90)

Age Distribution: (1985)

0-14	24.10%
15-64	65.50%
60+	10.40%

Median Age: 29.40 years (1985)

Maternal Mortality: 10 per 100,000 live births (1983)

Infant Mortality: 11 per 1,000 live births (1985-90)

HEALTH CARE

Hospital Beds: 97.90 per 10,000 population (1985-90)

Doctors: 15.69 per 10,000 population (1985-90)

ETHNIC COMPOSITION: White (of European descent) - 87%; Maori - 9%; Pacific Islander - 2%; other - 2%.

RELIGION: Christian - 81%; none or unspecified - 18%; Hindu, Confucian and other - 1%.

LANGUAGE: English is the official language. Maori is also used.

EDUCATION: Illiteracy: 2%. In 1984, there were 2,503 primary schools with 465,353 students; 330 secondary schools with 228,621 students; 35 area schools providing both primary and secondary education with 3,036 students; 21 technical colleges with 138,799 students; 7 teacher training schools with 2,728 students; and 7 universities with 58,242 students.

ECONOMIC DATA

Expenditures by Function [as % of total]: (1983)

General public services	7.29%
Defense	4.94%
Education	11.87%
Health	12.65%
Social security and welfare	29.25%
Housing and community amenities	0.94%
Other community and social services	0.32%
Economic services	17.64%
Agriculture, forestry, fishing and hunting	7.62%
Roads	2.44%
Other transportation and communication	1.91%
Other purposes	15.11%

GDP per capita: $5,973 (1984)

TRAVEL NOTES

Climate: With temperatures averaging 52°F, the climate is temperate and moist, except in the far north where higher temperatures are reached.

Health Precautions: No serious endemic diseases exist except for hepatitis and hydatids, a type of tapeworm infestation. The damp climate may be troublesome to arthritis, rheumatism and sinusitis sufferers.

Miscellaneous: The principal tourist attractions are the high mountains, lakes, hot springs and beaches. New Zealand is also particularly well known for its fishing.

GOVERNMENT

New Zealand (Dominion of New Zealand) achieved full independence as a sovereign state within the Commonwealth of Nations, with the British monarch as nominal head of state, in 1947. It is a constitutional monarchy with a parliamentary form of government based on the British pattern. Effective political authority rests with the majority party in Parliament.

Constitution: New Zealand has no formal single constitutional document, but its political institutions are set forth in an "unwritten Constitution" consisting of British Common Law and constitutional traditions, decrees and instructions of the British Crown, and "constitutional legislation" passed by the British and/or New Zealand Parliaments.

NICARAGUA
Republic of Nicaragua

LOCATION: Nicaragua lies in the Central American isthmus and is bounded on the west by the Pacific Ocean, on the east by the Caribbean Sea, on the north by Honduras and on the south by Costa Rica.

AREA: 46,430 sq. miles

Land Use: 50% forest; 7% prairie and pasture; 7% cultivable; 36% urban, waste or other.
Arable Land: 11%
Arable Land per capita: 0.98 acres

POPULATION: 3,342,000 (1986)

Population Density: 71.98 inhabs. per sq. mile (1986)
Population Distribution: 55.30% urban (1983)
Population Growth Rate: 3.30% per year (1986)

VITAL STATISTICS

Average Life Expectancy: 59.85 years (1985)
Male: 58.70 years (1985)
Female: 61.00 years (1985)
Age Distribution: (1985)
0-14 . . . . 46.70%
15-64 . . . . 50.70%
65+ 2.50%
Median Age: 16.50 years (1985)
Maternal Mortality: (not available)
Infant Mortality: 85 per 1,000 live births (1984)

HEALTH CARE

Hospital Beds: 1.68 per 10,000 population (1980)
Doctors: 4.49 per 10,000 population (1980)

ETHNIC COMPOSITION: Mestizo - 69%; white - 17%; black - 9%; Indian - 5%.

RELIGION: Roman Catholic - 95%; other - 5%.

LANGUAGE: Spanish is the official language. There are English- and Indian-speaking minorities on the east coast.

EDUCATION: Illiteracy: 34%. In 1981, there were 4,577 primary schools with 503,497 students; 377 secondary schools with 139,743 students; and 6 higher schools with 34,710 students.

ECONOMIC DATA

Expenditures by Function [as % of total]: (not available)
GDP per capita: $1,164 (1983)

TRAVEL NOTES

Climate: The climate is tropical, with a rainy season from May to October. The average annual temperature is 78°F.
Health Precautions: Malaria is present, especially in the beach areas. Intestinal diseases are common. Vaccinations for typhoid, polio, tetanus, diphtheria and yellow fever are all advised, and since infectious hepatitis is endemic, gamma globulin is also recommended. The standard of health care has reportedly substantially improved in the last 5 years.
Miscellaneous: While there are many tourist attractions, the tourist industry has been badly affected by guerrilla warfare. Among the attractions are the mountainous region of the Huellas de Acahualinca, the mineral baths of Tipitapa, Las Isletas archipelago and the abundant ocean and freshwater fishing.

GOVERNMENT

Nicaragua (Republica de Nicaragua—Republic of Nicaragua) gained its independence from Spain in 1821, along with other Spanish provinces in Central America. In 1838, after unions with Mexico (1822-23) and within a Central American federation, Nicaragua declared itself independent and a republic. After a fierce civil war, a three-member military-backed junta came to power in 1979, ending 46 years of domination of Nicaraguan politics by the Somoza family of the then-President Anastasio Somoza Debayle. The junta suspended the Constitution and dissolved the Congress, placing power in a Government of National Reconstruction. Presidential elections and elections to a National Constituent Assembly were held on Nov 4, 1984 and a new Constitution was promulgated Jan 9, 1987.

Constitution: A new Constitution drafted by the National Assembly came into effect Jan 9, 1987. It guarantees the right to lawful demonstrations, the right to hold meetings, to strike and to publish uncensored news. Between the time the junta suspended the Somoza Constitution of 1974 and the new Constitution came into effect, a Bill of Rights guaranteed religious and other individual liberties, along with freedom of the press.

NIGER
Republic of Niger

LOCATION: Niger lies in western Africa and is a landlocked country; it is bordered by Algeria and Libya to the north, Chad to the east, Nigeria and Benin to the south and Burkina Faso and Mali to the west.

AREA: 489,200 sq. miles

Land Use: 2.94% cropland; 7.28% permanent pasture; 2.15% forests and woodland; 87.63% other (mostly desert).
Arable Land: 2.94%
Arable Land per capita: 1.60 acres

POPULATION: 6,688,000 (1988 estimate)

Population Density: 14 inhabs. per sq. mile (1988 estimate)
Population Distribution: 16.17% urban (1985)
Population Growth Rate: 3.40% per year (1988 estimate)

VITAL STATISTICS

Average Life Expectancy: 44.50 years (1985-90 projection)
Male: 42.90 years (1985-90 projection)
Female: 46.10 years (1985-90 projection)
Age Distribution: (1985)
0-14 .... 46.71%
15-64 .... 50.02%
65+ 3.27%
Median Age: 16.60 years (1985)
Maternal Mortality: (not available)
Infant Mortality: 135 per 1,000 live births (1985)

HEALTH CARE

Hospital Beds: 5 per 10,000 population (1986)
Doctors: 0.34 per 10,000 population (1984)

ETHNIC COMPOSITION: Hausa - 56.00%; Djerma - 22.00%; Fula - 8.50%; Tuareg - 8.00%; Beri Beri - 4.30%; other (mostly Arab, Toubou and Gourmantche) - 1.20%.

RELIGION: Moslem (mostly Tijaniyya, Senoussi and Hamallist) - 80%; other (mostly indigenous beliefs) - 20%.

LANGUAGE: French is the official language; however, Hausa and Djerma are more widely spoken. Tuareg and Fulani are also spoken, and English is taught in schools.

EDUCATION: Illiteracy: 90%. In 1983, there were 1,728 primary schools with 261,531 students; 47,188 secondary school students; 1,593 teacher training students; 945 technical training students and 1 university with 2,450 students. In 1980 there were 69 secondary schools, and in 1979 there were 4 teacher training schools and 1 technical training school.

ECONOMIC DATA

Expenditures by Function [as %of total]: (1980)
General public services 19.59%
Defense 3.77%
Education 18.02%
Health 4.05%
Social security and welfare 1.67%
Housing and community amenities 2.10%
Other community and social services 2.21%
Economic services 32.24%
Agriculture, forestry, fishing and hunting ..6.81%
Roads 10.22%
Other transportation and communication ...3.62%
Other purposes 14.56%
GDP per capita: $295 (1985)

TRAVEL NOTES

Climate: The climate is marked by 4 distinct seasons. The most temperate of these lasts from November to March, when the weather is dry and daytime temperatures fall in the mid-90°F range. The hottest months of the year follow, from March to April, when daytime temperature in the shade reaches above 100°F and nightly temperatures are above 80°F. The rainy season lasts from May to September, during which an average of 22 inches of rain falls. Finally, a period of heat and humidity follows in October, when daily highs average 103°F and daily lows fall to an average of 75°F.
Health Precautions: Inoculations are recommended against yellow fever and cholera, in

addition to a gamma globulin inoculation. Other endemic diseases include malaria, hepatitis, dysentery, measles, tuberculosis and meningitis. The water is considered non-potable for travelers.

Miscellaneous: Tourist activities include hunting and fishing, touring the ancient cities of Agadez and Zinder and visiting the Niamey Museum, reputed to be one of the best western African museums.

GOVERNMENT

Niger (Republique du Niger—Republic of Niger), formerly a part of French West Africa, became an independent state on Aug 3, 1960. The armed forces under Brig. Gen. Seyni Kounteche seized power in a coup on Apr 15, 1974, declaring the main objectives of the new Government to be the elimination of corruption and effective famine resistance. Gen. Kounteche died of a reported brain tumor in a Paris hospital on Nov 10, 1987, and was succeeded by Col. Ali Saibou.

Constitution: The Constitution of 1960 was suspended in 1974 by the armed forces. However, on Jun 14, 1986, voters overwhelmingly approved a new national charter to form the basis for a new Constitution. The charter outlines 4 main objectives: national unity, social justice, the building up of the country and participatory democracy. The charter also sets rights for citizens and guidelines for the operation of government institutions and representatives.

NIGERIA
Federal Republic of Nigeria

LOCATION: Situated on the west coast of Africa, Nigeria is bounded by Niger to the north, Benin to the west and Cameroon to the southeast.

AREA: 356,669 sq. miles

Land Use: 33.64% cropland; 22.99% permanent pasture; 17.02% forests and woodland; 26.35% other.
Arable Land: 34%
Arable Land per capita: 0.87 acres

POPULATION: 111,812,000 (1988 estimate)

Population Density: 313 inhabs. per sq. mile (1988 estimate)
Population Distribution: 23.02% urban (1985)
Population Growth Rate: 2.90% per year (1988 estimate)

VITAL STATISTICS

Average Life Expectancy: 50.50 years (1985-90 projection)
Male: 48.80 years (1985-90 projection)
Female: 52.20 years (1985-90 projection)
Age Distribution: (1985)
0-14 ....48.26%
15-64 ....49.32%
65+ 2.42%
Median Age: 15.80 years (1985)
Maternal Mortality: (not available)
Infant Mortality: 127 per 1,000 live births (1985)

HEALTH CARE

Hospital Beds: 9 per 10,000 population (1983)
Doctors: 1 per 10,000 population (1984)

ETHNIC COMPOSITION: Hausa - 21%; Yoruba - 20%; Ibo - 17%; Fulani - 9%; other - 33%.

RELIGION: Moslem - 47%; Christian - 34%; other - 19% (mostly indigenous beliefs).

LANGUAGE: English is the official language. Hausa, Yoruba and Ibo are also widely used.

EDUCATION: Illiteracy: 70%. In 1983, there were 38,211 primary schools with 14,383,487 students and 5,030 secondary schools with 3,561,207 students. In 1984, there were 29 technical colleges and 50 teachers' colleges, and as of 1986 there were 23 universities.

ECONOMIC DATA

Expenditures by Function [as % of total]: (1987)
General public services 11.66%
Defense 23.49%
Education 4.50%
Health 2.51%
Social security and welfare 2.48%
Housing and community amenities 4.14%
Other community and social services 2.58%
Economic services 32.29%
Agriculture, forestry, fishing and hunting ..1.74%
Roads 11.51%

Other transportation and
communication 10.46%
Other purposes 16.36%
GDP per capita: $239 (1987)

TRAVEL NOTES

Climate: Nigeria's climate is tropical, with high humidity and an average temperature of 90°F. Up to 150 inches of rain may fall on the southern section of the country during the wet season. In the northern sections, the heat is offset slightly by cool, dry winds off the Sahara Desert, and rainfall is substantially less than in the south.

Health Precautions: Immunizations against yellow fever are required for entry into the country. Vaccinations for cholera, typhoid, tetanus/diphtheria and polio are recommended, as well as preventive measures against malaria. Tap water is not potable.

Miscellaneous: Nigeria's major tourist attractions are its beaches and scenic coastal landscapes. A large festival of Nigerian art is held annually, with its location varying from year to year.

GOVERNMENT

Nigeria (Federal Republic of Nigeria) became an independent member of the British Commonwealth on Oct 1, 1960. On the third anniversary of its independence, Nigeria revised its Constitution to form a republic. Prime Minister Abbakar Tafawa Balewa, a key figure in obtaining Nigeria's independence, was killed when instigators of a military coup seized power early in 1966. Various military regimes held control over the country until Oct 1, 1979, when authority was returned to a civilian Government under a new Constitution, which established a federal Government overseeing 19 state governments. Army officers seized control of the Government once more in December 1983 (at which time the Constitution was suspended and political parties were banned), and a subsequent coup in August 1985 brought Maj. Gen. Ibrahim Babangida to power. On Jan 13, 1986, Babangida pledged to return power to a civilian Government by Oct 1, 1990. A 5-year plan presented in July 1987 pushed back the formation of a civilian Government until 1992.

Constitution: The Constitution drafted in 1978 established three branches of government (executive, legislative and judicial) to administer a federal system dividing power between the federal and state governments. In January 1984 the Constitution was modified by decree to establish a federal military Government, consisting of a Supreme Military Council and a National Council of States. The Supreme Military Council was renamed the Armed Forces Ruling Council after the 1985 coup. Under Gen. Babangida's plan to return the country to civilian rule, a constituent assembly composed largely of elected members and charged with the task of drafting a new constitution was convened on May 2, 1988.

NORTH KOREA
Democratic People's Republic of Korea

LOCATION: North Korea is located on the Korean peninsula in Northeast Asia. It is bounded by China to the north and the Republic of Korea (South Korea) to the south.

AREA: 46,540 sq. miles

Land Use: 19.00% cropland; 0.42% permanent pasture; 74.50% forests and woodland; 6.08% other.
Arable Land: 19%
Arable Land per capita: 0.26 acres

POPULATION: 21,390,000 (1987 estimate)

Population Density: 460 inhabs. per sq. mile (1987 estimate)
Population Distribution: 63.80% urban (1985)
Population Growth Rate: 2.36% per year (1985-90 projection)

VITAL STATISTICS

Average Life Expectancy: 69.40 years (1985-90 projection)
Male: 66.20 years (1985-90 projection)
Female: 72.70 years (1985-90 projection)
Age Distribution: (1985)
0-14 . . . . 38.70%
15-64 . . . . 57.70%
65+ 3.60%
Median Age: 20.30 years (1985)
Maternal Mortality: (not available)
Infant Mortality: 24 per 1,000 live births

HEALTH CARE

Hospital Beds: 129 per 10,000 population (1982)
Doctors: 24 per 10,000 population (1982)

ETHNIC COMPOSITION: Korean

RELIGION: Buddhism, Confucianism, Daoism, Shamanism and Chundo Kyo are the principal beliefs, although religious practice is officially discouraged.

LANGUAGE: Korean is the official language.

EDUCATION: Illiteracy: 5%. In 1976, there were 4,700 primary schools with 2,561,674 students. In 1970, there were 500 higher technical schools. In 1982, there were 175 universities and colleges.

ECONOMIC DATA

Expenditures by Function [as % of total]: (not available)
GDP per capita: $2083 (1985)

TRAVEL NOTES

Climate: North Korea's climate is hot and humid during the summer and cold and dry in the winter. Temperatures range from 21°F to 77°F. Rainfall is concentrated in the summer months, with June and July usually being the wettest.
Health Precautions: (not available)
Miscellaneous: Travel in North Korea is permitted only in accompanied parties. Mount Keumgang and Mount Songdowon are among the country's most scenic attractions.

GOVERNMENT

North Korea (Choson Minchu-chui Inmin Konghwa-guk—Democratic People's Republic of Korea) was formerly an independent monarchy before being occupied by Japanese forces in 1905, and formally annexed by Japan in 1910. When Japan surrendered in August 1945, Korea was divided into separate occupation zones with the Soviet Union controlling the North and the US administering the South. On Sep 9, 1948, the Democratic People's Republic of Korea was proclaimed. The Korean Workers' Party, created by a merger of Communists in the North and South, was formed in June 1949 and, under the leadership of Kim Il Sung, has held effective political power ever since.

Constitution: The current 149-article Constitution (patterned largely on that of other Communist states) entered into effect on Dec 28, 1972, replacing the amended 1948 Constitution. The new Constitution instituted the offices of President and Vice President and established a new top-level policy-making body, the Central People's Committee. The Constitution declares North Korea to be an independent Socialist state that is guided by the Juche principle of the Korean Workers' Party. The new Constitution specifically commits the nation to the achievement of reunification of Korea by peaceful means. Authority to amend the Constitution rests with the Supreme People's Assembly.

NORTHERN IRELAND
See Britain

NORWAY
Kingdom of Norway

LOCATION: Situated in northern Europe, Norway forms the western part of Scandinavia. It is bordered to the east by Sweden and to the northeast (within the Arctic Circle) by Finland and the Soviet Union. Its long western coastline faces the Atlantic Ocean.

AREA: 125,025 sq. miles

Land Use: 21% forest; 3% cultivable; 2% meadow and pasture; 74% other.
Arable Land: 5%
Arable Land per capita: 0.91 acres

POPULATION: 4,165,000 (1986)

Population Density: 33.31 inhabs. per sq. mile (1986)
Population Distribution: 80% urban (1985)
Population Growth Rate: 0.30% per year (1986)

VITAL STATISTICS

Average Life Expectancy: 76.12 years (1983)
Male: 72.69 years (1983)
Female: 79.54 years (1983)
Age Distribution: (1985)
0-14 . . . . .20.10%

1.5-64 . . . . 64.30%
65+ 15.50%
Median Age: 34.50 years (1985)
Maternal Mortality: 3.90 per 100,000 live births (1983)
Infant Mortality: 8 per 1,000 live births (1985)

HEALTH CARE

Hospital Beds: 150 per 10,000 population (1981)
Doctors: 20.27 per 10,000 population (1981)

ETHNIC COMPOSITION: Germanic (Nordic, Alpine, Baltic) - 99.50%; Lapps - 0.50%.

RELIGION: Evangelical Lutheran - 94%; other Protestant and Roman Catholic - 4%; other - 2%.

LANGUAGE: The official language is Norwegian, which exists in two forms: the older form Bokmal, and the newer form Nynorsk. Lappish and Finnish are also spoken by small minorities.

EDUCATION: Illiteracy: 0%. In 1983, there were 3,539 primary schools with 596,910 students; 918 secondary and vocational schools with 188,040 students; 89 special colleges with 3,178 students; 30 teacher-training schools with 13,546 students; 182 non-university schools with 33,460 students; and 13 universities with 41,002 students.

ECONOMIC DATA

Expenditures by Function [as %of total]: (1985)
General public services 6.36%
Defense 8.61%
Education 8.80%
Health 10.55%
Social security and welfare 35.05%
Housing and community amenities 1.16%
Other community and social services 1.35%
Economic services 20.50%
Agriculture, forestry, fishing and hunting . . 7.28%
Roads 4.57%
Other transportation and communication . . 1.40%
Other purposes 9.63%
GDP per capita: $15,821 (1985)

TRAVEL NOTES

Climate: Temperate on the west coast, the climate is colder inland, with temperatures ranging from 28°F to 46°F.
Health Precautions: Sanitary conditions are considered above average; the water supply system is excellent.

Miscellaneous: Fjords, mountains, forests and lakes make Norway one of the most beautiful countries in the world. Norway is also a center for winter sports.

GOVERNMENT

Norway (Kongeriket Norge—Kingdom of Norway) is a constitutional monarchy. From 1814 to 1905, Norway was united with Sweden. The Swedish King was monarch, but Norway had its own Constitution. After the dissolution of the union (Oct 26, 1905), the Storting (legislative assembly) elected a new King from the Danish royal line.

Constitution: The Constitution of May 17, 1814 established a hereditary monarchy with legislative authority vested in the Storting, over which the King's authority was limited. Subsequent amendments increasingly democratized the political process and expanded the power of the Storting at the expense of the monarchy. Succession to the throne is in the direct male line.

OMAN
Sultanate of Oman

LOCATION: Situated on the eastern coast of the Arabian peninsula, Oman is bordered by the United Arab Emirates to the north, Saudi Arabia to the north and west and South Yemen to the southwest. Oman has a long coastline on the Arabian Sea.

AREA: 82,010 sq. miles

Land Use: 0.19% cropland; 4.71% permanent pasture; 0% forest and woodland; 95.10% other (mostly desert).
Arable Land: 0.19%
Arable Land per capita: 0.09 acres

POPULATION: 1,389,000 (1989 estimate)

Population Density: 17 inhabs. per sq. mile (1989 estimate)
Population Distribution: 8.86% urban (1985)
Population Growth Rate: 2.90% per year (1989 projection)

VITAL STATISTICS

Average Life Expectancy: 55.40 years (1985-90 projection)
Male: 54.10 years (1985-90 projection)
Female: 56.70 years (1985-90 projection)
Age Distribution: (1985)
0-14 .... 44.28%
15-64 .... 53.22%
65+ 2.50%
Median Age: 18.20 years (1985)
Maternal Mortality: (not available)
Infant Mortality: 115 per 1,000 live births (1985)

HEALTH CARE

Hospital Beds: 22 per 10,000 population (1986)
Doctors: 5 per 10,000 population (1986)

ETHNIC COMPOSITION: Arab - 88%; Baluchi - 4%; Persian - 3%; Indian - 2%; African - 2%.

RELIGION: Ibadhi Moslem - 75%; other (mostly Sunni Moslem, some Shiite Moslem and Hindu) - 25%.

LANGUAGE: Arabic is the official language. English and Urdu are also spoken in some areas.

EDUCATION: Illiteracy: 80%. In 1986/87, there were 354 primary schools and 295 secondary schools with a total of 244,657 students. Oman has a teacher training institute, an agricultural institute and a commercial institute. The Sultan Qabus University opened in 1986 and was attended by 520 students.

ECONOMIC DATA

Expenditures by Function [as % of total]: (1986)
General public services 13.62%
Defense 41.92%
Education 10.07%
Health 5.02%
Social security and welfare 0%
Housing and community amenities 1.39%
Other community and social services 2.36%
Economic services 20.84%
Agriculture, forestry, fishing and hunting .. 2.05%
Roads 3.94%
Other transportation and communication .. 0.83%
Other purposes 4.78%
GDP per capita: $8,347 (1985)

TRAVEL NOTES

Climate: In Muscat, temperatures range from 70°F to 90°F, and the average annual rainfall is just under 4 inches. Rainfall is somewhat higher inland, and there are summer monsoons in the southwestern province of Dhofar.
Health Precautions: Inoculations against typhoid, tetanus, cholera and polio are strongly recommended, as are gamma globulin shots and malaria suppressants. Tap water is not potable.
Miscellaneous: Old Muscat preserves the atmosphere of a medieval town with its narrow streets and surrounding wall. Muscat Harbor is guarded by two forts built by the Portuguese in the 15th and 16th centuries.

GOVERNMENT

Oman (Saltanat 'Uman—Sultanate of Oman) is a traditionalist Arab monarchy, in which the absolute authority of the Sultan is modified by Moslem law and tribal customs. Formerly the Sultanate of Muscat and Oman, the name was changed to Oman on Aug 9, 1970 by Sultan Qabus (Qaboos) bin Said, who seized power from his father on Jul 24, 1970, and launched a program to modernize Oman.

Constitution: There is no written Constitution, but the customs and usages of Moslem and tribal tradition provide some "unwritten" limits on the exercise of governmental power.

OUTER MONGOLIA
See Mongolia

PAKISTAN
Islamic Republic of Pakistan

LOCATION: Pakistan is located in southern Asia and is bordered on the east by India, on the northwest by Afghanistan and on the west by Iran. It has a short border with China to the northeast and coastline on the Arabian Sea to the south.

AREA: 310,403 sq. miles

Land Use: 24% cultivated; 3% forest; 73% urban, waste and other.
Arable Land: 40%
Arable Land per capita: 0.78 acres

POPULATION: 101,855,000 (1986)

Population Density: 328 inhabs. per sq. mile (1986)

Population Distribution: 29.80% urban (1985)

Population Growth Rate: 2.60% per year (1986)

VITAL STATISTICS

Average Life Expectancy: 50.65 years (1981)

Male: 51.60 years (1981)

Female: 49.70 years (1981)

Age Distribution: (1985)

0-14 .... 43.60%
15-64 .... 53.59%
65+ 2.81%

Median Age: 17.90 years (1985)

Maternal Mortality: (not available)

Infant Mortality: 119 per 1,000 live births (1983)

HEALTH CARE

Hospital Beds: 5.69 per 10,000 population (1981)

Doctors: 3.13 per 10,000 population (1981)

ETHNIC COMPOSITION: Punjabi - 66.00%; Sindhi - 13.00%; Pushtun - 8.50%; Baluchi - 7.60%; others - 4.90%.

RELIGION: Islam - 97%; Christian, Hindu and other - 3%.

LANGUAGE: Urdu and English are the official languages; Punjabi, Sindhi and Pushtu are also widely spoken.

EDUCATION: Illiteracy: 76%. In 1983/84, there were 6,412,000 primary school students; 1,676,000 middle school students; 611,000 secondary school students; 419,000 students in schools of arts and sciences; 87,737 students in professional schools; and 49,479 university students.

ECONOMIC DATA

Expenditures by Function [as % of total]: (1983)

General public services 8.01%
Defense 34.82%
Education 3.05%
Health 1.04%
Social security and welfare 6.08%
Housing and community amenities 3.19%
Other community and social services 1.81%
Economic services 27.98%
Agriculture, forestry, fishing and hunting .. 1.23%
Roads 1.42%

Other transportation and communication . . .6.78%
Other purposes 14.02%

GDP per capita: $288 (1985)

TRAVEL NOTES

Climate: The climate is generally dry and hot, with the annual average temperature around 80°F, except in the mountains of the north, where the winters are very cold.

Health Precautions: Giardia, malaria, hepatitis and amoebic and bacillary dysentery are common. A preventive rabies immunization series is recommended for anyone planning to reside in Pakistan. Drinking water should be boiled.

Miscellaneous: The magnificent scenery of the Himalayas are an important tourist attraction, while the climate is favorable for field sports, mountaineering and winter sports.

GOVERNMENT

Pakistan (Islami Jamhuria-e-Pakistan—Islamic Republic of Pakistan) became independent on Aug 15, 1947, as a result of the partition of British India, and became a republic on Mar 23, 1956. One of its two parts, East Pakistan, became the separate country of Bangladesh in 1971. (Pakistan resisted the separatist movement and did not recognize Bangladesh until 1974.) The 1973 Constitution provided for a parliamentary form of government, but on Jul 5, 1977, after an extended period of political violence that followed the March 1977 elections, the armed forces, led by Gen. Mohammad Zia ul-Haq, imposed a martial law regime in a bloodless coup against the Government of Prime Minister Zulfiqar Ali Bhutto, who was later hanged for alleged political murder. Martial law was lifted Dec 30, 1985, after amendments to the Constitution concentrated power in the hands of Gen. Zia. Zia was killed in a mysterious plane crash on Aug 17, 1988, and, following November 1988 National Assembly elections in which her party won the greatest number of seats, Benazir Bhutto, daughter of the overthrown Prime Minister, herself became Prime Minister.

Constitution: Pakistan's present Constitution entered into effect on Aug 14, 1973. On Mar 2, 1985, then-President Zia ul-Haq announced constitutional amendments that in effect indemnified all actions of the military regime and increased presidential power. Parts of the Constitution, including the provision of basic rights, were suspended under the martial law regime, but were restored Dec 30, 1985. The Constitution provides for an Islamic Republic and guarantees freedom of religion and the press, and equal rights for women.

PANAMA
Republic of Panama

LOCATION: Situated at the southern end of the isthmus separating North and South America, Panama is bounded by the Caribbean Sea to the north, Colombia to the east, the Pacific Ocean to the south and Costa Rica to the west.

AREA: 29,762 sq. miles

Land Use: 7.40% cropland; 15.28% permanent pasture; 53.69% forests and woodland; 23.63% other.
Arable Land: 7%
Arable Land per capita: 0.59 acres

POPULATION: 2,322,000 (1988 estimate)

Population Density: 78 inhabs. per sq. mile (1988 estimate)
Population Distribution: 52.40% urban (1985)
Population Growth Rate: 2% per year (1988 estimate)

VITAL STATISTICS

Average Life Expectancy: 72.10 years (1985-90 projection)
Male: 70.10 years (1985-90 projection)
Female: 74.10 years (1985-90 projection)
Age Distribution: (1985)

0-14	37.55%
15-64	57.96%
65+	4.49%

Median Age: 20.60 years (1985)
Maternal Mortality: 49.40 per 100,000 live births (1984)
Infant Mortality: 23 per 1,000 live births (1986)

HEALTH CARE

Hospital Beds: 36 per 10,000 population (1984)
Doctors: 11 per 10,000 population (1984)

ETHNIC COMPOSITION: Mestizo - 70%; West Indian - 14%; white - 10%; Indian - 6%.

RELIGION: Roman Catholic - 93%; Protestant - 6%; other - 1%.

LANGUAGE: The official language is Spanish, which is spoken by 86% of the population. Many Panamanians are bilingual, with 14% speaking English as their native tongue.

EDUCATION: Illiteracy: 10%. In 1985, there were 2,476 primary schools with 340,135 students; 329 secondary schools with 184,536 students; and 8 institutions of higher education with 55,644 students.

ECONOMIC DATA

Expenditures by Function [as % of total]: (1985)

General public services	21.37%
Defense	(not available)
Education	15.95%
Health	15.77%
Social security and welfare	12.94%
Housing and community amenities	3.76%
Other community and social services	0.68%
Economic services	9.04%
Agriculture, forestry, fishing and hunting	2.70%
Roads	3.86%
Other transportation and communication	0.47%
Other purposes	20.49%

GDP per capita: $2,300 (1986)

TRAVEL NOTES

Climate: Panama has a tropical climate. There is little seasonal variation in temperature, with coastal areas averaging between 73°F and 81°F. The rainy season lasts from April until December.
Health Precautions: The water is potable and health conditions are generally good in Panama City, but the usual health precautions should be taken in rural areas. Inoculations against yellow fever, typhoid and paratyphoid are recommended for longer visits.
Miscellaneous: The main tourist attractions include Panama City, the Canal, the ruins at Portobelo, the resort of Contadora, the San Blas Islands in the Atlantic and the many other tropical islands.

GOVERNMENT

Panama (Republica de Panama—Republic of Panama) was a member of the Confederation of Greater Colombia (Gran Colombia) from 1821 until Nov 3, 1903, when it declared its independence following the failure of Colombia to ratify the Hay-Herron treaty providing for a US-controlled zone for the construction of the trans-Panama canal. Under the Panamanian Constitution, executive power is vested in the President, but the nation's de facto ruler is the chief of the armed forces, Gen. Manuel Antonio Noriega (see below: Constitution). In June 1987, accusations that Noriega participated in electoral fraud and was involved in political murder led to widespread demonstrations and riots by people demanding the ouster of the military regime. After unsuccessfully attempting to dismiss Gen. Noriega, President Eric Arturo Delvalle was removed from office on Feb 26, 1988 by the National Assembly, which is dominated by Noriega supporters. Various efforts to oust Noriega have been made by the US, including the handing down of Federal indictments against Gen. Noriega and the implementation of economic sanctions, but the Panamanian leader has managed to retain power and solidify his power base.

Panama Canal and Canal Zone. Under the terms of the Panama Canal treaties between the US and Panama, which were signed in 1977 and entered into effect on Oct 1, 1979, Panama took over the administration of the Canal Zone. Operation of the canal was assigned to a new body, the Panama Canal Commission, which will be controlled by the US (with Panamanian representation) until 1989. The US will maintain military forces on the Canal until the year 2000, and will retain responsibility for the Canal's neutrality thereafter.

Constitution: Under the Constitutional arrangements of 1972, executive authority is held by a President and a Vice President, but real power in Panama is wielded by the armed forces, with the commander-in-chief of the National Defense Forces being the country's de facto ruler. In April 1983, a public referendum approved amendments to reform the Constitution. The amendments included the replacement of the existing National Assembly of Community Representatives (505 members) with a Legislative Assembly (67 members). The presidential term of office was reduced from 6 to 5 years and provisions were made for the election of two Vice Presidents. The amendments also barred armed forces from participation in the elections.

PAPUA NEW GUINEA

LOCATION: Comprising the eastern section of the South Pacific island of New Guinea, Papua New Guinea lies east of Indonesia and north of northeastern Australia.

AREA: 178,704 sq. miles

Land Use: 0.83% cropland; 0.22% permanent pasture; 84.86% forests and woodland; 14.09% other.
Arable Land: 1%
Arable Land per capita: 35.97 acres

POPULATION: 3,613,000 (1989 estimate)

Population Density: 20 inhabs. per sq. mile (1989 estimate)
Population Distribution: 14.24% urban (1985)
Population Growth Rate: 2.38% per year (1985-90 projection)

VITAL STATISTICS

Average Life Expectancy: 54.00 years (1985-90 projection)
Male: 53.20 years (1985-90 projection)
Female: 54.80 years (1985-90 projection)
Age Distribution: (1985)
0-14 . . . . .41.55%
15-64 . . . . .56.00%
65+ 2.45%
Median Age: 18.80 years (1985)
Maternal Mortality: (not available)
Infant Mortality: 91 per 1,000 live births (1985)

HEALTH CARE

Hospital Beds: 41 per 10,000 population (1985)
Doctors: 0.55 per 10,000 population (1985)

ETHNIC COMPOSITION: Mainly Melanesian and Papuan with Polynesian, Negrito and Micronesian minorities.

RELIGION: Protestant - 63%; Roman Catholic - 31%; pantheistic and other - 6%.

LANGUAGE: Pidgin English, English and Motu are the official languages in Parliament. There are over 700 native languages.

EDUCATION: Illiteracy: 68%. In 1986, there were 2,428 community (primary) schools with 368,455 students; 116 secondary schools with 47,299 students; 9 technical colleges with 1,507 students; and 94 vocational schools with 6,605 students.

ECONOMIC DATA

Expenditures by Function [as % of total]: (1985)
General public services 22.35%
Defense 4.52%
Education 17.01%
Health 9.62%
Social security and welfare 0.40%
Housing and community amenities 1.61%
Other community and social services 2.31%
Economic services 18.60%
Agriculture, forestry, fishing and hunting . . 5.01%
Roads 2.71%
Other transportation and communication . . 5.28%
Other purposes 23.58%
GDP per capita: $911 (1987)

TRAVEL NOTES

Climate: The country is tropical year-round, with an average maximum temperature of 91°F and an average minimum of 72°F. There is heavy rainfall on the coast. Annual rainfall ranges from 40 inches to 250 inches. There are two monsoon seasons: from May to October and from December to March.
Health Precautions: Malaria suppressants are recommended. Tap water is potable in the larger towns.
Miscellaneous: Tourist attractions include beautiful countryside and wildlife.

GOVERNMENT

Papua New Guinea became an independent state on Sep 16, 1975, although it had been internally self-governing since Dec 1, 1973. In the past, it was colonized by many different countries, most recently Australia. Papua New Guinea is a constitutional monarchy with the British monarch as the nominal head of state. It has a parliamentary form of government, with a multi-party system. Effective political authority rests with the Prime Minister and a Cabinet. The country's politics are strongly influenced by the diverse ethnic make-up of its population and the rugged nature of the country. These have spawned a number of movements for the decentralization of political authority, most notably a 1975 secessionist movement on Bougainville island.

Constitution: The Constitution, which took effect on Sep 16, 1975, set up a unitary form of government with a strong central authority. However, largely due to secessionist pressures, an amendment was adopted permitting the central Government to give provincial governments substantial autonomy. The Constitution bars discrimination based on race, color or sex, and provides for freedom of religion. The Constitution may be amended by a two-thirds vote of Parliament.

PARAGUAY
Republic of Paraguay

LOCATION: A landlocked country, Paraguay is located in central South America. It is bordered by Brazil to the east, Bolivia to the north and Argentina to the west and south.

AREA: 157,050 sq. miles

Land Use: 4.88% cropland; 39.14% permanent pasture; 51.47% forests and woodland; 4.51% other.
Arable Land: 5%
Arable Land per capita: 1.45 acres

POPULATION: 4,383,000 (1988 estimate)

Population Density: 28 inhabs. per sq. mile (1988 estimate)
Population Distribution: 44.44% urban (1985)
Population Growth Rate: 3% per year (1988 estimate)

VITAL STATISTICS

Average Life Expectancy: 66.10 years (1985-90 projection)
Male: 63.70 years (1985-90 projection)
Female: 68.60 (1985-90 projection)
Age Distribution: (1985)
0-14 . . . . .41.69%
15-64 . . . . .54.75%
65+ 3.56%
Median Age: 18.80 years (1985)
Maternal Mortality: 468.60 per 100,000 live births (1980)
Infant Mortality: 52 per 1,000 live births (1985)

HEALTH CARE

Hospital Beds: 10 per 10,000 population (1982)
Doctors: 7 per 10,000 population (1984)

ETHNIC COMPOSITION: Mestizo - 95%; other - 5%.

RELIGION: Roman Catholic - 97%; other - 3%.

LANGUAGE: Although Spanish is the official language, Guarani, an indigenous language, is spoken by about 90% of the people.

EDUCATION: Illiteracy: 19%. In 1983, there were 3,960 primary schools, 658 secondary schools and 2 institutions of higher education. In 1984, there were 559,080 primary school students, 150,556 secondary school students and 30,222 students in institutions of higher learning.

ECONOMIC DATA

Expenditures by Function [as % of total]: (1984)
General public services 12.76%
Defense 10.24%
Education 10.69%
Health 5.85%
Social security and welfare 30.41%
Housing and community amenities 2.51%
Other community and social services 0.16%
Economic services 22.24%
Agriculture, forestry, fishing and hunting . . 2.68%
Roads 13.32%
Other transportation and communication .. 0.16%
Other purposes 5.13%
GDP per capita: $809 (1986)

TRAVEL NOTES

Climate: Paraguay has a subtropical climate. The hot season lasts from October to March, and high temperatures average 94°F in January. The winter season lasts from April to September, and low temperatures average 51°F in June.
Health Precautions: Precautions should be taken against diphtheria, measles, tetanus, polio and typhoid fever. The water is not potable.
Miscellaneous: Tourists are attracted by the natural beauty of Paraguay, including the Chaco area, Iguazu Falls and Lake Ypacarai.

GOVERNMENT

Paraguay (Republica del Paraguay—Republic of Paraguay) gained its independence from Spain in 1811, and has since been governed by a series of dictatorships. A period of dispute with Bolivia during the 1930s and periods of authoritarian government and civil war in the 1940s were followed by the assumption of power by Gen. Alfredo Stroessner Mattiauda in a military coup in 1954. Gen. Stroessner—using repressive measures against opposition members and the media, a continuing state of siege and alleged election fraud—became the longest serving leader in Latin America until he was overthrown in a Feb 3, 1989 bloody coup. The leader of the coup, Gen. Andres Rodriguez, who had been second-in-command to Gen. Stroessner, was immediately sworn in as President, promising democratic reforms. In elections held May 1, Gen. Rodriguez easily won the position of President, and proceeded to carry out reforms, such as lifting press restrictions.

Constitution: The present Constitution, the country's 5th since independence, replaced the 1940 Constitution and came into force in 1968. The Constitution provides for a powerful executive and a bicameral legislature. The Constitution guarantees freedom of conscience, travel, residence, religion and the right of workers to organize and strike. However, Constitutional rights may be suspended under a presidentially-declared state of siege.

PEOPLE'S REPUBLIC OF CHINA
See China

PERU
Republic of Peru

LOCATION: Lying in western South America, Peru is bordered by Ecuador and Colombia to the north, by Brazil and Bolivia to the east and by Chile to the south. To the west is the Pacific Ocean.

AREA: 496,225 sq. miles

Land Use: 55% forest; 14% meadow and pasture; 2% cropland; 29% urban, waste, other.
Arable Land: 3%
Arable Land per capita: 0.46 acres

QUALITY OF LIFE INDICATORS

POPULATION: 20,727,000 (1987)

Population Density: 41.77 inhabs. per sq. mile (1987)
Population Distribution: 67.40% urban (1985)
Population Growth Rate: 2.60% per year (1986)

VITAL STATISTICS

Average Life Expectancy: 61.40 years (1985-90)
Male: 59.50 years (1985-90)
Female: 63.40 years (1985-90)
Age Distribution: (1985)
0-14 .... 40.50%
15-64 .... 55.90%
60+: 3.60%
Median Age: 19.40 years (1985)
Maternal Mortality: 103.40 per 100,000 live births (1978)
Infant Mortality: 88 per 1,000 live births (1985-90)

HEALTH CARE

Hospital Beds: 18.72 per 10,000 population (1977)
Doctors: 6.93 per 10,000 population (1979)

ETHNIC COMPOSITION: Indian - 45%; mestizo - 37%; white - 15%; black, Japanese, Chinese, other - 3%.

RELIGION: Over 90% of the population is Roman Catholic.

LANGUAGE: The official languages are Spanish, Quechua and Aymara.

EDUCATION: Illiteracy: 20%. In 1984, there were 22,876 primary schools with more than 3,412,769 students; 3,736 secondary schools with 1,429,219 students; 953 higher schools with 246,501 students; 35 universities with 315,701 students; and 159 special schools with 10,797 students.

ECONOMIC DATA

Expenditures by Function [as % of total]: (1981)
General public services 10.44%
Defense 13.81%
Education 11.34%
Health 5.30%
Social security and welfare 0.15%
Housing and community amenities 0.92%
Other community and social services 1.25%
Economic services .... (not available)
Agriculture, forestry, fishing and hunting .. 4.07%

Roads .... (not available)
Other transportation and communication .... (not available)
Other purposes .... (not available)
GDP per capita: $575 (1985)

TRAVEL NOTES

Climate: Varying with altitude, the climate includes a rainy season from October to April, with heavy rainfall in the tropical forests. Temperatures are about 20°F lower in the Andes mountains than in the coastal plains.
Health Precautions: New arrivals should be protected by gamma globulin every 4 months. Immunizations for typhoid, tetanus, measles, mumps, polio, German measles and yellow fever should be kept current. High altitudes may bring on headaches and nausea due to the lack of oxygen; visitors to the high Andean regions should prepare to rest 12 hours or more the first day.
Miscellaneous: Lima's Spanish colonial architecture and Cuzco's pre-Inca and Inca civilization, including the "lost city" of Machu Picchu, are main tourist attractions. There are also popular resorts at Lake Titicaca and in the Amazon jungle region to the northeast. Authorities plan to develop trekking, mountaineering and fishing holidays.

GOVERNMENT

Peru (Republica del Peru—Republic of Peru) was declared independent from Spain in 1821 and achieved independence in 1826. Its history has been marked by alternations of constitutional civilian and military rule. More than a decade of military rule ended in July 1980 when a civilian government assumed power. The succession of Alan Garcia Perez to the presidency in 1985 was the first such transfer of power from an elected President in 40 years.

Constitution: The Constitution, which came into force on Jul 28, 1980, deals extensively with human rights. State intervention in the economy is also elaborated on. The Constitution provides for the separation of executive, legislative and judicial powers and for a strong executive branch. The Chamber of Deputies is empowered to censure Cabinet Ministers.

PHILIPPINES
Republic of the Philippines

LOCATION: The Philippines are an archipelago located in the western Pacific Ocean, to the east of Southeast Asia.

AREA: 115,831 sq. miles

Land Use: 37.73% cropland; 3.76% permanent pasture; 40.41% forests and woodland; 18.10% other.
Arable Land: 26%
Arable Land per capita: 0.34 acres

POPULATION: 57,060,000 (1987)

Population Density: 492 inhabs. per sq. mile (1987)
Population Distribution: 39.63% urban (1985)
Population Growth Rate: 2.25% per year (1985-90 projection)

VITAL STATISTICS

Average Life Expectancy: 63.50 years (1985-90 projection)
Male: 61.70 years (1985-90 projection)
Female: 65.40 years (1985-90 projection)
Age Distribution: (1985)
0-14 .... 40.40%
15-64 .... 56.10%
65+ 3.40%
Median Age: 19.40 years (1985)
Maternal Mortality: 125 per 100,000 live births (1980)
Infant Mortality: 45 per 1,000 live births (1985-90 projection)

HEALTH CARE

Hospital Beds: 13 per 10,000 population (1984)
Doctors: 1.49 per 10,000 population (1981)

ETHNIC COMPOSITION: Christian Malay - 91.50%; Moslem Malay - 4.00%; Chinese - 1.50%; other - 3.00%

RELIGION: Catholicism - 83%; Protestantism - 9%; Islam - 5%; Buddhist and other - 3%.

LANGUAGE: Of the many languages spoken, the most common are Cebuano, Tagalog, Iloco and Ifugao. The national language is Pilipino, which is based on Tagalog. English is widely spoken, while the use of Spanish is declining.

EDUCATION: Illiteracy: 12%. In 1984/85, there were 32,809 primary schools with 8,794,000 students; 5,430 secondary schools with 3,323,000 students; and 1,157 colleges, universities and vocational schools with 1,054,000 students.

ECONOMIC DATA

Expenditures by Function [as %of total]: (1983)
General public services 19.70%
Defense 13.59%
Education 25.59%
Health 6.80%
Social security and welfare 2.97%
Housing and community amenities 1.94%
Other community and social services 0.87%
Economic services 44.62%
Agriculture, forestry, fishing and hunting .13.75%
Roads 10.37%
Other transportation and communication ...2.71%
Other purposes 11.12%
GDP per capita: $547 (1986)

TRAVEL NOTES

Climate: The climate in the Philippines is maritime and tropical. It is generally hot and humid, except in the mountains, and rainfall is frequent. The archipelago is often in the path of typhoons.
Health Precautions: Water is sometimes not potable and it should be boiled as a general precaution before consumption. Normal precautions should be adequate for avoiding such serious diseases as typhoid, cholera, diphtheria and poliomyelitis.
Miscellaneous: The Philippines' warm climate and tropical setting, and the cosmopolitan city of Manila, are its main tourist attractions.

GOVERNMENT

The *Philippines (Republika ng Pilipinas—Republica de Filipinas—Republic of the Philippines),* a Spanish colony from the 16th century until the US defeated Spain in the Spanish-American War in 1898, became independent on Jul 4, 1946, having been a self-governing Commonwealth under US control since 1935. From the time of independence until 1972, the Philippines had a governmental system modeled on that of the US, with separation of powers among executive, legislative and judicial branches, a strong President and a bicameral legislature. On Sep 23, 1972, President Ferdinand Marcos declared martial law, which remained in effect until Jan 17, 1981. Corazon C. Aquino assumed power after Marcos fled from the Philippines on Feb 25, 1986, in the midst of a popular and military uprising sparked by fraudulent elections. A new Constitution was passed in a popular referendum on Feb 2, 1987, creating a system of government modeled after that of the US, with Aquino being confirmed as President. The Government has been threatened by several coup attempts during 1987, as right-wing forces, led by the military, continually struggle with leftists over how the Government should deal with the country's Communist insurgents.

Constitution: The 1973 Constitution, while establishing a parliamentary form of government elected by and responsible to a unicameral legislature, also accommodated the martial law provisions imposed by President Ferdinand Marcos. On Mar 25, 1986, after the February downfall of Ferdinand Marcos, President Corazon C. Aquino abolished the National Assembly and suspended the Constitution. In October 1986, a presidential panel approved a new draft constitution, which was accepted by 81% of the voters in a national plebiscite on Feb 2, 1987. The new Constitution established a balanced government similar to the US Government, with executive, legislative and judicial branches. A Bill of Rights and a statement guaranteeing full respect of human rights was also incorporated into the new Constitution.

POLAND
Polish People's Republic

LOCATION: Situated in Eastern Europe, Poland is bounded by the Baltic Sea on the north, East Germany on the west, Czechoslovakia on the south and the Soviet Union on the east.

AREA: 120,727 sq. miles

Land Use: 49% arable; 27% forest; 14% other agricultural, 10% other.
Arable Land: 49%
Arable Land per capita: 1 acre

POPULATION: 37,753,000 (1987)

Population Density: 312.71 inhabs. per sq. mile (1987)
Population Distribution: 39% urban (1985)
Population Growth Rate: 0.70% per year (1985-90)

VITAL STATISTICS

Average Life Expectancy: 72.40 years (1985-90)
Male: 68.50 years (1985-90)
Female: 76.40 years (1985-90)
Age Distribution: (1985)
0-14 . . . . .25.30%
15-64 . . . . .65.40%
65+ 9.40%
Median Age: 30.90 years (1985)
Maternal Mortality: 81 per 100,000 live births (1980)
Infant Mortality: 17 per 1,000 live births (1985-90)

HEALTH CARE

Hospital Beds: 56.61 per 10,000 population (1985)
Doctors: 19.70 per 10,000 population (1985)

ETHNIC COMPOSITION: Polish - 98.70%; Ukrainian - 0.60%; Byelorussian - 0.50%; Jewish - less than 0.05%; other - 0.20%.

RELIGION: Roman Catholic - 95%; Uniate, Greek Orthodox, Protestant and other - 5%.

LANGUAGE: Polish.

EDUCATION: Illiteracy: 2%. In 1985, there were 16,429 primary schools with 4,770,600 students; 1,139 secondary schools with 375,000 students; 9,562 technical, art and vocational colleges with 1,516,800 students; 91 higher institutions with 349,800 students.

ECONOMIC DATA

Expenditures by Function [as % of total]: (not available)
GDP per capita: (not available)

TRAVEL NOTES

Climate: While temperate in the west, the climate is continental in the east. Summers are short and winters are cold and snowy. Warsaw temperatures range from 21°F to 75°F.

Health Precautions: Poland is reportedly considered a "jaundice area" and inoculation against typhoid is desirable, as are gamma globulin doses.

Miscellaneous: The Polish Tourist and Country Lovers' Society, responsible for tourism, maintains about 260 tourist hotels and hostels. There are a number of historically interesting cities, such as Wroclaw, Krakow and Warsaw, as well as 30 health and climatic resorts. The mountains, forests and rivers are appreciated by visitors for both their beauty and sports opportunities.

GOVERNMENT

Poland (Polska Rzeczpospolita Ludowa—Polish People's Republic) became a Communist People's Republic in 1947, in the aftermath of the Soviet defeat of German forces in World War II. Effective political authority resides in the United Workers' (Communist) Party. On Dec 13, 1981, a Military Council for National Salvation, headed by Gen. Wojciech Jaruzelski, imposed nationwide martial law. Martial law was officially lifted in July 1983. The National Defense Committee was empowered by the Sejm in November 1983 to assume martial law powers in any future emergency, however. In 1989, after round-table agreements with the formerly outlawed Solidarity trade union, elections were held for a new Parliament and on Jul 19, 1989, General Jaruzelski was elected President by the Parliament.

Constitution: The July 1952 Constitution, as amended in 1976, describes Poland as a socialist state and the Polish United Workers' Party as the "leading political force in the building of socialism."

PORTUGAL
Portuguese Republic

LOCATION: Bordered by Spain to the north and east, the mainland portion of Portugal lies in western Europe, on the Atlantic side of the Iberian peninsula. The archipelagos of Azores and Madeira are in the Atlantic Ocean.

AREA: 33,549 sq. miles

Land Use: 38.72% cropland; 5.78% permanent pasture; 39.73% forests and woodland; 15.77% other.
Arable Land: 49%
Arable Land per capita: 1.02 acres

POPULATION: 10,341,000 (1987 projection)

Population Density: 308 inhabs. per sq. mile (1987)
Population Distribution: 31.20% urban (1985)
Population Growth Rate: 64% per year (1985-90 projection)

VITAL STATISTICS

Average Life Expectancy: 73.00 years (1985-90 projection)
Male: 69.40 years (1985-90 projection)
Female: 76.90 years (1985-90 projection)
Age Distribution: (1985)
0-14 . . . . .24.60%
15-64 . . . . .64.90%
65+ 10.50%
Median Age: 30.10 years (1985)
Maternal Mortality: 34 per 100,000 live births (1982)
Infant Mortality: 17 per 1,000 live births (1985-90 projection)

HEALTH CARE

Hospital Beds: 38.41 per 10,000 population (1985)
Doctors: 23.63 per 10,000 population (1985)

ETHNIC COMPOSITION: The majority is of homogeneous Mediterranean stock. There is a small African minority.

RELIGION: Roman Catholics - 97%; other - 3%.

LANGUAGE: Portuguese

EDUCATION: Illiteracy: 20%. In 1983/84, there were 13,111 basic primary and preparatory schools with 1,288,163 students; 1,563 secondary schools with 575,595 students; 51 higher schools with 95,414 students; 289 teacher training schools with 1,772; and 26,174 students in 75 other schools excluding private schools.

ECONOMIC DATA

Expenditures by Function [as % of total]: (1975)
General public services 17.26%

Defense 13.29%
Education 10.67%
Health 4.43%
Social security and welfare 26.81%
Housing and community amenities 3.72%
Other community and social services 0.48%
Economic services 10.91%
Agriculture, forestry, fishing and hunting .. 1.94%
Roads .... (not available)
Other transportation and communication .. 5.50%
Other purposes 4.77%
GDP per capita: $2,188 (1985)

TRAVEL NOTES

Climate: Portugal enjoys a mild and temperate climate, with an average annual temperature of 61°F. The weather is hotter and drier inland.

Health Precautions: While no special health precautions are necessary, health care is considered below US standards, mainly due to overcrowding and poor nursing care.

Miscellaneous: Earnings from tourism are an important source of revenue. Attractions include Lisbon and Algarve on the mainland, and Madeira and the Azores islands, which are popular winter resorts.

GOVERNMENT

Portugal (Republica Portuguesa—Portuguese Republic) is a republic with a parliamentary form of government and a strong President. The first civilian President since a military coup in 1926 was elected on Feb 16, 1986.

Constitution: The Constitution of Apr 25, 1976 envisaged the construction of a socialist society. It listed the organs of sovereignty in the following order: President, Council of the Revolution, Assembly and Government (Council of Ministers, or Cabinet). Amendments to the Constitution approved in August 1982 by the necessary two-thirds majority of Assembly members and entering into effect on Oct 30 abolished the Council of the Revolution and established a Constitutional Tribunal (composed of 13 judges), a Supreme Council of National Defense and an advisory 16-member Council of State instead. The amendments also modified the Constitution's pronouncements on socialism. Macao, which will be transferred to China in 1999, is governed by special statute, while the Azores and Madeira were granted autonomy in 1976.

PUERTO RICO
Commonwealth of Puerto Rico

LOCATION: The Commonwealth of Puerto Rico is located in the Caribbean Sea and consists of the main island of Puerto Rico and a number of smaller islands, including Culebra and Vieques. The Dominican Republic lies to the west and the Virgin Islands to the east.

AREA: 3,459 sq. miles

Land Use: (not available)
Arable Land: (not available)
Arable Land per capita: (not available)

POPULATION: 3,363,000 (1988 estimate)

Population Density: 972 inhabs. per sq. mile (1988 estimate)
Population Distribution: 70.70% urban (1985)
Population Growth Rate: 0.80% per year (1988 estimate)

VITAL STATISTICS

Average Life Expectancy: 74.70 years (1985-90 projection)
Male: 71.20 years (1985-90 projection)
Female: 78.30 years (1985-90 projection)
Age Distribution: (1985)
0-14 ....29.68%
15-64 ....62.03%
65+ 8.29%
Median Age: 25.50 years (1985)
Maternal Mortality: 4.60 per 100,000 live births (1983)
Infant Mortality: 15 per 1,000 live births (1985)

HEALTH CARE

Hospital Beds: 43 per 10,000 population (1980)
Doctors: 13 per 10,000 population (1980)

ETHNIC COMPOSITION: Hispanic - 99%; other - 1%.

RELIGION: Roman Catholic - 85%; other - 15% (mainly Christian).

LANGUAGE: Spanish is the official language, but English is also widely spoken.

EDUCATION: Illiteracy: 12% (1980). In 1984/85, there were 1,782 public schools with 692,923 students; 818 private schools with 102,255 students; 101,217 students at private colleges and universities; and 54,455 students at the University of Puerto Rico.

ECONOMIC DATA

Expenditures by Function [as % of total]: (not available)
GDP per capita: $6,373 (1986)

TRAVEL NOTES

Climate: Puerto Rico has a mild maritime-tropical climate. The average annual temperature is 75°F, with a normal range of 63°F to 97°F.
Health Precautions: None
Miscellaneous: Tourists are attracted to Puerto Rico by its beautiful beaches, spectacular mountain scenery and bountiful fishing. Other attractions include the Old Walled City of San Juan, the San Juan Cathedral, the forts of El Morro and San Cristobal, the Ponce Museum of Art, the Arecibo Observatory and the El Yunque Rain Forest.

GOVERNMENT

Puerto Rico (Estado Libre Asociado de Puerto Rico—Free Associated State of Puerto Rico), a colony of Spain until 1898, is a self-governing "commonwealth" that has chosen to remain in free association with the US. Puerto Rico is represented in the US House of Representatives by a popularly elected, non-voting Resident Commissioner, who holds a 4-year term.

Constitution: The Constitution was ratified by the people of Puerto Rico on Mar 3, 1952, and entered into effect on Jul 25, 1952. It replaced the Organic Act (Jones Act) of 1917, under which Puerto Ricans were granted citizenship. As US citizens, Puerto Ricans enjoy the same privileges and immunities as if Puerto Rico were a member state of the Union. Puerto Ricans are subject to Federal laws but not Federal taxes, except by mutual consent. The Constitution contains its own Bill of Rights, including provisions prohibiting discrimination on account of race, color, sex, birth or religion.

QATAR
State of Qatar

LOCATION: Qatar sits on a peninsula that projects northward from the Arabian mainland on the west coast of the Persian Gulf. It is bordered by Saudi Arabia to the west and the United Arab Emirates to the south.

AREA: 4,416 sq. miles

Land Use: 0% cropland; 5% permanent pasture; 0% forests and woodland; 95% other (mostly desert).
Arable Land: None
Arable Land per capita: None

POPULATION: 342,000 (1989 estimate)

Population Density: 77 inhabs. per sq. mile (1989 estimate)
Population Distribution: 87.93% urban (1985)
Population Growth Rate: 3.60% per year (1989 estimate)

VITAL STATISTICS

Average Life Expectancy: 69.20 years (1985-90 projection)
Male: 66.90 years (1985-90 projection)
Female: 71.60 years (1985-90 projection)
Age Distribution: (1985)
0-14 . . . . .34.50%
15-64 . . . . .63.81%
65+ 1.59%
Median Age: 23.90 years (1985)
Maternal Mortality: (not available)
Infant Mortality: 42 per 1,000 live births (1985)

HEALTH CARE

Hospital Beds: 27 per 10,000 population (1986)
Doctors: 15 per 10,000 population (1986)

ETHNIC COMPOSITION: Arab - 40%; Pakistani - 18%; Indian - 18%; Iranian - 10%; other - 14%.

RELIGION: Moslem - 95% (native Qataris are mainly Sunni Moslems of the strictly orthodox Wahhabi sect); other - 5%.

LANGUAGE: Arabic is the official language. English is also spoken.

EDUCATION: Illiteracy: 60%. In 1985/86, there was a total of 51,350 students enrolled at primary, preparatory and secondary schools. There were 5,000 students enrolled at the University of Qatar.

ECONOMIC DATA

Expenditures by Function [as % of total]: (not available)
GDP per capita: $16,066 (1986)

TRAVEL NOTES

Climate: The climate is extremely hot in summer, with temperatures reaching up to 120°F and high humidity along the coast. Rainfall is negligible and winters are relatively mild.
Health Precautions: None.
Miscellaneous: Qatar uses the Islamic lunar calendar.

GOVERNMENT

Qatar (Dawlat Qatar—State of Qatar) is a traditional Arab monarchy making a transition toward modern constitutional government. It became independent in 1971 when a British protectorate ended. The monarch, Emir Khalifa ibn Hamad al Thani, came to power on Feb 22, 1972, when he deposed his cousin, Sheik Ahmed bin Ali al Thani, in a bloodless coup.

Constitution: A provisional Constitution—the Basic Law—came into effect in July 1970, providing for a Council of Ministers and an Advisory Council. It also guarantees all basic rights.

REPUBLIC OF CHINA
See Taiwan

REUNION
Department of Reunion

LOCATION: Reunion is an island in the Indian Ocean that lies approximately 500 miles to the east of Madagascar.

AREA: 970 sq. miles

Land Use: 22% cropland; 4% permanent pasture; 35% forest and woodland; 39% other.
Arable Land: 22%
Arable Land per capita: 0.26 acres

POPULATION: 555,000 (1989 estimate)

Population Density: 572 inhabs. per sq. mile (1989 estimate)
Population Distribution: 59.70% (1985)
Population Growth Rate: 1.00% per year (1989)

VITAL STATISTICS

Average Life Expectancy: 71.00 years (1985-90 projection)
Male: 67.00 years (1985-90 projection)
Female: 75.20 years (1985-90 projection)
Age Distribution: (1985)
0-14 . . . . .29.94%
15-64 . . . . .65.91%
65+ 4.15%
Median Age: 23.60 years (1985)
Maternal Mortality: (not available)
Infant Mortality: 13 per 1,000 live births (1985)

HEALTH CARE

Hospital Beds: 72 per 10,000 population (1985)
Doctors: 14 per 10,000 population (1986)

ETHNIC COMPOSITION: Most of the population is of mixed ancestry, with French, African, Malagasy, Chinese, Pakistani and Indian being the main ethnic components.

RELIGION: Roman Catholic - 94%; other - 6%.

LANGUAGE: French is the official language; Creole is widely spoken.

EDUCATION: Illiteracy: 20%. In 1986/87, there were 499 primary and pre-primary schools with 113,819 students; 69 secondary schools with 71,014 students; and one university with 3,572 students. Reunion also has a technical institute, an agricultural college and a teacher training college.

ECONOMIC DATA

Expenditures by Function [as % of total]: (not available)
GDP per capita: $3,513 (1982)

TRAVEL NOTES

Climate: The climate varies with elevation. Coastal areas enjoy a tropical climate with average summer temperatures of 82°F and average winter temperatures of 68°F, while rainfall in the uplands averages 27 inches. Higher elevations receive much more rainfall, an average of 186 inches, and experience lower average temperatures. These areas have average temperatures of 66°F in summer and 46°F in winter.

Health Precautions: Inoculations against typhoid and measles, as well as DPT and gamma globulin shots, are recommended. City tap water is potable.

Miscellaneous: Many new hotels have been built to encourage tourism. Reunion has beautiful beaches and a scenic volcanic landscape.

GOVERNMENT

Reunion was first occupied by France in 1642. An overseas department of France since 1946, Reunion is represented in the French Parliament by 5 directly-elected deputies in the French National Assembly and three indirectly-elected representatives in the Senate.

Constitution: Reunion is administered under the Constitutional laws of France.

RUMANIA
Socialist Republic of Rumania

LOCATION: Lying in the southeast of Europe, Rumania is bordered in the north and northeast by the Soviet Union, in the northwest by Hungary, the southwest by Yugoslavia and the south by Bulgaria. The Black Sea forms the southeastern coastline.

AREA: 91,699 sq. miles

Land Use: 44% cultivable; 27% forest; 19% other agriculture; 10% other.
Arable Land: 44%
Arable Land per capita: 1.13 acres

POPULATION: 22,830,000 (1986)

Population Density: 244.10 inhabs. per sq. mile (1986)

Population Distribution: 49.00% urban (1985)
Population Growth Rate: 0.40% per year (1986)

VITAL STATISTICS

Average Life Expectancy: 70.55 years (1986)
Male: 69.30 years (1986)
Female: 71.80 years (1986)
Age Distribution: (1985)
0-14 . . . . .25.20%
15-64 . . . . .65.40%
64+ 9.40%
Median Age: 31.50 years (1985)
Maternal Mortality: 547 per 100,000 live births (1983)
Infant Mortality: 23.90 per 1,000 live births (1983)

HEALTH CARE

Hospital Beds: 93.46 per 10,000 population (1983)
Doctors: 20.46 per 10,000 population (1984)

ETHNIC COMPOSITION: Rumanian - 88.10%; Hungarian - 7.90%; German - 1.60%; Ukrainian, Serb, Croat, Russian, Turk, Gypsy and other - 2.40%.

RELIGION: Romanian Orthodox - 80%; Roman Catholic - 6%; Calvinist, Lutheran, Jewish, Baptist - 4%; other - 10%.

LANGUAGE: The official language is Rumanian. Minority groups also speak Hungarian, German and other languages.

EDUCATION: Illiteracy: 2%. In 1984, there were 14,213 primary and gymnasium schools with 3,067,446 students; 981 secondary schools with 1,272,245 students; 623 vocational schools with 160,662 students; 278 technical colleges with 20,862 students; and 44 higher education faculties with 174,042 students.

ECONOMIC DATA

Expenditures by Function [as % of total]: (1983)
General public services 0.84%
Defense 5.50%
Education 2.53%
Health 0.79%
Social security and welfare 23.34%
Housing and community amenities 1.57%
Other community and social services 0.28%
Economic services 50.42%
Agriculture, forestry, fishing and hunting . .6.96%

Roads 1.41%
Other transportation and communication . . 7.05%
Other purposes 14.73%
GDP per capita: (not available)

TRAVEL NOTES

Climate: Summers are hot and winters are cold. Rainfall is moderate.
Health Precautions: Although tap water meets US standards, drinking water is often boiled.
Miscellaneous: The principal attractions are the Carpathian mountains, the Danube delta and the Black Sea resorts.

GOVERNMENT

Rumania (Republica Socialista Romania— Socialist Republic of Rumania) gained its independence from the Ottoman Empire under the Treaty of Berlin of Jul 13, 1878. It was a constitutional monarchy until 1947, when the monarch was forced to abdicate under Communist pressure and a people's republic was proclaimed (Dec 30, 1947). Rumania designated itself a socialist republic in the Constitution of Aug 21, 1965. Rumania is a one-party Communist state, in which effective political authority rests with the *Partidul Comunist Roman* (PCR), the only legal political party.

Constitution: The Constitution of Aug 21, 1965 (as amended Mar 28, 1974) declares Rumania to be a socialist republic, in which the leading political force is the Rumanian Communist Party. It contains a statement of fundamental rights and duties and outlines the major institutions of the Government. The Constitution may be amended by a vote of the Grand National Assembly.

RUSSIA
See Union of Soviet Socialist Republics

RWANDA
Republic of Rwanda

LOCATION: Rwanda is located in east central Africa and is bounded by Zaire to the west, Uganda to the north, Tanzania to the east and Burundi to the south.

AREA: 10,208 sq. miles

Land Use: 33% cultivated; 33% pasture; 33% other.
Arable Land: 40%
Arable Land per capita: 0.42 acres

POPULATION: 6,246,000 (1985)

Population Density: 625 inhabs. per sq. mile (1985)
Population Distribution: 5.10% urban (1985)
Population Growth Rate: 3.70% per year (1985)

VITAL STATISTICS

Average Life Expectancy: 45.20 years (1983)
Male: (not available)
Female: (not available)
Age Distribution: (1984)
0-14 . . . . .50.80%
15-59 . . . . .46.20%
60+: 3.00%
Median Age: 16.70 years (1980)
Maternal Mortality: (not available)
Infant Mortality: 137 per 1,000 live births (1983)

HEALTH CARE

Hospital Beds: 15.63 per 10,000 population (1980)
Doctors: 0.36 per 10,000 population (1981)

ETHNIC COMPOSITION: Hutu - 85%; Tutsi - 14%; Twa - 1%.

RELIGION: Catholic - 65%; Protestant - 9%; Moslem - 1%; indigenous beliefs - 25%.

LANGUAGE: Kinyarwanda and French are the official languages and Kiswahili is used in commercial centers.

EDUCATION: Illiteracy: 77%. In 1984, there were 761,955 primary students, 14,761 secondary students, and 1,317 tertiary students.

ECONOMIC DATA

Expenditures by Function [as %of total]: (1980)
General public services 15.58%
Defense 12.98%
Education 18.83%
Health 4.54%
Social security and welfare 2.85%
Housing and community amenities 1.17%
Other community and social services 0.90%
Economic services 41.55%

Agriculture, forestry, fishing and hunting . 12.33%
Roads 7.14%
Other transportation and communication . . 2.59%
Other purposes 1.55%
GDP per capita: $270 (1983)

TRAVEL NOTES

Climate: The climate is tropical. Average annual temperature is 73°F. The major rainy seasons are February-May and November-December.
Health Precautions: Cholera, smallpox and yellow fever certificates are required. Tap water is not potable and food should be carefully prepared.
Miscellaneous: Tourist attractions include national parks, Lake Kivu and mountain scenery.

GOVERNMENT

Rwanda (Republika y'u Rwanda - Republique Rwandaise - Republic of Rwanda) became an independent state on Jul 1, 1962. A coup overthrew the civilian government in Jul 5, 1973. Effective political power rests with the armed forces and the only legal political organization, the National Revolutionary Movement for Development.

Constitution: A new Constitution approved by a referendum on Dec 17, 1978, provides for a return to civilian government and a one-party state.

SAN MARINO
Republic of San Marino

LOCATION: San Marino is a tiny, landlocked enclave within the Italian province of Emilia-Romagna.

AREA: 23 sq. miles

Land Use: 0% cropland; 0% permanent pasture; 0% forest and woodland; 100% other (mostly urban).
Arable Land: 17%
Arable Land per capita: 0.13 acres

POPULATION: 23,000 (1989 estimate)

Population Density: 983 inhabs. per sq. mile (1989 estimate)

Population Distribution: 90.50% urban (1985)
Population Growth Rate: 0.90% per year (1989)

VITAL STATISTICS

Average Life Expectancy: (not available)
Male: (not available)
Female: (not available)
Age Distribution: (1985)
0-14 . . . . .19.00%
15-59 . . . . .63.70%
60+ 17.30%
Median Age: (not available)
Maternal Mortality: (not available)
Infant Mortality: 9.60 per 1,000 live births (1987)

HEALTH CARE

Hospital Beds: (not available)
Doctors: (not available)

ETHNIC COMPOSITION: Sanmarinese - 88%; Italian - 11%; other - 1%.

RELIGION: Most of the population is Roman Catholic.

LANGUAGE: Italian is the official language.

EDUCATION: Illiteracy: 3%. In 1986, there were 14 primary schools with 1,370 students and 3 secondary schools with 940 students. San Marino also has 1 higher secondary school, 1 technical institute and several vocational training schools.

ECONOMIC DATA

Expenditures by Function [as % of total]: (not available)
GDP per capita: (not available)

TRAVEL NOTES

Climate: Temperatures in San Marino range from a low of 28°F in winter to a high of 86°F in summer. The winters are generally dry.
Health Precautions: In addition to the usual inoculations, immunizations against hepatitis and influenza are recommended. Tap water is potable.
Miscellaneous: A remnant of the feudal city-states from the Middle Ages, San Marino claims to be Europe's oldest republic. The city of San Marino was constructed around a hermitage in 441 A.D.

GOVERNMENT

San Marino (Serenissima Repubblica di San Marino—Most Serene Republic of San Marino) is an independent republic that traces its origins to the 4th century A.D.

Constitution: The Constitution dates from the year 1600.

SAO TOME AND PRINCIPE
Democratic Republic of Sao Tome and Principe

LOCATION: The country includes the two main islands of Sao Tome and Principe, as well as the islets of Pedras, Caroco, Tinhosas and Rolas. They are located in the Gulf of Guinea, off the west coast of central Africa.

AREA: 372 sq. miles

Land Use: 37% cropland; 1% permanent pasture; 62% other.
Arable Land: 38%
Arable Land per capita: 1.01 acres

POPULATION: 114,025 (1987)

Population Density: 306.52 inhabs. per sq. mile (1987)
Population Distribution: 24% urban (1980)
Population Growth Rate: 2.89% per year (1987)

VITAL STATISTICS

Average Life Expectancy: (not available)
Male: (not available)
Female: (not available)
Age Distribution: (not available)
Median Age: (not available)
Maternal Mortality: (not available)
Infant Mortality: 65 per 1,000 live births (1985)

HEALTH CARE

Hospital Beds: 69 per 10,000 population (1978)
Doctors: 4.42 per 10,000 population (1981)

ETHNIC COMPOSITION: Mestico; angolares; forros; servicais (contract laborers from Angola, Mozambique and Cape Verde) and their children, known as tongas if born on the island; and Europeans of mostly Portuguese origin.

RELIGION: Christian - 80% (Roman Catholic, Evangelical Protestant, Seventh-Day Adventist); other - 20%.

LANGUAGE: The official language is Portuguese. Native dialects are spoken extensively.

EDUCATION: Illiteracy: 50%. In 1984, there were 16,132 primary school students; and in 1983 there were 3 secondary schools with 6,436 students; and one technical college. In 1982 there were 64 primary schools.

ECONOMIC DATA

Expenditures by Function [as % of total]: (not available)
GDP per capita: $260 (1983 estimate)

TRAVEL NOTES

Climate: The climate is humid and warm. The annual average temperature is 77°F.
Health Precautions: (not available)
Miscellaneous: Sao Tome is a port of call for some cruise liners. A tourist center is under development at Praia das Concas.

GOVERNMENT

Sao Tome and Principe (Republica Democratica de Sao Tome e Principe—Democratic Republic of Sao Tome and Principe) became independent on Jul 12, 1975, after having been governed by Portugal since the mid-16th century.

Constitution: The present Constitution was approved on Dec 12, 1975, and revised in December 1982 and October 1987. The Constitution provides for the separation of Church and State. It further states that the *Movimento de Libertacao de Sao Tome e Principe* (MLSTP—see below: Political Parties) is the country's sole political party, "the leading political force of the nation."

SAUDI ARABIA
Kingdom of Saudi Arabia

LOCATION: Occupying about 75% of the Arabian peninsula in southwestern Asia, Saudi Arabia is bordered by Jordan, Iraq and Kuwait to the north, Yemen to the southwest, South Yemen to the south, Oman to the south and east and Qatar and the United Arab Emirates to the northeast. Its main coastline is in the west on the Red Sea, and faces Egypt, Sudan and Ethiopia. A shorter eastern coastline on the Persian Gulf faces Iran and the Bahrein archipelago, which is just offshore.

AREA: 864,869 sq. miles

Land Use: 98% desert, waste or urban; 1% agricultural; 1% forest.
Arable Land: 2%
Arable Land per capita: 0.96 acres

POPULATION: 11,519,000 (1986)

Population Density: 13.32 inhabs. per sq. mile (1986)
Population Distribution: 66.80% urban (1980)
Population Growth Rate: 3.20% per year (1986)

VITAL STATISTICS

Average Life Expectancy: 56.05 years (1985)
Male: 54.50 years (1985)
Female: 57.60 years (1985)
Age Distribution: (1980)
0-14: 45.50%
15-59: 51.80%
60+: 2.80%
Median Age: 17.30 years (1980)
Maternal Mortality: (not available)
Infant Mortality: 103 per 1,000 live births (1985)

HEALTH CARE

Hospital Beds: 24 per 10,000 population (1983)
Doctors: 3.84 per 10,000 population (1981)

ETHNIC COMPOSITION: Arab - 90%; Afro-Asian - 10%.

RELIGION: Sunni Moslem (mostly Wahhabi sect) - 85%; Shiite Moslem - 15%.

LANGUAGE: The official language is Arabic.

EDUCATION: Illiteracy: 48%. In 1984, there were 7,269 primary schools with 1,161,096 students; 3,158 secondary schools with 579,147 students; and 26 special colleges with 2,371 students (figures include technical and vocational schools).

ECONOMIC DATA

Expenditures by Function [as % of total]: (1982 proposed)
General public services . . . . (not available)

Defense . . . . (not available)
Education 4.79%
Health 1.36%
Social security and welfare 1.28%
Housing and community amenities 3.06%
Other community and social services 11.04%
Economic services 6.75%
Agriculture, forestry, fishing and hunting . .1.55%
Roads . . . . (not available)
Other transportation and communication . . .8.62%
Other purposes 61.55%
GDP per capita: $10,335 (1984)

TRAVEL NOTES

Climate: While most of the country is dry, the coastal regions have high humidity, with temperatures between 100°F and 120°F. Temperatures in the interior reach up to 129°F. Winters are mild, except in the mountains.
Health Precautions: None
Miscellaneous: Tourism is strongly boosted by the ritual visit to the holy cities of Medina (the burial place of Mohammed), and Mecca (his birthplace), attempted by all devout Moslems.

GOVERNMENT

Saudi Arabia (al-Mamlaka al-Arabiya as-Saudiya—Kingdom of Saudi Arabia) is an Islamic monarchy in which effective political power rests with the royal family, Ulema (religious leaders) and chieftains of important tribes. Their authority is buttressed by the armed forces and the government bureaucracy, which they dominate.

Constitution: The Government functions within a framework provided by the Sharia (Islamic law, which is the common law of the land, Arab tradition and the decrees of successive monarchs. Taken together, these form an "un-written" Constitution although there is no formal constitutional document.

SCOTLAND
See Britain

144

SENEGAL
Republic of Senegal

LOCATION: Bordered by Mauritania to the north, Mali to the east and Guinea and Guinea-Bissau to the south, Senegal lies on the west coast of Africa. Gambia forms a 200-mile-long enclave into the southern part of Senegal.

AREA: 75,750 sq. miles

Land Use: 27.21% cropland; 29.69% permanent pasture; 30.95% forests and woodland; 12.15% other.
Arable Land: 27%
Arable Land per capita: 1.87 acres

POPULATION: 7,704,000 (1989 estimate)

Population Density: 102 inhabs. per sq. mile (1989 estimate)
Population Distribution: 36.36% urban (1985)
Population Growth Rate: 3.30% per year (1989 estimate)

VITAL STATISTICS

Average Life Expectancy: 45.30 years (1985-90 projection)
Male: 43.70 years (1985-90 projection)
Female: 46.90 years (1985-90 projection)
Age Distribution: (1985)
0-14 .... 44.35%
15-64 .... 52.70%
65+ 2.95%
Median Age: 17.80 years (1985)
Maternal Mortality: (not available)
Infant Mortality: 101 per 1,000 live births (1985)

HEALTH CARE

Hospital Beds: 11 per 10,000 population (1978)
Doctors: 1 per 10,000 population (1981)

ETHNIC COMPOSITION: Wolof - 36%; Fulani - 17%; Serer - 17%; Toucouleur - 9%; Diola - 9%; Mandingo - 9%; European and Lebanese - 1%; other - 2%.

RELIGION: Moslem - 92%; indigenous beliefs - 2%; Christian (mainly Roman Catholic) - 2%; other - 4%.

LANGUAGE: The official language is French. Wolof, Pulaar, Diola and Mandingo are also spoken.

EDUCATION: Illiteracy: 90%. In 1985/86, there were 2,171 public primary schools with 583,507 students; 119 public first cycle primary schools with 67,666 students; 19 public general schools with 21,236 students; 5 public technical schools with 3,515 schools; one university with 11,276 students and 6 other institutions of higher learning.

ECONOMIC DATA

Expenditures by Function [as % of total]: (1983)
General public services 26.57%
Defense 9.69%
Education 17.57%
Health 4.72%
Social security and welfare 5.65%
Housing and community amenities 2.95%
Other community and social services 2.23%
Economic services 19.16%
Agriculture, forestry, fishing and hunting .. 7.45%
Roads 6.14%
Other transportation and communication ... 0.32%
Other purposes 10.06%
GDP per capita: $436 (1985)

TRAVEL NOTES

Climate: The weather is tropical, with a long dry season followed by a short wet season, and an annual average temperature of about 84°F.
Health Precautions: Malaria is endemic and hepatitis is prevalent. Visitors need a yellow fever immunization certificate to enter the country. Additional inoculations are recommended against tetanus, cholera, polio and typhoid.
Miscellaneous: Senegal has many fine beaches and 5 National Parks, including a wild animal reserve, Mikolo-Koba National Park.

GOVERNMENT

Senegal (Republique du Senegal—Republic of Senegal) gained its independence from France on Apr 4, 1960 as part of the Federation of Mali, from which it seceded on Aug 20, 1960. On Feb 1, 1982, Gambia and Senegal formally united in a confederation called Senegambia, which establishes an integration of armed forces and economic and foreign policies between the two countries.

Constitution: The present Constitution (adopted on Mar 7, 1963) replaced a parliamentary system with a strong presidential form of government, which has been modified by subsequent amendments. The President and members of the National Assembly may propose amendments, which require the approval of either three-fifths of the members of the Assembly or a majority in a national referendum.

SEYCHELLES
Republic of Seychelles

LOCATION: The Republic of Seychelles consists of over 100 widely scattered islands located in the Indian Ocean approximately 700 miles northeast of Madagascar and 1,000 miles east of Kenya.

AREA: 175 sq. miles

Land Use: 18% cropland; 0% permanent pasture; 18% forest and woodland; 64% other.
Arable Land: 18%
Arable Land per capita: 0.34 acres

POPULATION: 70,000 (1989 estimate)

Population Density: 400 inhabs. per sq. mile (1989 estimate)
Population Distribution: 37% urban (1978)
Population Growth Rate: 1.20% per year (1989 estimate)

VITAL STATISTICS

Average Life Expectancy: 66 years (1986)
Male: (not available)
Female: (not available)
Age Distribution: (1987)
0-14 .... 36.30%
15-64 .... 57.30%
65+ 6.40%
Median Age: (not available)
Maternal Mortality: (not available)
Infant Mortality: 15 per 1,000 live births (1986)

HEALTH CARE

Hospital Beds: 49 per 10,000 population (1986)
Doctors: 6 per 10,000 population (1986)

ETHNIC COMPOSITION: The population is composed mainly of Seychellois, a mixture of Asian, African and French.

RELIGION: Roman Catholic - 90%; Anglican - 8%; other - 2%.

LANGUAGE: English and French are the official languages; Creole is widely spoken.

EDUCATION: Illiteracy: 40%. In 1986, there were 25 primary schools with 14,663 students; 4 secondary schools with 2,433 students; 1 special education school with 73 students; and 1 polytechnic institute with 1,540 students.

ECONOMIC DATA

Expenditures by Function [as % of total]: (1978)
General public services 35.25%
Defense .... (not available)
Education 14.36%
Health 13.14%
Social security and welfare 6.79%
Housing and community amenities 6.66%
Other community and social services 0.12%
Economic services 25.19%
Agriculture, forestry, fishing and hunting ..6.85%
Roads 2.05%
Other transportation and communication ...2.18%
Other purposes 0.57%
GDP per capita: $2,705 (1986)

TRAVEL NOTES

Climate: The Seychelles climate is tropical, with an average temperature in Victoria of 80°F and an average annual rainfall of 93 inches.
Health Precautions: Inoculations for typhoid, measles, diphtheria and tetanus, as well as gamma globulin shots are recommended. The water in Victoria is potable.
Miscellaneous: The Seychelles are known for their pleasant climate and beautiful volcanic scenery. Coral reefs surrounding the islands provide a home for a variety of marine life.

GOVERNMENT

Seychelles (Republic of Seychelles) became an independent member of the Commonwealth of Nations on Jun 29, 1976. James R. Mancham, chief minister of the colonial Government, was named President of the new republic and France Albert Rene, opposition leader under the colonial government, was named Prime

Minister. On Jun 5, 1977, Rene engineered a bloodless coup while Mancham was attending a Commonwealth conference in London. Rene declared himself head of state, suspended the independence Constitution and instituted a one-party socialist state in which effective political power rests with the Seychelles People's Progressive Front (SPPF).

Constitution: Although the 1976 independence Constitution was modified to permit the President to rule by decree and reintroduced in July 1977, it was replaced by a new Constitution drafted by order of President Rene. The new Constitution, which protects fundamental human rights, establishes a unicameral National Assembly, an independent judiciary and a strong President, was put into effect on Mar 26, 1979. It espouses the principles of socialism and enshrines the SPPF as the sole legal political party.

SIERRA LEONE
Republic of Sierra Leone

LOCATION: Lying on the west coast of Africa, Sierra Leone is bordered by Guinea to the north and east, and Liberia to the south.

AREA: 27,699 sq. miles

Land Use: 24.73% cropland; 30.77% permanent pasture; 29.28% forests and woodland; 15.22% other.
Arable Land: 24.73%
Arable Land per capita: 1.17 acres

POPULATION: 3,741,000 (1987 estimate)

Population Density: 135.06 inhabs. per sq. mile (1987 estimate)
Population Distribution: 28.30% urban (1985)
Population Growth Rate: 1.93% per year (1985-90 projection)

VITAL STATISTICS

Average Life Expectancy: 36.00 years (1985-90 projection)
Male: 34.50 years (1985-90 projection)
Female: 37.50 years (1985-90 projection)
Age Distribution: (1985)
0-14 . . . . 41.40%

15-64 . . . . .55.60%
65+ 3.00%
Median Age: 19.40 years (1985)
Maternal Mortality: (not available)
Infant Mortality: 169 per 1,000 live births (1985-90 projection)

HEALTH CARE

Hospital Beds: 11.91 per 10,000 population (1980)
Doctors: 0.55 per 10,000 population (1980)

ETHNIC COMPOSITION: African - 99%; European and Asian - 1%.

RELIGION: Indigenous beliefs - 30%; Moslem - 30%; Christian - 10%; other - 30%.

LANGUAGE: The official language is English. Mende, Limba, Temne and Krio (Creole) are also widely spoken.

EDUCATION: Illiteracy: 85%. In 1984/85, there were 1,219 primary schools with 350,160 students; 171 secondary schools with 81,879 students; 6 technical colleges with 2,124 students; 6 teacher training institutions with 2,650 students; and 2 universities with 2,445 students.

ECONOMIC DATA

Expenditures by Function [as % of total]: (1984)
General public services 13.82%
Defense 4.45%
Education 16.76%
Health 7.63%
Social security and welfare 2.28%
Housing and community amenities 0.38%
Other community and social services 0.54%
Economic services 20.15%
Agriculture, forestry, fishing and hunting . .6.14%
Roads 3.52%
Other transportation and communication . . .3.07%
Other purposes 17.03%
GDP per capita: $311 (1984)

TRAVEL NOTES

Climate: Sierra Leone's climate is tropical, with consistently high temperatures and almost constant high humidity. The average annual temperature is 80°F. The rainy season lasts from May to November, but most of the rainfall occurs between July and September.
Health Precautions: Inoculations against yellow fever and cholera are required. Malaria

suppressants and immunizations against hepatitis, typhoid, tetanus and polio are strongly recommended. The tap water is not potable.

Miscellaneous: The country's main tourist attractions are its mountains, beaches, jungle and game reserves.

GOVERNMENT

Sierra Leone (Republic of Sierra Leone), formerly a British colony and protectorate, became independent Apr 27, 1961. Sir Milton Margai served as the first Prime Minister. Following an election dispute, the army assumed control of the country in March 1967, but a second army revolt restored civilian rule in April 1968, with Dr. Siaka Stevens as Prime Minister and leader of the All-People's Congress. The nation's first republican constitution was approved in 1971, making Stevens the first executive President. Maj.-Gen. Joseph Momoh won the 1985 presidential elections against Stevens and, in March 1987, survived an attempted coup that threatened his rule. A major Government reshuffle took place in April 1987, and some Cabinet members were dismissed due to alleged connections with the coup attempt.

Constitution: In June 1978 a nationwide referendum endorsed a new Constitution, which instituted a single-party system with the ruling *All-People's Congress* (APC) as the sole officially recognized party.

SINGAPORE
Republic of Singapore

LOCATION: Singapore lies in southeast Asia, with Peninsular Malaysia to the north, East Malaysia to the east and Indonesia to the south. The country consists of one main island and several smaller nearby islands.

AREA: 240 sq. miles

Land Use: 10.53% cropland; 0% permanent pasture; 5.26% forests and woodland; 84.21% other.
Arable Land: 11%
Arable Land per capita: 0.01 acres

POPULATION: 2,640,000 (1988 estimate)

Population Density: 11,000 inhabs. per sq. mile (1988 estimate)

Population Distribution: 100% urban (1985)
Population Growth Rate: 1.00% per year (1988 estimate)

VITAL STATISTICS

Average Life Expectancy: 72.80 years (1985-90 projection)
Male: 70.10 years (1985-90 projection)
Female: 75.70 years (1985-90 projection)
Age Distribution: (1985)
0-14 ....24.47%
15-64 ....70.37%
65+ 5.16%
Median Age: 27.20 years (1985)
Maternal Mortality: 4.70 per 100,000 live births (1981)
Infant Mortality: 9 per 1,000 live births (1985)

HEALTH CARE

Hospital Beds: 39 per 10,000 population (1986)
Doctors: 11 per 10,000 population (1986)

ETHNIC COMPOSITION: Chinese - 76.40%; Malay - 14.90%; Indian - 6.40%; other - 2.30%.

RELIGION: The majority of the Chinese population is Buddhist or atheist, while Malays are generally Moslem; other adherents are Taoist, Sikh, Christian, Hindu and Confucianist.

LANGUAGE: English, Malay, Chinese and Tamil are the official languages. The main Chinese dialects are Hokkien, Teochew, Cantonese, Hainanese, Hakka and Foochow.

EDUCATION: Illiteracy: 14% (1986). In 1986, there were 236 primary schools with 268,820 students; 157 secondary schools with 203,088 students; 16 technical and vocational institutes with 20,873 students; and 5 colleges and universities with 42,007 students.

ECONOMIC DATA

Expenditures by Function [as % of total]: (1985)
General public services 14.09%
Defense 22.48%
Education 21.59%
Health 6.47%
Social security and welfare 1.58%
Housing and community amenities 4.16%
Other community and social services 0.63%
Economic services 17.68%
Agriculture, forestry, fishing and hunting ..0.38%

Roads 4.73%
Other transportation and communication . . 5.23%
Other purposes . . . . (not available)
GDP per capita: $6,721 (1986)

TRAVEL NOTES

Climate: The climate is tropical with high humidity. The average annual temperature ranges between 75°F and 80°F, and the climate does not fluctuate greatly throughout the year. The average annual rainfall is 96 inches.

Health Precautions: Precautions should be taken against cholera, typhoid and typhus. Tap water is potable.

Miscellaneous: Tourist attractions include beach resorts, shopping bargains and the exciting cultural life.

GOVERNMENT

Singapore (Hsing-chia p'o Kung-ho Kuo—Republik Singapura—Republic of Singapore) was under various forms of British rule and Japanese occupation from 1867 until after the end of World War II. The country became a self-governing member of the Commonwealth of Nations on Jun 3, 1959, and subsequently joined the Malaysian Federation on Sep 16, 1963. Singapore finally became an independent sovereign state on August 9, 1965. It has a parliamentary form of government, dominated by the People's Action Party led by Prime Minister Lee Kuan Yew.

Constitution: Originally promulgated Jun 3, 1959 and coming into effect in its amended state in August 1965, the Constitution declared Singapore to be a republic, with a President as head of state, a Cabinet led by a Prime Minister and a unicameral Parliament. The structure and processes of government are largely patterned on the British parliamentary model. The Constitution may be amended by a special act of Parliament.

SOLOMON ISLANDS

LOCATION: The Solomon Islands is composed of a double chain of islands, approximately 900 miles long, located in the southwestern Pacific Ocean, with the 6 major islands being Guadalcanal, Santa Isabel, Choiseul, Malaita, San Cristobal and New Georgia. The country includes Rennel Island, Ontong Java Islands, the Santa Cruz Islands and the section of the Solomon Islands chain that is southeast of the Papua New Guinean territory of Bougainville.

AREA: 10,639 sq. miles

Land Use: 1.92% cropland; 1.42% permanent pasture; 92.96% forests and woodland; 3.70% other.
Arable Land: 1.92%
Arable Land per capita: 0.52 acres

POPULATION: 301,180 (1987)

Population Density: 28.31 inhabs. per sq. mile (1987)
Population Distribution: 9% urban (1985)
Population Growth Rate: 3.62% per year (1987)

VITAL STATISTICS

Average Life Expectancy: 54 years (1987)
Male: (not available)
Female: (not available)
Age Distribution: (1987)
0-14 . . . . 49.00
15-59: 45.50
60+: 5.50
Median Age: (not available)
Maternal Mortality: (not available)
Infant Mortality: 46 per 1,000 live births (1985)

HEALTH CARE

Hospital Beds: 27.00 per 10,000 population (1985)
Doctors: 2.29 per 10,000 population (1985)

ETHNIC COMPOSITION: Melanesian - 93.00%; Polynesian - 4.00%; Micronesian - 1.50%; Chinese - 0.40%; European - 0.30%; other - 0.80%.

RELIGION: Anglican - 34%; Roman Catholic - 19%; Evangelical - 17%; United Church - 11%; Seventh-Day Adventist - 10%; traditional - 6%.

LANGUAGE: English is the official language, but Solomons Pidgin is much more widely used. There are approximately 120 native dialects in all.

EDUCATION: Illiteracy: 40%. In 1986, there were 469 primary schools with 49,934 pupils; 20 secondary schools with 5,553 students; 2 teacher training schools and 1 technical school.

ECONOMIC DATA

Expenditures by Function [as %of total]: (1983)
General public services 28.62%
Defense 0%
Education 13.81%
Health 7.36%
Social security and welfare 2.64%
Housing and community amenities 4.28%
Other community and social services 1.50%
Economic services 21.95%
Agriculture, forestry, fishing and hunting . 10.59%
Roads 0.32%
Other transportation and communication . . 4.00%
Other purposes 19.83%
GDP per capita: $507 (1985)

TRAVEL NOTES

Climate: The Solomon Islands enjoy a tropical climate with little seasonal change. Yearly rainfall averages about 85 inches, and the average temperature is 81°F.

Health Precautions: Yellow fever vaccination certificates are required of travelers arriving from infected areas. Malaria risk is sometimes present.

Miscellaneous: The Solomons are rugged and covered by forests. Taxis, rental cars and buses are available in Honiara.

GOVERNMENT

Solomon Islands, a British protectorate for the majority of the 20th century, received internal self-government in January 1976, and became an independent state within the Commonwealth on Jul 7, 1978. On Nov 14, 1986, Prime Minister Sir Peter Kenilorea resigned amid charges of misallocation of aid after he had directed cyclone relief funds to his hometown. The National Parliament, on Dec 1, 1986, elected Ezekiel Alebua as successor.

Constitution: The Constitution, originated September 1977, provides for a constitutional monarchy with the British sovereign, as titular head of state, to be represented by an island native Governor General. It also provides for the introduction of a "leadership code," and the appointment of an Ombudsman.

SOMALIA
Somali Democratic Republic

LOCATION: Somalia is situated on the eastern coast of Africa, with Ethiopia lying to the northwest and Kenya to the west. There is also a short northwestern frontier with Djibouti.

AREA: 246,201 sq. miles

Land Use: 2% cropland; 46% permanent pasture; 14% forests and woodland; 38% other (mainly desert).
Arable Land: 2%
Arable Land per capita: 0.68 acres

POPULATION: 4,862,000 (1987 projection)

Population Density: 18.90 inhabs. per sq. mile (1987)
Population Distribution: 34.10% urban (1985)
Population Growth Rate: 2.11% per year (1985-90 projection)

VITAL STATISTICS

Average Life Expectancy: 41.90 years (1985-90 projection)
Male: 40.30 years (1985-90 projection)
Female: 43.50 years (1985-90 projection)
Age Distribution: (1985)
0-14 . . . . .44.80%
15-64 . . . . .52.10%
65+ 3.10%
Median Age: 17.60 years (1985)
Maternal Mortality: (not available)
Infant Mortality: 149 per 1,000 live births (1985-90 projection)

HEALTH CARE

Hospital Beds: 14 per 10,000 population (1978)
Doctors: 1 per 10,000 population (1980)

ETHNIC COMPOSITION: Somali - 85%; the remainder are mostly Bantu. There are also 30,000 Arabs, 3,000 Europeans and 800 Asians.

RELIGION: Islam is the state religion. Most Somalians are Sunni Moslems, but there is a small Christian community.

LANGUAGE: Somali is the official language; Arabic, Italian and English are also spoken.

EDUCATION: Illiteracy: 40%. In 1983, there were 220,680 primary school students; 53,591 secondary school students; and 7,828 vocational college students. There is one university that had approximately 4,600 students in 1985.

ECONOMIC DATA

Expenditures by Function [as % of total]: (1985)
General public services 47.51%
Defense 23.29%
Education 6.87%
Health 2.33%
Social security and welfare . . . . (not available)
Housing and community amenities . (not available)
Other community and social services 0.73%
Economic services 12.79%
Agriculture, forestry, fishing and hunting . . 7.10%
Roads and other transportation
    and communication: 4.63%
Other purposes 2.03%
GDP per capita: $326 (1982)

TRAVEL NOTES

Climate: The climate is generally hot and dry. It is very hot on the Gulf of Aden and in the interior, but cooler on the coast of the Indian Ocean.

Health Precautions: There are minimal health facilities available outside of the capital and major cities. Intestinal upsets are common, as are fungus and skin infections (particularly in the hot seasons).

Miscellaneous: Tourism remains undeveloped at this time, although there is abundant wildlife in the national park near Kismayu.

GOVERNMENT

Somalia (Jamhuuriyada Demugraadiga Soomaaliyeed—Somali Democratic Republic) became independent on Jul 1, 1960. On Oct 21, 1969 a revolutionary military regime was established and a one-party state was proclaimed in July 1976.

Constitution: The Constitution (endorsed by a referendum on Aug 25, 1979) commits the Somali Republic to support "the liberation of Somali territories under colonial occupation" (meaning, principally, the disputed Ogaden desert of southeast Ethiopia) by "peaceful and legal means." The document proclaims Islam the state religion. It also states that the Somali Revolutionary Socialist Party (SRSP) wields supreme political and economic authority and bars the establishment of any other political party. A two-thirds majority of the Assembly may amend the Constitution.

SOUTH AFRICA
Republic of South Africa

LOCATION: Situated at the southern tip of Africa, South Africa is bounded by South West Africa (Namibia) to the northwest, Botswana and Zimbabwe to the north, Mozambique to the northeast and Swaziland to the east. It completely surrounds the country of Lesotho.

AREA: 471,445 sq. miles.
Note: Total area includes the Bantu homelands of Transkei, Bophuthatswana, Venda and Ciskei.

Land Use: 11.16% cropland; 65.40% permanent pasture; 3.40% forests and woodland; 20.04% other.
Arable Land: 11.16%
Arable Land per capita: 0.96 acres

POPULATION: 34,944,000 (1988 estimate)

Population Density: 74 inhabs. per sq. mile (1988 estimate)
Population Distribution: 55.90% urban (1985)
Population Growth Rate: 2.53% per year (1985-90 projection)

VITAL STATISTICS

Average Life Expectancy: 55.50 years (1985-90 projection)
Male: 53.80 years (1985-90 projection)
Female: 57.20 years (1985-90 projection)
Age Distribution: (1985)
0-14 . . . . .41.04%
15-64 . . . . .54.94%
65+ 4.02%
Median Age: 19.30 years (1985)
Maternal Mortality: (not available)
Infant Mortality: 72 per 1,000 live births (1985-90 projection)

HEALTH CARE

Hospital Beds: 35 per 10,000 population (1980)
Doctors: 6 per 10,000 population (1984)

ETHNIC COMPOSITION: African - 69.90%; Caucasian - 17.80%; Colored (mixed race) - 9.40%; Asian - 2.90%.

RELIGION: The majority of Caucasians and Coloreds are Christian (with 40% of Caucasians belonging to the Dutch Reformed Church), and about 60% of Africans are Christian; 60% of Asians are Hindu and 20% are Moslem. Animist beliefs are also practiced.

LANGUAGE: The official languages are English and Afrikaans. While many African languages are spoken, the principal ones are Xhosa, Zulu and Sesotho.

EDUCATION: Illiteracy: Caucasians - 1%; Africans - 50%. In 1985, there were 17,180 primary and secondary schools, 67 teacher training colleges and 21 universities. In 1986, there were 6,450,439 primary and secondary school students, 41,239 teacher training students, 92,182 technical and commercial institute students and 230,441 university students.

ECONOMIC DATA

Expenditures by Function [as %of total]: (1985)
General public services 3.36%
Defense 3.96%
Education 2.75%
Health 0.56%
Social security and welfare 1.69%
Housing and community amenities 0.07%
Other community and
    social services .... (not available)
Economic services 2.27%
Agriculture, forestry, fishing and
    hunting .... (not available)
Roads .... (not available)
Other transportation and
    communication .... (not available)
Other purposes .... (not available)
GDP per capita: $1,926 (1986)

TRAVEL NOTES

Climate: Although generally subtropical, the South African climate varies widely according to region. In Cape Town, temperatures are usually between 45°F and 79°F, while Johannesburg has an annual mean temperature of 63°F.

Health Precautions: Health conditions in South Africa are generally good, but lakes and other freshwater bodies are infested with bilharzia and should be avoided. City water is potable.

Miscellaneous: The main tourist attractions are the climate, scenery and wildlife. The great game reserves, with Kruger National Park being the largest, are extremely popular and attract thousands of visitors from around the world.

GOVERNMENT

South Africa (Republiek van Suid-Afrika— Republic of South Africa) became an independent state within the British Commonwealth in June 1934. It became a republic on May 31, 1961, when it severed its ties with the British Crown. Effective political power rests with the white minority (about 18% of the population) under a system of "separate development" (apartheid) of the various racial groups in South African society. The white minority is dominated by the Afrikaans-speaking descendants of Dutch settlers (Boers), who make up about 60% of the white population. The separate development program envisages the establishment of self-governing tribal "homelands" (Bantustans) for the majority of South Africans, who are black, and the eventual independence of these territories. Arrangements have also been made for limited political participation by other racial minorities, including Coloreds (persons of mixed-race) and Indians.

Constitution: A new Constitution came into force on Sep 3, 1984. It vests legislative power in the State President and a tricameral Parliament that gives political representation to Indians and Coloreds, but not blacks, in the central Government. The President is elected by an electoral college presided over by the Chief Justice and made up of 88 members of Parliament in a specified ratio from each of the houses. The office combines the executive and legislative powers of head of state and Prime Minister, and lasts for the duration of the Parliament from which the electoral college was drawn.

SOUTH KOREA
Republic of Korea

LOCATION: South Korea lies in the southern part of the Korean peninsula in eastern Asia. North Korea, to the north, is the only country that borders South Korea. The Sea of Japan lies to the east, the East China Sea is to the south and the Yellow Sea is to the west.

AREA: 38,279 sq. miles

Land Use: 22.11% cropland; 0.70% permanent pasture; 66.55% forests and woodland; 10.64% other.
Arable Land: 22.11%
Arable Land per capita: 0.14 acres

POPULATION: 43,672,000 (1988 estimate)

Population Density: 1,115 inhabs. per sq. mile (1988 estimate)
Population Distribution: 65.35% urban (1985)
Population Growth Rate: 1.66% per year (1985-90 projection)

VITAL STATISTICS

Average Life Expectancy: 69.40 years (1985-90 projection)
Male: 66.20 years (1985-90 projection)
Female: 72.70 years (1985-90 projection)
Age Distribution: (1985)

0-14	31.24%
15-64	64.73%
65+	4.03%

Median Age: 23.70 years (1985)
Maternal Mortality: (not available)
Infant Mortality: 24 per 1,000 live births (1985-90 projection)

HEALTH CARE

Hospital Beds: 17 per 10,000 population (1984)
Doctors: 7 per 10,000 population (1984)

ETHNIC COMPOSITION: The population is mostly Korean, but there are approximately 30,000 Chinese.

RELIGION: Mahayana Buddhism - 11,000,000; Christian (mainly Protestant) - 9,000,000; Confucianism; Daoism; Chundokyoism - 1,500,000.

LANGUAGE: Korean is the official language, but Japanese and English are often understood.

EDUCATION: Illiteracy: 8% (1987). In 1985, there were 6,519 primary schools with 4,856,752 students; 2,371 middle schools with 2,782,173 students; 1,602 high schools with 2,152,882 students; 120 junior vocational colleges with 242,114 students; 11 junior teachers colleges with 18,174 students; 100 universities with 931,884 students and 201 graduate schools with 68,178 students.

ECONOMIC DATA

Expenditures by Function [as % of total]: (1987)

General public services	9.63%
Defense	27.78%
Education	18.21%
Health	2.62%
Social security and welfare	6.55%
Housing and community amenities	0.78%
Other community and social services	0.98%
Economic services	16.16%
Agriculture, forestry, fishing and hunting	7.41%
Roads	2.46%
Other transportation and communication	0.85%
Other purposes	17.28%

GDP per capita: $2,416 (1986)

TRAVEL NOTES

Climate: Winters are cold and dry, with an average temperature of 21°F, while summers are hot and humid, with an average temperature of 77°F. Monsoon rains strike in July and August, while snow usually falls from December through February.
Health Precautions: An international health certificate is required to enter the country. Precautions should be taken against typhoid, diphtheria, typhus, cholera and smallpox.
Miscellaneous: Many visitors are attracted by mountain scenery and examples of traditional Korean arts in the temples, museums and the Royal Palaces at Seoul. There is also excellent hunting and fishing.

GOVERNMENT

South Korea *(Taehan-Minguk—Republic of Korea)* was proclaimed an independent state on Aug 15, 1948. The military dominated South Korean politics and government between a 1961 coup led by Gen. (later President) Park Chung Hee and when President Chun Doo Hwan came to power in 1980. In 1987, following a series of

153

popular demonstrations, President Chun agreed to direct presidential elections to select his successor. The Government also negotiated with the opposition to produce a new Constitution that included several democratic reforms. On Dec 16, 1987, after opposition leaders Kim Young Sam and Kim Dae Jung had decided to run separately, thus splitting support for the opposition, Government-backed candidate Roh Tae Woo was elected President amid widespread allegations of election fraud.

Constitution: The present Constitution, approved in a referendum on Oct 27, 1987, provides for a Government with a separate presidency and legislature. The Constitution, which took effect on Feb 25, 1988, limits the powers of the President. A number of civil and personal rights are guaranteed under the Constitution, including the right of habeas corpus, freedom of expression and of the press, and the rights of workers in non-defense industries to form unions, engage in collective bargaining and to strike. The Constitution further establishes the political neutrality of the military.

SOUTH YEMEN
People's Democratic Republic of Yemen

LOCATION: Situated in the southern part of the Arabian Peninsula with a long coastline on the Gulf of Aden, South Yemen is bordered by the Yemen Arab Republic to the northwest, by Saudi Arabia to the north and by Oman to the east. The islands of Socotra, Perim and Kamaran are also part of South Yemen.

AREA: 130,066 sq. miles

Land Use: 0.50% cropland; 27.22% permanent pasture; 4.72% forest and woodland; 67.56% other (mostly desert).
Arable Land: 1%
Arable Land per capita: 0.37 acres

POPULATION: 2,415,000 (1988 estimate)

Population Density: 19 inhabs. per sq. mile (1988 estimate)
Population Distribution: 10% urban (1980)
Population Growth Rate: 3.00% per year (1988 estimate)

VITAL STATISTICS

Average Life Expectancy: 46.00 years (1985)
Male: 45.00 years (1985)
Female: 47.00 years (1985)
Age Distribution: (1988 estimates)
0-14 ....44.40%
15-59 ....51.40%
60+ 4.20%
Median Age: (not available)
Maternal Mortality: (not available)
Infant Mortality: 131 per 1,000 live births (1985)

HEALTH CARE

Hospital Beds: 17 per 10,000 population (1984)
Doctors: 2 per 10,000 population (1984)

ETHNIC COMPOSITION: Arab - 75%; Indian - 11%; Somali - 8%; other - 6%.

RELIGION: Sunni Moslem - 91%; Christian - 4%; Hindu - 3.5%; other - 1.5%.

LANGUAGE: Arabic is the official language.

EDUCATION: Illiteracy: 75% (1988). In 1984, there were 900 primary schools with 238,004 students; 51 secondary schools with 26,896 students; 3 technical colleges with 1,012 students; 10 teacher training colleges with 1,261 students; and 1 university.

ECONOMIC DATA

Expenditures by Function [as % of total]: (not available)
GDP per capita: $492 (1984 estimate)

TRAVEL NOTES

Climate: South Yemen's climate is hot and arid, with summer daytime temperatures reaching 130°F and an average annual rainfall of less than three inches.
Health Precautions: Inoculations for cholera, typhoid, tetanus/diphtheria and polio are recommended and precautions should be taken against schistosomiasis. The water is not potable.
Miscellaneous: Aden has been an important port city since Roman times, and reached its zenith as the chief port on the medieval Arab trading route between the Red Sea and India.

GOVERNMENT

South Yemen (Jumhuriyat al-Yamen al-Dimuq-ratiyah al-Sha'biyah—People's Democratic Republic of Yemen), formerly governed under the British protectorates of Aden and South Arabia, achieved independence when the British handed control of the territories over to the left-ist National Liberation Front, who formed the People's Republic of Southern Yemen on Nov 30, 1967. Three years later, the country's name was changed to the People's Democratic Republic of Yemen. Internal political unrest has been exacerbated by continuing tensions with the Yemen Arab Republic despite the stated commitment of both countries to eventual unification. Effective political authority current-ly rests with the only legal political party, the pro-Soviet Yemen Socialist Party. In January 1986, Moslem faction rivalries within the party led to the violent overthrow of President Ali Nasser Muhammad, and his replacement by then-Prime Minister Haider Abu Bakr el-Attas.

Constitution: The 1970 Constitution formed a government according to Marxist-Leninist guidelines and established a provisional 101-member unicameral legislature called the Supreme People's Council (SPC). Elections held in 1978 replaced the provisional SPC with a new SPC composed of 111 directly elected members. Constitutional amendments approved in December 1978 enshrined the Yemen Socialist Party as the only legal political party and decreed that elections be held every 5 years, but due to political instability elections have not been held that frequently.

SOTHWEST AFRICA
See Namibia

SOVIET UNION
Union of Soviet Socialist Republic

LOCATION: Extending from the Baltic Sea to the Pacific Ocean and for 3,107 miles from north to south, the Soviet Union is the largest country in the world. It is bordered in the north by the Arctic Ocean and on the west by Norway, Finland, Poland, Czechoslovakia, Hungary, Rumania and the Black Sea. To the south are Turkey, Iran and the Caspian Sea, Afghanistan, China, Mongolia and North Korea.

AREA: 8,649,540 sq. miles

Land Use: 35.00% forest; 16.70% pasture and hay; 10.10% cultivated; 37.70% other.
Arable Land: 27%
Arable Land per capita: 5.34 acres

POPULATION: 279,904,000 (1986)

Population Density: 32.36 inhabs. per sq. mile (1986)
Population Distribution: 64% urban (1984)
Population Growth Rate: 0.90% per year (1986)

VITAL STATISTICS

Average Life Expectancy: 69.65 years (1980)
Male: 65.00 years (1980)
Female: 74.30 years (1980)
Age Distribution: (1984)
0-19 . . . . .36.70%
20-59 . . . . .50.50%
60+ 12.70%
Median Age: (not available)
Maternal Mortality: (not available)
Infant Mortality: 27.90 per 1,000 live births (1982)

HEALTH CARE

Hospital Beds: 129 per 10,000 population (1984)
Doctors: 41.20 per 10,000 population (1984)

ETHNIC COMPOSITION: Russian - 52%; Ukrainian - 16%; Uzbeks - 5%; Byelorussians - 4%; over 100 other ethnic groups - 23%.

RELIGION: Russian Orthodox - 18%; Moslem - 9%; Jewish, Protestant, Georgian Orthodox or Roman Catholic - 3%; atheist - 70%.

LANGUAGE: The official language is Russian. There are more than 200 languages and dialects, among which 75% are Slavic, 8% Indo-European, 12% Altaic, 3% Uralian and 2% Caucasian.

EDUCATION: Illiteracy: 1%. In 1984/85, there were 44,570,000 general school students; 4,129,000 professional and technical school students; 4,512,000 specialized secondary school students; 5,280,000 students at higher educational establishments and 49,986,000 students taking professional courses.

ECONOMIC DATA

Expenditures by Function [as % of total]: (1984)
General public services . . . . (not available)
Defense 4.61%
Education 12.72%
Health . . . . (not available)
Social security and welfare 15.00%
Housing and community amenities . (not available)
Other community and
   social services . . . . (not available)
Economic services 57.00%
Agriculture, forestry, fishing and
   hunting . . . . (not available)
Roads . . . . (not available)
Other transportation and
   communication . . . . (not available)
Other purposes . . . . (not available)
GDP per capita: (not available)

TRAVEL NOTES

Climate: The climate is continental, with extreme variations, such as -94°F in winter in Siberia and 122°F in summer in Central Asia desert regions. Snows begin in late October and continue through March.

Health Precautions: Fruits and vegetables bought from open markets and city stores should be washed thoroughly. Water is potable. Special polyclinics are available for foreign residents and tourists.

Miscellaneous: Tourism contributes a valuable amount of foreign currency to the Soviet Union. Favorite areas to visit are Moscow, Kiev, Leningrad, Odessa, the Black Sea and Baltic resorts, the Urals and Altai mountains and the ancient central Asian cities of Samarkand and Bukhara.

GOVERNMENT

The Union Of Soviet Socialist Republics (Soyuz Sovyetskikh Sotsialisticheskikh Respublik—USSR) is a federation of 15 Soviet Socialist Republics (SSR). It was formally established on Dec 30, 1922, by a treaty linking the 4 original Union Republics. Effective political power rests with the Soviet Communist Party (CPSU).

Soviet Federalism. The Soviet Union is a highly centralized federal state in which preponderant power rests with the central Government, but in which the governments of the constituent Union Republics play an important, if subordinate, role. The operation of the Soviet federal system is strongly influenced by the dominant role of the Soviet Communist Party.

Division of Powers. In article 73, the Constitution specifically grants the central Government, the Supreme Soviet, broad jurisdiction over all major areas of political, social and economic policy-making (e.g., foreign affairs, defense, internal security, economic planning, civil and criminal law, family law and labor legislation). But the Union Republics exercise independent authority outside these areas and are influential in determining how central Government policies are implemented at the republic level. According to article 74, in cases of conflict, central Government laws prevail over those of the Union Republic.

Nationality Principle. Soviet federalism emerged not only because the vast territory to be administered demands some form of decentralization, but also because a large number of distinct cultural nationalities exist within its borders. Each of the 15 Union Republics represents a dominant national group (e.g., Armenians, Kazakhs, Latvians, Uzbeks), and the largest of the Union Republics, the Russian Soviet Federative Socialist Republic (RSFSR), is itself a federation, with 16 Autonomous Republics, 5 Autonomous Regions and 10 national areas, all based on the nationality principle. There are 4 Autonomous Republics and three Autonomous Regions in other Union Republics.

Equality of Member States. According to the Constitution, the Soviet federal state is "a voluntary union" of "equal" republics, but the RSFSR tends to dominate the federation. This is partly because of its size (it contains over 75% of the territory and over 50% of the population of the Soviet Union), but also due to Russian cultural ascendancy (e.g., Russian is the official language throughout the country and Russians are the most widespread ethnic group). The second largest republic, the Ukrainian, also tends to be much more influential and independent than other Union Republics.

Right to Secession. The Constitution in article 72 grants each Union Republic "the right freely to secede." For this reason, it is an unstated principle of Soviet federalism that Union Republics must have international borders. But secession moves by a Union Republic would invite central Government intervention, under its duty to ensure the Soviet Socialist form in the Union Republics.

Foreign Relations of Republics. The Union Republics are conceived in the Soviet system as distinct national entities, and therefore the Constitution grants them the right to have foreign relations (article 80). The Byelorussian and Ukrainian Republics are members of the United Nations.

Constitution: The Constitution of Oct 7, 1977, the Soviet Union's third, consists of a preamble and 9 sections, divided into 174 articles, most of which are grouped under 21 chapters. The Constitution declares that the Soviet Union is "a developed socialist society," in which "socialism is developing on its own foundations" and which is "an objectively necessary stage on the road to communism." It reaffirms that "the supreme goal of the Soviet state is the building of a classless communist society." The Constitution further declares that Soviet society is one with "mature socialist social relations," in which "a new historical community of people has been formed, the Soviet people," on the basis of the drawing together of all social classes, nationalities and ethnic groups. Under the Constitution, all powers of the state are vested in the people, who exercise it through Soviets (councils) at all levels of government. According to article 173, the Constitution has "supreme legal force," and all laws or other acts of state agencies must be in conformity with it. Amendments to the Constitution may be made by a two-thirds vote of both houses of the Supreme Soviet.

SPAIN
Spanish State

LOCATION: Spain occupies 80% of the Iberian Peninsula in southwestern Europe. It is bordered by France on the north and Portugal on the west, with a coastline on the Bay of Biscay to the north, the Atlantic Ocean to the west and southwest and the Mediterranean Sea to the southeast.

AREA: 194,897 sq. miles

Land Use: 41% arable and crop; 27% meadow and pasture; 22% forest; 10% urban and other.
Arable Land: 41%
Arable Land per capita: 1.31 acres

POPULATION: 39,075,000 (1986)

Population Density: 200 inhabs. per sq. mile (1986)
Population Distribution: 91.40% urban (1981)
Population Growth Rate: 0.60% per year (1986)

VITAL STATISTICS

Average Life Expectancy: 74.40 years (1985)
Male: 71.30 years (1985)
Female: 77.50 years (1985)
Age Distribution: (1985)
0-14 . . . . .24.30%
15-64 . . . . .64.60%
65+ 11.10%
Median Age: 31.20 years (1985)
Maternal Mortality: 68 per 100,000 live births (1979)
Infant Mortality: 10.30 per 1,000 live births (1982)

HEALTH CARE

Hospital Beds: (not available)
Doctors: 25.65 per 10,000 population (1981)

ETHNIC COMPOSITION: Spanish (Castilian, Valencian, Andalusian, Asturian) - 72.80%; Catalan - 16.40%; Galician - 8.20%; Basque - 2.30%; other - 0.30%

RELIGION: Roman Catholic - 99%; other - 1%.

LANGUAGE: Castilian Spanish is the principal language, while Catalan is spoken widely in the northeast, as are Basque and Galician in the northwest.

EDUCATION: Illiteracy: 3%. In 1981/82, there were 178,845 primary schools with 5,629,874 students; 2,488 secondary schools with 1,124,329 students; 2,323 vocational schools with 619,090 students; and 244 universities with 441,173 students.

ECONOMIC DATA

Expenditures by Function [as % of total]: (1983)
General public services 4.22%
Defense 4.42%
Education 5.95%
Health 0.60%
Social security and welfare 62.89%
Housing and community amenities 1.27%
Other community and social services 0.60%
Economic services 10.08%

Agriculture, forestry, fishing and hunting . . 3.62%
Roads 1.07%
Other transportation and communication . . 2.74%
Other purposes 9.98%
GDP per capita: $3,896 (1984)

TRAVEL NOTES

Climate: The climate is less temperate than in most areas of Western Europe. Summers are hot in most regions, with cold winters in the mountainous areas of the interior.

Health Precautions: Immunizations for tetanus, polio and typhoid are advisable. Tap water is normally safe for drinking in the major cities.

Miscellaneous: Tourist attractions include the warm climate, the beaches and the many historic cities, such as Madrid, Barcelona, Cordoba, Granada, Sevilla and Toledo.

GOVERNMENT

Spain (Estada Espana—Spanish State) is a hereditary constitutional monarchy and a parliamentary democracy, but its institutions are marked by a strong concentration of authority in the executive branch. Effective political authority rests with a Cabinet responsible to an elected bicameral parliament (Cortes) and with elected local regional government.

Constitution: The present Constitution was approved in a popular referendum on Dec 6, 1978. It consists of a Preamble and 169 articles, plus additional provisions. The Constitution includes a statement of "Fundamental Rights and Duties" and a provision for the establishment of regional self-governing authorities (Autonomous Regions). Article 148 of the Constitution lists a wide range of powers (including the power to decide on the form of its government) that may be delegated to Autonomous Regions, as well as a wide range of powers that belong exclusively to the central Government (e.g. foreign affairs, defense, administration of justice). The central Government or authorities of the Autonomous Regions may propose amendments to the Constitution, which must be approved by a three-fifths vote of both houses of the Cortes. A Constitutional Court deals with constitutional interpretation.

SRI LANKA
Democratic Socialist Republic of Sri Lanka

LOCATION: Sri Lanka consists of one primary island and many smaller islands in the Indian Ocean in southern Asia; the southern tip of India lies about 50 miles to the northwest.

AREA: 25,332 sq. miles

Land Use: 33.78% cropland; 6.80% permanent pasture; 36.80% forests and woodland; 22.62% other.
Arable Land: 34%
Arable Land per capita: 0.32 acres

POPULATION: 17,242,000 (1988 estimate)

Population Density: 681 inhabs. per sq. mile (1988 estimate)
Population Distribution: 22.40% urban (1988 estimate)
Population Growth Rate: 1.70% per year (1988 estimate)

VITAL STATISTICS

Average Life Expectancy: 70.00 years (1985-90 projection)
Male: 68.20 years (1985-90 projection)
Female: 71.80 years (1985-90 projection)
Age Distribution: (1985)
0-14 . . . . .38.74%
15-64 . . . . .57.72%
65+ 3.54%
Median Age: 22.80 years (1985)
Maternal Mortality: (not available)
Infant Mortality: 28 per 1,000 live births (1985)

HEALTH CARE

Hospital Beds: 28 per 10,000 population (1984)
Doctors: 1 per 10,000 population (1984)

ETHNIC COMPOSITION: Sinhalese - 74%; Tamil - 18%; Moor - 7%; Burgher, Malay and Veddha - 1%.

RELIGION: Buddhist - 69%; Hindu - 15%; Christian (mostly Roman Catholic) - 8%; Moslem - 8%.

LANGUAGE: Sinhala is the official language; Sinhala, Tamil and English are recognized as national languages.

EDUCATION: Illiteracy: 13%. In 1986, there were 3,918 primary schools, 7,903 secondary schools and 372 Pirivenas (for clergical and lay students of Buddhism) enrolling an overall total of 3,831,625 students. In 1988, there were 26 teacher training institutes, 13 polytechnic institutes, 8 junior technical colleges, 7 universities and 2 university colleges.

ECONOMIC DATA

Expenditures by Function [as %of total]: (1985)
General public services 9.58%
Defense 8.51%
Education 7.63%
Health 3.77%
Social security and welfare 11.38%
Housing and community amenities 0.21%
Other community and social services 0.56%
Economic services 10.57%
Agriculture, forestry, fishing and hunting .. 4.79%
Roads .... (not available)
Other transportation and communication .. 4.19%
Other purposes 47.80%
GDP per capita: $352 (1985)

TRAVEL NOTES

Climate: The climate is tropical—hot and humid on the coastal plains, and slightly cooler in the south-central mountains inland. Average annual temperatures range from 81°F in coastal Colombo to 60°F in the mountain regions. The southwest and the northeast monsoons generate two main rainy seasons, giving the country an overall average rainfall of 100 inches annually.
Health Precautions: Visitors must take precautions against malaria and hepatitis before arriving in Sri Lanka. Injections against rabies, which is common in many animals, can be obtained locally. Water in the cities is not potable and must be boiled 10 minutes before use.
Miscellaneous: Sri Lanka's spectacular natural beauty, ancient monuments and Buddhist festivals have long made it a leading Asian tourist spot, although tourist arrivals have declined in the past few years due to continuing ethnic communal violence.

GOVERNMENT

Sri Lanka (Sri Lanka Prajatantrika Samajawadi Janarajaya—Democratic Socialist Republic of Sri Lanka), formerly the Dominion of Ceylon, spent nearly 4 and a half centuries under foreign domination, starting with the Portuguese in 1505, then the Dutch (1658-1815) and the British (1815-1948). On Feb 4, 1948, the country became an independent state within the Commonwealth of Nations, and in May 1972 was redesignated the Republic of Sri Lanka. The country adopted its current Constitution on Aug 16, 1978, at which time it further modified its name to the Democratic Socialist Republic of Sri Lanka, and dropped its British-style parliamentary government in favor of a presidential system.

Constitution: The Constitution concentrates executive powers in the President, who is head of state, and establishes a unicameral Parliament to serve as the people's supreme legislative body. Among its provisions, the Constitution states that Buddhism is the country's preeminent religion, but assures citizens freedom of choice in worship. A 1983 Constitutional amendment bans activity espousing separatism and requires all members of Parliament to take an oath of loyalty to the unified state of Sri Lanka.

SUDAN
Republic of the Sudan

LOCATION: Lying in northeast Africa, Sudan is bordered by Egypt to the north, the Central African Republic, Chad and Libya to the west, Kenya, Uganda and Zaire to the south, and the Red Sea and Ethiopia to the east.

AREA: 967,500 sq. miles

Land Use: 3% cultivated; 33% desert, waste or urban; 15% grazing; 15% forest.
Arable Land: 37%
Arable Land per capita: 9.99 acres

POPULATION: 22,932,000 (1986)

Population Density: 23.70 inhabs. per sq. mile (1986)
Population Distribution: 20.20% urban (1983)
Population Growth Rate: -0.20% per year (1986)

VITAL STATISTICS

Average Life Expectancy: 47.80 years (1985)
Male: 46.60 years (1985)
Female: 49.00 years (1985)

Age Distribution: (1980)

0-14 .... 44.10%

15-64 .... 53.60%

65+ 2.00%

Median Age: 17.90 years (1980)

Maternal Mortality: (not available)

Infant Mortality: 118 per 1,000 live births (1985)

HEALTH CARE

Hospital Beds: 9 per 10,000 population (1981)

Doctors: 1.15 per 10,000 population (1981)

ETHNIC COMPOSITION: Black - 52%; Arab - 39%; Beja - 2%; others - 7%.

RELIGION: Sunni Moslem (in the north) - 70%; indigenous beliefs - 20%; Christian (mostly in the south) - 5%.

LANGUAGE: The official language is Arabic. Nubian, Ta Bedawie, Nilotic, Nilo-Hamitic, Sudanic languages and English are also spoken.

EDUCATION: Illiteracy: 80%. In 1982, there were 6,758 primary schools with 1,579,286 students; 313 secondary schools with 427,954 students; 40 technical colleges with 21,293 students; and 35 teacher training and other tertiary schools with 39,506 students.

ECONOMIC DATA

Expenditures by Function [as % of total]: (1982)

General public services 18.01%

Defense 9.51%

Education 6.07%

Health 1.34%

Social security and welfare 2.24%

Housing and community amenities 0.08%

Other community and social services 1.38%

Economic services 23.45%

Agriculture, forestry, fishing and hunting .. 8.50%

Roads 3.43%

Other transportation and communication .. 0.07%

Other purposes 38.81%

GDP per capita: $350 (1983)

TRAVEL NOTES

Climate: There is a marked transition from desert in the north to the rainy equatorial region in the south. Temperatures also vary widely with altitude and latitude, with the annual average being about 70°F.

Health Precautions: Medical facilities are limited and under certain conditions, water should be purified before drinking. Cholera, smallpox and yellow fever shots are required.

Miscellaneous: Tourists are attracted to the rain forests of the south, which teem with wild game. In the north, there are sites of several temples and pyramids of ancient Sudanese civilizations.

GOVERNMENT

Sudan (Jumhuriyat al-Sudan al-Dimuqratiyah— The Republic of the Sudan) was proclaimed an independent sovereign state on Jan 1, 1956, ending the joint British-Egyptian condominium that administered the territory since the late 19th century. Sudan's political history has been marked by coups, countercoups and abortive coups, as well as protracted rebellion in the southern provinces where the population differs racially and culturally from the rest of the country. On May 15, 1986, a coalition government was formed under former Prime Minister Sadiq Siddiq al-Mahdi of the New National Umma Party. However, Mahdi was overthrown in a Jun 30, 1989 military coup led by Brig. Omar Hassam Ahmed al-Bashir, who became head of state and Prime Minister, and announced the dissolution of the Parliament and the suspension of the Constitution. Brig. Bashir announced that the country would be governed by a new Revolutionary Council.

Constitution: The April 1973 Constitution was suspended following an Apr 6, 1985 military coup. An interim Constitution was approved in October 1985, but this, too, was suspended, following the Jun 30, 1989 military coup.

SURINAME
Republic of Suriname

LOCATION: Suriname is located on the northeast coast of South America, and is bordered by French Guiana to the east, Brazil to the south, Guyana to the west and the Atlantic Ocean to the north.

AREA: 63,037 sq. miles

Land Use: 0.36% cropland; 0.14% permanent pasture; 96.61% forests and woodland; 2.89% other.

Arable Land: 1%
Arable Land per capita: 1.09 acres

POPULATION: 394,000 (1988 estimate)

Population Density: 6 inhabs. per sq. mile (1988 estimate)
Population Distribution: 45.70% urban (1985)
Population Growth Rate: 1.60% per year (1988 estimate)

VITAL STATISTICS

Average Life Expectancy: 69.60 years (1985-90 projection)
Male: 67.00 years (1985-90 projection)
Female: 72.30 years (1985-90 projection)
Age Distribution: (1985)
0-14 .... 37.33%
15-64 .... 58.40%
65+ 4.27%
Median Age: 20 years (1985)
Maternal Mortality: (not available)
Infant Mortality: 21 per 1,000 live births (1985)

HEALTH CARE

Hospital Beds: 52 per 10,000 population (1985)
Doctors: 6 per 10,000 population (1985)

ETHNIC COMPOSITION: East Indian - 37.00%; Creole - 31.00%; Javanese - 10.30%; Bush black - 2.60%; Amerindian - 1.70%; Chinese - 1.00%; other - 16.40%.

RELIGION: Hindu - 27.40%; Protestant - 25.20%; Roman Catholic - 22.80%; Moslem - 19.60%; indigenous beliefs - 5.00%.

LANGUAGE: Dutch is the official language. Other languages include English, which is widely spoken, Chinese, French, Spanish, Javanese and the native language, Sranang Tongo or Taki-Taki.

EDUCATION: Illiteracy: 35%. In 1984/85, there were 299 elementary schools with 71,454 students; 87 secondary schools with 23,686 students; 1 vocational school with 4,202 students; 1 teacher training school with 1,696 students and 1 university with 1,247 students.

ECONOMIC DATA

Expenditures by Function [as % of total]: (1986)
General public services 30.59%
Defense 4.43%
Education 17.55%
Health 3.71%
Social security and welfare 6.23%
Housing and community amenities 1.23%
Other community and social services 2.11%
Economic services 25.23%
Agriculture, forestry, fishing and hunting . . 4.46%
Roads 0.11%
Other transportation and communication . . . 1.03%
Other purposes 1.40%
GDP per capita: $2,575 (1986)

TRAVEL NOTES

Climate: The climate is subtropical—humid and warm year-round. Daily temperatures average 80°F, and the annual rainfall averages 87 inches. The hottest time of the year is during September and October, while the wettest seasons are from December to February and April to August.
Health Precautions: Water is potable in the larger towns but should be boiled in small villages and in the interior. Precautions against malaria and yellow fever should be taken when traveling to the interior.
Miscellaneous: Tourist attractions in Suriname include the unspoiled interior region, the great variety of flora and fauna, hunting and fishing.

GOVERNMENT

***Suriname** (Republiek Suriname—Republic of Suriname)* gained independence from the Netherlands on Nov 25, 1975. After a February 1980 military coup, the Constitution was suspended and a National Military Council (NMC) took over effective power. Following a failed coup attempt in March 1982, the NMC appointed a largely civilian Council of Ministers, headed by a Premier, and introduced an interim Constitution. Subsequently, the Government was faced with a series of coup attempts and periods of internal dissension, which led to various forms of government, with Lt. Col. Desi Bouterse, who participated in the 1980 coup, ultimately being declared head of government. In 1987, Lt. Col. Bouterse announced that a new Constitution would be drawn up and elections held, paving the way for civilian rule. On Jan 12, 1988, the newly-elected National Assembly chose Ramsewak Shankar as the new President.

Constitution: On Sep 30, 1987, a new 26-chapter Constitution was approved by referendum. The Constitution provides for a President as head of government, to be assisted by a State Council, but also calls for the military, as the "vanguard of the people," to retain a certain degree of power under civilian rule. The Constitution further provides for a Security Council, chaired by the President, to take power in times of war or national emergency.

SWAZILAND
Kingdom of Swaziland

LOCATION: Swaziland is a landlocked country in southern Africa, near the Indian Ocean. It is bordered by Mozambique to the east, and South Africa to the north, west, south and southeast.

AREA: 6,704 sq. miles

Land Use: 8.26% cropland; 66.69% permanent pasture; 5.87% forests and woodland; 19.18% other.
Arable Land: 66.69%
Arable Land per capita: 4.14 acres

POPULATION: 691,000 (1987 projection)

Population Density: 103 inhabs. per sq. mile (1987 projection)
Population Distribution: 26.30% urban (1985)
Population Growth Rate: 3.14% per year (1985-90 projection)

VITAL STATISTICS

Average Life Expectancy: 50.50 years (1985-90 projection)
Male: 48.80 years (1985-90 projection)
Female: 52.20 years (1985-90 projection)
Age Distribution: (1985)
0-14 . . . . .46%
15-64 . . . . .51%
65+ 3%
Median Age: 17 years (1985)
Maternal Mortality: (not available)
Infant Mortality: 118 per 1,000 live births (1985-90 projection)

HEALTH CARE

Hospital Beds: 25.52 per 10,000 population (1984)
Doctors: 1.27 per 10,000 population (1984)

ETHNIC COMPOSITION: African - 96%; European - 3%; mulatto - 1%.

RELIGION: Christian - 57%; indigenous beliefs - 43%.

LANGUAGE: English and siSwati are the official languages.

EDUCATION: Illiteracy: 35%. In 1984, there were 467 primary schools with 134,528 students. In 1983, there were 89 secondary schools with 27,801 students. In 1981, there were 2 teacher training colleges with 538 students and 3 technical and vocational training institutes with 901 students. In 1986, there was 1 university with 1,200 students.

ECONOMIC DATA

Expenditures by Function [as %of total]: (1986)
General public services 19.65%
Defense 4.91%
Education 20.97%
Health 10.26%
Social security and welfare 0%
Housing and community amenities 5.91%
Other community and social services 5.52%
Economic services 32.19%
Agriculture, forestry, fishing and hunting . .6.82%
Roads 12.93%
Other transportation and communication . . .6.64%
Other purposes 6.12%
GDP per capita: $873 (1983)

TRAVEL NOTES

Climate: The Swazi climate varies according to the region. The Highveld has an average annual temperature of 61°F, while the Lowveld averages 72°F. The annual rainfall in the humid Highveld ranges from 40 to 90 inches, whereas the warmer and less humid Lowerveld averages 20 to 25 inches of rain each year.
Health Precautions: Water from the town supplies in Mbabane and Manzini is potable. Swimming, wading or washing in natural bodies of water should be avoided due to the presence of bilharzia. The usual precautions should be taken against tuberculosis and malaria.
Miscellaneous: Swaziland has splendid mountain scenery in the Highveld, especially in the Ezulwini Valley. There are big game reserves at Hlane and Mlilwane.

GOVERNMENT

Swaziland (Kingdom of Swaziland), a former British protectorate, became an independent state within the Commonwealth of Nations on Sep 6, 1968. It is a traditional monarchy. Effective political authority rests with the King and the royal family, buttressed by traditional Swazi customs and institutions.

Constitution: King Sobhuza II, who was monarch for 60 years, suspended the independence Constitution, which provided for a parliamentary form of government, on Apr 12, 1973. The decision, made with the agreement of both houses of Parliament, was taken on the grounds that parliamentary forms were unsuited to the traditions of the Swazi people. In March 1977, the King announced that, in the future, the Swazi system would be based on traditional Tinkhundla, open local assemblies headed by a chieftain. In October 1978, a new Constitution established that the Tinkhundla would be the basis for the indirect election of a new advisory legislature.

SWEDEN
Kingdom of Sweden

LOCATION: Sweden lies in northwestern Europe, on the Scandinavian peninsula. It is bordered by Finland to the northeast, Norway to the northwest and west, the Baltic Sea and Gulf of Bothnia to the east and the Kattegat and Skagerrak Straits to the southwest.

AREA: 173,732 sq. miles

Land Use: 7.30% cropland; 1.62% permanent pasture; 64.19% forests and woodland; 26.89% other.
Arable Land: 7.30%
Arable Land per capita: 0.93 acres

POPULATION: 8,340,000 (1987)

Population Density: 48 inhabs. per sq. mile (1987)
Population Distribution: 85% urban (1985)
Population Growth Rate: 0.10% per year (1986)

VITAL STATISTICS

Average Life Expectancy: 76.80 years (1985-90)
Male: 73.70 years (1985-90)
Female: 80.10 years (1985-90)
Age Distribution: (1985)
0-14 .... 18.20%

15-64 ....64.80%
65+ 16.90%
Median Age: 37.50 years (1985)
Maternal Mortality: 4 per 100,000 live births (1982)
Infant Mortality: 6 per 1,000 live births (1985-90)

HEALTH CARE

Hospital Beds: 148 per 10,000 population (1980)
Doctors: 22.02 per 10,000 population (1980)

ETHNIC COMPOSITION: Swedish - 95%; Finnish - 2%; other - 3%.

RELIGION: Evangelical Lutheran - 93.50%; Roman Catholic - 1.00%; other - 5.50%.

LANGUAGE: Swedish is the national language, though minorities speak Finnish and Lapp.

EDUCATION: Illiteracy: 1%. Education is compulsory for 9 years starting at age 7. In 1983/84, there were 4,826 primary and secondary schools (grades 1-9) with 976,346 students; 520 integrated upper secondary schools with 275,278 students; and 122 People's Colleges with 14,674 students. Teacher training institutes and colleges enrolled 223,295 students.

ECONOMIC DATA

Expenditures by Function [as % of total]: (1984)
General public services 6.75%
Defense 6.69%
Education 8.96%
Health 1.35%
Social security and welfare 46.67%
Housing and community amenities 3.38%
Other community and social services 0.74%
Economic services 7.40%
Agriculture, forestry, fishing and hunting ..1.41%
Roads...............................2.08%
Other transportation and
communication ....(not available)
Other purposes 20.43%
GDP per capita: $12,346 (1985)

TRAVEL NOTES

Climate: Summers are mild and winters cold. Rainy seasons are in early fall and spring.
Health Precautions: Public health standards are high. Tap water is potable and dairy products pure. No special precautions are required. Bronchial ailments, rheumatism and sinus

trouble may be aggravated during winter.

Miscellaneous: Known for the variety of its landscapes, Sweden offers visitors white sandy beaches in the south, the mountains of the "Midnight Sun" to the north and many forests and lakes. Stockholm is famous for its modern architecture.

GOVERNMENT

Sweden (Konungariket Sverige—Kingdom of Sweden) is a constitutional monarchy with a parliamentary form of government. Effective political authority rests with the democratically elected parliamentary majority.

Constitution: The Constitution consists of a series of fundamental laws that have been extensively revised over the years since 1809, when the first constitutional document was promulgated. The last major revisions (to the Instrument of Government and the Riksdag Act—components of the Constitution), which entered into effect on Jan 1, 1975, limited the monarchy to purely honorific roles. There is a legislative Constitution Committee to consider alterations to the Constitution.

SWITZERLAND
Swiss Confederation

LOCATION: Switzerland lies in central Europe; it is a landlocked country that is bordered by Austria to the east, Italy to the south, France to the west and West Germany to the north.

AREA: 15,943 sq. miles

Land Use: 10.36% cropland; 40.46% permanent pasture; 26.45% forests and woodland; 22.73% other.
Arable Land: 10.36%
Arable Land per capita: 0.16 acres

POPULATION: 6,386,000 (1988 estimate)

Population Density: 401 inhabs. per sq. mile (1988 estimate)
Population Distribution: 58.24% urban (1985)
Population Growth Rate: 0.04% per year (1985-90 projection)

VITAL STATISTICS

Average Life Expectancy: 76.50 years (1985-90 projection)
Male: 73.10 years (1985-90 projection)
Female: 80.10 years (1985-90 projection)
Age Distribution: (1985)
0-14 . . . . .17.62%
15-64 . . . . .68.36%
65+ 14.02%
Median Age: 36.50 years (1985)
Maternal Mortality: 1.40 per 100,000 live births (1984)
Infant Mortality: 7 per 1,000 live births (1985-90 projection)

HEALTH CARE

Hospital Beds: 103 per 10,000 population (1984)
Doctors: 23 per 10,000 population (1984)

ETHNIC COMPOSITION: German - 65%; French - 18%; Italian - 10%; Romansch - 1%; other - 6%.

RELIGION: Roman Catholic - 49.00%; Protestant - 48.00%; Jewish - 0.30%; other - 2.70%.

LANGUAGE: German, French and Italian are the official languages. Romansch is also spoken.

EDUCATION: Illiteracy: 1%. In 1985/86, there were 376,500 primary school students; 391,700 secondary school students; 242,900 vocational students and 110,100 students at institutions of higher education.

ECONOMIC DATA

Expenditures by Function [as %of total]: (1984)
General public services 4.84%
Defense 10.25%
Education 3.08%
Health 13.11%
Social security and welfare 49.93%
Housing and community amenities 0.63%
Other community and social services 0.31%
Economic services 12.20%
Agriculture, forestry, fishing and hunting . .4.32%
Roads 3.27%
Other transportation and communication . . .3.81%
Other purposes 6.04%
GDP per capita: $17,357 (1985)

TRAVEL NOTES

Climate: The climate is generally temperate, but varies throughout the country depending on altitude. During winter, temperatures can average 30°F, while summer temperatures may average 61°F.

Health Precautions: None

Miscellaneous: Switzerland boasts numerous beautiful lakes and mountains. Visitors enjoy hiking, mountaineering and winter sports, such as skiing and bobsledding.

GOVERNMENT

Switzerland (Schweizerische Eidgenossenschaft—Confederation Suisse—Confederazione Svizzera—Swiss Confederation) has its origins dating to 1291, and its present borders were established in 1815. It has a history of political isolationism and neutrality which has never been violated by another country. Switzerland is a federal republic (a union of 23 cantons, three of which are divided into half-cantons), with a modified presidential system of government. The Swiss system is strongly influenced in its operation by the executive use of the popular initiative and referendum, through which the electorate plays a direct role in the making of the most important political, economic and social decisions.

Constitution: The present federal Constitution entered into effect on May 29, 1874. It is a lengthy, often-amended document, due partly to the attempt to establish in detail the division of powers between the federal Government and the cantons and partly to the important role played by initiative and referendum in the Swiss political process. The Constitution sets forth a system of strict separation of powers between the legislative and executive branches. A new draft Constitution, prepared in 1978, is expected to be put to the Federal Assembly, and then a national referendum, in the 1980s.

Swiss Federalism. Switzerland is the world's oldest federation. The division of powers between the cantons and the federal Government is marked by a strong centralization of authority. The federal Constitution (which goes into considerable detail in outlining the division of powers) grants the cantons all authority not given specifically to the federal Government, but successive amendments to the Constitution have centralized increasing amounts of power. The central Government is supreme in foreign affairs, defense, national economic policy, transportation and communications, monetary and financial affairs, foreign trade, energy policy, public works, civil, criminal and commercial law, immigration, marriage, social insurance, education, law enforcement, the administration of justice and a number of other areas. The cantons each have their own constitutions establishing the cantonal governments.

Swiss Direct Democracy. Popular participation in policy-making (conformance to the Swiss tradition that the people are sovereign) occurs at all levels of government (federal, cantonal and communal). All amendments under which Switzerland would enter into a mutual defense pact or join an international organization must be submitted to the electorate. Other treaties and federal legislation may be submitted to national referendum, if requested either by 8 cantons or by 30,000 voters. Constitutional amendments for approval by the people may be initiated either by one of the houses of the federal legislature or by a request by 50,000 voters. In some cantons, all legislation must be submitted for popular approval, while in others only major financial measures need be.

SYRIA
Syrian Arab Republic

LOCATION: Syria is located in western Asia. Turkey lies to the north, Iraq to the east, Jordan to the south and Lebanon and Israel to the southwest. The Mediterranean Sea lies to the west.

AREA: 71,498 sq. miles

Land Use: 30.90% cropland; 45.30% permanent pasture; 2.69% forests and woodland; 21.11% other.

Arable Land: 48%

Arable Land per capita: 1.94 acres

POPULATION: 11,734,000 (1988 estimate)

Population Density: 164.12 inhabs. per sq. mile (1988 estimate)

Population Distribution: 49% urban (1986)

Population Growth Rate: 3.69% per year (1987)

VITAL STATISTICS

Average Life Expectancy: 65.00 years (1985-90 projection)
Male: 63.20 years (1985-90 projection)
Female: 66.90 years (1985-90 projection)
Age Distribution: (1985)

0-14	48.34%
15-64	48.91%
65+	2.75%

Median Age: 15.80 years (1985)
Maternal Mortality: 8.10 per 100,000 live births (1981)
Infant Mortality: 48 per 1,000 live births (1985-90 projection)

HEALTH CARE

Hospital Beds: 12 per 10,000 population (1984)
Doctors: 6 per 10,000 population (1984)

ETHNIC COMPOSITION: Arab - 90.30%; other - 9.70% (mainly Kurdish, Armenian and Turkish).

RELIGION: Sunni Moslem - 74%; Alawite Moslem - 12%; Christian - 10%; other Moslem sects - 4%.

LANGUAGE: Arabic is the official language. Kurdish, Armenian, Aramaic, Circassian and Turkish are also spoken, while French and English are widely understood.

EDUCATION: Illiteracy: 53%. In 1984, there were 1,789,455 public and private primary school students; 188,539 secondary school students; 53,745 vocational and technical college students; and 123,753 university students.

ECONOMIC DATA

Expenditures by Function [as % of total]: (1981)

General public services	3.45%
Defense	37.73%
Education	7.12%
Health	1.08%
Social security and welfare	8.23%
Housing and community amenities	3.17%
Other community and social services	1.31%
Economic services	30.91%
Agriculture, forestry, fishing and hunting	4.79%
Roads	3.75%
Other transportation and communication	0.97%
Other purposes	7.00%

GDP per capita: $2,074 (1986)

TRAVEL NOTES

Climate: Along the coast, summers are hot and winters are mild while inland, the winters are dry but cold. Average daytime temperatures range from 96°F in July to 55°F in January, while average yearly rainfall measures more than 5 inches.
Health Precautions: Precautions should be taken against diseases such as typhoid, dysentery, tuberculosis, cholera and hepatitis.
Miscellaneous: The Mediterranean coastline, the mountains, town bazaars and the antiquities of Damascus and Palmyra are among the tourist attractions in Syria.

GOVERNMENT

Syria (al-Jumhuriyah al-'Arabiyah al-Suriyah— Syrian Arab Republic) is a republic with a strong presidential form of government, in which effective political power rests with the *Baath Party* and leftist military officers led by President Hafez al-Assad.

Constitution: The 157-article Constitution (which entered into effect on Mar 14, 1973) proclaims Syria "a socialist popular democracy with a pre-planned socialist economy in which private property is recognized." The Constitution declares that Islamic traditional law (Sharia) is "a principal source of legislation," but it also guarantees freedom of belief and adds that all religions are to be respected by the state. Amendments to the Constitution are proposed by the President and approved by the legislature.

TAIWAN
Republic of China

LOCATION: Taiwan is an island nation located about 100 miles off the east coast of China. The main island, called Taiwan (or Formosa), has a northern coast on the East China Sea, an eastern coast on the Pacific Ocean, southern and southwestern coasts on the South China Sea and a western coast on the Taiwan Strait. The nation of Taiwan also includes a number of other smaller islands near the main island.

AREA: 13,900 sq. miles

Land Use: 24% arable; 1% permanent cropland; 5% meadows and pastures; 55% forests and woodland; 15% other.
Arable Land: 24%
Arable Land per capita: 0.11 acres

POPULATION: 19,768,035 (1987)

Population Density: 1,422 inhabs. per sq. mile (1987)
Population Distribution: 66% urban (1979)
Population Growth Rate: 1.24% per year (1987)

VITAL STATISTICS

Average Life Expectancy: 72.40 years (1987)
Male: 69.90 years (1987)
Female: 74.90 years (1987)
Age Distribution: (not available)
Median Age: (not available)
Maternal Mortality: (not available)
Infant Mortality: 11 per 1,000 live births (1983)

HEALTH CARE

Hospital Beds: 37 per 10,000 population (1985)
Doctors: 9 per 10,000 population (1985)

ETHNIC COMPOSITION: Taiwanese - 84%; mainland Chinese - 14%; aborigine - 2%.

RELIGION: Mixture of Buddhism, Confucianism and Taoism - 93.00%; Christian - 4.50%; other - 2.50%.

LANGUAGE: Mandarin Chinese is the official language.

EDUCATION: Illiteracy: 6%. In 1985/86, there were 2,486 primary schools with 2,321,700 students; 1,052 secondary schools with 1,678,767 students; and 105 institutions of higher education with 428,576 students.

ECONOMIC DATA

Expenditures by Function [as % of total]: (not available)
GDP per capita: $3,047 (1985)

TRAVEL NOTES

Climate: Taiwan has rainy summers and mild winters, with temperatures averaging about 79°F during the summer and about 59°F during the winter.
Health Precautions: (not available)
Miscellaneous: The major tourist attractions in Taiwan include its festivals, its treasures of ancient art and its scenery.

GOVERNMENT

Taiwan (Chung-hua Min Kuo—Republic of China) was a province of the Republic of China after World War II, but became the base for the Kuomintang Government, which fled the Communist revolution in China in 1949. The Kuomintang regime has since maintained that it is the rightful Chinese Government, and has in recent years rejected several reunification proposals from the People's Republic of China (PRC). In 1971, it was replaced by the PRC at the United Nations, and by 1983 was recognized by no more than 23 countries. Domestically, martial law was lifted on Jul 14, 1987, for the first time in 38 years.

Constitution: The Constitution is based on the Kuomintang Constitution promulgated in Nanking, China on Jan 1, 1947. It incorporates a 5-power system composed of Yuans (governing bodies); the Executive Yuan, Legislative Yuan, Judicial Yuan, Examination Yuan and Control Yuan. A President acts as a mediator and arbiter among the Yuans.

TANZANIA
United Republic of Tanzania

LOCATION: Lying on the east coast of Africa, mainland Tanzania (Tanganyika) is bounded by Uganda and Kenya to the north; Rwanda, Burundi and Zaire to the west; Zambia, Malawi and Mozambique to the south, and the Indian Ocean to the east. Zanzibar and Pemba are Tanzanian islands located in the Indian Ocean. Lake Victoria is located along Tanzania's northern border.

AREA: 364,900 sq. miles (Tanganyika 363,950 sq. miles; Zanzibar 950 sq. miles)

Land Use: 5.86% cropland; 39.50% permanent pasture; 48.42% forests and woodland; 6.22% other.
Arable Land: 6%
Arable Land per capita: 0.69 acres

POPULATION: 23,938,000 (1988 estimate)

Population Density: 66 inhabs. per sq. mile (1988 estimate)

Population Distribution: 20% urban (1984)

Population Growth Rate: 3.30% per year (1988 estimate)

VITAL STATISTICS

Average Life Expectancy: 52 years (1986)
Male: 50 years (1985)
Female: 54 years (1985)
Age Distribution: (not available)
Median Age: (not available)
Maternal Mortality: (not available)
Infant Mortality: 110 per 1,000 live births (1985)

HEALTH CARE

Hospital Beds: 11 per 10,000 population (1984)
Doctors: 0.51 per 10,000 population (1984)

ETHNIC COMPOSITION: Mainland Tanganyika: African - 99%; other - 1% (mainly Asian, European and Arab). Zanzibar's population is almost 100% Arab.

RELIGION: Mainland Tanganyika: Christian - 33%; Moslem - 33%; indigenous beliefs - 33%; other - 1%. Zanzibar's population is almost 100% Moslem.

LANGUAGE: Swahili and English are the official languages, although many indigenous languages, as well as Arabic, are also spoken.

EDUCATION: Illiteracy: 21%. In 1986, there were 10,147 primary schools with 3,160,000 students; 95 secondary schools with 43,363 students; 39 teacher training colleges with 12,409 students; 2 technical colleges with 1,547 students; and 2 universities with 3,342 students.

ECONOMIC DATA

Expenditures by Function [as % of total]:
General public services 23.52%
Defense 12.31%
Education 13.27%
Health 6.02%
Social security and welfare 1.24%
Housing and community amenities 1.44%
Other community and social services 1.34%
Economic services 40.26%
Agriculture, forestry, fishing and hunting . 11.07%

Roads 6.16%
Other transportation and communication . . .3.26%
Other purposes 6.54%
GDP per capita: $212 (1987)

TRAVEL NOTES

Climate: The climate varies with altitude, ranging from tropical (in Zanzibar, Pemba and on the coast and plains) to semi-temperate (in the highlands). Heavy rains fall during the country's two monsoon seasons.

Health Precautions: Immunizations against cholera and yellow fever are required, while vaccinations against diphtheria-tetanus, measles, mumps, polio, rabies, rubella and typhoid are recommended. Malaria is endemic, and gamma globulin immunizations are also suggested. Tap water is not potable.

Miscellaneous: Tourists are attracted by Tanzania's natural beauty; Mount Kilimanjaro, Africa's tallest mountain, is located in Tanzania. There are also several parks and reserves.

GOVERNMENT

Tanzania (Jamhuri ya Muungano wa Tanzania— United Republic of Tanzania) was created on Apr 26, 1964 with the union of the independent republics of Tanganyika and Zanzibar. Tanganyika, originally a German colony and later under British rule, had become an independent state on Dec 9, 1961, with the British monarch as its formal head of state; on Dec 9, 1962, Tanganyika was proclaimed a republic. Zanzibar, previously a British protectorate, became an independent state on Dec 10, 1963, and a republic was proclaimed on Jan 12, 1964. Effective political power rests with the sole political party, Chama Cha Mapinduzi (CCM—Revolutionary Party), led by President Ali Hassan Mwinyi, who succeeded long-time President Julius K. Nyerere in 1985.

Constitution: Tanzania's first permanent Constitution was proclaimed on Apr 26, 1977. It specifically recognizes the leading position of the Chama Cha Mapinduzi as the nation's sole political party. In matters of local concern, the Constitution provides for separate, but not completely autonomous, government ministries for mainland Tanganyika and the island of Zanzibar. Zanzibar still retains its own Constitution, President, Cabinet and House of Representatives. However, the union Government retains exclusive control over foreign affairs, defense, police and foreign trade. Constitutional amendments approved in October 1984 provide for the post of a second Vice President (to be held by the Prime Minister) and more directly elected Assembly seats.

THAILAND
Kingdom of Thailand

LOCATION: Lying in southeast Asia, Thailand is bordered on the west and north by Burma, to the northeast by Laos and to the southeast by Cambodia (Kampuchea).

AREA: 198,115 sq. miles

Land Use: 56% forest, 24% agriculture, 20% other.
Arable Land: 36%
Arable Land per capita: 0.87 acres

POPULATION: 52,438,000 (1986)

Population Density: 265 inhabs. per sq. mile (1986)
Population Distribution: 17% urban (1984)
Population Growth Rate: 1.70% per year (1986)

VITAL STATISTICS

Average Life Expectancy: 62.30 years (1986)
Male: 59.50 years (1986)
Female: 65.10 years (1986)
Age Distribution: (1984)
0-14 .... 38.50%
15-59 .... 54.90%
60+ 6.60%
Median Age: 18 years (1980)
Maternal Mortality: (not available)
Infant Mortality: 51.40 per 1,000 live births (1985)

HEALTH CARE

Hospital Beds: 15.43 per 10,000 population (1980)
Doctors: 1.46 per 10,000 population (1980)

ETHNIC COMPOSITION: Thai - 75%; Chinese - 14%; other - 11%.

RELIGION: Buddhist - 95.50%; Moslem - 4%; other - 0.50%.

LANGUAGE: Thai is the official language, while English is the secondary language of the elite. Ethnic and regional dialects are also widely spoken.

EDUCATION: Illiteracy: 16%. In 1980, there were 30,460 primary schools with 6,390,285 students; 4,613 secondary schools with 2,906,323 students; 1,478 technical colleges with 530,260 students; and 50 teacher training schools with 63,983 students.

ECONOMIC DATA

Expenditures by Function [as %of total]: (1984)
General public services 9.34%
Defense 19.87%
Education 20.73%
Health 5.45%
Social security and welfare 3.07%
Housing and community amenities 1.31%
Other community and social services 0.49%
Economic services 19.74%
Agriculture, forestry, fishing and hunting .10.04%
Roads 5.51%
Other transportation and communication ...0.40%
Other purposes 19.95%
GDP per capita: $766 (1985)

TRAVEL NOTES

Climate: Tropical and humid, Thailand has three main seasons: hot, rainy and cool. The annual average temperature is 85°F, with temperatures between 68°F and 95°F in Bangkok.
Health Precautions: In many cases, smallpox and cholera vaccinations are required. Hepatitis is common.
Miscellaneous: Major attractions are Thailand's temples, palaces and pagodas. The most famous tourist attractions are the Royal Palaces of Bangkok. Tourism is the largest source of foreign exchange.

GOVERNMENT

Thailand (Prathet Thei—Kingdom of Thailand) is a monarchy. The monarchy was absolute until 1932, when a regime dominated by military leaders placed constitutional limits on the royal authority. Since then Thailand has been mostly under the control of one military regime or another. Attempts to set up constitutional parliamentary governments have usually been short-lived. A Constitution was drawn up by a military regime in 1978. The Constitution is still in force, but the military continues to play an important role in political affairs. On Jul 31, 1986, the Democratic Party, Thai Nation Party, Social Action Party and Rassadorn agreed to form a coalition Government, with Gen. Prem Tinsulanonda as its head.

Constitution: Thailand's 14th Constitution since 1932 was approved on Dec 18, 1978, by an appointed assembly set up by the military regime that took power in October 1976. The Constitution establishes a parliamentary form of government with a strong Prime Minister.

TOGO
Republic of Togo

LOCATION: Togo lies on the west coast of Africa, with Burkina Faso to the north, Ghana to the west, Benin to the east and the Gulf of Guinea to the south.

AREA: 21,925 sq. miles

Land Use: 26.24% cropland; 3.68% permanent pasture; 28.50% forests and woodland; 41.58% other (mostly savanna).
Arable Land: 26.24%
Arable Land per capita: 1.32 acres

POPULATION: 3,146,000 (1987 estimate)

Population Density: 143.49 inhabs. per sq. mile (1987)
Population Distribution: 22.10% urban (1985)
Population Growth Rate: 3.06% per year (1985-90 projection)

VITAL STATISTICS

Average Life Expectancy: 52.50 years (1985-90 projection)
Male: 50.80 years (1985-90 projection)
Female: 54.30 years (1985-90 projection)
Age Distribution: (1985)
0-14 . . . . 44.80%
15-64 . . . . 52.00%
65+ 3.20%
Median Age: 17.50 years (1985)
Maternal Mortality: (not available)
Infant Mortality: 93 per 1,000 live births (1985-90 projection)

HEALTH CARE

Hospital Beds: 13.31 per 10,000 population (1982)
Doctors: 0.52 per 10,000 population (1980)

ETHNIC COMPOSITION: Ewe - 35%; Kabye - 22%; Mina - 6%; other indigenous peoples - 37%.

RELIGION: Animist - 70%; Christian - 20%; Moslem - 10%.

LANGUAGE: French is the official language. Kabiye and Ewe are the national languages. Mina and Dagomba are widely spoken.

EDUCATION: Illiteracy: 82%. In 1984, there were 2,329 primary schools with 454,209 students; 85,745 secondary school students; 5,187 technical school students; 58 teacher training students; and 1 university with 4,192 students. In 1982 there were 358 secondary schools and in 1980 there were 19 technical schools and 2 teacher training schools.

ECONOMIC DATA

Expenditures by Function [as % of total]: (1985)
General public services 10.84%
Defense 6.91%
Education 11.69%
Health 3.61%
Social security and welfare 7.37%
Housing and community amenities 1.78%
Other community and social services 1.35%
Economic services 23.48%
Agriculture, forestry, fishing and hunting . .8.09%
Roads 5.13%
Other transportation and communication . . .0.45%
Other purposes 19.30%
GDP per capita: $212 (1984)

TRAVEL NOTES

Climate: The Togolese climate is tropical. The south is humid, with temperatures ranging between 70°F and 89°F. In the north, temperatures range from 65°F to greater than 100°F.
Health Precautions: Malaria is a risk. Inoculation against yellow fever and cholera is required. Avoid tap water and unwashed fruits and vegetables.
Miscellaneous: Visitors are attracted by good beaches, hunting and fishing. Air travel is the best way to get to Lome. Uncertain road conditions or frontier difficulties can complicate automobile travel to neighboring Benin.

GOVERNMENT

Togo (Republic of Togo—Republique Togolaise) became independent on Apr 27, 1960. After two coups and at least one attempted coup, both the President and a new proposed Constitution were endorsed in 1979 elections, leading to the proclamation by the President of the "Third Republic" in January 1980. The President, running as a single candidate, was almost unanimously reelected for another 7-year term on Dec 12, 1986.

Constitution: The Constitution provides for single-party rule, with a highly centralized form of government.

TONGA
Kingdom of Tonga

LOCATION: Tonga consists of more than 160 volcanic and coral islands in the South Pacific, located south of Western Samoa and east of Fiji.

AREA: 289 sq. miles

Land Use: 80% cropland; 6% permanent pasture; 12% forests and woodland; 2% other.
Arable Land: 80%
Arable Land per capita: 1.48 acres

POPULATION: 108,000 (1989 estimate)

Population Density: 269 inhabs. per sq. mile (1989 estimate)
Population Distribution: 50% urban (1985)
Population Growth Rate: 1.30% per year (1989 estimate)

VITAL STATISTICS

Average Life Expectancy: 58 years (1988)
Male: (not available)
Female: (not available)
Age Distribution: (1984)
0-14 .... 44.40%
15-59 .... 50.50%
60+ 5.10%
Median Age: (not available)
Maternal Mortality: (not available)
Infant Mortality: 45 per 1,000 live births (1985)

HEALTH CARE

Hospital Beds: 30 per 10,000 population (1985)
Doctors: 5 per 10,000 population (1985)

ETHNIC COMPOSITION: Mixed Polynesian and Melanesian - 98%; other Pacific islander and European - 2%.

RELIGION: The population is mainly Christian, with the primary denomination being Free Wesleyan.

LANGUAGE: Tongan and English are spoken.

EDUCATION: Illiteracy: 5-10%. In 1985, there were 112 primary schools with 17,019 students; 54 secondary schools with 14,655 students; 10 technical and vocational schools with 430 students; and 1 teacher training school with 126 students.

ECONOMIC DATA

Expenditures by Function [as % of total]: (not available)
GDP per capita: $630 (1983)

TRAVEL NOTES

Climate: The climate is mild, with a rainy season from December through March.
Health Precautions: (not available)
Miscellaneous: Attractions include the mild climate and beautiful vistas.

GOVERNMENT

Tonga (Pule' anga Fakatu'i 'o Tonga—Kingdom of Tonga) became an independent nation within the Commonwealth on Jun 4, 1970, after having been a British protectorate since 1900.

Constitution: Tonga's Constitution, promulgated at independence, is based on the 1875 Constitution passed by King Tupou I, and provides for a constitutional hereditary monarchy.

TRINIDAD AND TOBAGO
Republic of Trinidad and Tobago

LOCATION: Trinidad and Tobago is a nation made up of two Caribbean islands of the Lesser Antilles—Trinidad, off the coast of Venezuela and the southernmost Caribbean island, and Tobago, about

20 miles to the northeast. The island of Grenada is the nearest country to the north.

AREA: 1,979 sq. miles

Land Use: 30.99% cropland; 2.14% permanent pasture; 44.25% forests and woodland; 22.62% other.
Arable Land: 31%
Arable Land per capita: 0.32 acres

POPULATION: 1,242,000 (1988 estimate)

Population Density: 628 inhabs. per sq. mile (1988 estimate)
Population Distribution: 63.90% urban (1985)
Population Growth Rate: 1.50% per year (1988 estimate)

VITAL STATISTICS

Average Life Expectancy: 70.20 years (1985-90 projection)
Male: 67.60 years (1985-90 projection)
Female: 72.90 years (1985-90 projection)
Age Distribution: (1985)
0-14 . . . . 32.90%
15-64 . . . . 61.70%
65+ 5.40%
Median Age: 23 years (1985)
Maternal Mortality: 78.90 per 100,000 live births (1977)
Infant Mortality: 21 per 1,000 live births (1988 estimate)

HEALTH CARE

Hospital Beds: 38.24 per 10,000 population (1982)
Doctors: 6.89 per 10,000 population (1980)

ETHNIC COMPOSITION: Black - 43%; East Indian - 40%; mixed - 14%; white - 1%; Chinese - 1%; other - 1%.

RELIGION: Roman Catholic - 36%; Hindu - 23%; Protestant - 13%; Moslem - 6%; other - 22%.

LANGUAGE: The official and primary language is English. French, Spanish, Chinese and Hindi are also spoken.

EDUCATION: Illiteracy: 11%. In 1983/84, there were 166,638 primary students; 13,039 Government secondary students; 17,602 assisted secondary students; 39,205 junior secondary students; and 22,190 senior comprehensive students. There

are 2 teacher training colleges, 3 vocational institutes and 3 universities.

ECONOMIC DATA

Expenditures by Function [as % of total]: (1981)
General public services 27.27%
Defense 2.03%
Education 11.23%
Health 5.91%
Social security and welfare 5.95%
Housing and community amenities 11.40%
Other community and social services 1.23%
Economic services 31.08%
Agriculture, forestry, fishing and hunting . .4.43%
Roads 9.06%
Other transportation and communication . . .3.27%
Other purposes 3.56%
GDP per capita: $4,249 (1985)

TRAVEL NOTES

Climate: The climate is tropical, but the islands are kept cool by the prevailing northeast trade winds. A rainy season lasts from June to December, with a slight interruption in September. The average rainfall is 64 inches per year and the average daytime temperature is 84°F.
Health Precautions: No vaccinations are required but the standard immunizations are recommended. The water is not potable and should be boiled and filtered before drinking.
Miscellaneous: The annual carnival festival attracts thousands of visitors from other Caribbean nations, the US and Canada.

GOVERNMENT

Trinidad-Tobago (Republic of Trinidad and Tobago), formerly a British colonial possession, became an independent member of the Commonwealth of Nations on Aug 31, 1962, and a republic on Aug 1, 1976.

Constitution: A new Constitution, which took effect on Jul 27, 1976, replacing the 1962 Constitution, provided for the establishment of a republic and the supersession of the British monarch by a President as head of state.

TUNISIA
Republic of Tunisia

LOCATION: Tunisia is located on the northern coast of the African continent and is bounded by the Mediterranean Sea to the north, Libya to the east and Algeria to the west.

AREA: 63,170 sq. miles

Land Use: 30.15% cropland; 19.68% permanent pasture; 3.58% forests and woodland; 46.59% other.
Arable Land: 30%
Arable Land per capita: 1.56 acres

POPULATION: 7,760,000 (1988 estimate)

Population Density: 123 inhabs. per sq. mile (1988 estimate)
Population Distribution: 56.80% urban (1985)
Population Growth Rate: 2.20% per year (1988 estimate)

VITAL STATISTICS

Average Life Expectancy: 63.10 years (1985-90 projection)
Male: 62.60 years (1985-90 projection)
Female: 63.60 years (1985-90 projection)
Age Distribution: (1984)
0-14 .... 39.20%
15-64 .... 56.40%
65+ 4.40%
Median Age: 19.60 years (1985)
Maternal Mortality: (not available)
Infant Mortality: 53 per 1,000 live births (1985)

HEALTH CARE

Hospital Beds: 21 per 10,000 population (1984)
Doctors: 1 per 10,000 population (1985)

ETHNIC COMPOSITION: Arab - 98%; European - 1%; other - 1% (mainly Jewish).

RELIGION: Moslem - 98%; Christian - 1%; other - 1% (mainly Jewish).

LANGUAGE: Arabic is the official language, but French is also widely used in education, administration and trade. A small percentage of the population also speaks Berber.

EDUCATION: Illiteracy: 38%. In 1984/85, there were 3,214 primary schools with 1,238,968 students; 349 secondary schools with 385,445 students; and 1 university with 5,019 students.

ECONOMIC DATA

Expenditures by Function [as % of total]: (1984)
General public services 8.32%
Defense 7.95%
Education 14.32%
Health 6.55%
Social security and welfare 6.35%
Housing and community amenities 6.04%
Other community and social services 2.67%
Economic services 33.06%
Agriculture, forestry, fishing and hunting . 18.10%
Roads 1.51%
Other transportation and communication . . . 3.63%
Other purposes 14.74%
GDP per capita: $1,140 (1986)

TRAVEL NOTES

Climate: The Tunisian climate is temperate on the coast, with mild winters and hot summers. The central and southern sections of the country are hot and dry most of the year. Temperatures in Tunis range between 43°F and 91°F.
Health Precautions: Inoculations are required for yellow fever and immunizations are recommended for polio and diphtheria-tetanus. The water is potable in Tunis and the surrounding suburbs, but precautions should be taken with water in other parts of the country.
Miscellaneous: Popular tourist attractions include beautiful sandy beaches on the Mediterranean coast, architectural remains of the Roman Empire and the site of the ancient Phoenician city of Carthage.

GOVERNMENT

Tunisia (al-Jumhuriyah al Tunisiyah—Republic of Tunisia), formerly a French protectorate (1883-1956), became an independent state on Mar 20, 1956, with the Bey of Tunis as its monarch. On Jul 25, 1957, a Constitutional Assembly proclaimed Tunisia a republic, deposed the Bey and elected Prime Minister Habib Bourguiba as President. Bourguiba ruled the nation until Nov 7, 1987, when he was replaced by his Prime Minister, Zine El Abidine Ben Ali, who declared that the President was senile and unable to run the country. Effective political power rests with the ruling *Parti Socialiste Destourien* (PSD).

Constitution: Tunisia's Constitution, which entered into effect in June 1959, establishes a strong presidential system, in which the chief executive exercises broad discretionary powers while the authority of the legislature to take independent initiatives is limited. The operation of the basic political institutions is also strongly modified by the pervasive influence throughout the government structure of the *Parti Socialiste Destourien*.

TURKEY
Republic of Turkey

LOCATION: Turkey is located at the northeastern end of the Mediterranean Sea, with most of the country (Anatolia) considered part of western Asia, and a small portion (Thrace) part of southeastern Europe. It is bounded by the Aegean Sea to the west, Greece and Bulgaria to the northwest, the Black Sea to the north, the Soviet Union and Iran to the east and Iraq and Syria to the south.

AREA: 300,948 sq. miles

Land Use: 35.08% cropland; 11.94% permanent pasture; 26.21% forests and woodland; 26.77% other.
Arable Land: 35.08%
Arable Land per capita: 1.31 acres

POPULATION: 51,390,000 (1987 estimate)

Population Density: 171 inhabs. per sq. mile (1987 estimate)
Population Distribution: 45.90% urban (1985)
Population Growth Rate: 2.06% per year (1985-90 projection)

VITAL STATISTICS

Average Life Expectancy: 64.10 years (1985-90 projection)
Male: 62.50 years (1985-90 projection)
Female: 65.80 years (1985-90 projection)
Age Distribution: (1985)
0-14 . . . . 36.40%
15-64 . . . . 59.40%
65+ 4.20%
Median Age: 21.40 years (1985)

Maternal Mortality: (not available)
Infant Mortality: 76 per 1,000 live births (1985-90 projection)

HEALTH CARE

Hospital Beds: 21.24 per 10,000 population (1982)
Doctors: 6.55 per 10,000 population (1982)

ETHNIC COMPOSITION: Turkish - 85%; Kurd - 12%; other - 3%.

RELIGION: Moslem - 98%; other - 2% (mainly Christian and Jewish).

LANGUAGE: Turkish, the official language, is spoken by the majority of the population. Kurdish and Arabic are also spoken.

EDUCATION: Illiteracy: 30%. In 1984/85, there were 48,533 primary schools with 6,532,000 students; 7,545 secondary schools with 2,757,000 students; and 302 teacher training institutes, vocational schools and universities with 398,000 students.

ECONOMIC DATA

Expenditures by Function [as % of total]: (1985)
General public services 54.01%
Defense 10.90%
Education 9.95%
Health 1.81%
Social security and welfare 1.04%
Housing and community amenities 2.59%
Other community and social services 0.08%
Economic services 19.61%
Agriculture, forestry, fishing and hunting . .1.29%
Roads 6.81%
Other transportation and communication . . .1.01%
Other purposes 0%
GDP per capita: $1,028 (1986)

TRAVEL NOTES

Climate: The interior part of the country endures climatic extremes, with hot, dry summers and cold, snowy winters. Ankara averages 14 inches of annual rainfall and has a temperature range of 25°F to 86°F. The Mediterranean coastline has milder winters and warmer summers.
Health Precautions: Immunizations against polio, tetanus, typhoid and diphtheria are recommended. The water is not potable.

Miscellaneous: Tourists are attracted to Turkey by its pleasant climate, fine beaches and ancient monuments.

GOVERNMENT

Turkey (Turkiye Cumhuriyeti—Republic of Turkey) is the secular republic that succeeded the disbanded Ottoman Empire in 1923. The armed forces seized control of the Government on Sep 12, 1980, following several years of widespread political violence. The 1961 Constitution was suspended, and supreme political authority was vested in a 5-member National Security Council.

Constitution: A Nov 7, 1982 referendum approved a new Constitution that included the nomination of National Security Council chairperson Gen. Kenan Evren to a 7-year term as President. The Constitution also abolished the National Security Council in favor of a Presidential Council.

TUVALU

LOCATION: Tuvalu, located in the western Pacific Ocean, is made up of 9 small atolls scattered over 350 miles. Its closest neighbors are Kiribati to the north, Solomon Islands to the west, Fiji to the south and Samoa to the southeast.

AREA: 10 sq. miles

Land Use: 0% cropland; 0% permanent pasture; 0% forests and woodland; 100% other (mostly coral reefs).
Arable Land: None.
Arable Land per capita: None.

POPULATION: 9,000 (1989 estimate)

Population Density: 900 inhabs. per sq. mile (1989 estimate)
Population Distribution: (not available)
Population Growth Rate: 1.70% per year (1989 estimate)

VITAL STATISTICS

Average Life Expectancy: 58.50 years (1988)
Male: 57 years (1988)
Female: 60 years (1988)

Age Distribution: (not available)
Median Age: (not available)
Maternal Mortality: (not available)
Infant Mortality: 35 per 1,000 live births (1985)

HEALTH CARE

Hospital Beds: 90 per 10,000 population (1981)
Doctors: 5 per 10,000 population (1981)

ETHNIC COMPOSITION: Most Tuvaluans are ethnically Polynesian.

RELIGION: Christian - 98% (mostly Protestant); other - 2%.

LANGUAGE: English is the official language. Tuvaluan is widely spoken.

EDUCATION: Illiteracy: 50%. In 1984, there were 11 primary schools with 61 teachers and 1,349 students, and one secondary school with 243 students. The University of the South Pacific center, built in 1987, is located on Tuvalu's Funafuti atoll.

ECONOMIC DATA

Expenditures by Function [as % of total]: (not available)
GDP per capita: $346 (1987 estimate)

TRAVEL NOTES

Climate: The climate in Tuvalu is warm throughout the year with a mean annual temperature of 84°F and an average rainfall of 120 inches.
Health Precautions: (not available)
Miscellaneous: Tourism in Tuvalu is limited due to the island's remoteness. There is one hotel, located on Funafuti.

GOVERNMENT

Tuvalu was formerly a British protectorate known as the Ellice Islands, which was part of the Gilbert group, now known as Kirabati. Tuvalu, which gained its independence on Oct 1, 1978, is a constitutional monarchy with a special membership in the British Commonwealth.

Constitution: The Constitution, promulgated in February 1978 and amended in June 1986, provides for all basic democratic rights.

UGANDA
Republic of Uganda

LOCATION: A landlocked East African country, Uganda is surrounded by Zaire to the west, Sudan to the north, Kenya to the east and Rwanda and Tanzania to the south. Lake Victoria straddles the southern border.

AREA: 93,100 sq. miles

Land Use: 31.11% cropland; 25.04% permanent pasture; 29.59% forests and woodland; 14.26% other.
Arable Land: 31%
Arable Land per capita: 1.28 acres

POPULATION: 16,240,000 (1988 estimate)

Population Density: 174 inhabs. per sq. mile (1988 estimate)
Population Distribution: 9.52% urban (1985)
Population Growth Rate: 3.50% per year (1988 estimate)

VITAL STATISTICS

Average Life Expectancy: 51.00 years (1985-90 projection)
Male: 49.30 years (1985-90 projection)
Female: 54.80 years (1985-90 projection)
Age Distribution: (1984)
0-14 .... 48.08%
15-64 .... 49.42%
65+ 2.50%
Median Age: 15.90 years (1985)
Maternal Mortality: (not available)
Infant Mortality: 113 per 1,000 live births (1985)

HEALTH CARE

Hospital Beds: 14 per 10,000 population (1983)
Doctors: 0.47 per 10,000 population (1984)

ETHNIC COMPOSITION: Indigenous peoples (including the Bantu, Nilotic, Nilo-Hamitic and Sudanic tribes) - 99%; other - 1%.

RELIGION: Roman Catholic - 33%; Protestant - 33%; indigenous beliefs - 18%; Moslem - 16%.

LANGUAGE: English is the official language. Luganda and Swahili are also widely used, along with numerous other Bantu and Nilotic dialects.

EDUCATION: Illiteracy: 48%. In 1982, there were approximately 5,300 primary schools with 1,616,791 students; 132,051 secondary schools students; 4,181 vocational secondary school students; 9,157 teacher training students; 4,854 university students; and 2,458 other students of higher education.

ECONOMIC DATA

Expenditures by Function [as % of total]: (1986)
General public services 21.66%
Defense 26.34%
Education 15.01%
Health 2.39%
Social security and welfare .... (not available)
Housing and community amenities 0.77%
Other community and social services 1.26%
Economic services 14.77%
Agriculture, forestry, fishing and hunting ..4.67%
Roads 6.18%
Other transportation and communication ...0.35%
Other purposes 15.69%
GDP per capita: $408 (1983)

TRAVEL NOTES

Climate: The Ugandan climate is tropical, although temperatures vary with altitude, ranging from 60°F to 85°F. Rainfall varies considerably, but the country receives an average of 64 inches per year.
Health Precautions: Precautions should be taken against malaria, cholera and yellow fever. Tap water should be boiled and filtered.
Miscellaneous: Uganda boasts a beautiful countryside, and tourists are attracted to Lake Victoria, as well as Kabalega and Rwenzori National Parks.

GOVERNMENT

Uganda (Republic of Uganda) became an independent state within the Commonwealth on Oct 9, 1962. It was initially a federation, in which traditional kingdoms retained a large degree of autonomous authority, but on Sep 8, 1967, it became a unitary republic under a new Constitution. The Constitution was first suspended by Maj. Gen. Idi Amin Dada, who seized power in a 1971 coup. The Government of Milton Obote, which succeeded the Amin dictatorship after the reestablishment of the 1967 Constitution and holding of National Assembly elections in December 1980, was ousted in a July 1985 military coup headed by Brig. Basilio Olara

Okello. Lt. Gen. Tito Okello was sworn in as head of state and the Constitution was again suspended, but Okello was in turn ousted in another coup in January 1986 led by Yoweri Museveni.

Constitution: The 1967 Constitution, which has been suspended, provided for a parliamentary form of government. A pact in June 1988 between the Government and rebel forces provides for a new Constitution to be drawn up in 1989.

UNION OF SOVIET SOCIALIST REPUBLICS
See Soviet Union

UNITED ARAB EMIRATES

LOCATION: The United Arab Emirates is located in the eastern portion of the Arabian peninsula and is bordered on the northwest by Qatar, on the west and south by Saudi Arabia and on the east by Oman. It has a long coastline on the Persian Gulf to the north and a short coastline on the Gulf of Oman to the west.

AREA: 30,000 sq. miles

Land Use: 0.18% cropland; 2.39% permanent pasture; 0.04% forests and woodland; 97.39% other (mostly desert).
Arable Land: 1%
Arable Land per capita: 0.13 acres

POPULATION: 1,437,000 (1987 projection)

Population Density: 38 inhabs. per sq. mile (1987)
Population Distribution: 71.82% urban (1985)
Population Growth Rate: 3.46% per year (1985-90 projection)

VITAL STATISTICS

Average Life Expectancy: 69.25 years (1985-90)
Male: 71.60 years (1985-90)
Female: 66.90 years (1985-90)
Age Distribution: (1985)
0-14 . . . . 31.80%
15-64 . . . . 66.70%
65+ 1.50%

Median Age: 26.50 years (1985)
Maternal Mortality: (not available)
Infant Mortality: 32 per 1,000 live births (1985-90 projection)

HEALTH CARE

Hospital Beds: 31 per 10,000 population (1981)
Doctors: 20 per 10,000 population (1981)

ETHNIC COMPOSITION: South Asian - 50%; Emirian - 19%; other Arabic - 23%; other - 8%.

RELIGION: Moslem - 96%; Christian, Hindu and other - 4%.

LANGUAGE: Arabic is the official and most widely spoken language, while the languages of various South Asian groups are also spoken. English is used as a second language in commerce.

EDUCATION: Illiteracy: 43.70% (1985). In 1985, there were 395 schools with about 180,000 students. In 1982/83 there were 126,726 primary school students; 51,277 students in general secondary schools; 615 students in vocational secondary schools; and 5,615 university students.

ECONOMIC DATA

Expenditures by Function [as % of total]: (1981)
General public services 16.68%
Defense 41.10%
Education 7.56%
Health 6.20%
Social security and welfare 2.53%
Housing and community amenities 1.28%
Other community and social services 1.33%
Economic services .5.51%
Agriculture, forestry, fishing and hunting . .0.88%
Roads 0%
Other transportation and communication . . .1.46%
Other purposes 15.47%
GDP per capita: $20,590 (1984)

TRAVEL NOTES

Climate: The climate is very hot and humid during the summer, with the average high temperature over 100°F. From late fall to spring, temperatures range from 45°F to 80°F. Average annual rainfall is very low, between 4 and 6 inches.
Health Precautions: Malaria suppressants should be taken in advance by anyone traveling to the eastern coast or to the inland oasis of Al-Anin.

Dubai tap water is generally safe, though Abu Dhabi water should be filtered and boiled.

Miscellaneous: There is currently an established tourist industry in Sharjah, and Dubai has plans to foster tourism.

GOVERNMENT

United Arab Emirates (al-Imarat al-'Arabiyah al-Muttahida) proclaimed its independence on Dec 2, 1971, after Britain formally ended its special treaty responsibilities for the foreign affairs and defense of the 7 Trucial Coast Sheikdoms. It is a confederation of the 7 emirates of Abu Dhabi, Dubai, Sharjah, Ajman, Fujairah, Umm al-Qaiwain and Ras Al-Khaima. Effective political authority rests with the ruling families of the 7 constituent emirates and their traditional supporters. The rulers of Abu Dhabi and Dubai, however, have tended to play a leading role in federation affairs, due to the superior wealth and population of their domains.

Constitution: A 5-year provisional Constitution entered into effect at independence. It has been extended three times by decree (the most recent extension was voted on Oct 14, 1986). It provides for a relatively decentralized federal system under which the central Government has exclusive jurisdiction over foreign affairs, defense of the federation as a whole, the union armed forces, federal finances and similar matters of a nationwide concern. The constituent emirates retain extensive residual powers in all matters not assigned exclusively to the federal Government (including control over taxation, local police powers and mineral rights).

UNITED STATES OF AMERICA

LOCATION: Occupying a major portion of the North American continent, the United States is bounded by Canada to the north, the Atlantic Ocean to the east, the Caribbean Sea and Mexico to the south and the Pacific Ocean to the west. The non-contiguous states of Alaska and Hawaii lie to the northwest of Canada and in the central Pacific Ocean respectively.

AREA: 3,618,770 sq. miles

Land Use: 20.72% cropland; 26.34% permanent pasture; 28.93% forests and woodland; 24.01% other.
Arable Land: 21%
Arable Land per capita: 1.98 acres

POPULATION: 245,302,000 (1988 estimate)

Population Density: 68 inhabs. per sq. mile (1988 estimate)
Population Distribution: 73.90% urban (1985)
Population Growth Rate: 0.90% per year (1988 estimate)

VITAL STATISTICS

Average Life Expectancy: 75.00 years (1985-90 projection)
Male: 71.30 years (1985-90 projection)
Female: 78.80 years (1985-90 projection)
Age Distribution: (1985)
0-14 . . . . .21.88%
15-64 . . . . .66.43%
65+ 11.69%
Median Age: 32.10 years (1987)
Maternal Mortality: 8 per 100,000 live births (1983)
Infant Mortality: 10 per 1,000 live births (1985)

HEALTH CARE

Hospital Beds: 55 per 10,000 population (1984)
Doctors: 22 per 10,000 population (1983)

ETHNIC COMPOSITION: White - 83.15%; black - 11.70%; Asian - 1.57%; Native American - 0.60%; other (mainly Hispanic) - 2.98% (1980 census).

LANGUAGE: English is the predominant language, but a substantial minority speaks Spanish.

EDUCATION: Illiteracy: 1%. In 1985, there were 26,900,000 primary school students; 12,400,000 secondary school students; and 3,200 colleges and universities with 12,000,000 students.

ECONOMIC DATA

Expenditures by Function [as %of total]: (1986)
General public services 5.32%
Defense 25.76%
Education 1.74%
Health 11.55%
Social security and welfare 28.42%

Housing and community amenities 2.59%
Other community and social services 0.26%
Economic services 8.84%
Agriculture, forestry, fishing and hunting . . 3.31%
Roads 1.39%
Other transportation and communication . . 1.14%
Other purposes 15.99%
GDP per capita: $17,415 (1986)

TRAVEL NOTES

Climate: The climate varies substantially, with average annual temperatures ranging from 77°F in Florida to 10°F in Alaska. The average annual rainfall is 29 inches, with Alabama receiving 65 inches and Arizona having 7 inches of rain each year.

Health Precautions: None

Miscellaneous: The US offers an unlimited range of tourist attractions, from winter sports to summer leisure activities. Natural wonders include the Grand Canyon, the Everglades and large national parks in the west, such as Yellowstone and Yosemite. Other items of interest include modern urban architecture, museums, art galleries and diverse cultural events.

GOVERNMENT

United States of America is a federal republic of 50 member states. Its independence was proclaimed by the 13 original states on Jul 4, 1776. It is a constitutional democracy, with a presidential form of government, but with strong independent authority vested in the legislature. Effective political authority rests with the elected officials of the state and federal governments.

Federalism. Political authority is divided between the Federal Government and the governments of the 50 states. Within their jurisdiction state governments exercise a broad range of independent powers, wider than the members of any other federal system. Although the growth of federal authority has been a feature of the 20th century, the power of the states has also grown. Nevertheless, the trend since World War I has been toward a centralization of power and responsibility in the Federal Government.

Constitution: The First US Constitution. The US had two national Constitutions: the Articles of Confederation and the Federal Constitution of 1787. The Continental Congress approved the Articles of Confederation for submission to the 13 original states on Nov 15, 1777. Ratification by the states was delayed by disputes over a number of issues and it was not until Mar 1, 1781, that the Articles of Confederation officially entered into effect as the first US Constitution. It remained in effect until Mar 4, 1789.

The Federal Constitution of 1787. By the middle of the 1780s, a widespread consensus existed in favor of some changes in the system set up under the Articles of Confederation. On Feb 21, 1787, the Congress endorsed a call for a national convention, to meet in Philadelphia on May 5, to propose amendments to the Articles. Of the 13 states, 12 sent delegates—Rhode Island refusing to participate. Of the 65 delegates selected, 55 participated in the Philadelphia Convention, which formally opened on May 15, with George Washington as presiding officer. The convention decided to submit an entirely new Constitution, rather than just propose amendments to the Articles. On Sep 17, 1787, 39 delegates signed the document, which was then submitted to state conventions for ratification. Technically, the new Constitution was ratified on Jun 21, 1788, when New Hampshire became the ninth state to approve it. However, the later endorsements by Virginia (Jun 25, 1788) and New York (Jul 26, 1788) are generally regarded as the key ratifications. Of the two remaining states, North Carolina did not approve until Nov 21, 1789 and Rhode Island not until May 29, 1790, after the new Federal Government was functioning. The first congress under the new Constitution met on Mar 4, 1789, in New York. On Apr 30, 1789, George Washington was inaugurated as the first President. The Original Written Constitution consists of a Preamble and 7 Articles. The Articles are divided into sections and clauses. The Constitution grants "all legislative powers" of the national Government to a bicameral Congress, consisting of a House of Representatives and a Senate; gives Congress the power to lay and collect taxes, to "regulate commerce with foreign nations, and among the several states" and to make such laws as are "necessary and proper" to implement the specific powers granted to the national Government; vests the executive power in the President, who is elected by the electoral college; and appoints the President as commander-in-chief of the armed forces and outlines the President's powers, including supervision of the executive departments, treaty-making (with the advice and consent of the Senate), and appointing federal officials (with the advice and consent of the Senate). The Constitution also establishes the Supreme Court and vests it (and such other courts as Congress may create) with the judicial power; outlines the jurisdiction of the courts, grants Congress the power to regulate the appellate jurisdiction of the Supreme Court and requires jury trials for all crimes except in cases of impeachment; provides that no state may infringe upon the "privileges and immunities" of a citizen of the US; and establishes the procedure for admission of new states into the federal union and grants Congress the power to govern territories that have not achieved statehood. Amendments to the Constitution may be proposed by Congress or by a convention called by Congress upon application of two-thirds of the states. Proposed amendments must be submitted to the states, and take effect only if three-fourths of the states approve.

Constitutional Amendments. Since 1789, Congress has formally proposed 33 amendments to the Constitution. The states have ratified 26 of these proposals. The first 10 amendments are called the Bill of Rights, because they were proposed to meet criticism that the original Constitution of 1787 did not sufficiently protect individual and states rights. The Bill of Rights was specifically intended to limit the power of the Federal Government. The first 10 amendments entered into effect on Dec 15, 1791. They guarantee freedom of religion, speech, press and peaceful assembly, the rights to petition for redress of grievances and separation of church and state; ensure the right to keep and bear arms (as a means for maintaining a militia); forbid forced quartering of troops in private homes in peacetime and in time of war except as provided by law; guarantee the security of persons, homes and property against "unreasonable searches and seizures"; provide that no person is to be held for a crime unless charged by a grand jury and is not to be tried twice for the same offense, nor to be compelled to bear witness against himself in a criminal case, nor "deprived of life, liberty or property without due process of law"; and provide no private property is to be taken for public use without just compensation. The Bill of Rights further grant the right of a person in a criminal case to a "speedy and public trial," to be informed of the nature of the accusation and confronted with witnesses against him, and to obtain witnesses in his favor; the right to trial by jury in civil suits at common law when the value in controversy exceeds $20; bars excessive bail and "cruel and unusual punishments"; and provides that "The powers not delegated to the United States by the constitution, nor prohibited by it to the States, are reserved to the States respectively, or to the people." Amendments to the Constitution provide that: states may not be sued in federal courts without their consent; separate ballots are to be used for election of President and Vice President by the electoral colleges; the abolition of slavery and "involuntary servitude" except as punishment for crime; states may not "deprive any person of life, liberty or property, without due process of law" or to "deny any person . . . the equal protection of the laws"; the right of citizens to vote "shall not be denied or abridged . . . on account of race, color, or previous condition of servitude"; Congress is authorized to levy income taxes without apportionment among the states according to population; senators are to be elected by direct popular vote instead of by state legislatures; introduces and later repeals the prohibition of production and sale of "intoxicating liquors"; the right to vote "shall not be denied or abridged . . . on account of sex"; advancement to Jan 20 of the date of inauguration of the President and Vice President, and abolition of "lame duck" session of Congress by calling for Congress to assemble in January instead of early December; "No person shall be elected to the office of President more than twice, and no person who has held the office of President or acted as President, for more than two years of a term to which some other person was elected President shall be elected to the office of President more than once"; the District of Columbia is granted the right to vote for the President and Vice President, being given three electoral votes in presidential elections; forbids collection of poll taxes as a requirement for voting in primaries and elections for President and Vice President and members of Congress; enables Vice President to become acting President in the event of a presidential disability; enables President to nominate a new Vice President in the event of a vice presidential vacancy; and lowers to 18 years the minimum voting age in all elections.

UPPER VOLTA
See Burkina Faso

URUGUAY
Eastern Republic of Uruguay

LOCATION: Lying on the southeastern coast of South America, Uruguay is bordered by Brazil to the north and east, Argentina to the west and the Atlantic Ocean to the south.

AREA: 68,037 sq. miles

Land Use: 8.33% cropland; 78.52% permanent pasture; 3.63% forests and woodland; 9.52% other.
Arable Land: 8%
Arable Land per capita: 1.22 acres

POPULATION: 2,983,000 (1989 estimate)

Population Density: 44 inhabs. per sq. mile (1989 estimate)
Population Distribution: 85.00% urban (1987)
Population Growth Rate: 0.40% per year (1989 estimate)

VITAL STATISTICS

Average Life Expectancy: 71.00 years (1985-90 projection)
Male: 67.80 years (1985-90 projection)
Female: 74.40 years (1985-90 projection)
Age Distribution: (1984)
0-14 .... 26.89%
15-64 .... 62.39%
65+ 10.72%
Median Age: 29.80 years (1985)
Maternal Mortality: 55.90 per 100,000 live births (1978)
Infant Mortality: 26 per 1,000 live births (1985)

HEALTH CARE

Hospital Beds: 79 per 10,000 population (1983)
Doctors: 20 per 10,000 population (1986)

ETHNIC COMPOSITION: Caucasian (mainly Spanish and Italian origin) - 89%; mestizo - 10%; other - 1%.

RELIGION: Roman Catholic - 66%; Protestant - 2%; Jewish - 2%; other - 30%.

LANGUAGE: Spanish is the official language.

EDUCATION: Illiteracy: 6%. In 1984, there were 2,321 primary schools with 350,390 students; 176,885 general secondary students; 30,778 vocational secondary students; and 63,734 post-secondary students. There is one university.

ECONOMIC DATA

Expenditures by Function [as % of total]: (1986)
General public services 10.98%
Defense 10.25%
Education 7.12%
Health 4.77%
Social security and welfare 49.43%
Housing and community amenities 0.05%
Other community and social services 0.95%
Economic services 8.30%
Agriculture, forestry, fishing and hunting ..1.37%
Roads 3.92%
Other transportation and communication ...1.68%
Other purposes 10.79%
GDP per capita: $2,046 (1987)

TRAVEL NOTES

Climate: Uruguay experiences a temperate climate with an average winter temperature of 57°F to 61°F and an average summer temperature of 70°F to 82°F. Winter lasts from June through August, while summer occurs between December and February. The spring season is wetter and cooler than fall.
Health Precautions: Precautions are recommended against polio, hepatitis and typhoid. Tap water is potable in the larger cities.
Miscellaneous: Uruguay is known for beautiful harbors and beaches, as well as inland forests. Montevideo is the furthest south of all capital cities in the Western Hemisphere.

GOVERNMENT

Uruguay (Republica Oriental del Uruguay— Oriental Republic of Uruguay) achieved independence from Spain in 1825 and from Brazil in 1828 following a conflict between Argentina and Brazil over its possession. Civil wars caused by conflicts between the main political parties dominated the 1800s. Between 1967 and 1972, left-wing Tupamaro guerrillas waged an unsuccessful war against the Government, while the military ruled the country between 1973 and 1985. On Nov 25, 1984, the first general election in 13 years launched a transfer of power from the military to a civilian government led by Dr. Julio Maria Sanguinetti. Legislative power was returned to civilians on Feb 15, 1985, three days after the military President stepped down.

Constitution: The current Constitution was approved by plebiscite on Nov 27, 1966 and implemented in 1967. The Constitution provides for a President and bicameral legislature. Universal suffrage and freedom of religion are guaranteed. In a 1980 referendum, voters rejected a new Constitution.

U.S.S.R.
See Union of Soviet Socialist Republics

VANUATU
Republic of Vanuatu

LOCATION: Located in the southwestern Pacific, Vanuatu consists of an archipelago of about 80 islands. Fiji lies 600 miles to the east and New Caledonia lies 250 miles to the southwest.

AREA: 4,706 sq. miles

Land Use: 6% cropland; 2% permanent pasture; 1% forests and woodland; 91% other.
Arable Land: 6%
Arable Land per capita: 1.28 acres

POPULATION: 145,000 (1988 estimate)

Population Density: 31 inhabs. per sq. mile (1988 estimate)
Population Distribution: 4% urban (1980)
Population Growth Rate: 3% per year (1988 estimate)

VITAL STATISTICS

Average Life Expectancy: 55.00 years (1987)
Male: 56.20 years (1984)
Female: 53.70 years (1984)
Age Distribution: (not available)
Median Age: (not available)
Maternal Mortality: (not available)
Infant Mortality: 78 per 1,000 live births (1985)

HEALTH CARE

Hospital Beds: 59 per 10,000 population (1980)
Doctors: 2 per 10,000 population (1983)

ETHNIC COMPOSITION: Melanesian - 90%; French - 8%; other - 2% (including Vietnamese, Chinese, Pacific Islanders).

RELIGION: A majority of the population is Christian, with a number of denominations being represented.

LANGUAGE: English, French and pidgin (Bislama) are the official languages. There are also numerous Melanesian languages and dialects.

EDUCATION: Illiteracy: 80-90% (1987). In 1984, there were 246 primary schools with 23,465 students. There were 10 secondary schools in 1981, and 2,904 secondary school students in 1983.

ECONOMIC DATA

Expenditures by Function [as % of total]: (not available)
GDP per capita: $608 (1984)

TRAVEL NOTES

Climate: Vanuatu has an oceanic tropical climate, with southeasterly trade winds occurring between the months of May and October.
Health Precautions: (not available)
Miscellaneous: Vanuatu serves as a port of call for cruise ships in the Pacific. Port Vila and South Efate provide limited tourist accommodations.

GOVERNMENT

Vanuatu (Republique de Vanuatu—Ripablik blong Vanuatu—Republic of Vanuatu) was colonized by French and British nationals during the beginning of the 19th century. The Anglo-French Condominium of the New Hebrides was formed by Britain and France in 1906. Vanuatu became an independent nation and adopted its present name on Jul 30, 1980.

Constitution: The Constitution came into effect at independence on Jul 30, 1980. It designates the Republic of Vanuatu as a sovereign democratic state. The Constitution establishes French and English as the official languages, with Bislama (a pidgin dialect) recognized as a "national language." Custom law and decentralization is emphasized in the Constitution, and indigenous Vanuatuans and their descendants are considered the rightful owners of all land in the Republic. The Constitution also provides for a National Council of Chiefs, which deals with local affairs and makes recommendations to Parliament on matters related to the culture and languages of Vanuatu. Provisions are also made for public finance, a civil service, a judiciary, a national ombudsman and a leadership code.

VENEZUELA
Republic of Venezuela

LOCATION: Venezuela is located on the northern coast of South America; Colombia lies to the west, Brazil to the south, Guyana to the east and the Caribbean Sea to the north.

AREA: 352,150 sq. miles

  Land Use: 4.26% cropland; 19.67% permanent pasture; 36.51% forests and woodland; 39.56% other.
  Arable Land: 4%
  Arable Land per capita: 0.59 acres

POPULATION: 18,757,000 (1988 estimate)

  Population Density: 53 inhabs. per sq. mile (1988 estimate)
  Population Distribution: 81.29% urban (1987)
  Population Growth Rate: 2.60% per year (1988 estimate)

VITAL STATISTICS

  Average Life Expectancy: 69.70 years (1985-90 projection)
  Male: 66.70 years (1985-90 projection)
  Female: 72.80 years (1985-90 projection)
  Age Distribution: (1985)
  0-14 .... 39.49%
  15-64 .... 57.10%
  65+ 3.41%
  Median Age: 19.90 years (1985)
  Maternal Mortality: 64.70 per 100,000 live births (1979)
  Infant Mortality: 37 per 1,000 live births (1985)

HEALTH CARE

  Hospital Beds: 29 per 10,000 population (1978)
  Doctors: 14 per 10,000 population (1984)

ETHNIC COMPOSITION: Mestizo - 67%; white - 21%; black - 10%; Indian - 2%.

RELIGION: Roman Catholic - 96%; Protestant - 2%; other - 2%.

LANGUAGE: Spanish is the official language. Native dialects are spoken by some of the 200,000 indigenous people in the remote interior region.

EDUCATION: Illiteracy: 14%. In 1985, there were 13,184 primary schools with 2,770,520 students; 1,037,950 secondary school students and 443,064 students in institutions of higher learning. In 1982/83, there were 106 institutions of higher learning.

ECONOMIC DATA

  Expenditures by Function [as % of total]: (1985)
  General public services 7.24%
  Defense 4.92%
  Education 19.76%
  Health 8.10%
  Social security and welfare 6.69%
  Housing and community amenities 7.29%
  Other community and social services 0.85%
  Economic services 17.95%
  Agriculture, forestry, fishing and hunting ..3.21%
  Roads 2.15%
  Other transportation and communication ...1.98%
  Other purposes 28.93%
  GDP per capita: $1,566 (1986)

TRAVEL NOTES

  Climate: The Venezuelan climate varies according to region, but ranges from tropical to moderate. The rainy season lasts from May through November. The average annual temperature in Caracas is 69°F.
  Health Precautions: Precautions should be taken against typhoid, tetanus and hepatitis. The water is not potable.
  Miscellaneous: Tourists are attracted by the natural beauty of the Andes Mountains and numerous historical places of interest, such as the birthplace of Simon Bolivar.

GOVERNMENT

  Venezuela (Republica de Venezuela—Republic of Venezuela) is a federal republic. It achieved independence from Spain in 1821 as part of the Republic of Gran Colombia, and became a separate state in 1830, largely due to efforts by

Simon Bolivar ("The Liberator"). Various dictatorships and the military dominated the Government until 1958, when the dictatorship of Gen. Marcos Perez Jimenez was overthrown and a federal constitutional system was established.

Constitution: The Constitution, promulgated Jan 23, 1961, establishes a federal republic and provides for the separation of executive, legislative and judicial powers, and for a strong executive. The Constitution also calls for equitable participation by all in the enjoyment of natural wealth.

VIETNAM
Socialist Republic of Vietnam

LOCATION: Located in Southeast Asia, Vietnam is bordered on the north by China and on the west by Laos and Cambodia, with a long eastern coastline on the South China Sea and a short western coastline on the Gulf of Siam.

AREA: 127,246 sq. miles

Land Use: 20.57% cropland; 0.84% permanent pasture; 40.47% forests and woodland; 38.17% other.
Arable Land: 23%
Arable Land per capita: 0.30 acres

POPULATION: 62,177,000 (1987)

Population Density: 489 inhabs. per sq. mile (1987)
Population Distribution: 20.30% urban (1985)
Population Growth Rate: 2.05% per year (1985-90)

VITAL STATISTICS

Average Life Expectancy: 60.80 years (1985-90)
Male: 58.70 years (1985-90)
Female: 63.10 years (1985-90)
Age Distribution: (1985)
0-14 .... 39.30%
15-64 .... 56.70%
65+ 4.00%
Median Age: 19.50 years (1985)
Maternal Mortality: (not available)
Infant Mortality: 67 per 1,000 live births (1985-90)

HEALTH CARE

Hospital Beds: 37 per 10,000 population (1981)
Doctors: 2.46 per 10,000 population (1981)

ETHNIC COMPOSITION: Vietnamese - 90%; Chinese - 3%; other - 7%.

RELIGION: The principal religion is Buddhism.

LANGUAGE: Vietnamese is the official language. French, English, Khmer and some tribal languages are also spoken.

EDUCATION: Illiteracy: 22%. In 1980, there were 7,887,439 primary school students and 3,846,737 secondary school students; in 1981/82 there were 109,142 professional education students and 43,883 technical professional education students; and in 1985 there were 93 colleges and universities with 115,000 students.

ECONOMIC DATA

Expenditures by Function [as % of total]: (not available)
GDP per capita: (not available)

TRAVEL NOTES

Climate: Humid year-round, the climate ranges from hot during the summer to relatively cold during the winter. Monsoon rains may occur during both winter and summer. The average temperature in Hanoi is generally between 55°F and 91°F.
Health Precautions: Among the diseases to be guarded against are malaria and trachoma.
Miscellaneous: Little information on tourism is available.

GOVERNMENT

Vietnam (Cong-Hoa Xa-Hoi Chu-Nghia Viet Nam—Socialist Republic of Vietnam) formally came into existence on Jul 2, 1976, with the official unification of North Vietnam and South Vietnam. The Government of the reunified country is dominated by officials of North Vietnam. Effective political power rests with the Vietnamese Communist Party.

Constitution: In December 1980, the National Assembly adopted a new Constitution (replacing the North Vietnamese Constitution of 1960) that provides for a collective presidency.

WEST GERMANY
Federal Republic of Germany

LOCATION: West Germany is located in north-central Europe and is bordered by the Netherlands, Belgium, Luxembourg and France on the west; Switzerland and Austria on the south; Czechoslovakia and East Germany on the east; and the Baltic Sea, Denmark and the North Sea on the north.

AREA: 96,062 sq. miles

Land Use: 33% cultivated; 29% forests; 23% meadow and pasture; 13% waste or urban; 2% inland water.
Arable Land: 30%
Arable Land per capita: 0.30 acres

POPULATION: 60,734,000 (1986)

Population Density: 632 inhabs. per sq. mile (1986)
Population Distribution: 84.70% urban (1980)
Population Growth Rate: -0.40% per year (1986)

VITAL STATISTICS

Average Life Expectancy: 73.78 years (1983)
Male: 77.09 years (1983)
Female: 70.46 years (1983)
Age Distribution: (1985)
0-14 . . . . 15.90%
15-59 . . . . 64.10%
60+ 20.00%
Median Age: 37.70 years (1985)
Maternal Mortality: 11.40 per 100,000 live births (1983)
Infant Mortality: 10.30 per 1,000 live births (1983)

HEALTH CARE

Hospital Beds: 115 per 10,000 population (1980)
Doctors: 23 per 10,000 population (1980)

ETHNIC COMPOSITION: Mostly German, with a Danish minority.

RELIGION: Protestant - 44%; Catholic - 45%.

LANGUAGE: German is spoken.

EDUCATION: Illiteracy - 1%. In 1983, there were 18,356 primary schools with 4,246,700 students;

5,426 general secondary schools with 3,399,800 students; 2,800 special schools with 301,900 students; 4,992 vocational secondary schools with 2,512,900 students; 2,824 trade and technical schools with 205,500 students; 94 universities with 971,500 students; 26 colleges of art and music with 20,100 students; and 188 vocational colleges with 275,700 students.

ECONOMIC DATA

Expenditures by Function [as % of total]: (1983)
General public services 4.14%
Defense 9.32%
Education 0.83%
Health 18.64%
Social security and welfare 49.97%
Housing and community amenities 0.31%
Other community and social services 0.10%
Economic services 7.00%
Agriculture, forestry, fishing and hunting . .0.31%
Roads 1.38%
Other transportation and communication . . .3.13%
Other purposes 9.68%
GDP per capita: $12,251 (1985)

TRAVEL NOTES

Climate: The climate is generally temperate, though there is much variation between the lowlands in the north, and the highlands in Bavaria. The average annual temperature is about 48°F.
Health Precautions: None
Miscellaneous: Tourist attractions include the medieval towns and villages, the spas, summer and winter resorts, the mountains in Bavaria, the North Sea coast, the Rhine Valley and the Black Forest.

GOVERNMENT

West Germany (Bundesrepublik Deutschland— Federal Republic of Germany) is a federation of 10 states (Laender) and West Berlin, established in 1949, with parliamentary forms of government at both federal and state levels.

Constitution: The Basic Law (Grundgesetz) of May 23, 1949, consisting of a preamble, 146 articles and several amendments, serves as the constitutional basis for the Federal Republic. It emphasizes the protection of individual rights and civil liberties and the division of power in a federal structure. The Basic Law can be amended by a majority of two-thirds in both legislative chambers.

Federalism. The Basic Law describes the Federal Republic of Germany as a democratic and social federation with authority shared between the states and the federal Government (Bundesregierung). Each state (Land) has its own legislature, elected by universal adult suffrage, empowered to legislate in such matters as education, police and broadcasting. The federal Government is exclusively responsible for the foreign affairs and defense of the Republic and for such matters as immigration, citizenship, customs and excises, posts and telecommunications, currency and weights and measures. In other matters concurrent legislation exists. Where there is incompatibility of state and federal authority, federal law supersedes state law. Rights and duties of citizens are the same in every state.

WESTERN SAMOA
Independent State of Western Samoa

LOCATION: Western Samoa consists of a group of 9 islands, including two main ones, located in the South Pacific Ocean about 1,500 miles north of New Zealand.

AREA: 1,093 sq. miles

Land Use: 43% cropland; 0% permanent pasture; 47% forests and woodland; 10% other.
Arable Land: 43%
Arable Land per capita: 1.87 acres

POPULATION: 169,000 (1989 estimate)

Population Density: 155 inhabs. per sq. mile (1989 estimate)
Population Distribution: 21.20% urban (1981)
Population Growth Rate: 0.90% per year (1989 estimate)

VITAL STATISTICS

Average Life Expectancy: 64 years (1988)
Male: 62.60 years (1986)
Female: 65.60 years (1986)
Age Distribution: (1984)
0-14	50.40%
15-59	45.40%
60+	4.30%

Median Age: (not available)
Maternal Mortality: (not available)
Infant Mortality: 28 per 1,000 live births (1985)

HEALTH CARE

Hospital Beds: 46 per 10,000 population (1982)
Doctors: 4 per 10,000 population (1981)

ETHNIC COMPOSITION: Most of the population is Samoan, although about 7% of the population is mixed European and Polynesian. Less than 1% of the population is European.

RELIGION: Almost all of the population is Christian.

LANGUAGE: Samoan and English are spoken.

EDUCATION: Illiteracy: 10%. In 1983, there were 164 primary schools with 31,447 students; 8,643 intermediate school students; and 11,961 secondary school students.

ECONOMIC DATA

Expenditures by Function [as % of total]: (1984 provisional)
General public services	25.76%
Defense	0%
Education	13.86%
Health	9.31%
Social security and welfare	0%
Housing and community amenities	0.34%
Other community and social services	1.58%
Economic services	40.76%
Agriculture, forestry, fishing and hunting	8.24%
Roads	5.79%
Other transportation and communication	9.82%
Other purposes	8.42%

GDP per capita: $618 (1986 estimate)

TRAVEL NOTES

Climate: Western Samoa enjoys a tropical climate with temperatures ranging from 73°F to 86°F. November to April is the rainy season.
Health Precautions: (not available)
Miscellaneous: Western Samoa's tropical climate and natural beauty attract visitors.

GOVERNMENT

Western Samoa (Malo Sa'oloto Tuto'atasi o Samoa i Sisifo—Independent State of Western Samoa) became a German protectorate in 1899, and came under the administration of New Zealand in 1919. Some responsibility for self-governing was assumed in 1954, culminating in independent nation status on Jan 1, 1962.

Constitution: The Constitution was adopted by a Constitutional Convention on Oct 28, 1960, and was approved by a UN-supervised plebiscite in 1961, finally coming into force on Jan 1, 1962. The Constitution states that following the death of Paramount Chief Malietoa Tanumafili II, the O le Ao o le Malo (the mainly ceremonial position of head of state), future heads of state will be elected by the Legislative Assembly for 5-year terms.

YEMEN
Yemen Arab Republic

LOCATION: Located in the southwestern corner of the Arabian peninsula, Yemen is bordered by South Yemen to the southeast, Saudi Arabia to the north and east and the Red Sea to the west.

AREA: 77,220 sq. miles

Land Use: 6.93% cropland; 35.90% permanent pasture; 8.21% forests and woodland; 48.96% other (mainly desert).
Arable Land: 14%
Arable Land per capita: 1.07 acres

POPULATION: 6,937,000 (1989 estimate)

Population Density: 90 inhabs. per sq. mile (1989 estimate)
Population Distribution: 20.05% urban (1985)
Population Growth Rate: 3.10% per year (1989 estimate)

VITAL STATISTICS

Average Life Expectancy: 50.90 years (1985-90 projection)
Male: 49.40 years (1985-90 projection)
Female: 52.40 years (1985-90 projection)
Age Distribution: (1985)
0-14 .... 46.85%
15-64 .... 49.79%
65+ 3.36%
Median Age: 16.50 years (1985)
Maternal Mortality: (not available)
Infant Mortality: 137 per 1,000 live births (1985)

HEALTH CARE

Hospital Beds: 9 per 10,000 population (1986)
Doctors: 2 per 10,000 population (1984)

ETHNIC COMPOSITION: Arab - 90%; mixed Arab and African - 10%.

RELIGION: Sunni Moslem - 50%; Shiite Moslem - 50%.

LANGUAGE: Arabic is spoken.

EDUCATION: Illiteracy: 85% (estimate). In 1983, there were 731,989 primary school students, 78,665 general secondary school students, 4,489 teacher training students, and 1,681 vocational students. In 1980, there were 4,519 students enrolled in institutes of higher learning.

ECONOMIC DATA

Expenditures by Function [as % of total]: (1986 provisional)
General public services 21.59%
Defense 28.82%
Education 22.52%
Health 4.71%
Social security and welfare 0%
Housing and community amenities 0%
Other community and social services 2.69%
Economic services 7.80%
Agriculture, forestry, fishing and hunting ..2.29%
Roads 4.85%
Other transportation and communication ...0.40%
Other purposes 1.17%
GDP per capita: $505 (1986)

TRAVEL NOTES

Climate: Yemen is divided into two main climate zones; the coastal area is hot and humid, while inland the country is cooler, with heavy rainfall (which makes it one of the most important agricultural areas of the Arabian peninsula).
Health Precautions: Vaccinations against cholera, typhoid and yellow fever are recommended, as are gamma globulin shots. Tap water is not potable.
Miscellaneous: The country is renowned for its well-preserved traditional way of life. Tourism has only been permitted since 1970.

GOVERNMENT

Yemen (al-Jumhuriyah al-'Arabiyah al-Yamaniyah—Yemen Arab Republic) is an independent Islamic republic. It was under Ottoman Turkish rule from the 1500s to 1918, when a hereditary monarchy was established. Yemen became a republic on Sep 27, 1962 in the wake of a military coup that deposed the monarchy. The republican regime has been strained by the assassination of two of the country's presidents (in 1977 and 1978), as well as several reported coup attempts. Its stability has also been undermined by continuous tension with South Yemen, which has periodically resulted in open warfare. (Both Yemen and South Yemen are on record as supporting the unification of the two countries.)

Constitution: A provisional Constitution was announced on Jun 19, 1974 after the Dec 28, 1970 Constitution was suspended following a military coup. The interim Constitution, which remains in effect pending the drafting of a permanent one, establishes an Islamic Arab republic, headed by a president.

YUGOSLAVIA
Socialist Federal Republic of Yugoslavia

LOCATION: Yugoslavia is located in southern Europe on the Adriatic Sea. It shares borders with Italy to the west, Hungary and Rumania to the north, Bulgaria to the east and Albania and Greece to the south.

AREA: 98,766 sq. miles

Land Use: 30.55% cropland; 24.97% permanent pasture; 36.29% forest and woodland; 8.19% other.
Arable Land: 31%
Arable Land per capita: 0.86 acres

POPULATION: 23,753,000 (1989 estimate)

Population Density: 240 inhabs. per sq. mile (1989 estimate)
Population Distribution: 46.27% urban (1985)
Population Growth Rate: 0.60% per year (1989 projection)

VITAL STATISTICS
Average Life Expectancy: 71.70 years (1985-90 projection)
Male: 69.00 years (1985-90 projection)
Female: 74.70 years (1985-90 projection)
Age Distribution: (1985)
0-14 . . . . .23.81%
15-64 . . . . .67.96%
65+ 8.23%
Median Age: 31.40 years (1985)
Maternal Mortality: 22.40 per 100,000 live births (1982)
Infant Mortality: 30 per 1,000 live births (1985)

HEALTH CARE

Hospital Beds: 60 per 10,000 population (1985)
Doctors: 16 per 10,000 population (1985)

ETHNIC COMPOSITION: Serb - 36.30%; Croat - 19.70%; Bosnian Moslem - 8.90%; Slovene - 7.80%; Albanian - 7.70%; Macedonian - 5.90%; Yugoslav - 5.40%; Montenegrin - 2.50%; Hungarian - 1.90%; other - 3.90%.

RELIGION: Eastern Orthodox - 50%; Roman Catholic - 30%; Moslem - 10%; Protestant - 1%; other - 9%.

LANGUAGE: Serbo-Croatian, Slovene, Macedonian, Albanian and Hungarian are spoken. Under the 1974 Constitution, all languages of the Yugoslav people are official.

EDUCATION: Illiteracy: 9.50%. In 1984/85, there were 12,213 primary schools with 2,823,248 students; 923,435 secondary school students; and 340 institutions of higher learning with 359,175 students.

ECONOMIC DATA

Expenditures by Function [as % of total]: (1986)
General public services 6.06%
Defense 59.95%
Education . . . . (not available)
Health . . . . (not available)
Social security and welfare 9.01%
Housing and community amenities (not available)
Other community and social services 0.29%
Economic services 15.38%
Agriculture, forestry, fishing and
  hunting . . . .(not available)
Roads . . . . (not available)
Other transportation and

communication . . . . (not available)
Other purposes 9.30%
Gross Material Product per capita: $2,358 (1986)

TRAVEL NOTES

Climate: The Yugoslav climate varies from region to region; coastal areas enjoy a Mediterranean climate with mild winters and warm summers while inland areas experience greater contrasts between winter and summer. Belgrade, located in the interior, has an average yearly temperature of 71°F, but its average winter temperature is 32°F.

Health Precautions: Apart from the usual inoculations recommended for traveling abroad, no special precautions are necessary for visiting Yugoslavia. Tap water is potable.

Miscellaneous: Sarajevo, famous as the site of Archduke Francis Ferdinand's assassination in 1914, is a beautiful city with fine examples of Turkish architecture.

GOVERNMENT

Yugoslavia (Socijalisticka Federativna Republica Jugoslavija—Socialist Federal Republic of Yugoslavia) is an independent Communist state. It was proclaimed a republic on Nov 29, 1945, after efforts to restore the pre-World War II monarchy failed. Effective political power rests with the League of Communists of Yugoslavia (LCY), the only legal political party. The Yugoslav political system is marked by a high degree of decentralization; decision-making power is spread among regional and local governments and economic enterprises (within limits set by the LCY). A unique feature of the social and political system is Yugoslavia's "self-management system," designed to ensure and enhance the control of social, political and economic institutions by the working class. Recently, the country has been destabilized by a combination of ethnic strife and economic woes. A clash with Parliament over fulfilling the conditions of an IMF economic recovery program brought down the Government of Prime Minister Branko Mikulic in December 1988. The man chosen to succeed Mikulic as Prime Minister, Ante Markovic, is a reform-minded Croatian economist who recently stated that Yugoslavia should pursue a market economy.

Constitution: The present Constitution (adopted Feb 21, 1974) is the 4th full-scale constitutional revision to be passed since the founding of modern Yugoslavia. Like the previous Constitutions, it represents an attempt to codify the changes that occurred in the evolving institutions and processes since the last revision, and to provide guidelines for future development. The Constitution is composed of an Introduction (consisting of 10 chapters outlining the basic principles of the Yugoslav political, social and economic system) and 6 Parts (with a total of 406 articles). Amendments to the Constitution must be passed by a two-thirds vote of both houses of the Federal Council and ratified by the 6 republics and two autonomous regions.

ZAIRE
Republic of Zaire

LOCATION: Zaire is located in central Africa, bounded by the Congo to the northwest; the Central African Republic and Sudan to the north; Uganda, Rwanda, Burundi and Tanzania to the east; and Zambia and Angola to the south. There is a short coastline where the Zaire River flows into the Atlantic Ocean.

AREA: 905,328 sq. miles

Land Use: 2.85% cropland; 4.07% permanent pasture; 77.89% forests and woodland; 15.19% other.

Arable Land: 3%

Arable Land per capita: 0.55 acres

POPULATION: 31,796,000 (1987 estimate)

Population Density: 35.12 inhabs. per sq. mile (1987 estimate)

Population Distribution: 36.60% urban (1985)

Population Growth Rate: 3.04% per year (1985-90 projection)

VITAL STATISTICS

Average Life Expectancy: 52.00 years (1985-90 projection)

Male: 50.30 years (1985-90 projection)

Female: 53.80 years (1985-90 projection)

Age Distribution: (1985)

0-14 . . . . .45.20%

15-64 . . . . .51.90%

65+ 2.90%

Median Age: 17.30 years (1985)

Maternal Mortality: (not available)
Infant Mortality: 98 per 1,000 live births (1985-90 projection)

HEALTH CARE

Hospital Beds: 27 per 10,000 population (1982)
Doctors: 0.73 per 10,000 population (1982)

ETHNIC COMPOSITION: African - 99%; European - 1%.

RELIGION: Roman Catholic - 50%; Protestant - 20%; Moslem - 10%; Kimbanguist - 10%; other - 10% (mainly syncretic sects and traditional beliefs).

LANGUAGE: French is the official language. The majority of the population speaks Bantu languages, including Swahili, Kingwana, Lingala, Tshiluba and Kikonga.

EDUCATION: Illiteracy: 39%. In 1983, there were 10,065 primary schools with 4,654,613 students. There were 1,570,887 general secondary students; 365,823 teacher training students; and 215,190 vocational institution students. In 1982, there were 3 universities with 31,643 students.

ECONOMIC DATA

Expenditures by Function [as % of total]: (1982)
General public services 22.09%
Defense 7.93%
Education 16.36%
Health 3.21%
Social security and welfare 0.39%
Housing and community amenities 0%
Other community and social services 2.10%
Economic services 16.86%
Agriculture, forestry, fishing and hunting .. 3.00%
Roads 0.62%
Other transportation and communication .. 0.78%
Other purposes 31.06%
GDP per capita: $87 (1985)

TRAVEL NOTES

Climate: Zaire's climate is tropical, with an average high temperature of 86°F and an average low of 70°F. The rainy season lasts from October to May and the annual rainfall ranges from 60 to 80 inches.
Health Precautions: Yellow fever and cholera inoculations are required. Immunizations against tetanus, typhoid, poliomyelitis and rabies are recommended. Precautions should be taken against malaria and hepatitis, too. The tap water is not potable.
Miscellaneous: Zaire has an abundance and diversity of natural resources, with extensive lake and mountain scenery.

GOVERNMENT

Zaire (Republique du Zaire—Republic of Zaire), formerly the Republic of the Congo, attained its independence from Belgium on Jun 30, 1960. The first Constitution established a parliamentary form of government, which was overthrown by a military coup on Nov 24, 1965, after a lengthy period of instability. Effective political power rests with the armed forces and the Mouvement Populaire de la Revolution (MPR—Popular Movement of the Revolution), the sole legal political party.

Constitution: A 1967 Constitution established a strongly centralized presidential system. Constitutional amendments adopted in 1974 formally linked the leadership of the MPR with the leadership of the Government. A new Constitution promulgated on Feb 15, 1978 consolidates presidential and party power.

ZAMBIA
Republic of Zambia

LOCATION: Situated in central Africa, Zambia is bordered by Zaire and Tanzania to the north; Malawi and Mozambique to the east; Zimbabwe, Botswana and Namibia to the south; and Angola to the west.

AREA: 290,586 sq. miles

Land Use: 6.96% cropland; 47.25% permanent pasture; 39.95% forest and woodland; 5.84% other.
Arable Land: 7%
Arable Land per capita: 2.09 acres

POPULATION: 7,522,000 (1988 estimate)

Population Density: 26 inhabs. per sq. mile (1988 estimate)
Population Distribution: 49.46% urban (1985)
Population Growth Rate: 3.20% per year (1988 estimate)

VITAL STATISTICS

Average Life Expectancy: 53.30 years (1985-90 projection)
Male: 51.60 years (1985-90 projection)
Female: 55.10 years (1985-90 projection)
Age Distribution: (1985)
0-14 .... 47.33%
15-64 .... 50.00%
65+ 2.67%
Median Age: 16.30 years (1985)
Maternal Mortality: (not available)
Infant Mortality: 107 per 1,000 live births (1985)

HEALTH CARE

Hospital Beds: 35 per 10,000 population (1982)
Doctors: 1 per 10,000 population (1982)

ETHNIC COMPOSITION: African (various Bantu tribes) - 98.70%; European - 1.10%; other - 0.20%.

RELIGION: Christian - 70%; indigenous beliefs - 29%; other (mostly Hindu) - 1%.

LANGUAGE: English is the official language. Nyanja, Bemba, Tonga, Lozi, Lunda and Luvale are some of the many native languages spoken.

EDUCATION: Illiteracy: 46%. In 1986, there were 3,164 primary schools with 1,442,133 students; 276 secondary schools with 150,298 students; 14 technical colleges with 5,410 students; 14 teacher training colleges with 4,277 students; and 2 universities with 3,831 students.

ECONOMIC DATA

Expenditures by Function [as % of total]: (1982)
General public services .... (not available)
Defense .... (not available)
Education 15.10%
Health 8.35%
Social security and welfare 2.11%
Housing and community amenities 2.03%
Other community and social services 2.11%
Economic services 23.77%
Agriculture, forestry, fishing and hunting . 16.39%
Roads 4.75%
Other transportation and communication .. 0.55%
Other purposes 7.29%
GDP per capita: $300 (1986 estimate)

TRAVEL NOTES

Climate: Zambia has a pleasant climate, with summer temperatures rarely exceeding 90°F and winter lows rarely dipping below 43°F. The rainy season runs from November to April, with annual rainfall averaging 34 inches.
Health Precautions: Malaria suppressants are strongly recommended, and care should be taken to avoid wading or bathing in lakes and ponds infested with schistosomiasis. City water is potable.
Miscellaneous: The spectacular Victoria Falls are twice as high and half again as wide as Niagara Falls. Zambia is also the home of many beautiful lakes and game reserves.

GOVERNMENT

Zambia (Republic of Zambia) became an independent state within the Commonwealth of Nations on Oct 24, 1964. From 1953 to 1963 Zambia (the former British protectorate of Northern Rhodesia) formed part of the Central African Federation, together with the self-governing British colony of Southern Rhodesia and the British protectorate of Nyasaland, now Malawi. In October 1964, the former British protectorate of Barotseland was incorporated as part of the newly independent Republic of Zambia.

Constitution: The present Constitution entered into effect on Aug 25, 1973, replacing the 1964 Constitution. It provides for a "one-party participatory democracy" with a strong President and a unicameral legislature. Government policy is largely formulated by the Central Committee of the United National Independence Party (UNIP). The Constitution also includes a Bill of Rights ensuring basic freedoms for the citizens of Zambia.

ZIMBABWE
Republic of Zimbabwe

LOCATION: Landlocked in southern Africa, Zimbabwe is bordered by Mozambique to the east, Zambia to the northwest, Botswana to the southwest and South Africa to the south.

AREA: 150,873 sq. miles

Land Use: 7.02% cropland; 12.56% permanent pasture; 61.85% forests and woodland; 18.57% other.
Arable Land: 40%
Arable Land per capita: 4.10 acres

POPULATION: 9,340,000 (1987)

Population Density: 62.50 inhabs. per sq. mile (1987)
Population Distribution: 24.60% urban (1985)
Population Growth Rate: 3.60% per year (1985-90)

VITAL STATISTICS

Average Life Expectancy: 57.80 years (1985-90)
Male: 56.00 years (1985-90)
Female: 59.70 years (1985-90)
Age Distribution: (1985)
0-14 .... 47.60%
15-64 .... 49.60%
65+ 2.70%
Median Age: 16.10 years (1985)
Maternal Mortality: (not available)
Infant Mortality: 80 per 1,000 live births (1985-90)

HEALTH CARE

Hospital Beds: 30.16 per 10,000 population (1980)
Doctors: 1.63 per 10,000 population (1981)

ETHNIC COMPOSITION: Black - 96% (with over 73% members of Shona-speaking sub-tribes, and 19% Ndebele-speaking); white - 3%; mixed and Asian - 1%.

RELIGION: Syncretic (part Christian, part indigenous beliefs) - 50%; Christian - 25%; indigenous beliefs and a few Moslem - 25%.

LANGUAGE: The official language is English. ChiShona and Si Ndebele are widely spoken.

EDUCATION: Illiteracy: 45-55%. In 1985, there were 2,229,396 primary school students, 497,766 secondary school students, 15,084 technical college students, 943 agricultural college students, 9,504 teachers' training college students and 4,742 University of Zimbabwe students.

ECONOMIC DATA

Expenditures by Function [as % of total]: (1983)
General public services 11.71%
Defense 18.34%
Education 21.49%
Health 6.15%
Social security and welfare 6.37%
Housing and community amenities 1.45%
Other community and social services 1.53%
Economic services 20.85%
Agriculture, forestry, fishing and hunting ..6.09%
Roads 2.85%
Other transportation and communication ...1.25%
Other purposes 12.11%
GDP per capita: $854 (1983)

TRAVEL NOTES

Climate: Tropical, the climate is modified significantly by altitude. In the highveld (savanna-covered plateau), average monthly temperatures range from 55°-72°F, while in the low-lying Zambezi river valley, they range from 68°-86°F.
Health Precautions: Aralen or Nivaquine are often recommended to suppress malaria. While tap water is safe for drinking, most lakes and standing bodies of water are infested with bilharzia, and swimming in them is unhealthy.
Miscellaneous: Tourist attractions include the magnificent Victoria Falls, the Hwange Game Park, man-made Lake Kariba, the Great Zimbabwe ruins at Masvingo and the Matopos mountains near Bulawayo. The scenic mountainous Eastern Highlands are also popular.

GOVERNMENT

Zimbabwe (Republic of Zimbabwe), a former British colony, became an independent nation on Apr 18, 1980. However, as Rhodesia, the country practiced autonomous government under the terms of Prime Minister Ian Smith's illegal unilateral declaration of independence (UDI) announced on Nov 11, 1965. In January 1979, following several years of escalating violence between the Smith regime and black activist groups opposed to white minority rule, a cease-fire was negotiated and a majority rule constitution was accepted. In April 1979, the nation's first elections by universal adult suffrage were held and the following December, Parliament voted to renounce independence and revert temporarily to the status of a British colony. In February 1980, new elections supervised by a British Electoral Commissioner led to independence for the new state of Zimbabwe in April.

Constitution: The British-drafted Constitution was approved by the Assembly on Jan 20, 1979, and entered into effect on Apr 18, 1980. It establishes a parliamentary form of government, and includes a Declaration of Rights. Amendments to the Constitution require the support of two-thirds of the senators and 70 House members. Executive President Robert Mugabe has restructured the government and overseen the merger of political parties in order to create a one-party socialist state, which will be permitted under the Constitution in 1990.

Bibliography

Banks, Arthur S., ed. *Political Handbook of the World*. Binghamton, New York: CSA Publications, 1984/85–.

Caribbean UPDATE. 2, no. 7– (Aug 1986–).

Central Intelligence Agency. *The World Factbook*. Washington, D.C., 1983–.

Defense Marketing Services. *DMS Market Intelligence Reports*. Greenwich, Conn., 1984–.

Europa Publications. *The Europa Year Book*. London, 1978–.

Facts on File. *Facts on File: World News Digest with Index*. 41– (1981–).

————. *World Elections on File*. 2 vols. New York, 1987.

Gale Research Company. *Cities of the World*. 2nd–3rd eds. 4 vols. Detroit, 1985, 1987.

Harper & Row. *World Resources 1987*. New York, 1987.

International Institute for Strategic Studies. *The Military Balance*. London, 1964–.

International Monetary Fund. *Government Finance Statistics Yearbook*. Washington, D.C., 1977–.

————. Bureau of Statistics. *International Financial Statistics*. Washington, D.C., 1948–.

Longman. *Keesing's Record of World Events*. 30– (Jan 1984–).

Merriam-Webster. *Webster's New Geographical Dictionary*. Springfield, Mass., 1984.

Pharos Books. *The World Almanac and Book of Facts*. New York, 1979–.

Sivard, Ruth Leger, ed. *World Military and Social Expenditures 1987–88*. Washington, D.C.: World Priorities, 1987.

United Nations. *Monthly Bulletin of Statistics*. New York, 1947–.

————. Department of International Economic and Social Affairs. *World Population Prospects: Estimates and Projections as Assessed in 1984*. New York, 1986.

————. Statistical Office. *Demographic Yearbook*. New York, 1985/86–.

U.S. Bureau of the Census. *World Population Profile: 1985*. U.S. Department of Commerce, 1985.

World Health Organization. *World Health Statistics Annual*. Geneva, 1983–.